STRUGGLE FOR KENYA

STRUGGLE FOR KENYA

The Loss and Reassertion
of Imperial Initiative,
1912–1923

Robert M. Maxon

Rutherford • Madison • Teaneck
Fairleigh Dickinson University Press
London and Toronto: Associated University Presses

Associated University Presses
440 Forsgate Drive
Cranbury, NJ 08512

Associated University Presses
25 Sicilian Avenue
London WC1A 2QH, England

Associated University Presses
P.O. Box 338, Port Credit
Mississauga, Ontario
L5G 4L8 Canada

The paper used in this publication meets the requirements
of the American National Standard for Permanence of Paper
for Printed Library Materials Z39.48-1984.

Library of Congress Cataloging-in-Publication Data

Maxon, Robert M.
    Struggle for Kenya : the loss and reassertion of imperial
initiative, 1912–1923 / Robert M. Maxon.
        p.   cm.
    Includes bibliographical references and index.
    ISBN 0-8386-3486-9 (alk. paper)
    1. Kenya—Politics and government—To 1963.   2. Kenya—Economic
conditions—To 1963.   I. Title.
DT433.57.M394   1993
320.96762—dc20   91-58952
                                                          CIP

335048

To the late Robert Munn,
Dean of Libraries
at West Virginia University

Contents

Abbreviations

ASAPS	Anti-Slavery and Aborigines Protection Society
CNC	Chief Native Commissioner
CO	Colonial Office
EACB	East African Currency Board
EAD	East African Department
EAINC	East African Indian National Congress
EAP	East Africa Protectorate
EAS	*East African Standard*
Execo	Executive Council
H.M.G.	His Majesty's Government
IO	India Office
IOA	India Overseas Association
Legco	Legislative Council
M.P.	Member of Parliament
NLC	Native Labour Commission
S of S	Secretary of State

Maps and Tables

Maps

Tables

11

Preface

The eleven years covered by this study of imperial relations encompass one of the most crucial time periods in the history of Britain's association with her East African dependency known after 1920 as Kenya.[1] It is this time of intense struggle, which would go far towards determining the framework within which future policy towards Kenya would be developed, that is the focus of this work. The Colonial Office (CO) in London struggled to maintain initiative and control in these years in the face of several, often contradictory, interested parties and pressure groups; among the most influential were Kenya's colonial state, the European settlers and Indians resident there, the India Office (IO) and the government of India, missionaries, humanitarians, and capitalists in Britain itself, and the African majority in Kenya.

Relying primarily on CO records, this work describes the struggle that made Kenya one of the most controversial dependencies in the British empire after World War I. From 1919 through the early months of 1922, for example, white supremacy was at a peak in Kenya. Strongly backed by the colonial state, Kenya's small European settler population seemed poised on the brink of economic dominance, resting on the exports of white-owned farms and plantations and of southern African–style minority self-government. Between the spring of 1922 and July 1923, however, this rush to white supremacy was checked through the reassertion of imperial control over Kenya that culminated in the policy decisions announced in the Devonshire Declaration of July 1923. The answers as to why and how this transpired can be understood not only by examining imperial relations in the postwar era, but also in the preceding years. Thus while concluding with the decisions announced by the CO in mid-1923, this study begins in 1912.

The latter date is chosen as the starting point because in the years prior to the outbreak of World War I, the CO was clearly in control in its relations with the East Africa Protectorate. With the onset of the war, however, the CO rapidly lost the initiative. As will be shown, a number of factors were responsible for the loss. Most significant were the impact of the war in East Africa and the economic gains made by settler agriculture during the conflict. Both magnified the economic and political influence of the settlers, who made significant breakthroughs during and after the war.

Those gains and the policy decisions taken by the colonial state to support the settlers provoked a period of intense struggle over the direction of imperial policy towards Kenya that clearly exposed the CO's loss of control. Pressured by protests from Kenya, India, and Britain, the CO finally intervened to regain the initiative in Kenya affairs in 1922 and 1923 through the sacking of governor Sir Edward Northey, the development of a new policy agenda for Kenya, and the issuing of the Devonshire white paper. Yet of all the pressures and protests brought to bear on the CO between 1920 and 1923, the most significant in forcing the CO into action was the colony's economic situation. The colonial state's reliance on settler production had driven Kenya to the brink of bankruptcy, thus endangering the continued existence of colonial rule. Economic factors and African protest, greatly overshadowed in previous scholarly emphasis on the missionary/humanitarian lobby in Britain, played the key role in bringing about the reassertion of imperial control and direction. Of the numerous published accounts that deal with the subject and the declaration of African paramountcy that marked the reassertion of CO control, only Professor E. S. Atieno Odhiambo has grasped this point.[2] This book demonstrates and documents the importance of economic factors in that process, providing a needed reassessment of the accounts, such as those noted in the text, that have given far too significant an impact on CO policy to the missionary/humanitarian lobby in Great Britain.

The main sources of this study, unlike most earlier work on the imperial relations of the period, are the CO archives. Although CO-Kenya relations in the 1912–23 period have been touched upon by a variety of published studies, none have made extensive use of CO records for the whole of the time period. These accounts have therefore failed to provide a complete and definitive picture. The several works of the late George Bennett, to take but one example, have had considerable impact on interpretations of imperial policy towards Kenya.[3] Yet none of these works used CO records as the basis for the account and interpretation provided. This book seeks to redress that situation by primary reliance on the CO records and a careful description of the economic realities upon which CO policies came to be based. The evolution of British policy towards Kenya between 1912 and 1923 is therefore examined from "inside" the metropole. Thus it is possible to describe exactly how a number of important issues in Kenya's colonial history, such as land and the Crown Lands Ordinance, 1915, settler political rights, the Indian question, the postwar labor controversy, the annexation of Kenya as a colony, and the currency and exchange alterations of 1920–21, came to evolve.

As the focus of this work has been on primary sources, the majority of the research was carried out at the Public Record Office in London. Through the assistance of a grant from West Virginia University, I was able to obtain, moreover, a portion of the relevant records, dating from 1912 to 1916, on microfilm. West Virginia University's Wise Library supplemented the research grant by purchasing additional reels of microfilm. These are now housed there. I was also able to obtain documents from the CO 533/ series on loan from the Syracuse University Library.

I am grateful, therefore, to the West Virginia University Senate grants program, the staff of the Public Record Office, the Rhodes House Library at Oxford, and the Syracuse University Library for their kind assistance. Research for this book was begun with the aid of a sabbatical from West Virginia University and a grant for research overseas from the U.S. Office of Education. Their assistance is also gratefully acknowledged. The support of Neil Bucklew, President of West Virginia University, and S. O. Keya, Vice-Chancellor of Moi University, was especially important as they enabled me to spend sabbatical leave at Moi University during the 1989–90 academic year. I completed the manuscript during that time. Others to whom I owe a large debt for advice and encouragement with this work include my colleagues Phyllis Boanes, Wilbert Jenkins, and Joe Trotter. I am also thankful for the assistance of E. S. Atieno Odhiambo, William R. Ochieng', Peter Ndege, and Robert Gregory for reading and commenting on earlier drafts of the work, and to William Little, Director of the Center for Black Culture and Research at West Virginia University for his encouragement and assistance in the preparation of the manuscript. In the lengthy period of research and writing that went into its completion, I was very fortunate to have the support, first and foremost, of my family; I received valuable research assistance from my daughter Trudy. Most particularly, I am grateful to Dr. Robert Munn, the late Dean of Libraries at West Virginia. Dean Munn not only came up with additional funding to purchase CO records for my research, he, as Provost, brought me to West Virginia University, and he continued to guide and assist me in my interest in Kenya history, which he shared. This book is respectfully dedicated to his memory.

STRUGGLE FOR KENYA

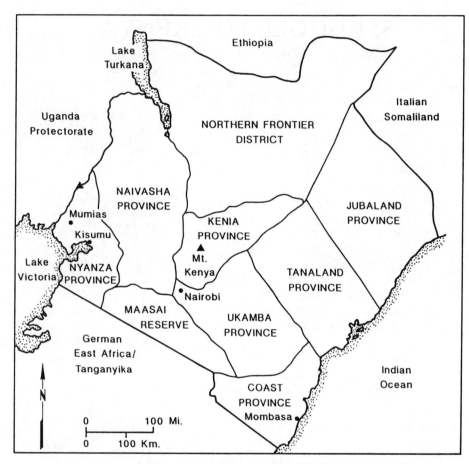

Lake
Turkana

Ethiopia

Uganda
Protectorate

Italian
Somaliland

NORTHERN FRONTIER
DISTRICT

NAIVASHA
PROVINCE

JUBALAND
PROVINCE

Mumias

KENIA
PROVINCE

Kisumu

Mt.
Kenya

NYANZA
PROVINCE

Lake
Victoria

TANALAND
PROVINCE

Nairobi

MAASAI
RESERVE

German
East Africa/
Tanganyika

UKAMBA
PROVINCE

Indian
Ocean

N

0   100 Mi.

0   100 Km.

COAST
PROVINCE
Mombasa

East Africa Protectorate in 1912

1
The Colonial Office and Kenya

The Colonial Office (CO) was the most important department of state so far as the framing and implementation of policy for Britain's African colonies such as the East Africa Protectorate (EAP) was concerned. It would play a central role in the struggle for Kenya. It is thus important to understand the CO and the various other institutions and groups, such as the colonial government of the EAP, the India Office (IO), or British humanitarians, that played a part in the struggle. That is the purpose of this introductory chapter.

This introduction also seeks to set the major theme of the study in the context of the time period covered by the book, which begins in early 1912. Prior to that time, the CO was clearly in control in its relations with the government of the EAP. While CO officials did not call all the shots for the EAP from London, it maintained a last word as it had considerable say in shaping and altering the significant policy initiatives of the colonial state. It was particularly noteworthy that none of the major demands made by the protectorate's European settler community were totally accepted by the CO during this period. Moreover, the CO was still capable of initiating important policy proposals, as in the case of land, down to 1912, and, as the dismissal of governor Sir Percy Girouard would demonstrate, the CO was capable of intervening decisively in EAP affairs.

The CO

For the most part, the prewar CO in fact stood as supervisor or final arbiter rather than initiator of day to day policy. It had long been accepted in the CO that the colonial governor "administers" and the CO "supervises."[1] Real initiative lay with the territory's governor, the "man on the spot," as the CO had no executive powers. In exercising its essentially supervisory role, however, the CO was able to exert influence on policy through approval of colonial budgets, legislation, and appointments. Under the colonial regulations, the right of appointment in the colonial service lay with the Secretary of State (S of S) for the Colonies, and the annual estimates of each dependency required the prior approval of the CO.[2] It had long been established that major policy initiatives, whether involving legislative or administrative action, had to be approved by the S of S. Moreover, the CO often laid out general policy to be followed and suggested the administrative aims to be accomplished, for example on the appointment of a new governor, in the colonies it supervised. As this study will demonstrate, the relationship between CO and colonies was not normally one of direct command; rather it involved a lengthy process of negotiation and bargaining.

It was in the economic sphere, in particular, that CO supervision had to try to achieve a balance between metropolitan interests and those of indigenous groups to which the colonial government was linked. This involved, in Berman's words, "managing the exploitation of a colony to find a stable division of its surplus products that would on the one hand satisfy metropolitan needs, and yet, on the other, maintain local production and political control."[3] Nevertheless, the CO did not feel that it should assume the role of economic manager nor take the responsibility to initiate proposals for economic development. Such initiatives were the responsibility of private enterprise and individual colonial states. A major assumption of the CO in this regard was that it would become involved in economic development projects only if private enterprise was unwilling, or unable, to take the lead.[4]

As far as the CO was concerned, the maintenance of law and order was far more important than economic development or social engineering. This emphasis on law-and-order colonialism was tinged with the doctrine of trusteeship. In theory, this meant that the CO sought to exercise its supervision on behalf of the welfare of the indigenous population of the empire. In 1912, and generally throughout the period to 1923, the CO held to a "preservationist interpretation" of that trust. In Constantine's words, "certainly the preservationist interpretation of trusteeship formed a part of the mental baggage carried by the permanent staff at the CO before the war, and it constituted a standard against which to judge proposals for economic change."[5] The preservationist ideal, in particular, sought to hold back or slow down those forces which had the potential for producing economic, political, and social change away from what were perceived as the traditional patterns of authority and production. This meant that the CO, and the colonial state, were particularly concerned that rapid captialist penetration in Africa would have negative, and indeed disruptive, effects on indigenous societies.[6]

Before turning to the specifics of the CO position and policies as regards Kenya, it will be useful to briefly describe the organization of the office and the individuals who were most responsible for dealing with matters effecting that East African territory. The CO, in 1912, was responsible for both the affairs of dependent colonies and self-governing dominions. The affairs of the dependent empire were handled by six separate departments. Those of the EAP fell within the purview of the East African Department (EAD). In 1912, the EAD consisted of three second class clerks and a principal clerk, H. J. Read, who served as head of the department.

Among those who served in the EAD and in other sections of the CO during the period 1912–14 were several who would be intimately involved with Kenya affairs over the next decade. In addition to Read, F. G. A. Butler, H. F. Batterbee, A. C. C. Parkinson, and W. C. Bottomley would play a part in helping to shape the CO's stance towards Kenya. Most came from a middle-class, establishment background. All, save Bottomley, took degrees at Oxford. As a group, their academic records were truly exceptional, probably surpassed by few other units in the British civil service at that time.

Of them all, Herbert Read was the only official from what might be termed a commercial or petit bourgeois background. His father was a drapery store owner in Devon. Read gained a first class degree from Oxford, and immediately joined the civil service as a clerk at the War Office. He entered the CO in 1889, and, shy and reticent in public, he distinguished himself by his "genius for committee work," particularly those dealing with scientific and medical subjects in the tropics.[7] Of all those in the EAD, Read had the least confidence in, and sympathy for, Kenya's European settlers. Yet as will be seen, Read was not always capable of successfully articulating this point of view in the face of differing opinions of colleagues and superiors. This inability was undoubtedly a major reason for the nickname, "Broken Read," by which he became known in the colonial service.

Frederick G. A. Butler also attended Oxford, gaining two firsts in classics. After a brief stint in the Admiralty, he joined the CO in 1897. By 1912, he had served as private secretary to two under-secretaries of state, and in that year, he was tapped to serve as S of S Lewis Harcourt's private secretary. He held that position until Harcourt left office in May 1915, and continued in the same capacity under Harcourt's successor. Although out of the EAD during that period, his minutes still appeared in several key EAP issues (e.g. the Maasai move of 1911-12). A contemporary described Butler as " 'a very able conscientious, but inflexible civil servant, who came and went by the same trains every day.' "[8] He would briefly head the EAD in 1917.

W. Cecil Bottomley and Henry F. B. Batterbee joined the CO after Butler. Batterbee, seven years Butler's junior, was also educated at Oxford where he took firsts in classics and mathematics. He joined the CO in 1905, and he worked in both the EAD and West African department prior to 1912. In 1912, he became secretary to the West African Lands Committee, and in December he was appointed assistant private secretary to the S of S. From October 1914 through May 1915, Batterbee served as private secretary to the parliamentary under-secretary, and from December 1916 to January 1919, he was private secretary to the S of S. Bottomley was the only Cambridge man among those who served in the EAD before the war. He distinguished himself in mathematics at Cambridge, and he joined the CO in 1901. Between 1911 and his elevation to first class clerk in 1913, Bottomley served as private secretary to the three individuals who held the position of parliamentary under-secretary of state (Colonel Seely, Lord Lucas, and Lord Emmott). Upon his promotion, he came to the EAD, and from that time forward, he

was more deeply involved with the affairs of Kenya than any other single
individual at the CO. He served as head of the EAD from 1918 to 1927.
Bottomley had an excellent memory for detail, and his remarkable skill in
writing minutes that captured the crucial factors in despatches and telegrams
from the colonies was much appreciated and respected by his superiors.
Parkinson later remembered Bottomley as "a Cambridge wrangler, who
found pleasure in working through a ghastly book of advanced mathematical
problems in his spare time. . . ."[9]

In 1912, A. C. Cosmo Parkinson was quite the junior member of the EAD.
Born in 1884, the son of a doctor, Parkinson took firsts in classics and literature at Oxford and joined the CO in 1909 after a year at the Admiralty.
Parkinson quickly earned a reputation for efficiency, and prior to World War
I he served as secretary to the committee appointed to investigate sleeping
sickness and its relationship to wild game. From October 1914 though May
1915, he served as assistant private secretary to the S of S. From the latter
date, he was on military service in East Africa. Parkinson rose furthest of all
those serving in the EAD before the war; he became permanent under-
secretary of state in 1937.[10]

The department that these individuals staffed was the first important point
of contact for despatches, telegrams, and letters that arrived at the CO from,
or concerning, the EAP. The actual opening of the correspondence was carried out by registry clerks who entered each item in a register, linked it up
with previous and/or closely related documents and sent it to the EAD.[11] One
of the second class clerks in the department would then read the document
and minute it on the accompanying minute paper. The minute was meant to
summarize the despatch, telegram, or letter and to propose a possible course
of action and response by the CO. At the close of each minute, the author
placed his initials and the date.[12] The document was then passed to the assistant under-secretary of state responsible for the EAD.

The major exceptions to this procedure had to do with cipher, or coded,
telegrams, and confidential and secret despatches. It was the job of a second
class clerk in the department to decode the arriving telegrams. After that, the
document was forwarded to the registry for typing. For confidential and
secret despatches, the second class clerks were charged with opening and
registering the document without involving the CO registry. Most secret
despatches, of which there were relatively few, were seen by the S of S.[13]

From the assistant under-secretary the file could pass up the CO chain of
command to the permanent under-secretary of state, the parliamentary
under-secretary of state, and finally the S of S himself. The great majority of
correspondence never got that far. It could be stopped along the way by the
head of the department or one of the more senior civil servants if that individual felt he could properly dispose of it.[14] Disposal normally either involved
sending a despatch, telegram, or letter in reply or doing nothing more than
keeping the item of correspondence on file. The latter action was suggested

by the minute, "put by". When a reply was to be sent, the file was returned to the EAD for drafting a suitable one. This was almost always done by the second class clerk and then passed up the chain of command again for possible revision and final approval. When approved, the despatch or telegram was sent to the registry for typing. When ready for signature, it was returned to the appropriate official. All correspondence addressed to the governor of the EAP went out over the name of the S of S. On the other hand, correspondence directed to other government ministries or to private individuals or organizations normally went out over the signature of the assistant under-secretary of state responsible for the department.[15]

From 1912 until 1916, that individual was Sir George V. Fiddes. Fiddes took a second in classics at Oxford, but two years later he ranked first in the Home civil service exam. He entered the CO as a second class clerk. It is generally acknowledged that "his great qualities as an official became apparent after the Jameson Raid" of 1895.[16] For the next seven years, Fiddes's work would be closely tied to South African affairs. In September 1897, he went out to South Africa as imperial secretary to the high commissioner, Lord Milner. Fiddes served through the Boer War, and from 1900-1902, he was secretary to the administration set up by Britain to govern the Transvaal. As a result "of friction on Milner's staff," however, he returned to the CO in 1902 to take charge of the Far Eastern department.[17] Fiddes quickly distinguished himself through his knowledge of financial affairs and skill as an accountant; he was thus appointed accounting officer for the CO in 1907. In 1909, he was promoted to assistant under-secretary of state, and in addition to his other duties, he assumed responsibility for the affairs of British territories in tropical Africa.[18]

Thus from 1912 until his retirement from the CO in 1921, Sir George Fiddes would be deeply involved in Kenya affairs considered important by the CO. His impact on official thinking and policy was not small, especially since from 1916 to 1921 he served as permanent under-secretary of state. Besides his financial expertise, Fiddes was known at the CO for the "lucid and concise writing" of his minutes.[19] Thanks to his sharp, and often sarcastic, minuting and his arid and pedantic personality, Fiddes appeared a very formidable figure whose negative comments provoked fear among those below him in the CO hierarchy.[20] Always an advocate of economy in government, Fiddes was, nevertheless, the least liberal, in the sense of traditional nineteenth century liberalism, of all the CO officials who dealt with EAP affairs during his period at the CO.[21]

In the latter, and in several other ways, Sir John Anderson, the permanent under-secretary of state[22] and next individual in the CO hierarchy who would have something to do with EAP affairs, provided a stark contrast to Fiddes. Unlike the other officials mentioned, Anderson attended neither Oxford or Cambridge. He took an undergraduate and M.A. degree at the University of Edinburgh with first class honors in mathematics; indeed, he won the gold

medal as the most distinguished graduate of 1877. Two years later, he joined
the CO as a second class clerk.[23] His rise within the office was steady as he was
promoted to first class clerk in 1896. In 1904, Anderson left the CO to take up
appointment as governor of the Straits Settlements and high commissioner for
the Federated Malay States. A major reason for acceptance of a post abroad
was marital problems.[24] Getting away from his wife, Anderson governed
Malaya for seven years. In mid-1911, S of S Harcourt offered the position of
permanent under-secretary to Anderson. The latter first refused since his wife
insisted that he live with her if he was in Britain, but eventually a compromise
was reached so that Anderson accepted the appointment.[25] As a result of his
service abroad, Anderson, unlike other CO officials, had considerable experience as a governor. As far as Kenya affairs were concerned, Anderson would
be distinguised, in striking contrast to Fiddes, by a lack of enthusiasm for
European settlement and little sympathy for the settlers demands.

Above Anderson in the CO hierarchy were the parliamentary under-
secretary and the S of S. For the period 1912 to 1914, these positions were
held, respectively, by Lord Emmott and Lewis Harcourt. Both were stalwarts
of the then governing Liberal Party. Very much a free trade Liberal and an
advocate for the midlands textile industry, Emmott served as M.P. for Oldham from 1899 to 1911. In the Commons, he had taken considerable interest
in African affairs, and he spoke out strongly against what he perceived as the
evil system set up by King Leopold in the Congo Free State. So insistent was
his advocacy of the reform measures pushed by E. D. Morel and the Congo
Reform Association that Bernard Porter dubbed him "the mouthpiece of the
Liverpool trading interest."[26] As deputy and counsellor of the S of S, he
would continue to look with suspicion on policies in Africa which might have
what he considered a negative impact on the indigenous population. Emmott
accepted a peerage when he took up the position at the CO.[27]

Lewis Harcourt was the only surviving son of the prominent nineteenth
century Liberal politician Sir William Harcourt. Commonly known to his
friends as Lulu (or Loulou), Harcourt served for several years as his father's
private secretary. Eschewing a political career during that period, he finally
agreed to enter active politics in 1904 as he won a seat in the House of
Commons.[28] A free trader, and initially a lukewarm imperialist, Harcourt was
given, largely as a result of his father's place in the Liberal Party, the post of
First Commissioner of Works when the Liberals returned to power, after
almost a decade out of office, in December 1905.[29] Only in 1910 was he included in the cabinet as Prime Minister Asquith appointed him S of S for the
Colonies. This promotion was not the result of any perceived colonial expertise on Harcourt's part; rather it was the result of Asquith's personal and
political calculations in restructuring his cabinet at the time.[30]

Harcourt's term as S of S was marked by efficiency of organization and
direction. Although heavily dependent on Anderson for advice on major policy decisions and the running of the office, Harcourt took a greater interest in

East African affairs than would any of his successors down to 1924. He was very well regarded by his staff, probably because of his readiness to defend the CO and support their work.[31] Moreover, Harcourt's years at the CO appear to have transformed him into an imperialist. At the end of his tenure as S of S, he would become the leading spokesman in the cabinet for adding to Britain's imperial holdings during World War I.[32] Although Harcourt's attentiveness to CO work and his own interest in EA lagged, as we shall see, after late 1914, the S of S had considerable impact on several EAP issues which the CO viewed as important in the 1912–14 period.

Struggle for Kenya:
The CO and External Pressure Groups in Britain

As intimated earlier, the determination of policy for the EAP was not exclusively the obligation of the CO staff, whether political or permanent. The colonial state and various individuals and groups sought to press varied, and often contradictory policies for Kenya. Among the most influential in addition to the colonial state were the European settlers and Indian residents of Kenya, the IO and the government of India, missionaries in Kenya and Britain, humanitarians and capitalists in the metropole, and the African majority in Kenya. This was certainly the case between 1912 and 1923 as a struggle emerged over specific policies being implemented in that colonial dependency and the general direction that it should take. The struggle was particularly intense during 1919–23, and the intensity was to a considerable degree the result of the fact that the CO had lost control during the war years. During the immediate postwar period, the CO attempted to regain the initiative while several interested parties, in Kenya and outside, attempted to influence the course of events and future policy.

The struggle was not merely over specific policies, such as land tenure or labor regulations, but it was also about such broader issues as the meaning of trusteeship and the future direction Kenya would take. Many British humanitarians and capitalists advocated the "West African" model; an extroverted economy based on peasant production. After World War I, Kenya's small European settler community achieved dominance in the colony's export economy and obtained considerable political influence. The settlers seemed poised to achieve white supremacy on the South African model. That this did not occur was largely the product of the struggle for Kenya that involved protest and advocacy of varying types from a variety of groups and institutions. Such protest was particularly directed at the CO, and it led, in the end, to the CO reasserting its control.

It is thus important to identify in more detail the various interests involved in the struggle to influence and shape British policy in Kenya. Individuals and groups in Britain external to the CO had an impact to be sure. From time to time, such individuals and groups in Britain, and indeed other departments of the British government, raised questions about Kenya or directed protests against policies or actions of the colonial state that demanded CO attention and action.

In theory, the most important groups external to the CO were parliament and the cabinet. The S of S was responsible to both for the actions of the CO as regards any colonial dependency. In fact, neither parliament nor the cabinet exerted continuous or direct influence on policy for Kenya. On the few occasions when Kenya issues were discussed by the cabinet between 1912 and 1923, it was the CO or another department of state (e.g. IO) that initiated the discussion rather than the cabinet assuming any policy initiative. Questions relating to Kenya were regularly raised by members of parliament, but other than the period 1920–22, these did not have a significant impact on CO policy. Questions about, or criticism of, CO policy could also be raised during the annual debate on the CO estimates or vote for the coming financial year. On the whole, this was not an occasion for any lengthy consideration of policy alternatives, though it did provide opportunities for criticism of the actions of the colonial state, especially after World War I. However, most M.P.s, like the general British public, were, unless roused by a particular issue or cause, little interested in the colonies.[33]

In the House of Commons, interest in Kenya affairs was confined to a relatively small group of M.P.s, mainly drawn from the Liberal and Labour parties. Their concern and interest was usually marked by criticism of specific actions of the colonial state or by a fear that the exploitation of African resources (principally land and labor) was being too brutally carried out for the benefit of Kenya's settlers. Africans, they felt, should not be subjected to forced labor or injustice, and the indigenous peoples should retain and cultivate their own lands. Prominent among such parliamentary critics were "Radicals" such as the Liberal member Edmund Harvey and the Liberal (and later Labour) M.P. Josiah Wedgwood.[34] The latter was not only a strong advocate of African rights; he supported Indian demands for equal rights after the war. The bulk of Conservative M.P.s, if interested in Kenya affairs at all, were generally supportive of the settlers and the colonial state. One notable exception to this tendency was the attitude of William Ormsby-Gore. Prior to entering the government in late 1922, Ormsby-Gore was critical of the trend of economic policy in Kenya that gave excessive state support to European agriculture and little to African production.

M.P.s could not only gain the attention of the CO by questions, motions, and contributions in parliament. Those mentioned above, and others, from time to time addressed personal letters to the S of S or the parliamentary under-secretary, or they approached them directly while at the Commons or Lords. Such approaches usually merited a reply, and the CO staff were thus forced to investigate the questions raised, or allegations made; on some occasions, these necessitated contact with the governor in Nairobi, but seldom did they lead to serious CO policy initiatives.

A major source of criticism of Kenya policies, on the other hand, came from non-parliamentary individuals and groups that for convenience may be termed the humanitarian lobby. This rough grouping included church and missionary groups on the one hand, and the moralists of the Anti-Slavery and Aborigines Protection Society (ASAPS) on the other. The latter was always ready to cast a critical eye on labor policies in the EAP, while the former were concerned that the work of the protestant missions in Kenya not be compromised by exploitative or excessively pro-settler policies. The interests of the humanitarians were overwhelmingly the result of moral concerns. Missionary and church groups, effectively marshalled by J. H. Oldham, would take a great interest in Kenya affairs during the period 1920–23, and they exerted considerable pressure on the CO. As this study will demonstrate, Oldham and the missionary lobby have been credited, in scholarly studies, with a degree of influence on CO policy that is not warranted by a close examination of CO records.

Though much less vocal than the humanitarian lobby, colonial officials, in Britain either on leave or retirement, actually had a much greater impact on the CO's decision making process in initiating significant policy changes in Kenya. Lord Lugard, never shy to share his views with the CO after his retirement, was one such figure. Colonial officers who had served in East Africa could not be dismissed as mere do gooders; their knowledge of Kenya earned them a respectful hearing from CO officials. As will be seen in chapters 6 and 7, two such officials, John Ainsworth and O. F. Watkins, played crucial roles in forcing the CO to recognize the need to intervene in Kenya to try to bring about the alteration of unwise policies that had been adopted by the colonial state. Another former colonial servant whose criticism the CO was often forced to consider was the former medical officer, Dr. Norman Leys. He was one of the strongest and most persistent critics of Kenya policies after the war. Leys often made common cause with the humanitarian lobby, and he was an influential member of the Labour party's colonial advisors.[35] Though Leys's criticisms were usually unsympathetically received by CO officials, he did play a significant role in initiating the process of CO review that led to the alteration of Kenya labor policy in 1921.

Another category of individuals to whom the CO was forced to give attention during the period 1912–23 were those representing metropolitan capital. The latter's interests were mainly in economic policy. As Brett has shown, the "most pervasive and effective influence on policy was almost certainly exerted by the representatives of British capital directly or indirectly involved in East Africa."[36] The fractions of British capital most involved in Kenya were finance and merchant, and their interests in, and influence on, CO policy fell largely into two categories: those representatives whose intersts and activity was continuous and those who merely intervened with the CO when particular issues arose of concern to them.

Finance capital fell into the latter category. Representatives of the three British banks operating in Kenya had little contact with the CO until the 1919–21 period when a consideration of changes in currency and exchange policy caused them considerable distress. Even then, it was the CO that initiated contact. Although the currency crisis of 1919–21 would clearly illustrate the tremendous muscle the bankers could bring to bear on the CO if they wished to do so, finance capital was hardly a major factor in determining imperial policy towards Kenya. George Lloyd's brief interest in investment in railway construction prior to the war provides another example of a brief, and ultimately unfruitful, interest in Kenya by a British financier.

Neither, as this study will show, was merchant capital "pulling the strings" for CO officials. Representatives of merchant capital normally were only in contact with the CO regarding specific issues or grievances. A major exception is provided, however, by Sir Humphrey Leggett, managing director of the British East Africa Corporation. Leggett's firm had considerable commercial interests in the EAP and Uganda, and he was in fairly regular communication with the CO both before and after the war. Leggett also headed the East Africa section of the London Chamber of Commerce after 1918. His influence would be considerable in the post war debates over currency and exchange policy, but Leggett's greatest impact will be noted in the 1922 CO decision to reassert its control over Kenya for economic reasons.

In addition to capitalists, the CO was, on occasion, forced to consider criticisms and suggestions from other departments of state. During the period covered by this study, the IO and the Treasury were the departments with the greatest impact. The CO had to take note of Treasury advice prior to 1913 since the EAP received an annual grant-in-aid from the Treasury. After that date, the CO was still forced to grudgingly seek Treasury approval for loan projects and currency and tariff changes. The IO relationship with the CO was somewhat different. After the war, the IO was in regular contact with the CO regarding the so-called Indian question. IO pressure certainly would have a major impact on CO policy, though the latter would never go as far as the IO wished in meeting East African Indian demands.

One final external pressure group that deserves mention was the Kenya settlers and their sympathizers in Britain. Some settlers, particularly those with good connections to the establishment in Britain, could bring pressure to bear on both the CO and the colonial state in support of the policies they advocated.[37] Settler leaders, such as Lord Delamere and E. S. Grogan, often wrote to CO officials or visited the office while in London so as to voice their desires and criticisms of Kenya policy and practice. Others, such as Lord Cranworth and W. M. Crowdy, placed their views before the CO on a less regular basis. After the war, a pressure group, Associated Producers of East

Africa, took shape as a loose grouping of people in Britain with agricultural interests in East Africa. The settler pressure groups were not without impact on the CO, but it is perhaps worth noting that CO officials held rather low opinions of them, particularly Grogan and Delamere.

The CO and the EAP

Groups external to the CO would influence CO machinery and policies and be involved in the struggle for Kenya, but the most important factor in CO policy towards the EAP was its relations with the protectorate itself and the colonial state that had taken shape to govern it. It is important to recognize that the colonial state was not static; it was continually evolving. As Berman has persuasively suggested, it was "a set of institutions and practices that both reflected and shaped the contradictions and crises of the political economy in which it was set."[38]

Although a British protectorate had been formalized a decade earlier, the CO had only assumed responsibility for the EAP in 1905.[39] It inherited a position with regard to this part of Africa that involved coping with a number of contradictions. The roots of these contradictions were varied and complex, and in practically every instance the colonial state was the institution that had to try to deal with them rather than the CO. Yet since the most fundamental of the contradictions were difficult to resolve, had the potential to have an impact on wider imperial interests, and threatened to cause parliamentary questions and scrutiny, the CO was inevitably deeply involved as well in attempting to frame satisfactory solutions.[40]

The most crucial of the contradictions that the CO had to grapple with stemmed from the EAP's economic situation. Although the British taxpayer had underwritten the construction of the Uganda Railway, the EAP had not been able to pay its way prior to 1912. Since 1895, the colonial state required annual grants-in-aid from the imperial government. The colonial state had conquered and exercised coercive authority in the most populous parts of the EAP by 1912, but it had yet to see production for export reach a level which would provide sufficient state revenue to balance expenditure.[41] Though the conquest of the EAP had been gradual and piecemeal, the cost proved a substantial charge on the protectorate's meager revenues.[42] Thus not only were grants-in-aid necessary, but the British Treasury exercised direct budgetary supervision over the EAP and the CO so long as Britain provided such grants.

What Lonsdale and Berman have called the contradiction of accumulation and control was complicated by the presence of two alien groups of capitalists; a small, but vocal, group of European settler farmers and a significantly larger group of Indian merchants and artisans.[43] The colonial state had encouraged, and the imperial government acquiesced in, the settlement of these two groups. Both offered the potential of promoting production for export that would enable the grant-in-aid to be terminated while at the same time assisting metropolitan capital by producing increasing amounts of the kind of commodities desired by the latter (e.g. cotton, oil seeds) and expanding markets for British manufactured goods.[44] This concern that the African dependencies should assist metropolitan accumulation in those ways was consistently voiced by Harcourt during his years at the head of the CO.[45]

Although the Indian and settler offered alternative routes to increased production for export, they both depended on the indigenous African population. Far more numerous than either of the immigrant communities, the overwhelming bulk of the African population were, prior to 1895, characterized by pre-capitalist modes of production. They comprised a network of economies that have been described as "an overlapping patchwork of hunting, cultivating and herding peoples" who "exploited varied ecological arenas: forest, hills, and plains."[46] Capitalist penetration of the EAP was at first slow as conquest was gradual and piecemeal because the colonial state had as its top priority the completion of the Uganda Railway to Lake Victoria. Such penetration speeded up after the latter had been accomplished in 1901; this was accompanied by the arrival of increasing numbers of Europeans and Indians. The result was to bring about a pattern of capitalist penetration dependent upon African peasant production and settler estate production. Both were reliant on African labor and access to land for cultivation and grazing.

On the one hand, the colonial state, and the CO, encouraged peasantization. Through taxation, distribution of seeds, and coercion by chiefs and headmen, the state encouraged commodity production from African households. Using household labor and land available to the family unit, increasing numbers of African households began to produce surplus commodities for sale. This surplus came largely from new crops, such as improved maize, sim sim, groundnuts, and cotton, made available to African households after the introduction of colonial rule. On the whole, this increased production was made possible by the cultivation of additional land.[47] Indian merchants handled the marketing of the surplus commodities for sale within the protectorate and for export. By 1912, peasant production had become entrenched in the Kikuyu-inhabited districts of Kiambu, Fort Hall (now Murang'a), and Nyeri, and the Luo- and Luyia-inhabited districts of Central and North Kavirondo (later Central and North Nyanza).[48]

At the same time, the colonial state encouraged production for export from European settler farms, estates, and ranches. The most significant ways in which the colonial state favored settler production was through the land and labor policies it adopted; railway rates were also lowered as an incentive to settler exports. For the African population, the major impact of these policies were felt in the start of the process of proletarianization. Administrative and economic policies were adopted that had the effect of forcing African men to become workers on settler farms and estates. Large tracts of land were granted to the Europeans with the result that substantial areas were lost, then and in the future, for African cultivation and grazing.[49] Taxation was another way the colonial state fostered the process of proletarianization. The purpose of the 1902 hut tax was not only to raise government revenue, but to force African men to work, either for the colonial state or the settlers, for wages. From the first days of settlement, Europeans bombarded the state with calls of assistance in obtaining cheap labor. This pressure brought about the inauguration of the poll tax in 1908; it hit young men over the age of sixteen (normally bachelors) who did not have to pay hut tax. Despite the economic pressure afforded by these taxes, a leading student of Kenya's labor history concluded that the major factor in bringing Africans into the labor market prior to World War I was coercion. The colonial state, through its administrative apparatus (largely the colonial chiefs), simply forced men out to work for wages.[50]

State attempts to promote both estate and peasant production spawned the most fundamental contradiction in colonial Kenya's history. It led to severe competition for land, labor, and markets that produced land and labor problems and crises through most of the first half of the twentieth century. Most of these were major concerns for the CO as well. The economic realities which underlay this contradiction were the most essential single factor determining the stance the CO would take as arbiter in that competition and the struggle that ultimately raged over Kenya's destiny.

For the CO, the fundamental factor in the imperial equation was not the mode of production but the fact of production for export. This was important because, as noted earlier, colonies were expected to pay for themselves and to provide raw materials and markets as a means of aiding the metropolitan economy. Prior to 1913, moreover, the CO had another pressing reason for desiring increased production for export: a strong desire to escape what was viewed as Treasury control. Since the EAP received an imperial grant-in-aid, Treasury approval had to be obtained for the protectorate's annual estimates.[51] It was a source of some unhappiness among CO officials that the final word as to EAP revenue and expenditure was not theirs but the Treasury's. This served to heighten the well established "suspicion and hostility" that existed between the two departments.[52] It was with considerable satisfaction that CO welcomed the end of the grant-in-aid and Treasury control in the 1912–13 financial year as the EAP's revenues finally came to surpass expenditure.[53]

It is crucial to understand what brought about this situation. Without question, the reason lay in a dramatic expansion in the value of exports between 1908 and 1913. This amounted to an increase of 5,164,383 rupees (£344,292 at the then rate of exchange).[54] This rise fuelled increases in customs revenue and hut and poll tax collection and growth in railway revenue sufficient to

balance the EAP budget. Between 1909 and 1912, for example, customs
revenue increased by 43 per cent, hut and poll tax collection by 28 per cent,
and railway revenue by 48 per cent.[55]

Table 1.1.   Percentage Value of Agricultural Exports, 1908–13

	1908	1909	1910	1911	1912	1913
African						
Hides and Skins	26	40	40	33	23	37
Maize	*	1	5	see mixed category**		
Beans and Peas	1	3	4	3	5	5
Sim Sim	*	16	13	15	14	20
Oil seeds (linseed, cotton, castor, sim sim)	*	1	*	2	1	*
Other grain (millet, rice)	*	*	*	*	1	*
Cotton	6	7	5	2	13	1
Groundnuts	1	*	1	1	2	2
Ghee	5	2	3	3	3	1
Potatoes	6	5	3	2	4	2
% of total	45	75	74	61	66	68
European Settler						
Coffee	*	1	1	3	2	5
Sisal	–	–	–	*	1	2
Other fibre	–	–	–	–	1	2
Plantation rubber	–	–	–	1	1	1
Wool	2	*	2	3	3	2
% of total	2	1	3	7	8	12
Miscellaneous						
Coconuts/copra	29	14	15	11	4	7
Gum copal	1	1	1	1	*	1
Bees wax	19	5	6	5	3	2
Wild animal skins	3	3	1	1	1	1
Wild rubber	–	–	–	5	2	1
Mangrove bark	1	1	*	*	*	–
% of total	53	24	23	23	10	12
Mixed						
Maize				9	16	8
% of total				9	16	8
Total value (rupees)	647,607	1,168,740	2,168,504	2,943,389	4,780,717	5,811,990

Notes: *Denotes exports, but less than half of one percent of total.
         **After 1910, maize exports came from both African and European farms.
         –Denotes no recorded export.
Source: East Africa Protectorate, *Department of Agriculture British East Africa Annual Report
         1916–17* (Nairobi, 1918), 27.

As Table 1.1 clearly illustrates, the bulk of the increases in agricultural exports came from peasant households. From 45 per cent of agricultural exports in 1908, Africans generated well over half the total exports in 1909 and the African proportion remained at that level down to 1913. Key elements in this increase were maize, sim sim, cotton, beans, and peas. The example of sim sim was most remarkable. From less than one half of one per cent in 1908, sim sim exports had come to constitute 20 per cent of the protectorate's agricultural exports by the end of 1913. In terms of value received, this more than 4500 per cent rise came to a £76,416 difference.[56] The sim sim exports, as with cotton and most of the maize, came from Nyanza province. Thus while the end of the imperial grant-in-aid was largely the result of the efforts of African producers in Nyanza, the colonial state had done relatively little to foster this development. Rather it was the result of local initiative undertaken by the provincial commissioner, John Ainsworth.[57]

By contrast, European settler crops made up but a small share of the EAP's agricultural exports by the beginning of 1914. Clearly the African sector responded more quickly than did the settler farms and estates to the opportunities offered by the colonial economy. Settler-generated exports made up more than 14 per cent of the total if account is taken of the fact that after 1911 a portion of the protectorate's maize exports came from settler farms. The primary stimulus for this was the reduction of railway rates for maize intended for export starting in 1910.[58] Coffee, grown on relatively small number of estates, had shown healthy increases in exports from a value of £185 in 1908 to £19,486. Yet this still represented a very small share of the protectorate's total exports. Sisal, the other major settler estate crop, had made even less headway; only in 1912 could the director of agriculture state that it had finally been "proved in the affirmative" as a paying cash crop.[59]

A discussion of the lack of success of settler production should not focus only on export figures, however. There were alternative avenues for settlers to obtain an income. One such route that continued to be a concern to the CO was land speculation. A number of early settlers obtained huge amounts of land at very cheap prices. Before the end of the first decade of the twentieth century, there had emerged a group of "largemen" who held colossal tracts of land in several parts of the protectorate. Lord Delamere and E. S. Grogan were examples of this type of landowner, and much of their, and others, accumulation was for speculative purposes. Land regulations had done little to check such speculation as development and occupation clauses in leases were circumvented. After 1910, land values began to rise because of a growing demand from new settlers. Already established European landowners were able to capitalize through subdivision of their farms and estates. Thus it is important to bear mind that land dealings were "an integral part of the pre-war settler economy."[60] This was an easier route, in the short term, to profit than agricultural development.

The most important factor in the EAP's agricultural economy prior to 1914, nevertheless, was African peasant production. When adding maize to the others shown in Table 1.1, the African contribution to exports constituted at least 70 per cent of the total in 1912 and 1913. Using slightly different data, John Overton concluded that African products made up 66.7 per cent of the protectorate's exports in 1912–13; settler products constituted 9.3 per cent and miscellaneous 24 per cent.[61] Leaving exports aside, it is Overton's estimate that with the heavy African contribution to taxation, railway earnings, customs duties, fees, and fines, by 1914 "the cost of governing the Protectorate was being borne to the extent of at least 70 per cent by Africans."[62]

What is even more striking about the dominance of African production is the fact that it had come about despite the fact that the colonial state had done little comparatively to stimulate it and a great deal to spur that of the settler sector. African agriculture had shown itself very responsive to new market opportunities and had required very limited state intervention. By contrast, settler agriculture had experienced considerable state intervention but had shown itself relatively unresponsive to market opportunities.[63] It was African production that, in fact, provided the means to meet the costs of colonial administration, to say nothing of terminating the imperial grant-in-aid. Overton has demonstrated that Nyanza and Kenia provinces, where the great majority of African production for export took place, were large net exporters of revenue to the rest of the protectorate.[64] Even more significant than this, African peasant production was underwriting and subsidizing European settlement!

Thanks to the work of Overton and E. A. Brett,[65] this most fundamental fact of colonial Kenyan history is well known to students of that subject. Yet for purposes of this study, it is important to attempt to ascertain if CO officials had grasped it. The answer is that they were certainly aware that European settlement was not paying its way and "had not proved itself" by 1914.[66] As to why they had not taken steps to do something about the situation, the answer seems to lie with the position of the colonial state. The coming of European settlers and metropolitan concessionaires, in Berman's words, "created political processes that progressively undermined the colonial state's control over the terms of development."[67] Thus political factors would always be as significant, and sometimes more, than economic in defining the colonial state's stance towards European settlement and the settlers' economic demands and pressures. The CO would be subject to adopt a similar stance.

One rather radical step that had occurred to at least some at the CO in 1908 was the liquidation of the experiment in European settlement. This possibility had been discussed by CO officials in light of the fact that "no one in the white highlands had made any money and many have lost what they had."[68] W. D. Ellis suggested that "it would probably pay the British taxpayer to repatriate all the whites and forbid their entry except on payment of a heavy poll tax."[69] This was certainly "one of the most startling suggestions to emanate from the Colonial Office" at least until 1940 when Harold Macmillan would make a similar recommendation, but, though the EAP governor's views were sought, the proposal was never seriously taken up.[70]

While it is true that CO sympathies were broadly anti-settler and pro-African, this did not translate itself into a firm resolve to force the colonial state to slow down and halt the subsidization of settlement by African production, dramatically expand the latter by increased levels of support, and resist settler political and economic demands. CO officials who dealt with it thought that the African population of the EAP was particularly "backward" and "primitive", a long way from "civilization" (by which was meant western civilization and values). Fully sharing the "paternalistic authoritarianism"[71] that characterized colonial administrators and the racist thinking of the time, they could not, on the one hand, conceive of rapid African economic development. All officials held, as gospel, the racist stereotype of the "lazy native" that was loudly and repeatedly propagated by Kenya settlers. According to this view, the African male was inherently lazy and utterly resistant to any of the kinds of economic pressures that forced individuals to work under capitalism.[72]

Although this gospel was contradicted by the economic facts of the pre–World War I period, CO officials were utterly convinced of its correctness. On the other hand, the CO preservationist interpretation of trusteeship provided a different, but quite persuasive, argument against the speeding up and expanding of capitalist penetration of African areas. CO officials felt that such initiatives held the potential for undermining the "traditional" political and social structure. The desire to avoid what was seen as destructive social change that would accompany the commercialization of African production and lead to the breakdown of "tribal" control was thus strong in CO thinking.[73]

There were few indeed prepared to argue that Kenya would be better off economically by emphasizing African production, rather than settler. In economic terms, the EAP was one of Britain's poorest dependencies. Prior to 1912, it had proven largely lacking in precious minerals, and its small contribution to the imperial economic order was clearly evident to metropolitan capitalists. Nevertheless, merchant capital in Great Britain had shown some interest in promoting African cotton production in the protectorate. The British Cotton Growing Association, representing textile interests there, played a part in starting cotton cultivation in Nyanza province after 1906, but their interest in Nyanza cotton growing soon lagged. Cotton planting there expanded, thanks to strong support from Ainsworth who became provincial commissioner in 1907.[74] These efforts, nevertheless, had not been very effective down to the start of 1914 as a huge rise in exports in 1912 was followed by a drastic drop in the following two years. Factors responsible included problems with seed distribution, lack of substantial government support and investment, unwise government strategies for dealing with planting and plot location, lack of economic incentives, and too frequent reliance on commu-

CO was losing its grip on the EAP, here was a clear indication that the CO had not lost it completely.[86] The CO intervened decisively in EAP affairs; yet the reasons for its intervention were not essentially economic or political. While it brought about the end of a governor's administration, the CO did little to solve Kenya's fundamental economic contradiction.

Girouard's downfall stemmed from his handling of two incidents in particular. These were the aftermath of the trial of Galbraith Cole and the Maasai move of 1911. Both raised, in the minds of CO officials, issues of British justice. Moreover, they came to believe, with good reason, that Girouard had failed to keep London informed of the course of events, had followed opportunist policies aimed at winning support from the settlers at the expense of London, had been extremely dilatory in carrying out instructions from the CO, and had actually lied to the S of S.

The CO's difficulty with Girouard over what may be termed the Cole affair began with the murder trial of Galbraith Cole on 31 May 1911. Cole was one of the most wealthy and prominent of the EAP's early settlers. Son of the Earl of Enniskillen and brother-in-law of settler–political leader Lord Delamere, Cole held a large ranch near Lake Elementeita.[87] At his trial, held in the heart of the white highlands at Nakuru, Cole admitted shooting an African he suspected of stealing some of his sheep and not reporting the matter to police. Despite the charge of the judge to "confine yourselves to the evidence," the jury of nine white men took but five minutes to acquit Cole.[88]

The first reports of the case from Girouard reached the CO by telegram on 7 June. The governor mentioned the possibility of an appeal against the verdict, but stated that his legal adviser counseled against any such action. Girouard went on to inform the CO: "The crime is due to the prevalence of unrestrained stock theft."[89] The EAD had already learned more details of the case through press reports of the preliminary inquiry held on 26 April. Read reacted angrily to Girouard's telegram. "In spite of Sir P. Girouard's apologetics," he minuted, "it seems to me that murder is murder and that it is out of the question to let the matter slide in the easy manner he appears to contemplate."[90] Read thus proposed a strong telegraphic reply. Approved by Fiddes, who felt Girouard had a "plain duty to appeal in such a particularly atrocious case," and S of S Harcourt himself, a telegram was sent to Girouard on 12 June which stated that "a callous and unjustifiable murder" had been committed and that there had been "a gross miscarriage of justice."[91] Despite the fact that the CO legal adviser doubted that an appeal was possible in the case, the CO telegram urged Girouard "to appeal from the order for acquittal if you are advised that it is possible."[92]

Following confirmation from Girouard a week later that an appeal was legally impossible, no more was heard of the case in London until the end of July. At that time, an official despatch and a private letter arrived from the governor providing further detail about the case. The despatch enclosed a complete copy of the court proceedings, and Girouard reiterated that the crime was "due to prevalence of unchecked stock thefts."[93] In his private letter, Girouard confided to the S of S two possible lines of administrative action open to him: "1 To recommend the suspension of trial by jury. 2 The deportation of Mr. Cole." The governor asked for guidance as he was "unsure of my exact rights and your possible orders in the case."[94]

On receipt of the full details of the Cole case, CO officials were even more outraged by the miscarriage of justice. H. F. Batterbee of the EAD was aghast that the defense counsel "did not attempt to set up any defense, and evidently relied upon the jury to acquit simply because he was a white man."[95] Permanent under-secretary Sir John Anderson vehemently advocated the adoption of Girouard's second suggestion, the deportation of Cole. Anderson argued that Cole's testimony at the trial established that in the language of Section 25.1 of the 1902 East Africa Order-in-Council "he is conducting himself so as to be dangerous to peace, order and good government in East Africa." All the governor needed was a single affidavit attesting to Cole's actions, and he could order the latter's deportation.[96] Harcourt agreed with Anderson. It was, he wrote, "a very horrible case. . . . Cole must be deported."[97]

As a result, a telegram was sent to Nairobi on the same day. "On reading papers in Cole case," it stated, "have come to the conclusion that he must be deported under section 25.1 of order-in-council. If you have any observations to make telegraph them at once as I wish to direct deportation immediately."[98]

The wording and the haste with which the telegram was despatched clearly indicated the CO's desire for a rapid reply. Considerable consternation was therefore felt when days went by and no word relating to the Cole case came from Nairobi. Short telegrams of reminder were sent to Girouard on 3 and 7 August requesting a response. Finally Harcourt ordered a stern telegram sent to the governor on 9 August demanding a reply "at once on receipt of this telegram" and an explanation "why you have omitted to do so earlier."[99]

This strong message finally evoked a response from Girouard on 10 August, but it stunned CO officials by raising legal difficulties to any deportation of Cole. The governor had consulted judges of the High Court and his Executive Council (Execo) and concluded that an individual who had been acquitted in a criminal case could not be deported. If Cole applied for a writ of habeas corpus and it was granted, no deportation could ensue.[100] Shocked that Girouard had consulted the judges on a matter that might later come before them, the London officials did not agree with the governor's assessment. They believed that the order-in-council gave the governor power to order a deportation of any individual "conducting himself so as to be dangerous to the peace and good order in East Africa. . . ."[101]

The CO quickly replied, informing the governor that he seemed to have "entirely misapprehended" the reason for the deportation. The only connection with the trial was that evidence given there established that Cole "is conducting himself so as to be dangerous to peace and good order whose continued presence in the protectorate may provide reprisals by natives." The CO legal advisors held that no appeal could be made against a deportation order under section 25.1 of the 1902 order-in-council. Thus Girouard was ordered to undertake the necessary steps to effect the deportation.[102]

Upon receipt of this telegram, Governor Girouard was still not prepared to act as the CO desired. He telegraphed London on 22 August expressing doubts that section 25 and 26 of the order applied in the Cole case. He did, however, wire the substance of an affidavit sworn by the acting crown advocate, and he stated that if the law officers of the crown in London considered the evidence adduced in the affidavit adequate, he would issue the deportation warrant at once.[103]

CO officials decided not to refer the affidavit to the legal advisors, and Harcourt ordered a short telegraphic reply to the governor transmitting that fact.[104] Harcourt and the permanent officials undoubtedly felt that upon receiving this reply Sir Percy would issue the deportation order as he had indicated he would in his telegram of 22 August.

If that was the case, they were soon disappointed. Girouard telegraphed to London on 5 September stating, after consulting his Execo, that he was issuing the deportation order under protest and only on orders from London. Girouard's strangely worded wire expressed his doubts as to the applicability of the 1902 order-in-council. He stated that as "the order-in-council of October 1906 directs me to carry out your instructions" he was issuing a deportation warrant "ordered in your telegram of July 28."[105]

CO officials were not amused by what seemed clearly to have been an attempt by Girouard to "divest himself of all responsibility in the matter."[106] After consultation with the CO legal advisor, a strong telegram, personally approved by Harcourt, was sent to Nairobi. It informed the governor that the provisions of the 1902 order had to be complied with exactly. He was asked if he had done so or "have you in order, as in the telegram under reply, attempted to divest yourself of responsibility in the matter and cite instructions from me. . . ." The telegram concluded with a very pointed observation suggested to Harcourt by Read: "I regret that throughout this case I have failed to receive from you the cooperation to which I consider myself entitled."[107]

Girouard's subsequent reports that Cole had been served with the deportation order and a further explanation of the reasons for his actions in the case cut little ice at the CO.[108] Read felt that "this is not very convincing" and then parliamentary under-secretary Lord Lucas argued that Girouard's despatch furnished "no justification or explanation."[109] The CO replied with a personal letter to the governor that was highly critical of his conduct in the Cole case. The S of S told Girouard: "So far from lending me ready assistance, you continued to raise difficulties which appeared to me to be adequately covered by the instructions and opinions already sent to you."[110] The CO had eventually had its way in the Cole case, and in the process Harcourt and the permanent officials lost confidence in Girouard.

Girouard's handling of the Maasai move was, as noted earlier, an even more powerful factor in bringing a premature end to his governorship. It was not so much the bungling of the attempts to move the Maasai from the Laikipia plateau following the treaty forced on them in 1911 that caused the CO to lose confidence in his leadership. Rather the crucial issue was the promise of farms to European settlers on the Laikipia plateau. Suggestions that Girouard had promised such farms to settlers prior to the 1911 treaty reached the CO in the form of allegations and rumors to that effect at the time Harcourt was considering approving the treaty.[111] The move from Laikipia began, but it soon broke down. As rumors of promises of Laikipia land to settlers continued to make their way to London, the CO sent a wire to Girouard on 5 October 1911, warning against the grant of, or promise of, land there and inquiring whether any grants or promises to such land had already been made. Girouard replied on the 7th that no such rights had been given or promised, but that Europeans who had given up 130,000 acres for the extended southern Maasai reserve had to be accommodated elsewhere.[112] The S of S accepted the governor's statement, and on the strength of it, Harcourt replied to a question in the House of Commons in mid-April 1912 that "no allocations of land occupied by the Northern Masai had yet been made."[113]

Much to Harcourt's annoyance, it soon became clear that promises of land for Europeans on Laikipia had indeed been made. Even before his Common's reply, Harcourt had been told by a provincial commissioner in the EAP, C. R. W. Lane, that farms had been promised. In fact Girouard had promised settlers land on Laikipia in April 1910.[114] Harcourt raised the issue with Girouard at an interview on 8 May 1912 while the governor was on home leave, and to the S of S's astonishment Sir Percy stated that lands on Laikipia had been promised to settlers who gave up land for the expanded southern Maasai reserve. When reminded of his 7 October telegram, the governor could say nothing more than that he saw no inconsistency in his statement then and his recollection at the CO.[115]

This interview was, in effect, the last straw. Just as in the Cole case, Girouard had been caught not playing straight with the CO. Whether he deliberately misled Harcourt or was guilty of forgetful incompetence, the governor had to go. His favoritism for the settlers had proved a huge embarrassment and laid the groundwork for events that were likely to provide future difficulty for the CO as the Maasai had filed, through European attorneys, a law suit asking for the return of Laikipia to them. Girouard "resigned" from the colonial service in July 1912.

The passage of years would not soften the CO view of Girouard's behavior. Bottomley wrote, in a 1918 memo that

the mark he left on the protectorate at the end of his administration in 1912 was rather one of promise than of performance. His promises in fact were the chief difficulty in the way of his successor and Sir Henry Belfield was continually in a position of having to refuse to recognize alleged promises made to settlers by Sir

Percy Girouard. . . . there is nothing in his [Girouard's] record in East Africa to shew that his efforts would be directed to the permanent welfare of the country rather than to the expediency of the moment and his own popularity.[116]

Yet the victory for the CO in the case of the Laikipia land was only partial. Girouard might be sacked, but his promises were kept. On the advice of Anderson, Harcourt concluded that "obligations contracted in 1910 must therefore be discharged."[117]

Despite giving the land to the settlers, the removal of Sir Percy Girouard and the deportation of Cole demonstrated that the CO could intervene decisively in EAP affairs. The CO had the means to exercise control over policy, if it was prepared to use it, to put a brake on the implementation of unsound policies that benefitted the European settlers at the expense of the protectorate's African and Indian populations. Girouard's governorship was not, as Hyam asserts, "a major turning point in the wayward evolution of Kenya, enabling the settlers to entrench themselves in a way far removed from official intention."[118] The CO was still in control. The real major turning point would come in the succeeding governorship.

2
Belfield and the CO Before the War, 1912–14

With the resignation of Sir Percy Girouard, the CO moved quickly to appoint a successor. If the purpose was to gain a firmer grip on the protectorate and to slow down or halt the direction of government policies favoring the European settlers, CO officials would be quickly disappointed. Sir Henry Conway Belfield was not a man suited for such a task. He soon became an advocate, and indeed a chief supporter, of settler political, economic, and, above all, land demands. Yet in spite of the governor's pro-settler orientation, the CO managed to retain the initiative in EAP affairs to the extent that by the start of World War I, it had vetoed or considerably watered down these demands in practice. Yet on the crucial question of land policy, the CO would all but give over control to the new governor.

Belfield Takes Over

The choice of Sir Henry Belfield as the EAP's new chief administrator is, at first glance, difficult to understand since he had almost no African experience. The new governor's background was impressive enough. Born in 1855, Belfield, son of a justice of the peace, attended Rugby school and Oxford. He then qualified as a barrister in 1880 and practiced law in England until 1884. In that year, he joined the colonial service as a magistrate in the Malay states. There he remained for the next twenty-eight years, serving in a variety of posts (including commissioner of lands in Selangor), learning the Malay language, and becoming, as he described himself, "a tropical creature."[1] He rose to serve as British Resident in three of the states, concluding his career in Malaya as resident of Perak. His only African experience during that time was exceedingly brief. In 1911, he undertook, at the behest of the CO, a special mission to the Gold Coast to report on land alienation there.

Belfield's lack of acquaintance with Africa is not the only reason why his appointment is difficult to fathom. At age 57, he was in M. P. K. Sorrenson's words, "in the twilight of his career."[2] Shy and not a good mixer, Belfield did not possess the strong and dynamic personality that had characterized

Girouard. It must have been abundantly clear to CO officials that he would not provide vigorous leadership for the protectorate.[3]

Yet it was undoubtedly this very fact that strongly recommended Belfield's appointment to the CO. They did not want another "dynamic" Girouard. In the CO view, what the EAP needed was "a period of steady, sober-minded administration."[4] Throughout his years in Malaya, Belfield had shown himself an able, and above all, a loyal civil servant. He could be counted on to follow orders, implement policy directives from London, report fully to his superiors, and make no attempt to mislead them. Belfield's experience with colonial land issues was another plus as far as the CO was concerned. After years of study and wrangling, there were a number of outstanding land issues that needed to be decided,[5] and Belfield seemed especially well qualified to do so. His report on land alienation in the Gold Coast suggested that he had an appreciation of "native rights" and would not be likely to support settler demands for additional alienation of African land.[6]

Perhaps the most obvious, and telling, reason for the appointment of Belfield was that he was Sir John Anderson's choice. Anderson had governed Straits Settlements and been high commissioner of the Malay states from 1904 to 1911. Belfield had served under him during that period, and Anderson was convinced that Belfield was the right man for the job in the EAP. The permanent under-secretary would remain a supporter of Belfield in most critical circumstances.

Once the choice of Belfield had been made, the CO was faced with two difficulties that complicated the appointment. The first was the hostility of the Kenya settlers that took the form of protest resolutions when the CO made public Girouard's resignation and Belfield's appointment in mid-July. Because of Girouard's popularity with the settlers, protest against the resignation did not likely come as a surprise. However, the vehemence of the criticism of Belfield and his qualifications came as a bit of a shock to London. The protests emanated from a "mass meeting" of Europeans called by A. G. W. Anderson, editor of the *East African Standard* (*EAS*), one of Nairobi's two daily newspapers. He told the meeting that "the experience of the gentleman now proposed as Governor in itself could not justify the appointment."[7] As a result of Anderson's initiative, a telegram was sent to the CO, through the acting governor. It reported the meeting's "consternation" at Girouard's resignation and recorded its "grave anxiety at the change of policy indicated by the appointment of another gentleman . . . whose record as shown by published statistics appears to contain nothing in the nature of previous colonial experience. . . ."[8] The telegram asked the CO to reconsder the appointment.

It caused an angry reaction in the CO. Upon reading it, Butler, the S of S's private secretary, minuted: "It is difficult to characterize this telegram adequately. A mild man might call it 'damned cheek' based on ignorance."[9] A week after the receipt of the telegram, the CO replied with a very brief one of its own. "In view of Mr. Belfield's long career in the colonial service your telegram not understood," the CO wire stated, "but I presume it was sent under a misapprehension."[10]

The arrival of the CO telegram found the Nairobi settlers in a much less combative mood. The reply from London was considered at the annual general meeting of the Landholders Association on 29 July. Although criticism of Belfield's appointment was voiced, the meeting passed a motion expressing the hope that the new governor "will follow the progressive policy inaugurated by the late Governor and thereby obtain the cordial support of the whole white community."[11] Even before this meeting had been held, chief secretary C. C. Bowring, who acted as governor during Girouard's absence, had sent a despatch to the CO downplaying the importance of the protest orchestrated by Anderson.[12]

A more serious hitch in Belfield's appointment than this minor flap emerged, however, in the attitude taken by the Treasury. This difficulty came forth as Belfield was preparing to leave London for East Africa in August. Following acceptance of the post on the same terms as Girouard, Belfield had spent a good deal of time during July and August in study and consultation at the CO on such issues as land and the protectorate's finances. As a matter of course, the CO applied to the Treasury for approval to start paying Belfield's emoluments. The reply left CO officials surprised. The Treasury maintained that Girouard's salary of £3,000 per year plus a duty allowance of £1,000 was personal to him. The Treasury Lords had approved the sums in his case because that had been his salary and allowance as governor of Northern Nigeria. Although it agreed to keep the duty allowance at £1,000, the Treasury would not assent to Belfield receiving as high a salary as his predecessor. The new governor would have to get by on £2,000 per year.[13] CO officials were most unhappy with this position, but their appeal to Sir R. Chalmers at the Treasury produced less than satisfactory results. Chalmers wrote to Anderson on 10 August, stating that the Treasury would agree to a salary of £2,500. It was, the Treasury official wrote, "the furthest I am able to go."[14]

CO officials felt that even this was an absurdly small salary for a protectorate as important as the EAP, and, following Read's advice, Anderson decided that the personal intervention of the S of S was required. In a minute to Harcourt on 13 August, Anderson reminded him that, unaware that the salary was personal to Girouard, they had already offered the post to Belfield at a salary of £3,000 per year. Upon reading Anderson's minute and the correspondence with the Treasury the next day, Harcourt exploded: "This is absolutely out of the question." The S of S ordered Anderson to see Chalmers and "tell him I consider £3,000 and £1,000 duty allowance to be vital." If this was turned down, Harcourt went on, "we must cancel Belfield's appointment and refuse to make a new one til the salary is settled on proper lines and we must announce publicly why the appointment is cancelled."[15] Harcourt closed his instruction to Anderson with the order that if the matter was not settled by the 15th, the permanent under-secretary was to telegraph to Harcourt the vacation addresses of the chancellor of the exchequer and the prime minister so that he could appeal to them.

Harcourt's intervention caused the Treasury to give way. Chalmers wrote to Anderson on the 29th to agree that "as public faith has been pledged," the Treasury had no option but to agree that Belfield would receive the same emoluments as drawn by his predecessor.[16] This incident was indicative of tension that existed between the Treasury and the CO during the period of Treasury control over EAP finances.

Salary matters settled, Belfield sailed for Mombasa, accompanied by his wife and two daughters, on 9 September. He arrived at the port city on 3 October, and proceeded to Nairobi where he received a pleasant welcome.[17] Having survived the flaps with the Treasury and the Nairobi settlers, Belfield could now apply himself to the task of governing. As he did so, however, the new governor soon became, despite the settlers' initial chilly response, a strong advocate for policies they supported or which would prove beneficial to their interests.

Belfield and Settler Political Demands

One example of this is provded by the new governor's treatment of the settler political demands. The main demand was that the Europeans be granted the right to elect members to the Legco. This was in no way a new request. Settlers had raised such ideas from the time the CO had taken over control of the protectorate in 1905. There was little sympathy with such requests in London, but the CO provided for unofficial (meaning non–civil servant) white representation when a Legco was inaugurated in 1907.[18] By late 1911, there were five European and one Indian unofficial members while the colonial state maintained a large official majority.[19] This level of representation was not sufficient for the most politically conscious settlers. They used the numerous organizations that had been set up to articulate various interests: the Land-holders Associations, the Colonists Association, and particularly the Convention of Associations, established in 1910 as a means of giving all settler associations a single voice; all were used as vehicles for the call for elective representation. A petition in support of such a demand had been sent to London in November 1911. It did not receive a positive recommendation from Girouard, and the CO rapidly turned it down.[20]

This rebuff did not dampen the enthusiasm of settlers for elective representation. At the same time that Belfield's appointment was being mooted in London, calls for dramatically increased settler influence in the EAP's government were being made from various quarters in Nairobi. In mid-July, the *EAS* called editorially for settlers "to have a direct voice in the Government of the country."[21] Continued assertions that the time was ripe for electoral representation appeared in the Nairobi press during August as well. In the first week of September, the *EAS* published an editorial titled "Our Farcical

Council". The Legco was said to be farcical because it had been given as a sop "with a hope of weakening our insistent cry for a right to popular representation."[22]

Thus Belfield's arrival coincided with calls for the franchise for settlers, but the calls did not translate themselves into political action until some months later. The political action at that time was largely the result of the lead supplied by Lord Delamere. One of the protectorate's first, and most wealthy, settlers, Delamere was invariably able to exercise political influence on his fellows. Although he had been relatively inactive politically during the latter part of 1912 because of ill health, Delamere would take the lead in the campaign for electoral representation in 1913. He started his campaign at the Nakuru agricultural show in December 1912 where he launched, with what Belfield called remarks of a rather inflammatory nature, his Popular Representation Petition.[23] Until the start of the war, Delamere's main concern, in the words of his biographer, "was to win from the Colonial Office recognition of the settlers' right to elect their representatives to the Legislative Council."[24]

The petition would not be the only route chosen by Delamere. In January 1913, Belfield decided to invite Delamere to fill one of the vacant unofficial seats in the Legco. Before approaching him, the governor wired to London for approval.[25] Officials at the CO were not enthused, but, as Read noted, he was "as good a choice as can be made." Approval to offer the seat was given.[26] To the surprise of Belfield, Delamere refused to accept nomination, claiming that whites should now have elections since the territory was self-supporting and the settlers now paid direct taxes (the non-native poll tax had been introduced the previous year).[27]

By the end of July, Delamere's campaign had gained sufficient momentum to attain the support of the Convention of Associations for yet another petition to the CO. This time the petition, dated 29 July, was backed by the resignation of three of the four remaining unofficial Legco members. It was now made clear that those who supported Delamere's position would not accept nomination to the council. Only elections would be acceptable.[28] The petition was sent to the governor's office for transmission to the CO on 7 August.

The petition began by recalling the 1911 document and asking for a reconsideration of the S of S's decision not to grant "popular representation." Conditions in the EAP had greatly changed since the previous petition had been submitted; these included a large increase in the white population, the end of the imperial grant-in-aid, the precedent of popular representation in other British colonies, and the fact that the country was "now in reality more of a Colony than a Protectorate."[29] The petitioners dwelt not only on the termination of the grant-in-aid and the reliance of the EAP on its own revenue. They maintained that "such revenue is either directly contributed by us or indirectly by reason of our settlement and the consequent increased earnings of the coloured population. . . ." The petitioners added one additional rationale.

Since the EAP had no imperial garrison, the settlers would have to bear "the burden of defence" in the event of "any internal trouble", but this position was made difficult in that circumstance because they were "without a voice in the Government. . . ."

The CO received the petition in the first week of September, but officials refrained from comment on it until the governor's views had been received. Belfield's confidential despatch containing these arrived some two weeks later. He backed the settlers' demand that they be granted electoral representation on the Legco and "other bodies of public nature." Indeed, Belfield supported the grant of elections with great enthusiasm. His only disagreement was with the tactics of those who followed Delamere in resigning their seats in the council. Belfield asserted that the white population had "very materially increased" even during the eleven months he had been in the EAP, and development was expanding rapidly. He felt that the amount of capital now invested in the country "justifies the claims of the investors to be allowed some share . . . in the administration of the country." Belfield also gave great weight to his view that the grant of electoral rights would greatly reduce friction since the public (by which he meant the whites) would have more confidence that the government was working efficiently on its behalf. He wrote:

> I venture therefore to request that you will give due weight to my opinion that a concession in respect of this question of representation will go a long way towards allaying misapprehension and will do much to remove the erroneous idea that the interests of the people are consistently disregarded.[30]

Belfield pointedly reminded the CO that if elections were not granted, most settlers would refuse nomination to the Legco, officials would dominate there, and government would be difficult to carry out. This was a significant point since much of Belfield's governorship would be marked by concessions to settler demands so as to make his own position in relation to that community easier.

W. C. Bottomley, who had joined the EAD earlier in the year, was the first official to read and comment on the petition and the governor's despatch. He advocated conceding elective representation to the settlers. Bottomley advanced two reasons for that point of view. First he noted that the protectorate's position had been altered as a result of the agreement with the Treasury to cease their financial control at the end of 1913. Second, Bottomley maintained that the only way to secure "effective representation of the unofficial element" was by election. He concluded: "I think the events of the last month or two show that we cannot hope to keep a nominated council together."[31] Bottomley thus proposed a reply to Nairobi accepting the principle and asking the governor to work out detailed proposals for implementation, but he added some thoughts of his own on the latter point. He felt that there should be nominated European members to represent the Indian, Arab, and African communities. Direct Arab or African representation was, in his view, "hopeless", and "the experience of a nominated Indian on the council was a failure, and I see no chance of an Indian elected by Indians being more successful."[32]

Other officials at the CO were not prepared to go this far without more information and study. At the direction of Read and Fiddes, A. C. C. Parkinson got together the latest population statistics for the EAP as well as those for Southern Rhodesia. These showed a total population of 3,175 Europeans, 11,886 Indians, and 2,750,170 Africans in the EAP at the end of 1911.[33] These figures weighed heavily in Read's lengthy appraisal of the petition a week after Bottomley had written his.

In examining the size of the European population in the EAP, Read came to the obvious conclusion that it was extremely small, and this fact caused him to put a very strong case forward for not acceding to the request for European elections. Read reduced the white unofficial population to those who would actually be qualified to vote (males over twenty-one years of age). From the 3,175, he obtained a probable electorate of only 865 individuals. Even though the European population had been growing steadily during 1912 and 1913, the potential electorate was still minuscule. Read therefore recommended the S of S reply that since the petition "emanates from only one section of the community," he would not be prepared "to consider proposals which do not provide for the community as a whole." Before conceding the demands of the settlers, the CO must know how "it is proposed to provide for the representation of the Eurasian, Indian, Arabic, native and other sections of the population which vastly outnumber the European section. . . ."[34]

The small size of the European population was not the only ground advocated by Read for turning down the settlers request. He took extremely strong exception to the petition's assertion that the improved revenues of the protectorate were, directly or indirectly, the result of European settlement. He called attention to the fact that revenue from the Uganda Railway, to take one example, made up more than half the total for the EAP. Some 50 per cent of the railway's revenue was derived from the traffic of Uganda, German East Africa, and the Belgian Congo. He further urged that Belfield and the petitioners be reminded that the imperial government was paying debt charges on the Uganda Railway amounting to £319,000 per annum.[35]

Read's analysis and his proposed reply to the governor were accepted by his superiors. Fiddes urged that there must be no question of any acceptance of the principle of election while Anderson expressed a preference for nominated representation on the Legco. Harcourt approved a reply along lines suggested by Read's minute on 1 October.[36]

The CO thus made no commitment to allow European elections in its reply to the petition which took the form of a lengthy confidential despatch dated 14 October. It stated that the S of S would "preserve an open mind on the subject pending the receipt of further information on various important aspects of the question raised in the petition." This position was buttressed by an important observation:

> the petition emanates from one section only of the community in the East Africa Protectorate, and I feel that I should not be fulfilling one of the most important of the charges entrusted to the Secretary of State for the Colonies if I were to favourably consider proposals for elective representation which do not provide for the community as a whole.[37]

This statement of general principles was followed by requests for additional information that would be needed before the CO could make any decision in the matter. The S of S sought to know how it was proposed to provide for the representation of those other sections of the community that vastly outnumbered the European. He also called for up-to-date and accurate statistics on the white population, and, even though the question of elective representation had not been settled, Harcourt asked for suggestions for dealing with such issues as the need for educational, property, or other qualifications for the vote.

On the question of the financial position of the protectorate, the despatch followed Read's minute in refusing to "admit the claim of the signatories of the petition that the local revenue is contributed by them either directly or indirectly as a result of their settlement in the country."[38] This was one of the more significant parts of the CO despatch. It showed that the London officials understood the economic realities of the EAP, even if Belfield and the settlers did not. Not only did peasant production undergird the improved revenue picture of the time; economic realities warranted strong consideration in any policy decisions that would involve giving greater authority in the protectorate's affairs to the European settlers, who for their part had their sights set not just on elections but ultimately on minority self-government on the South African model.[39]

As the CO doubtlessly anticipated, the settlers were not pleased with this response to their petition. At a January 1914 meeting, the Convention of Associations agreed on a reply, and it was sent to London on 16 February.[40] It sought to answer the points raised in the CO despatch. First to be dealt with was the question of the representation of the other communities. The settler politicians began by rejecting any form of representation of the African population. It was impossible due to the "present state of practical barbarism" of the latter. The colonial state could look after their interests. Turning to the question of franchise rights for Indians, the convention was adamant in its feeling that their inclusion in elections would lead to complications. Among the most serious these settlers foresaw that "the Indians would in seriously contested elections vote solid . . . thus giving them the practical power of controlling the unofficial policy of the Protectorate."[41] Although opposing electoral rights for the Indian population, the settlers felt they could accept the appointment "of one additional unofficial European member of council directly to represent Eastern interests."

Passing to voter qualifications for a European electorate, the convention took a liberal stand. Their guiding principle was "one white man one vote" with no educational or property qualifications. Twelve months residence in what the settler document referred to throughout as "the Colony" was all that would be required.

These settlers then went on to express their disagreement with the CO position with regard to the generation of revenue in the EAP. They came to a preposterous conclusion:

It is only the establishment of the progressive and energetic Colony of East Africa which has made that traffic possible and we submit that the present conditions would not have obtained but for the presence of white settlers, who have sunk a very large amount of capital in the country.[42]

The convention concluded their lengthy reply with a justification of the actions of those who had resigned from the Legco.

The arrival of the despatch at the CO a month later coincided with Delamere's request for an interview with Harcourt to personally push the case of the settlers. The S of S agreed to meet Delamere, but no commitments were made by the former pending receipt of the views of Belfield.[43]

The governor had been on tour in Nyanza province at the time the Convention's reply had been sent to London, and he forwarded his views some three weeks later. On the question of franchise arrangements for all sections of the community, Belfield fell in very strongly with the settlers. He agreed that it was "out of the question" to confer voting rights on Africans. Turning to Indians and Arabs, the governor acknowledged that he had, at the conclusion of his 23 August 1913 despatch, suggested that it might be necessary to confer "some degree of voting power" on those communities, but he had now changed his mind. He wrote:

I have never been in favour of placing a native upon the Council, and I should never make recommendation to that effect, because I believe that an Indian or Arab member would either be apathetic or useless or active only in matters where his personal or commercial interests are concerned and that the section of the community which he is supposed to represent would derive no sort of benefit from his occupation of that position.[44]

The governor further explained his opposition to voting rights for "Asiatic communities" by referring to his plans, yet to be formalized, for reorganizing the protectorate's administration by separating it into two parts, one for the whites and the other to be responsible "for the administration of all native areas." The new scheme would provide for a commissioner who would "specially represent all native communities" in the Legco; the settlers would be represented by their unofficial members. Even without the most recent population statistics for whites, which he promised to send as soon as possible, the governor strongly endorsed the settlers' stance.

Since the requested information as to the size of the European population had yet to be received, CO officials took no action on the settlers' letter or the governor's despatch.[45] Belfield finally sent a despatch containing the population figures at the end of June. His count showed 2,944 male Europeans over twenty-one years of age; 2,624 of these were British.[46] By the time this information reached London, other matters seemed more important than answering the settlers. However, the start of World War I only postponed consideration of the issue; the CO would be forced to return to voting rights for whites well before the conclusion of the conflict.

The Indian Question

As noted in the preceding discussion, raising the question of voting rights for Europeans inevitably raised it for the other immigrant community, the Indians. Thus Belfield's governorship marks the beginning of what would be a most contentious issue for the CO in dealing with Kenya after World War I. Nor did the Indian question emerge solely as the result of consideration of voting rights by the EAP and British governments. Indians in the EAP, deprived of representation in the Legco since September 1911, put forward demands for an Indian to be a member of the council. In early April 1912, moreover, the Mombasa Indian Association sent a petition to the governor protesting against the new non-native poll tax. The major basis for their protest was that as there was no Indian member of the Legco, the measure was equivalent to taxation without representation. In forwarding the petition to London, acting governor Bowring maintained that the absence of an Indian member was "not because we refuse the principle of Indian representation but because no suitable member of the British Indian community is available."[47] This would form the usual argument put forward by the EAP government prior to the war. The CO agreed as the experience of having Jevanjee on the council had not been a success.[48]

Indian protests did not stop here, however. In addition to the franchise question, Indian leaders had good reason to be concerned about the EAP government's favoritism for the settler community on the issues of land availability in the white highlands and urban segregation. They thus constituted a more inclusive organization to articulate their grievances; the new organization, formed in March 1914, was known as the East African Indian National Congress (EAINC).[49]

At its initial meetings in Mombasa, the organization adopted resolutions calling attention to a number of grievances that would, over the next nine years, form the heart of the Indian question. Among the resolutions for-warded to the government of the EAP were those demanding "full and com-plete equality of treatment in the eyes of the law" for Indians, representation on the Legco, an end to the prohibition of Indians acquiring land in the high-lands, and the abolition of segregation of Indian businesses and residences, allegedly for health and sanitary reasons, in townships.[50] However, Governor Belfield was totally unsympathetic. In forwarding the congress resolutions to London, he rejected them all out of hand. He forcefully suggested that there could be no equality between whites and Indians in any sphere. In the gov-ernor's view:

It would be well that the aspirations of its members should be checked at the outset by an intimation from yourself which leave them in no doubt that further agitation on the same or similar subjects will not be sympathetically received.[51]

Despite this recommendation, officials at the CO were unprepared to take such a hard line. Two months earlier, Sir John Anderson had expressed the opinion that "a good Indian," if one could be found, would be useful in the Legco in a minute on Belfield's 6 March 1914 despatch supporting settler political claims. Lord Emmott had agreed with that position.[52] Bottomley, obviously aware of these views of his superiors, altered his earlier opinion and in minuting Belfield's despatch enclosing the EAINC demands, stated: "If a good Indian candidate could be found, I think it would be worthwhile to nominate him."[53] Bottomley also felt that the CO could not reply "quite as harshly as the Governor seems to desire" to the Indian claims.[54]

In sending their grievances, the EAINC also took the most significant step of requesting that a copy of their resolutions also should be sent to the S of S for India. The involvement of the IO in Kenya affairs relating to Indians would be a constant thorn in the side of the CO in years to come. In forward-ing a copy of the resolutions to the IO, the CO stated that it was "unable to admit that any injustice is involved in the present position of British Indians in the East Africa Protectorate."[55] This also would be a consistent theme in years ahead.

The CO finally sent a reply to Belfield in August. It repeated the position transmitted to the IO. Nevertheless, the governor was told that he should "give further consideration to the question of nominating an Indian member to the Legislative Council should a suitable individual for the position be available at any time. . . . "[56] The CO was thus more liberally inclined and less willing to back the racist positions voiced by most settlers than was the colonial state in 1914. This was made extremely clear in Belfield's reply. He proclaimed that he was not aware "of any differentiation that now exists to the detriment of Indians except in respect of ownership of farm lands in the high-lands." He reiterated his belief that there were no Indians qualified to serve on the Legco, but he promised to give the matter careful consideration.[57] The position of the colonial state in the Indian question would continue to be out of step with the Indian claims to equality as citizens of the British Empire that would burst forth as a major issue of controversy after the war.

In Search of a Land Policy for the EAP

The issues of electoral representation for Europeans and equal rights for Indians were not the only ones to occupy the attention of H. C. Belfield during the first period of his governorship. EAP land questions took an even greater portion of his and CO time and energy. From the time it assumed control of the EAP in 1905, a major objective of the CO had been to establish a workable land policy for the EAP that would make land available for European settlement but would provide safeguards against excessive accumulation and land speculation, provide some government control over land dealings, and insure beneficial development of land holdings. These objectives, and others, had finally been translated into effective policy proposals by the CO under then S of S Lord Elgin's direction; they were sent to Nairobi in March 1908. Lord Elgin's despatch laid down a number of principles upon which a new land ordinance could be framed. Among the most important was an insistence on ninety-nine-year leases with a revaluation of rent every thirty-three years at 5 per cent of the unimproved value of that land. Also the CO proposed to introduce a graduated land tax, and it insisted that its proposed new land ordinance should prevent dummying.[58]

Despite CO instructions that these concepts be put into law through passage of a new land ordinance, nothing of the sort had been accomplished down to the time Belfield assumed office. The main reason for this was the opposition raised to the CO proposals by EAP settlers. They protested strongly against the revaluation of rentals and the very idea of a land tax when a land bill was introduced in the Legco in 1909. They also called for a longer term of tenure for leases.[59] For the settlers, a limited tenure period, revaluation, land taxes, and requirements that a land holder make improvements over a specified time period were opposed because these "worsened the prospects for profits from both agriculture and land speculation."[60] Thus when a bill was finally passed by the Legco in March 1910, the land tax and anti-dummying measures desired by the CO were dropped and revaluation of rentals altered to a fixed rental thanks to settler influence.[61]

This bill was not acceptable to the CO, and it was left to Sir Percy Girouard to put through legislation that would be more palatable to London. As in other areas of policy, Girouard entirely adopted the settler position (or perhaps more precisely Delamere's position, as the two had become close friends and confidants); he therefore advocated approval of the 1909 bill. The CO refused to give way on the question of revaluation of rents, land tax, and the anti-dummying provisions, and Girouard was instructed to draft a new land bill, including in it the principles deleted or altered in the 1909 legislation.[62] Nothing had been decided, however, by the time of Girouard's resignation other than an indication by Harcourt that he was ready to drop the land tax.

The continued delay in the passage of an effective ordinance was obviously not something the CO was happy about. As Belfield was preparing to take up the reins of the EAP, the CO itself was undertaking a major review of land policy in the hopes of finally moving forward to the passage of an ordinance. One such action was the CO's invitation to A. C. Tannahill, a land ranger in the EAP land department, to submit memoranda on alienation and dummying. In wide ranging memoranda dated 2 June and 26 June 1912, Tannahill provided a review of land policy in the protectorate together with suggestions for improvement. His major proposal was to introduce 999-year leases with revision of rent every thirty-three years. The revision would be made according to the capital value of the land (1 per cent on first revision, 2 per cent on the second, and 3 per cent on all subsequent revisions rather than the 5 per cent of the unimproved value of the land laid down by the 1908 despatch). He also strongly recommended an auction system for land allocation. He argued that the enforcement of development and occupation conditions would remove the concern with land accumulation since development was, in Tannahill's view, more crucial than how much land a man held.[63]

A "small committee" within the CO was charged to review and comment on Tannahill's memoranda. This consisted of Read and Batterbee of the EAD plus Butler and J. S. Risley, the CO legal adviser. The committee agreed that allotment by auction was to be perferred and, in general, endorsed the development conditions proposed by Tannahill. In the case of his proposed change in the revision formula, the committee pointed out that this would involve higher payments for the renter in the long run, and it felt that it could not take responsibility for "recommending rates in advance of those laid down in Lord Elgin's despatch." Their major area of disagreement with Tannahill, however, lay with his proposal of the 999-year lease. The committee recommended holding fast to the period of ninety-nine years.[64]

In August 1912, these recommendations, Tannahill's memoranda, and other papers relating to the land bill, dating back to the time of Lord Elgin, were placed before Belfield so that he might acquaint himself with land policy and make comments and recommendation. The new governor produced a thirteen and a half page memorandum that was critical of previous CO policy. Belfield began with not very subtle criticism of past land policy and those in the CO who had formulated it. As a result of his review of the correspondence, he concluded: "I have been unable to find an instance in which any officer or member of the public has expressed approval or agreement with the principles and procedure embodied in the directions issued by the Colonial Office." It was his impression that no one at the CO or in the EAP was really satisfied that the proposed bill was "framed on lines which are likely to be beneficial to the country."[65]

Belfield went on to say that he viewed the prospect of enacting the land ordinance along the lines the CO proposed with grave apprehension. In the hope that it was not too late to obtain Harcourt's approval for "a substantial modification" of the conditions to be incorporated in the draft ordinance, Belfield put forward his own views. First and foremost, the new governor called for a grant of 999 years or perpetuity. Ninety-nine years was too short a term in his view as most leaseholders would wish to see the land they held passed on to their heirs, and that term would impose re-alienation responsibility on the government. He strongly opposed the idea of a land tax. It would be difficult to administer and not really necessary. Belfield endorsed, based on his Malay experience, auction as the appropriate means of allotment. Belfield favored free transfers except that none should be allowed to Indians. Such a suggestion would work, he believed, if all transfers were effectively registered with the Land Office. Belfield, like Tannahill, held that there should be no bar to the accumulation of holdings so long as effective development conditions were enforced.[66] As Sorrenson noted, Belfield did not have to go to the EAP to be converted by the settlers; "he accepted their case before he left England."[67]

This expression of view by the new governor sent shock waves through the EAD. His recommendations were so at odds with Elgin's 1908 despatch and previous CO positions on land that Read recommended further review by the EA land committee and eventual decision by the S of S on points of dispute.[68] F. G. A. Butler went even further. He asked for a preliminary statement of views by the S of S before the committee began its review. It was his belief that the committee had always previously "been bound to adhere to the main principles laid down in Lord Elgin's despatch of 19 March 1908," but since Belfield wished "to bury those principles," Butler desired to know if the committee would have a free hand to make any recommendations they felt to be necessary or if the principles in Lord Elgin's despatch were "immutable." Butler identified three important points where Belfield had advocated departing from the 1908 despatch: the 999-year lease instead of ninety-nine, the abandonment of the progressive land tax, and his views "as to the accumulation of holdings are at variance with those expressed throughout Lord Elgin's despatch."[69]

Butler's unusual action forced the senior CO officials to comment on the matter before the committee began its work. Sir John Anderson remarked that "the Elgin Scheme was hopelessly impracticable and what we want is a practicable scheme. . . ."; he did not think the committee should be fettered by any more specific instructions than that an adequate price should be paid for the rise of land value and that the community received the benefit of the "enhanced value of the land due to the economic causes other than the exertions of the landholder."[70] Harcourt followed Anderson's advice, but he perceptively added one important condition.

I wish the committee to be free to examine and comment on Mr. Belfield's suggestions, but I do not see my way at present to depart from the principle of 99 year leases variable every 33 years. The EAP will be self-governing long before 99 years have passed and they ought not to find themselves with all their land finally alienated.[71]

The committee completed its review and produced a seventeen-page report by 8 October even though Read was absent from the CO during that period. Risley, Butler, and Batterbee's report concurred with Belfield's recommendations in practically every particular. They agreed that auction "provides the best method of allotment," and they approved Belfield's proposals for carrying it out. The governor's thinking as to development and occupation conditions found general favor with the committee except that they felt it essential to insist on personal occupation by the lease holder for at least the period of the occupation license. The committee also expressed concurrence with the method of revaluation proposed by Tannahill; it would have the added advantage of bringing greater revenue to the state than the system proposed in the 1908 despatch.[72]

On two of the three points Butler had previously identified as ones on which Belfield's views diverged from those of the 1908 despatch, the committee supported the governor's desire to "bury" them. They agreed in advocating "the abandonment of the graduated land-tax on account of the difficulties with which they are convinced that its administration would be attended." They also concurred that the conditions proposed by the governor (auctions, personal attendance by bidders, restriction of purchases to one block only at a single sale, stringent development conditions, and personal occupation) would provide sufficient safeguards against accumulation. In the committee's words: "there will be no need for further special safeguards against the land speculator." So also did the committee adopt the governor's view on land transfers, including the right of the governor to veto sales to Indians.[73]

Thus the committee had, with the exception of some relatively minor points, accepted Belfield's position with one deviation, the length of lease. In his minute on the committee's report, Fiddes expressed his preference for 999 years.[74] Anderson did not agree, however, and both Emmott and Harcourt strongly advocated the ninety-nine-year lease. In a lengthy minute, Emmott admitted that there were disadvantages with short leases, but, he concluded, "I do not like the idea of tieing up the land of the EAP which is available for white settlers for 1000 years."[75] Harcourt approved the drafting of a despatch based on the committee's report, but, he emphasized, "*I must adhere to the 99 years.*"[76]

The despatch summarizing the CO decisions regarding what would be a considerably changed land bill from that of previous years was sent to Belfield on 8 November together with the Tannahill and Belfield memoranda as enclosures. After a review of the preceding months's discussions regarding land policy, Harcourt made known his decisions. Restating his belief that the EAP would be a self-governing colony before 99 years elapsed and the settlers ought not then to find all crown lands finally alienated, Harcourt made clear that he would not depart from the principle of a ninety-nine-year lease. In other respects, the S of S accepted the governor's and the committee's recommendations. The governor was ordered to begin the preparation of a new land ordinance, but, in the meantime, it was desirable, in order to avoid further delay in allotting new farms for settlement, that rules should be issued under the 1902 Crown Lands Ordinance prescribing conditions for land alienation. The governor was instructed to draft such rules as quickly as possible.[77]

Belfield's Implementation of CO Land Policy

Even before the receipt of the despatch, Belfield was anxious to provide farms for settlers so as to meet the substantial land demand in the protectorate. After receipt, he informed London that prescribing conditions of alienation under the 1902 ordinance presented "great practical difficulties." Drafting the new ordinance would also take time, and the governor asserted that since there were a number of farms ready for immediate allotment and a large number of settlers clamoring for land, he required authority to recommence alienation of land.[78] The CO approved these proposals in January and urged Belfield to hasten drafting of the new ordinance.[79] Belfield then moved quickly to put one hundred farms up for auction in May.[80]

When Belfield replied formally to the CO despatch of 8 November, he identified some problems, but he expressed no opposition to the ninety-nine-year lease. "I find since my arrival in the country," he wrote, "that the community is generally satisfied with a lease of that duration, and that term will be retained in the draft ordinance."[81] Nevertheless, the governor did desire some changes from the policy laid down by the CO. He wished to reduce the term of an occupation license from three to two years if development conditions had been fulfilled, allot land at fixed prices in exceptional cases, auction all farm land at a uniform starting rent of ten cents per acre, and abolish the distinction between grazing and agricultural land. The CO approved these proposals by telegraph with no comment.[82]

While the CO may have assumed that the key principles for the drafting of a new crown lands ordinance had now been settled, it would soon be apparent that such was not the case. Belfield continued to bring forward proposals for alterations over the remaining months of 1913. The first instance occurred in April as a result of discussions with leading settlers and such officials as the chief secretary, the attorney general, and the land officer. Belfield was not averse to bending further than ever to settler desires on land. He decided that occupation licenses should no longer be continued. Instead, "a lease should be granted in respect of each block of land as soon as sold." The motivation for this change was to insure that all land titles could be immediately negotiable. Belfield felt that though the intent of the occupation license was to prevent the obtaining of title before the completion of development, it had not worked in the EAP. Development conditions would still apply; thus this measure would not be harmful, and it would "go a long way towards meeting the views of the general community" (i.e., the settlers).[83]

Belfield did not stop there. He went on to insist that his six months experience in the EAP had confirmed him in his belief that it was not possible to prevent dummying and illegal land transfers "if capitalists are determined . . . so we should legalize them rather than compel people to resort to subterfuge and hide from Government dealings we should have full knowledge of."[84]

The governor's proposals met with little enthusiasm in London. Bottomley's perceptive minute summarized official feeling. "The Governor in this despatch turns upside down the whole policy—as regards country land at least—formulated by himself . . . at a moment's notice."[85] In its reply, the CO refused to consider the abolition of occupation licenses until development conditions for leases had been submitted for approval. Nor would London "lightly relinquish this principle on non-transferable licenses." The CO despatch went on to ask for a fuller explanation of the reasons why the governor felt enforcement of anti-dummying and legal transfer measures was "impracticable."[86] It was, after all, one of the last precautions against land accumulation.[87]

Belfield sent his justification for the change in July. He felt the three year, non-transferable license would serve no useful purpose, but "will place considerable difficulties in the way of the bona fide farmer who is anxious to develop his farm." Development was emphasized by Belfield; if the lease holder could not manage to undertake it, he should be free to transfer his holding to someone who would. Clearly the governor reckoned that measures whose object was to limit land accumulation did not afford the most effective path to development.[88]

The CO was not overwhelmed by the force of the governor's argument, but, anxious to finalize the land ordinance, it was willing to give way to Belfield's insistence that the three-year license was unnecessary. Bottomley found the governor's explanation "not altogether clear", but because evasions were taking place and their effect was bad, the official lamely held that the CO had to adopt Belfield's proposal. This was advanced with the clear recognition that the effect of dropping the occupation license would be to aid the big man, the land speculator, and harm "the man of moderate means." Bottomley further suggested that stringent development conditions would help control speculation, and he concluded with an extremely weak rationalization. "I think we can only adopt the Governor's view that all we can do is get as much land properly cultivated as possible."[89]

Bottomley's view formed the basis for the CO concession on that point. On 20 August, the governor was informed that, since the license conditions could not be enforced, the S of S had "no alternative but to accept your recommendation that immediate leases shall be granted."[90] Even though the CO maintained in the despatch its belief in the rightness of limiting holdings to a moderate area had not wavered, it was clear that Belfield and the settlers had won yet another round in the battle over the land bill.[91]

This would not be the last surrender, however. In November, Belfield made further proposals for changes in land regulations. Most significant was that on the coming into operation of the new ordinance, all persons holding land, by whatever title or license, should have the option of tenure under the new law. He stated that a clause to that effect was being put in the new ordinance.[92] Bottomley urged accepting the governor's view "if we are ever to arrive at a finality" even though he recognized, as did Read and other officials, that the governor's proposal would result in automatic conversion of occupation licenses into more valuable, because they were negotiable, leasehold titles without any increase in the premium paid.[93] Though with many doubts, Harcourt agreed, and the CO approved the conversion of existing titles when the ordinance would come into effect.[94]

By the time the CO response was sent to Nairobi, the crown lands bill had been completed and introduced in the Legco. On 8 January 1914, Belfield sent copies to London. CO officials were in for what would be one last jolt; completely ignoring Harcourt's May request that the governor communicate in advance any new matters of principle so as to avoid delay when the ordinance itself was submitted, Belfield did just that. The governor noted the four modifications that had been accepted by the CO since Harcourt's despatch of 8 November 1912, and reported that a special committee of the Legco had been appointed to hear evidence and report on the bill before the council. However, the bill itself was still, in his view, not acceptable to the settlers. He wrote: "I feel strongly that general discontent with our Land Laws will continue until provision is made for a grant in perpetuity or some long term lease without revision of rent."[95] Belfield reminded the CO that he had advised a 999-year lease in 1912, and, admitting the opinion he had expressed in January 1913 that ninety-nine years was acceptable to settlers was "premature and erroneous," he concluded: "my experience of the country has strengthened my opinion that the point should be conceded."[96]

CO officials were quick to grasp the significance of the governor's request even though he had placed it in the seventh paragraph of his despatch. On reading the despatch, Bottomley maintained that if the CO position "that no term of more than 99 years shall be granted is to be adhered to, we shall do well to make the fact clear to the Governor at once."[97] Others agreed that the CO would have to make a fairly rapid decision, but the situation was complicated by a personal letter Belfield had sent to Sir George Fiddes. In that communication, Belfield expressed the hope that even at "this eleventh hour" the S of S would concede the principle of tenure in perpetuity, with revision of rent. He made clear that a primary motivation for his request was his desire to placate the settlers.

This land measure gives us such a chance of bringing the people to really better relations with the Government that it will be a thousand pities if the opportunity is lost and the forcing of the Bill upon them in its present form perpetuates and accentuates (as it will) hostility to the Government.[98]

CO officials found it inconsistent that in this letter the governor advocated grants in perpetuity (999 years) with revision of rent while in his despatch he called for such a grant without revision.

Rather than delay the CO deliberations, however, this inconsistency actually provided the justification for giving up the ninety-nine-year term for one of 999 years. The decision was made by the political leadership of the CO. Of the permanent officials, only Read was not in favor of caving in to the settlers.[99] Fiddes had already expressed a preference for 999 years, and the experience with the issue of electoral rights previously described suggests that Bottomley found it convenient to fall into line with the views of his superiors in the office. In this case, Fiddes urged only that if the ninety-nine-year term could not be changed, the governor should be told at once. If so, he added, "we must be prepared for a very unpleasant agitation."[100] Anderson stated his agreement with Belfield's preference for "a perpetual title with periodical reassessment," but he stopped short of recommending the dropping of the ninety-nine-year term.[101] It was Lord Emmott who, after reading both documents, made a virtue of the inconsistency by his conclusion that the settlers' fundamental objection was to revision of rents. He wrote: "So long as we stick to reassessment the terms of the original lease is not so vitally important altho I prefer the 99 yrs lease to the 999 yrs."[102]

This would become the CO position. The political and permanent officials, having convinced themselves that revision of rent (rather than length of lease) was the critical issue, now decided they could alter a position that had been one of the CO's most fundamental tenets of land legislation over the preceding two years. This decision was sent to Belfield by a private and personal telegram on 17 February. The CO asked for more information, but indicated its willingness to accept a longer term of lease. Carefully drafted by Fiddes after discussion with Anderson and Harcourt, the telegram was for the governor's "personal information as it may be useful in your negotiations." In the key passage, Harcourt stated: "Though with much hesitation I should be prepared to go as far as Federated Malay States system of perpetual lease with revision up or down at intervals of 30 or 33 years but only if I am assured that this will be accepted by settlers as a fair and final settlement."[103]

Belfield was afforded much satisfaction by this response. He was unwilling to "hazard an opinion" as to whether the CO concession would be accepted by the settlers as "a fair and final settlement," but he was "confident that they will go a long way towards effecting an adjustment of differences." Belfield reported that the Convention of Associations had appointed a committee to consider the bill, and when their views were in hand, he would lay them before the Legco special committee. The governor used this despatch, moreover, to clear up the inconsistency between the views expressed in his 8 January despatch and his letter to Fiddes. The latter contained his personal opinion (lease in perpetuity with revision) while in the despatch he had described "what I understood to be the views of the settlers."[104] For the CO, it appeared that there was nothing to do now but to wait for the outcome of the committee reviews in the EAP.[105]

By this time, the CO had been forced to give attention to another portion of the new bill not previously considered in London. It was not compelled to do so by representations from the EAP, but because of a strong protest against portions of the proposed ordinance by Liberal M. P. Edmund Harvey. Harvey, a strong parliamentary champion of African land rights,[106] objected to the bill's inclusion of all lands occupied by and reserved for Africans in the category of crown lands. Harvey accurately felt that legislating this "would be a monstrous act of theft" that was likely to produce future grave injustice to the African population. Harvey also objected to the power the bill gave to the colonial state to exclude from reserves land required for mining and public purposes.[107]

Harvey's criticism of the legislation jolted the CO into examination of what would become, in the future, perhaps the most significant facet of the crown lands ordinance. The examination began with a recognition that this provision of the bill did not emanate from the CO but from the EAP. It was an addition that had not appeared in the 1911 draft. Caught on the defensive, the CO did little more than hand the matter back to the colonial state. In a lengthy minute considering Harvey's protests, Bottomley could see no danger in making all African land crown land nor any proof of a potential "monstrous act of theft." In particular, he did not think "that there can be any great objection to placing the Reserves under the crown lands definition . . . provided that the rights of the natives are properly secured."[108] The CO merely decided to send Harvey's letter to the governor, asking for a full statement of his views on the bill's provisions regarding African land. On one point only did the CO make a significant policy pronouncement. As a result of Anderson's concern that the occupancy rights of individual Africans or tribes be safeguarded and that should these be "disturbed for reasons of public policy compensation should be paid," Belfield was explicitly told in the early March despatch to safeguard those rights and to provide for payment of compensation for disturbance due to reasons of public policy.[109]

Belfield replied in April that the points raised by Harvey would be put before the special committee of the Legco.[110] No more would be heard from the governor regarding the projected land bill until after the start of the war. Thus the final consideration and decisions by the CO were still some time off. Yet it is certainly correct that the most significant and far-reaching decisions had already been made through the CO's assent to the changes proposed by Belfield from the time of his arrival in the EAP. This had culminated in Harcourt's agreement in principle to drop his insistence on ninety-nine-year leases. CO officials felt that this did not constitute a final commitment on the point, but Belfield certainly did. He and the EAP settlers would get their way when the bill was finally passed into law in 1915.

It is therefore a point of some interest to try to ascertain how it could have happened that the desires of the settlers (particularly those of the large men) could have so fully been met and the CO could have departed so far from the policies laid down in the 1908 despatch. First of all, the CO was ever more desirous of a settlement of the land question as time went by, and the controversy dragged on. Sick of the whole business, the staff, both permanent and political, gave up the struggle to impose land legislation on an unwilling governor and settlers.[111]

But that was not all; the CO were certainly "heartily sick of the whole controversy," but the most important officials dealing with the land question retained great faith in Belfield's expertise in land matters. It is especially noteworthy that this was the position of Anderson. The permanent under-secretary had personally played a large part in Belfield's selection, and he was one of the governor's strongest supporters. Anderson's feelings were well captured by a minute he wrote in December 1913. He strongly asserted that "the Governor is a man with a very wide experience of land matters, and we should not press it [the CO view on conversion of titles] against his judgement."[112]

Another factor which caused the CO to support Belfield's recommendations on the land bill related to the governor's health. At the end of August 1913, Belfield fell gravely ill. He contracted a severe case of malaria, and this caused him to suffer a heart attack.[113] Although his doctors thought the governor too weak to travel to Britain on 13 September, Belfield had recovered sufficiently to return to duty on 1 October.[114] Belfield's illness and the likelihood that he would be forced to resign caused the CO concern as to the final disposition of the land bill. Officials did not want to start again with a new governor. Bottomley expressed the view in September 1913 that the CO would "feel Mr. Belfield's continued absence greatly" with land as in several other matters.[115] Of all the CO officials, only Fiddes felt that Belfield's illness required that the governor "must come away—and probably shd not return."[116]

The CO's Favorable Assessment of Belfield

In addition to the CO confidence in Belfield's expertise in land questions and its desire that he see the land bill through to passage, it is also important to note that, at least during his first two years of office, the CO was generally quite pleased with the governor's performance. Belfield consulted the CO fully and kept it informed of important developments and policy issues to a greater degree than during Girouard's time. The move of the Maasai from

Laikipia to the extended southern reserve was carried out with little difficulty under his administration.[117] Not only was the move of the Maasai carried through; Belfield toured the southern reserve in June and July 1913. Upon his return to Nairobi, he sent an extensive report to London in which he stated, much to the relief of the CO, that he "had met a uniformly contented people, thousands of head of fine cattle in grand condition and ample abundant pasturage."[118] This was exactly what the CO required for use against potential parliamentary critics of the Maasai move.

Moreover, Belfield's efforts at "damage control" for Girouard's actions won strong praise from the CO. Girouard had made many verbal promises of land to Europeans but had kept no written record, and he, of course, had not informed London of his actions. Belfield sorted these out satisfactorily, and in the process provided the S of S with "the smoking pistol" needed if it became necessary to publicly explain the reason for Girouard's resignation.[119]

Perhaps the greatest "success" of the initial period of Belfield's administration was his handling of the events leading up to the verdict in the lawsuit filed by the Maasai for the return of Laikipia plateau to them. From the moment the Maasai retained two European lawyers to file the case, Belfield led his government in an obstructionist posture. The main aim, and outcome, of that stance was to make it as difficult as possible for the advocates to consult their clients and to collect fees for their legal work both before and after the case was filed in 1912. Although Belfield never stated that he was following an obstructionist line, it is impossible, in reviewing the voluminous correspondence, not to obtain the impression that obstruction was his aim. It was certainly the outcome of his policy.[120] The advocates continued to protest to Belfield and to Harcourt, but the governor did not cease to make the lawyers' efforts to meet their clients as difficult as possible.[121]

From the very beginning, Belfield was absolutely certain that the Maasai had no grounds for a case and that the government would triumph. After meeting Maasai leaders, including those who instigated the law suit, in December 1912, Belfield came away convinced that "only a minority of the tribal elders . . . are responsible for this action." The governor was satisfied "that those who now oppose the move have no valid ground for their objection. . . ."[122]

Few CO officials were as confident of the strength of the government's position in the lawsuit. Even after reading a commentary by a CO legal assistant that presented a pessimistic assessment of the Maasai chances in the case, Harcourt minuted: "I suppose if the case went against us in the EAP we could take it to the Privy Council."[123] When Belfield telegraphed the fact that the Maasai case had been dismissed with costs, Harcourt was still not easy about the position. He had already discussed the case with a predecessor as S of S, A. Lyttleton, and the latter suggested "that if there was any chance—which he thought possible—of a decision against us; we should settle by a money payment."[124] Harcourt and the other officials were no more confident after they read the complete judgement in July 1913. Anderson exclaimed: "I do not like the decision at all . . . to call the Agreement a Treaty is abuse of language." He concluded that he could not imagine the Privy Council "supporting the judgement if it is brought before them on appeal." Harcourt agreed.[125]

But the Maasai did not meet the conditions set down for appeal to the Privy Council, and their legal challenge to the move from Laikipia failed.[126] The relief of CO officials was matched by their respect for Belfield. He had carried out the move, supported CO policy effectively, and helped obstruct legal proceedings against the government. Belfield's handling of the Maasai clearly represented the high point of his governorship in CO eyes.

One final reason for the CO sympathy with Belfield's position on the land bill is suggested by the officials' appreciation of the difficult position in which Belfield found himself in his relations with the settlers. Not only was he replacing a popular governor, but Belfield himself, not outgoing or "a good mixer", never was popular or liked by the settlers. Lord Delamere, it was said, commonly referred, disparagingly, to the governor as "that very admirable servant of the Crown. . . ."[127] To cite another example, Belfield became embroiled in a controversy with the *EAS* and its editor that was indicative of the low esteem in which his administration was held in some European quarters.[128] In short, it was not so much that the settlers had "captured" Belfield as much as that he was laboring under the handicap that they seemed to be holding him at arms length. The CO was aware of the difficulties Belfield had because of the attitude of the settlers, and as a result, officials there did not take as strong exception to Belfield's attitudes and tactics in the land issue as they might have.[129] In fact, Belfield was made K.C.M.G. in 1914 as a recognition of London's satisfaction with the initial period of his tenure.[130]

Labor

As with the land ordinance and settler political demands, Sir Henry Belfield encountered labor questions almost immediately on his arrival. The most pressing matter in so far as labor was concerned was the growing shortage of African workers experienced by settlers in 1912. From the second quarter of that year, demand for employees—the result of increased settlement—increasingly outstripped supply. Protests and expressions of concern by European settlers culminated in a July Convention of Associations call for a commission of inquiry. This was accepted by the EAP government and a Native Labour Commission (NLC) had been appointed by acting governor Bowring prior to Belfield's arrival.[131] The commission was given wide-ranging terms of reference in investigating the reasons for, and possible solutions to, the labor shortage. It held numerous sittings and accumulated a large volume of evidence; it did not finalize its report until August 1913. Belfield's only involvement with the commission's work, from his arrival to that date, was through the appointment of additional members. Although the labor shortage continued to be felt by settlers, there was no particular pressure on the governor to take extensive action prior to the completion of the commission's work.

The CO was, on the other hand, not able to await the completion of the commission's investigations before undertaking a review of the system for recruiting labor in the EAP. This was forced on them by settlers and merchants in Britain who had interests in large farms and estates in the EAP. These, with the assistance of Major Henry Guest, a Liberal M.P., urged intervention of the CO as a major means to solving the labor shortage, in December 1912. Guest actually approached Harcourt at the end of November to inquire if the S of S would receive a deputation of capitalists interested in the EAP. Harcourt requested that they submit their views prior to such a meeting, finally set for 17 December, and Guest forwarded a five page memorandum on 2 December.[132]

The memorandum was signed, in addition to Guest, by Major E. Humphrey Leggett of the British East Africa Corporation and such "large men" as E. S. Grogan, Galbraith and Barcly Cole, and Lord Cranworth. Increasing demands for labor and the inability of the "larger interests" they represented to obtain substantial numbers of workers in the EAP suggested to the authors of the memorandum the need for reorganization of the labor recruiting system. The main thing desired was that the government should take a much larger part in labor recruitment. The memorandum called for government recruitment and an employers' labor federation to administer the labor when recruited. It demanded increased taxation of Africans and justified this with the remarkable, and totally untrue, assertion that Africans had made little contribution to the "increased wealth and prosperity" and revenue of the protectorate. It went on to maintain that the "advancing development" of the EAP necessitated a system of registration and identification. The report concluded by advocating "greater facilities" for the laborer to enable him to bring his family to his place of work, deferment of pay, and the restriction of the drink trade, especially at the coast.[133]

CO officials found the latter points worthy of further discussion and investigation, but the major demands of the large planters and their friends were received with very little favor. Bottomley voiced a long-held CO position when he declared that government interference in labor recruiting was "liable to lead to abuse." CO policy was that government officials must not recruit. Bottomley showed that this had been made very clear to the EAP in the past by quoting from a 1908 despatch. The CO had then condemned government assistance in finding labor for settlers and concluded: "The proper course would appear to be for the Government to introduce legislation laying down the conditions for employment and proper treatment of native labourers and then stand aside leaving the settlers to make their own arrangements to procure the labour."[134] Bottomley interpreted, no doubt correctly, the memorandum's remarks on taxation to mean "that the native is too well off to work and must therefore be taxed to make him poor." He was thus not convinced of the need for increased taxation, nor was he satisfied that "the difficulty of identification was greater in EAP than in other parts of tropical Africa. . . ."[135]

An even stronger statement of opposition to the ideas expressed in the memorandum was made by Sir John Anderson. He took a remarkably liberal view for the times.

> I hope there will be no encouragement given to Government recruiting. After the recent experience of Southern Rhodesia we have had enough of that. It would be equivalent to a system of forced labour, not for Government purposes and under Government supervision, but for planters work and under planters supervision.
>
> Nor should we under any circumstances agree to contracts being signed except before a Government Officer responsible for seeing that the terms of the contract are explained to the natives.
>
> After all, the country belongs to the native and the doctrine that they must be compelled to furnish labour to enable the white men to develop the country is not one to which we can subscribe. It may be very irritating to see the natives idle and the land lying fallow, but if he can afford to be idle, until we can get to the ideal socialist state, he has as much right to do so as the white man.[136]

What is remarkable about Anderson's minute is not just the blunt statement of view. It illustrates the degree to which the CO would lose control in Kenya in the years ahead since postwar labor policy there would depart from Anderson's ideals in practically every particular.

In meeting the settler delegation at the House of Commons on 16 December, Harcourt made it clear he adhered to Anderson's point of view. Besides Guest, the delegation was made up of Leggett, Cranworth, E. Powys-Cobb, a large landowner, A. J. B. Wavill, owner of coast sisal plantations, Colonel Owen Thomas, general manager of East African Estates, and a representative of the London Chamber of Commerce. Harcourt reminded them that he had continued the policy of refusing to allow labor recruiting by government officials. He called attention to the fact that the memorandum had made little reference to the subject of increases in wages as a means to obtaining more labor; rather, testimony of settlers before the NLC suggested that their desire was to keep them down.[137]

After his statement reacting to the delegation's memo, Harcourt listened to the complaints and suggestions raised by the individuals who stressed the shortage of labor and the necessity to find some solutions. Leggett was especially prominent. A former officer in the Royal Engineers, he had been seconded for duty in the EAP after an extended tour in South Africa during and after the Boer War.[138] His company had extensive involvement in East Africa and he was particularly outspoken in his dissent from the view that African production in Nyanza was an important element in the protectorate's economy. He argued that Africans had shown little incentive to production. It will be important to remember that this representative of metropolitan merchant capital would come to dramatically alter this point of view in the postwar depression. The S of S promised to raise specific points with Governor Belfield but stated that he wished to await the findings of the NLC before making further judgments.[139]

At the direction of the S of S, a copy of the minutes of the meeting and the memorandum prepared by the deputation were sent to Belfield. The accompanying despatch asked the governor to inquire into a number of issues, but stated that the CO had no desire to anticipate the recommendation he might make as a result of the report of the commission. On what he referred to as the most important point, however, Harcourt made it clear that he endorsed the view expressed by Lord Crewe in 1908 that there must be no possibility "of direct Government intervention in labor recruiting."[140]

Having strongly made this point, the CO gave no more detailed consideration to issues relating to labor until it received a copy of the NLC report and the governor's recommendations arising from it. This proved to be some considerable time. Although the commission produced its report in August 1913, Belfield, desirous to consult settler opinion, did not send his views to London until March of the following year. The governor endorsed most of the recommendations made by the commission, and his comments demonstrated that, as in other matters, Belfield was only too ready to adopt positions advocated by the most influential settlers. He made this clear at the outset of his commentary cataloguing the reasons for the previous labor shortage. Among these the governor counted the African's suspicion of attempts to get him out to work, his disinclination to perform manual labor, and "his lack of ambition to improve the condition of his existence."[141]

From this commentary on labor shortage, Belfield moved to comment on the various recommendations, requesting the S of S to intimate the extent of the latter's agreement with the proposals put forward by the governor. In the latter's view, "the most important and far-reaching" recommendation of the NLC did not directly relate to the labor shortage. It called for the restructuring of the administration of the protectorate into African and European areas, each with its own separate system. This had been advocated by settlers as had the creation of a new administrative position, chief native commissioner (CNC), to oversee African administration.

The governor then went on to comment on what made up the other significant recommendations. Belfield supported the commission calls for inspection of labor and enforcement of health and sanitary conditions relating to workers. He had directed the officers concerned to prepare legislation to impose the necessary obligations on employers, and he proposed to do what was possible to improve the transport of laborers. The NLC had recommended that Africans could pay a higher rate of taxation, but opposed an increase merely to force out labor. Belfield merely stated: "I can not consider that the question of taxation is so intimately connected with the labour problem as to be properly included within the scope of this inquiry. . . ."[142] He agreed completely with the NLC's call, echoing that of the settlers, for the start of a system of African registration and pass laws. It was necessary, he felt, to deal with desertion from the job. He hoped London would view the idea with favor; in which case the governor promised to adapt the law in force in Southern Rhodesia to local conditions.

Belfield's views as to the proper role of government in recruitment would be of particular interest at the CO. This was because they diverged significantly from those forcefully expressed to him in Harcourt's despatch of December 1912. In Belfield's opinion:

> It is of the utmost importance that all officers entrusted with duties of native administration should impress upon the people the desire of the Government that their young men should go out to work and should keep that fact always prominently before them. I am taking steps to see that more attention is paid to the subject than has been the case, in some instances, in the past.[143]

Such views were literally light years away from those of his patron, Sir John Anderson.

CO officials quickly realized that the NLC report and the governor's lengthy commentary would need careful and detailed study. In fact, they did not send a reply until more than two months had passed from the time Belfield had completed his despatch. Moreover, all officials, while they agreed that taxation had to be considered independently of labor supply, found themselves at odds with some of the points advocated by the governor and the commission. Bottomley, for example, found himself out of step with them, and in step with views expressed to him personally and before the NLC by Nyanza provincial commissioner John Ainsworth. The CO official held, as did Ainsworth, that higher wages and better working conditions would produce more labor. Bottomley emphasized the fact that there was to be no government assistance in labor recruitment; as for registration, he would wait for the governor's detailed report on the subject before altering his previously expressed lack of enthusiasm.[144]

Sir George Fiddes felt that before embarking on the same path as South Africa or Southern Rhodesia had taken, it was important to consider what had happened in those two territories. After discussion with Anderson, he asked Sir H. C. Lambert of the Dominions Division of the CO to have a memo drawn up detailing the experience in southern Africa with labor problems.[145] Lambert quickly completed his memo. In it he argued that the South African experience suggested that a reorganization of administration would be beneficial and that government had an important role to play in labor inspection and control. On the other hand, the CO official strongly maintained that the southern African experience suggested that "the Governor is on very dangerous ground" in wishing to use government officials to impress on African the need to go out to work. The latter were likely to confuse a suggestion to go to work with an order that had to be obeyed.[146] Having read this, Fiddes urged that the CO make it clear that the EAP government should do nothing that suggested compulsion. He considered that the CO could examine a detailed proposal for registrtion, but it was only one of several points that he urged reserving a decision pending receipt of detailed suggestions from Belfield.[147]

After further review by Anderson, Emmott, and Harcourt, the CO reply was sent to Nairobi on 20 May. Significantly, Lambert's memo and another on the Southern Rhodesia experience werȩ sent as enclosures. The CO despatch expressed general approval for the reorganization of the administration, and it endorsed the commission's recommendations regarding labor inspection, the enforcement of health regulations, and improvement of transport for laborers. On points of detail, such as registration, the governor was told, it was necessary for the S of S to reserve decision until the proposals for carrying them out had been provided by Nairobi.

On the question of recruiting labor, however, the CO did have a good deal to say. Although the matter was one of great difficulty, it was of "utmost importance that Government officers should do nothing which could in any way suggest Government compulsion." The CO maintained that the African would not always be able to discriminate between advice and compulsion. "For this reason," wrote the S of S, "I am inclined to think that the proposal that officials should impress on the people the need to work may have dangerous consequences unless it is carefully limited and defined."[148] The CO despatch concluded with a reminder that rapid development, while desirable, should not compromise the interests of the African population.

With the strong statements on labor recruiting and its refusal to commit itself in advance on Belfield's proposals, the CO seemed to have retained a good deal of leverage for itself over labor policy in the EAP. In fact, this did not prove to be the case. As Clayton and Savage have demonstrated, Belfield's government provided the settlers with a watered-down version of the CO despatch. Belfield added to the S of S's statement his own decision to instruct the provincial and district administrators to urge Africans to go out to work.[149] More significant than this, however, was the fact that the CO had reserved some very important policy decisions for a future which would be fundamentally changed by the impact of the first World War.

Within a month of sending its response to the EAP, the CO heard from other parties concerned about the labor situation there. The ASAPS addressed a letter to the S of S on 11 June, expressing concern with some of the NLC's recommendations and much of the testimony given before it. Two matters particularly concerned the society: it opposed the idea that African reserves should be reduced and Africans discouraged from agricultural production, and it vehemently objected to the contention that it was the duty of government to secure labor for private enterprise. The latter would, sooner or later, lead to compulsion, and forced labor for private work was, in the society's opinion, slavery. The ASAPS therefore requested assurance that the reserves would not be curtailed and that the British government accept the proposition that forced labor for private enterprise "is a form of slavery" which would not be tolerated.[150]

The CO returned a noncommittal reply to the society two weeks later, but the ASAPS pressed Harcourt for a statement of his views; did he believe that "forced labour for private profit amounts to slavery?"[151] Read finally responded for the S of S on 9 July that "the proposition that forced labour for private profit amounts to slavery appears to him to be self-evident."[152]

This would not be the last time that the ASAPS would express concern over labor policies in the EAP. British humanitarians would form an important pressure group on the subject after the war.

African Reserves

The interest in the sanctity of African reserves that the society had expressed was one that was shared by many at the CO. It had arisen because the NLC had been asked to report on the effects of the African reserves on the labor supply. Many settler witnesses before the commission had demanded a reduction of African land as a means of forcing more men out to work. CO concern with the reserves, their adequacy, and possible excisions of land from them had existed well before the appointment of the commission. In theory the CO favored extensive and inalienable reserves, but this was not translated into effective policy before 1912. Reserves had been proclaimed for the Maasai in 1904, only to be altered by a treaty in 1911. Kikuyu reserves had been declared in 1907, but no other African inhabited areas had been officially demarcated and recognized as reserves.[153]

A report on trouble among the Kipsigis, submitted by Governor Belfield in late 1912, raised CO concerns about the adequacy of reserves. In his report, Belfield had spoken of the need to keep the people "within their boundaries," and this brought a strong reaction from Sir John Anderson. The governor's report gave him "an uncomfortable impression" that Europeans were being granted land irrespective of African claims and that the Kipsigis did not have sufficient land.[154] The CO therefore asked the governor if the Kipsigis had sufficient land for their needs.[155]

Prior to receipt of this despatch, Belfield had forwarded to London a more extensive statement of view on African reserves in a memorandum drawn up in response to claims for compensation by Kikuyu from Kiambu. He admitted that the alienation of areas that Africans desired to retain had caused widespread dissatisfaction and given rise to feelings of insecurity. The governor maintained that provision should be made in the new land ordinance for safeguarding the reserves. But he viewed the question of reserves as part of a

railway rolling stock since the present Uganda railway stock was being worked to the utmost capacity, £200,000 for road and bridge construction, and
£65,000 for Lake Victoria steamers. The £1,665,000 was a larger portion of
the total loan than either Uganda or Nyasaland would receive.[166]

It is particularly significant that the EAP projects were targeted to help
both settler (roads, harbour, Thika railway extension) and African (roads,
harbour, Thika and Mumias railway extensions) production. As strong an
advocate as Belfield was of the settler position, he recognized the contribution of peasant production to the protectorate's exports. He was so impressed
with the potential for increased exports from Nyanza province that he encouraged Ainsworth to contact the CO, while on leave in 1913, to seek assistance
for development projects there.[167]

The CO gained approval for the loan in 1914. In both its submissions to the
Treasury and in Harcourt's defense of the loan act in parliament, the CO
emphasized that the money would aid both peasant and estate production.
This would enable the EAP to pay its own way and cease to be a drain on the
British taxpayer. As Constantine has shown, moreover, arguments in favor of
the loan bill also pointed to the benefits it would provide to Britain itself. The
EAP and the other protectorates would provide more raw materials and jobs
for British industries and better markets for British manufactured goods. In
looking to benefit the British economy as well as that of the EAP, these
arrangements foreshadowed postwar development ideas.[168]

The major private development initiative that marked these years also
sought to provide improved communications and increased exports. Yet the
proposal to build a railway to open up the Uasin Gishu plateau, in the western
portion of the white highlands, demonstrated the strength and importance of
African production. The plateau had been thrown open to European settlement in 1908, but the farmers (both South African boers and English settlers)
produced few viable exports. The settlers ascribed their economic difficulties
to poor transportation facilities, and their complaints were received sympathetically by Governor Belfield.[169] Belfield visited the Uasin Gishu plateau
in February 1913, and he had been impressed with what he viewed as "excep-
tionally favourable natural conditions for agriculture."[170]

Belfield's desire to see a railway built to open up the Uasin Gishu plateau
was matched by the desire of two non-officials to achieve the same result.
These were George Lloyd and E. S. Grogan. The former, a member of the
Lloyd banking family and a Tory M.P., visited the EAP in 1913 as a representative of a number of British investors seeking avenues for profitable investment. Lloyd's interest was particularly drawn to the Uasin Gishu by Grogan, one of the most prominent and outspoken members of the Kenya settler
community. Grogan had obtained a timber concession of almost 200,000
acres in the Eldama Ravine area, and he needed a railway to effectively exploit this timber.[171] The concession lay to the east of the Uasin Gishu plateau.

Lloyd returned to Britain in May 1913 and quickly approached the CO with his willingness to raise money and arrange construction of a railway to the Uasin Gishu plateau if the government would provide a guarantee. At the CO, he met Fiddes and Read who were not enthusiastic about mixing private and government enterprise in the way Lloyd proposed. Fiddes told the M.P. that there was little chance of a guarantee being given, a view that Harcourt supported when the proposal was put before him a few days later. The CO told Lloyd in mid-May that "there is no prospect whatever" of such a guarantee by the British or EAP governments.[172]

The financier was not put off by this rebuff. Lloyd now turned to seek private capital to build the railway even without a government guarantee. In August he wrote Harcourt to propose a scheme in which private capital would find money for construction according to plans and contractors approved by the government. Once the line was complete, the protectorate government would lease it from private enterprise for a fixed rent with an option to purchase.[173] This proposal seemed almost too good to be true to CO officials. They would have to bear little risk for the project. Harcourt therefore approved another meeting between Lloyd and Fiddes.[174]

When Lloyd met Fiddes on 12 September, he brought Grogan with him; they painted an optimistic picture of the prospects of raising money for construction and the profitability of the rail line. One new factor added to the scheme by Grogan particularly had this potential: the extension of the line across the Uasin Gishu plateau to Mumias in North Kavirondo, Nyanza province's most productive district. Lloyd not only committed himself to finding the necessary capital; he and his fellow investors would require as rent only the equivalent of their loss of interest.[175] Fiddes, understandably, now began to view the scheme in a much more positive light. "I have struck a philanthropist," he wrote four days after the meeting, "and I have not yet recovered from the shock."[176] When Lloyd confirmed his offer in writing, the CO decided to seek the views of the EAP government on the matter. Significantly, the CO despatch of 19 September now recognized the possibility of extension beyond the Uasin Gishu plateau. As it noted:

> It was claimed by the promoters that the line would give not merely the shortest and least hilly route to Uasin Gishu plateau but also that in the event of the railway being required in North Kavirondo district an extension on the line now proposed would have equal or greater advantages in the development of that region also.[177]

The EAP government was also at this time seriously considering the possibility of a rail line to the Uasin Gishu. As a result of pressure from Grogan, Belfield had sent the general manager of the Uganda railway, H. B. Taylor, to examine the region between Nakuru, on the Uganda railway, and Eldoret, headquarters for the Uasin Gishu district. Although he recognized that it would take time to develop traffic from the largely undeveloped settler farms, Taylor recommended that a detailed railway survey be carried out.[178]

Lloyd and Grogan gained what proved to be an even more powerful ally than Taylor in October 1913. John Ainsworth, on home leave, met Lloyd in London. Ainsworth had been the prime moving force behind the scheme to build a railway line from Kisumu, the railway terminus on Lake Victoria, north to Mumias. Since 1910, Ainsworth had pushed for a railway to open up what was now the most productive region of the EAP. It was the railway's best customer in 1912, and Ainsworth maintained that a huge increase in production for export would result. Ainsworth had convinced Girouard of the need for such a railroad, and by mid-1913, as noted earlier, the CO had accepted the extension as one of the projects to be financed from the loan bill to be submitted to parliament.[179]

After meeting Lloyd, Ainsworth dropped his advocacy for a rail line from Kisumu to Mumias and adopted the alternative from Nakuru to Eldoret and then to Mumias.[180] Ainsworth's description of the productive possibilities of North Kavirondo greatly impressed Lloyd. The financier was now even more determined to gain CO approval for a railway through to Mumias. He wrote to Fiddes making his reason very clear:

all doubts as to the prospects of adequate returns on the Uasin Gishu section would be eliminated; for it is perfectly clear that the productive wealth of the Mumias district would provide rich and immediate traffic on this last section and offer an immediate heavy freightage over the Uasin Gishu section. . . .[181]

The unproductive settler section on the Uasin Gishu plateau would be easily carried by the traffic from the Mumias region. Thus Lloyd suggested the utilization of African agriculture to subsidize European settlement.

Lloyd and Ainsworth's letters forced CO officials to once again seriously examine the scheme, now altered to provide a line through to Mumias. Read favored a Kisumu-Mumias over the Uasin Gishu route. The former would be shorter and much cheaper to construct. He contrasted North Kavirondo, "the most productive part of the E.A.P." and "the best source of labour we have in that country—another reason for having a railway through it" with the Uasin Gishu where he had observed on a 1911 visit that the small number of European settlers "were doing practically nothing in the way of development."[182] Fiddes was not so hostile to the Uasin Gishu proposal, but it was decided to take no final decision on the route until the governor's views had been obtained.[183]

The CO thus sent a confidential despatch to Belfield on 7 November that asked him to consider the matter carefully and decide "which of these extensions would be most advisable." The CO gave authority to undertake expenditure for a survey of the Nakuru-Eldoret-Mumias line. That and the despatch's favorable reference to Ainsworth's view that such a line would be more advantageous to the protectorate as a whole indicated CO preference for that route as well.[184]

Even before receipt of this despatch, Belfield had expressed a preference for a Nakuru–Uasin Gishu–Mumias line. He included it among a list of development projects he sent to London in response to an earlier CO request.[185] The governor expressed several reasons for favoring it over the route from Mumias to Kisumu, but primary among these was the advantage of using the traffic from North Kavirondo to subsidize the plateau settlers. General manager Taylor made clear that this was the primary advantage of the scheme in an accompanying letter. He stated that the region around Mumias "would certainly pay if opened out by railway connections, and if we do this in the manner suggested it will mean that the Uasin Gishu Railway, which in itself can not bring much traffic in its first few years, will if extended to Mumias, have an assured traffic from the very outset amounting to a couple of trains per day."[186]

It would come, therefore, as no surprise to the CO that Belfield expressed a strong preference for the Uasin Gishu to Mumias route when he finally answered the November despatch. Supported by another letter from Taylor, the governor urged the subsidization of the Uasin Gishu settlers by the North Kavirondo traffic.[187] With the governor's strong preference before them, CO officials felt able to go forward to finalize negotiations with Lloyd for construction. All that was lacking was a final estimate of cost. In February 1914, the CO sent a request for such an estimate to Nairobi.[188]

When the estimate arrived at the CO, however, it actually produced further delay. This was because the estimate of £1,000,000 (£5,000 per mile for 200 miles) shocked officials at the CO. A previous estimate had put the cost at £450,000.[189] This huge discrepancy meant that a detailed survey would have to be carried out before any arrangements with Lloyd could be taken in hand. The CO engaged engineers to undertake the work.[190] The survey was actually completed, but World War I intervened before the CO had a chance to consider the scheme further. No consideration would be given to this kind of railway extension until 1918.

Nevertheless, the Uasin Gishu–Mumias railway scheme was extremely significant. It clearly demonstrated that the great importance of African peasant production was recognized by both the CO and the colonial state. This would not be the last time that the state would contemplate using African production to subsidize that of the European settlers. The project provides, moreover, a good example of what would later be termed the dual policy; the state would, at least in theory, foster both settler and African production. Finally, the consideration of the scheme clearly demonstrates that the CO was still in control as far as major economic policy decisions for the EAP were concerned. Unwilling at first to support such a development project that promised to benefit European settlement but be very costly, the CO finally backed a railway extension to Mumias via the Uasin Gishu to stimulate African production for export.

The CO in Control

The CO's attitude in the case of railway extension was hardly the only one that demonstrates that London was not merely dancing to the tune of the settlers, backed by Belfield, on all issues, large and small. The CO stance in the case of Galbraith Cole provides another example.

As described in Chapter 1, Cole had been deported from the EAP in October 1911 on orders from Harcourt. Cole attempted to bring considerable pressure to bear on the CO to rescind this order and allow him to return. Cole received an interview with Harcourt on 3 July 1912, and he tried to show, in Fiddes words, "that his conduct was not as black as was represented." Harcourt listened patiently, but the S of S told Cole that he would not allow the settler to return to the EAP as long as he remained in office.[191]

Harcourt maintained that stance throughout 1912 and 1913. Cole's former commanding officer wrote, without success, to Harcourt to plead for the latter's return in July 1912. Cole next convinced Lord Stamfordham, the king's private secretary, to intercede on his behalf. Stamfordham came to see Butler on 25 October, but Harcourt would not change his mind. "My decision is final," he wrote.[192] Lady Delamere pleaded with the S of S in November to allow her brother to return to the EAP. Since Cole suffered from rheumatoid arthritis, he found the climate of Britain very difficult to bear. Harcourt stuck to his decision.[193] In March 1913, Lord Crewe, Harcourt's cabinet colleague, wrote to pass on a request from his "very good friend," the Earl of Enniskillen, that Cole be allowed to see Anderson and state his position. Crewe's request drew a favorable response from Harcourt, but he told Crewe in no uncertain terms that he would not allow Cole to return to the EAP as long as he was at the CO.[194] Cole had an interview with Anderson, but the S of S did not alter his previous stand.[195]

Thus at the end of the first year and a half of Belfield's governorship, the CO remained in control of the initiative as far as the EAP was concerned. In their pronouncements on African reserves and labor, moreover, CO officials had staked out positions quite at variance with those advocated by the settlers and the governor. Nevertheless, the CO would not be able to sustain these and other positions and its control in the succeeding two years. The changed conditions brought about by the war would help to create a climate in which the CO would give way, as in the question of land policy during the period under review, to settler demands advocated by the colonial state. The result would be a clear loss of CO control over the direction of policy in the EAP.

3
The CO Loses Control, 1914–16

The period that began with the outbreak of World War I was an extremely important one in terms of CO relations with the EAP. It, rather than Girouard's governorship, represents a major turning point for the settlers, with the strong backing of the colonial state, now firmly entrenched themselves as the major factor in protectorate affairs. At the outset of the war, the CO was still in charge, but by the end of 1916, it had clearly lost control.

The loss of initiative would manifest itself in CO acceptance of all the demands advocated by the settlers. The most compelling reason for this was the war. Its impact on Kenya produced changed economic and political realities that very much favored the European settlers. The colonial state, largely bereft of leadership in this initial period of the war, became an even more enthusiastic advocate for the economic and political demands of the settlers.

The CO and the War in East Africa

At the start of the First World War, the CO was in direct charge of the military forces in the EAP (the Kings African Rifles). As German East Africa shared a large common border with the EAP, it was soon evident that the British colony would be involved in military operations against its German neighbor. The CO, through Governor Belfield and the protectorate's military leaders, played a role in developing and guiding war policy in the East African theatre. However, the CO did not have complete control of war policy in East Africa for very long. The cabinet quickly decided that German East Africa should be conquered using, in the main, troops from India. The EAP armed forces adopted a "mainly defensive" posture until the arrival of an expeditionary force from India (known as Force B).[1] The Indian troops were under direct control of the IO; thus direction of operations in East Africa would be shared with the CO.[2]

For the CO, the period of joint control never worked well. It began with a lack of communication; the CO was not told when Force B left India.[3] It ended with the disaster of the British defeat at the battle of Tanga in early November.

The defeat was a shock for Governor Belfield and for the CO. Belfield had met with General Aitken, commander of the Indian expeditionary force, on the latter's arrival at Mombasa at the end of October. Belfield was little involved in the military planning, but he did throw himself enthusiastically into plans for administering the northeastern portion of German East Africa that Aitken expected to conquer quickly.[4] This exercise in dividing the German territory proved quite premature, and even before the battle of Tanga, CO officials had expressed disquiet over the detailed plan Aitken had developed for division of the spoils before the defeat of the enemy.[5]

The plan was never implemented. Belfield sent news of the defeat at Tanga by telegram on 5 November. He now concluded that the protectorate's military forces must assume the defensive, and that considerable reinforcements would be needed to "reduce German East Africa." The CO resignedly accepted those conclusions.[6] However, the CO's direct participation in operations would be terminated just over two weeks later by decision of the cabinet in London. All operations in East Africa would, after 22 November, come under the control of the War Office.[7] Once this decision was made, the CO was taken out of any direct role in military operations in East Africa. CO officials could only console themselves that the operations, all defensive, that they had responsibility for had been successful.[8]

This CO loss of command was most significant; it was one way in which World War I reduced the CO's control over Kenya. It is easy to see the disappointment reflected in the minutes of CO officials that marked the end of their direction of the EAP's troops, and this would have a very real impact. Unable to influence the military decisions in East Africa, CO officials increasingly let the initiative in most important policy matters slide to the colonial state. In light of previous experience, this would mean that the European settlers would have a far greater say in such matters than ever before.

That the war strengthened the settlers' political influence was quickly apparent. No sooner had the conflict begun than had the S of S reversed a decision he had affirmed just a few months prior to the war. That decision concerned Galbraith Cole, the prominent settler deported from the EAP in 1911. In mid-September 1914, the CO received word from Cole's mother that his services were required by the military authorities in East Africa. When Parkinson learned that the governor had not known of this request for Cole's services, he felt that this was "a very discreditable 'try-on' and I trust that a curt refusal to reconsider the previous action of the CO will be sent."[9] Fiddes shared this sentiment, but Harcourt, to the surprise of the two permanent officials, took a completely different line. He minuted: "I must certainly cancel the G. Cole deportation in view of the general amnesty to Suffragettes and S A deportees. I am sorry I did not think of it sooner."[10] Harcourt thereafter ordered Belfield to cancel the deportation order.[11] The war thus undermined (at least for the S of S) the principles that had undergirded the Cole deportation and, above all, ultimate control over EAP affairs. This had been especially significant in a case like Cole's: even when the governor's views had not been supportive, the CO had intervened in the name of justice and morality. Several years would pass before the CO could undertake even remotely similar action.

During the initial period of the war, moreover, the CO experienced a substantial reduction in external questions about, or criticisms of, policies in the protectorate. Whether in parliament or outside, the humanitarian lobby and other groups that had been interested in affairs in the EAP were now conspicuous by their silence. The war in Europe provided an obviously more compelling cause for concern among most people in Britain, and it is not surprising that non-military interest in East Africa would lapse. This would have an impact on the CO, moreover, since officials would not be called upon to counter criticism of the gains the settlers would make in the EAP during the war. This must be counted as a not insignificant factor in facilitating the CO loss of control that marked these years.

Another factor that produced a weakening of CO control in the early stage of the war had little to do directly with the conflict. This was the illness of Harcourt. In early November 1914, he suffered a heart attack.[12] The S of S was not completely incapacitated, but his direct involvement in EAP affairs was, as a result, greatly reduced. For the next few months, he spent most of his time in bed or on his home sofa, doing his paperwork there. He left bed only to attend cabinet meetings and to undertake essential interviews.[13] During his illness, Harcourt left much of the work to his young, unpaid private secretary, J. C. C. Davidson. The latter had full authority to act as S of S during Harcourt's absence.[14]

Hazelhurst is rightly critical of Harcourt's actions:

> That anyone in Harcourt's condition should have contemplated, for a moment, continuing to undertake responsibility of the Colonial Office is, to say the least, surprising. That he should have done it in time of war is so little short of incredible that it can not be recorded without comment.[15]

Harcourt stayed on at the CO until May 1915, but he never was to display the vigor and interest in EAP affairs that he had before his illness that had fatefully coincided with the CO loss of influence over military operations in East Africa. In his last two months at the CO, his great concern was what should be done with Germany's colonies in Africa and the Pacific region that had been conquered by allied forces.[16] He had little time for the EAP. This was a matter of no small significance. More than any other S of S of the period 1912–23, Lewis Harcourt had taken an interest in all aspects of EAP affairs. As several examples in chapters 1 and 2 clearly showed, Harcourt had been virtually the only one at the CO to take a stand against settler demands. When he could no longer play that active role, the initiative, in a very real sense, passed to the colonial state and the settlers.

Land

One of the first issues where this was apparent was the EAP land bill. On 25 August, Belfield sent copies of the revised bill to London with a strong plea that the changes made by a Legco special committee be given rapid approval. He recognized the ordinance had been constructed on "broader lines" than the principles laid down by the CO in 1908 or 1912 had anticipated, but the governor urged that the new ordinance would insure a prosperous future "by the removal of vexatious restrictions which must inevitably imperil the process of regular development. . . ."[17]

The change that Belfield could not urge too strongly on the CO was the substitution of a lease in perpetuity (999 years) for the ninety-nine-year term. This undoubtedly did not surprise anyone at the CO, but the new bill did retain the principle of reassessment of rent at 30-year intervals which the CO had come to regard as more important than length of lease. The governor also pushed for the dropping of clauses requiring continuous residence on the property by the landholder in favor of new development conditions. Although he had not been certain of the impact of these provisions on the settlers earlier in the year, he had no doubts now. The new ordinance would "prove to be a practical and acceptable measure." His two years in the country had convinced Belfield that the settlers' objections to the ninety-nine-year lease were well founded. Landholders would hesitate before embarking on large expenditure under the shorter term of tenure. The longer term, he was sure, would "so restore confidence that the rate of development will be substantially enhanced."

Responding also to previous CO concerns about making the African reserves crown lands under the ordinance, Belfield strongly supported the special committee's view that such classification was essential. No African ethnic group in the EAP recognized anything more than occupier's rights, asserted the governor; and from that rather doubtful proposition, he went on to justify placing all such land under the direct control of the colonial state. This was, he held, the only effective safeguard, preserving for the African peoples "the rights and privileges which they are unable to protect for themselves." Belfield had strong words for critics, such as Liberal M.P. Harvey, whose protests had forced the CO to raise the issue with the EAP government. He was certain that

> those gentlemen in England who are anxious that the rights of the natives should remain inviolate need be under no misapprehension that the Government is actuated by any predatory instinct or is preparing to despoil the native for the benefit of the settler. On the contrary, the arrangement proposed is the most effective means of placing the barrier of official authority between the desire of the settler to acquire and the temptation to the native to part with what is not his to dispose of.

For all his enthusiasm for the bill, one potential difficulty was noted by the governor. This had to do with the best means for restricting transfers of land in the white highlands to Europeans. The new ordinance, urged Belfield, had to give to the governor power to prohibit participation in land transfers in the highlands "by people of Asiatic or African birth" while at the same time allowing transfers to other Europeans.[18]

The CO received the governor's despatch on 21 September, and officials undertook a lengthy review of it. The EAD first examined what were regarded as important matters of principle in the bill. These included the 999-year lease, with revision of rent, dropping insistence on continuous occupation by the lessee, the definition of African reserves as crown land, and the governor's veto on land transfers in the highlands to non-Europeans. Bottomley and Read concurred with most of the governor's recommendations, but on the latter two matters, they expressed some doubts. In the case of African lands, Bottomley thought that "practically every tribe had a system of tribal tenure" and that the governor's view of the pre-colonial past seemed "rather out of place." However, he accepted that defining the reserves as crown lands was a good idea, as did Read. On land transfers, Bottomley thought it was a pity "to drag our 'Asiatic' distinction into legislative print at a time when Indian opinion agreed to sink its grievances for the time." Fiddes agreed that the present was the worst possible time for discrimination, in name, against Indians.[19]

With Anderson's approval, the bill was next examined in detail by a special committee made up of Bottomley, Read, and the CO legal assistant C. B. Tennyson. The latter emphasized in his comments there should be no discrimination against Indians, by name, as "it would give a bad impression in India." The lawyer suggested retaining the governor's veto on land transfers without spelling out that such veto power would only apply to transfers to Indians and Africans.[20] Although the committee's review was not complete, they placed this and other matters of principle before the S of S for his decisions on 5 October.

Three days later, Harcourt laid out the final CO position on the land ordinance that it had initiated more than six years before. He agreed to the 999 years with revision at thirty-year intervals and to African reserves being defined as crown land. He could not, however, accept discrimination by name against Indians. He proposed two alternatives: an unrestricted governor's veto "with no pledge that it will be only exercised against Asiatics," or "free transfer, which will leave a possibility of Asiatic purchases in the Highlands." The S of S directed that the governor be asked to state which seemed best from the point of view of the settlers and the government.[21]

Therefore, a telegram was sent to the EAP the next day, requesting that Belfield express his preference for one of the two alternatives posed by Harcourt.[22] The governor replied on 20 October that in the present circumstances it was "difficult to ascertain feeling of the community as to relative merits of free transfer and unrestricted veto." He suggested letting the question stand over for a time as "dealing in land is practically at a standstill and the bringing into operation of the new law is not, therefore, now a matter of urgency."[23]

The EAD were not particularly happy to learn that passing the ordinance into law was no longer urgent; nevertheless, they completed their review upon receipt of the governor's telegram. On the issue of the veto, Bottomley proposed an innovative solution. He suggested limiting the power of veto to transactions in which a European and a non-European were concerned as the two parties. He maintained: "this would meet the case as regards the Asiatic in the highlands so long as individual tenure by natives is not recognized outside the coast strip, and it would tend to protect the Indian land holder and the coast native or Arab against the wiles of the European concession hunter."[24] Bottomley's superiors found the suggestion acceptable, and the EAD could now move forward to draft a despatch to Nairobi, summarizing the CO decisions on the bill.[25]

This was despatched to Belfield on 7 November. On most questions of principle, the CO came around to the governor's view. However, for the final time, Harcourt stated his reluctance. He had changed his mind because of the governor's representations, based on his two years experience in the EAP, and "of the extreme desirability of putting an end to the uncertainty and discontent which have for so long been felt in the Protectorate."[26] First and foremost was the extension of the lease period from ninety-nine to 999 years. The S of S formally stated that he had no alternative but to accept this principle as it appeared that "a 99 years tenure is unduly retarding development of the Protectorate. . . ." Harcourt also stated that he would have preferred to retain "some safeguard against speculation other than that afforded by conditions as to expenditure on and maintenance of development," but he agreed with the governor's position here also. The CO rejected the governor's proposal as to vetoes of land transactions between people of different races and suggested instead Bottomley's proposal giving the governor power to veto all transfers of agricultural land, whether in the highlands or elsewhere, to which the parties were a European and a non-European. The S of S also concurred that "the inclusion of reserves in the definition of Crown Lands is in no way injurious to the natives and forms the only satisfactory means of exercising the necessary Government control."[27]

With this approval from the CO, the ordinance was passed, in final form, by the Legco early the following year. It would thus be known to posterity as the Crown Lands Ordinance, 1915.[28] In transmitting the ordinance to London in February, Governor Belfield expressed "profound satisfaction" at the outcome of the lengthy struggle over the land ordinance. The changes and concessions that the CO had now accepted would have the effect of pleasing the settlers while adequately safeguarding the interests of the African population.[29]

This did not prove to be the case. Rather than protecting African land rights the ordinance had the effect of depriving Africans of all rights in land. Ghai and McAuslan have provided a succinct summary of the bill's impact:

> Thus not only did the protectorate government now have complete control of all land occupied by Africans, but it was made clear that Africans had no right to alienate any of the land, whether they occupied it, or it was reserved for their use. In addition, land reserved for their use could at any time be cancelled and thereafter alienated to settlers. The disinheritance of Africans from their land was complete.[30]

The ordinance would long be a source of dissatisfaction to Kenya's Indian and African peoples, and it stimulated much political protest in the future. Harcourt had closed his November 1914 despatch with the rationalization that if the result of the ordinance's enactment was "to end the dissatisfaction and friction of the past" and give a stimulus to prosperity of the EAP, "which could not have been hoped for from a more restricted measure, I shall have little cause to regret the concessions on points of principle which I have made in this and former despatches."[31] The dissatisfaction of the settlers might be removed, but that of the other peoples in the protectorate would not.

This was the logical outcome of the position of retreat followed by the CO on land issues after 1912. Repeatedly pushed by Belfield to make changes acceptable to the settler community, the CO, and most particularly Harcourt, gradually gave way. The retreat became a rout in the first months of World War I as the CO literally gave over control of land policy to the man on the spot. The settler "victory" is perhaps all the more remarkable when it is recalled that for most of the initial period of Belfield's governorship, the settlers had given up their membership in the Legco.[32]

Registration

Unlike the land ordinance, Governor Belfield was able to obtain approval of a registration ordinance within a year of his September 1914 despatch, in which he mentioned his intention to prepare a bill to effect an identification and pass law for Africans. The ordinance was based on Southern Rhodesia legislation. Every "adult male native" would be supplied with a registration number and a paper "which will be both a means of identification and a record of the native's labour history."[33] After its second reading, the bill was placed before a special committee for further consideration; the only major change that resulted was the raising of the age of adulthood from fourteen to sixteen.

At the CO, there was no opposition to the ordinance. In the preceding year officials had shown themselves willing, in principle, to accept such legislation. Read thought that "we can sanction if the legal adviser agrees it is proper legal form." When the legal adviser reviewed the bill, he approved it.[34] At this point, however, Anderson intervened. He wondered about the timing of the measure. Britain was on the defensive in East Africa. "Had it not better wait," he wrote to Read, "til our position is more secure? It cannot fail to be unpopular amongst the natives."[35] Read felt that there would be no risks if the ordinance was suspended until the end of the war. Anderson accepted that suggestion because, as he put it, "the natives everywhere dislike registration and the consequent restriction on their movements. In the present temper of our East African natives I think we should run no avoidable risk."[36] Belfield was thus informed by despatch that the ordinance should be suspended until after the war.[37]

The compulsory registration of African men did not actually begin until after the war. It was a measure strongly demanded by the settlers and the colonial state. Since the CO had shown no interest in blocking or holding back the concept from becoming law, it is difficult to see how, in this case, the war served to speed up the approval of a measure demanded by the settlers. Rather, the war probably had the effect of delaying its implementation.

Changes at the CO

Several significant changes in personnel occurred at the CO during the period that stretched from the start of World War I to the end of December 1916. These had, and would have in the future, considerable impact on CO policy towards the EAP. The cumulative impact of the changes was to further loosen the CO's grip on the protectorate's affairs.

The first changes to take place, in August 1914 and May 1915, affected the political heads of the CO. With the restructuring of the government at the start of the war, Lord Emmott was raised to the cabinet as first commissioner of works. As was noted in the previous chapter, Emmott's views were not inconsequential where EAP affairs were concerned. A traditional liberal, he was no friend of the European settlers. Emmott was replaced as parliamentary under-secretary of state by Lord Islington. An M.P. from 1892 to 1910, Islington came to the CO from a stint as governor of New Zealand (1910–12) and service as chair of a commission on the Indian civil service. During Islington's brief period of service (August 1914 to May 1915), he had little impact and took little part in the CO deliberations on significant East African issues.

The succeeding changes in political leadership at the CO were more sweeping and far reaching than that of 1914. Prime minister H. H. Asquith formed a coalition government with the Conservative party in May of 1915. The prime minister's restructuring of his cabinet sent Harcourt to replace Emmott as first commissioner of works and brought Andrew Bonar Law, leader of the Conservative party, to the CO. At first glance, the choice of the CO for his coalition partner seems a strange decision for Asquith to have made as there were certainly cabinet posts more directly concerned with the war to which he might have been sent. Bonar Law's biographer suggests, however, that Asquith "neither found Bonar Law a congenial character nor thought highly of his talents."[38] Lord Blake judges Bonar Law's administration at the CO to have been "quiet and competent. Beyond that there is little to be said."[39] Indeed, Blake devotes only a single paragraph to Bonar Law's CO work during the year and half he held the position of S of S!

The impact of this change on CO policy toward East Africa over the next nineteen months would be difficult to exaggerate. Harcourt had taken an active part in all the important policy decisions that effected the EAP during his tenure of office. He had a profound impact on policy, and he actively sought to defend his concept of trusteeship and African rights. He had finally given way on the crown lands ordinance, but he was no friend of the European settlers in the EAP. Bonar Law, on the other hand, took virtually no part in matters relating to the EAP. He took notice only of those papers directly involving the war. With Bonar Law as S of S, there was no involvement from the top as there had been with Harcourt. The contrast was utterly striking.

With the formation of the coalition, moreover, Lord Islington moved to the IO as under-secretary, and he was replaced at the CO by Arthur Steel-Maitland, another Tory. For Steel-Maitland, this was his first government appointment. He had first entered parliament in 1910, coming to politics from a brilliant scholarly career at Oxford, where besides taking two firsts in classics, he served as president of the Oxford Union Society. He had developed a reputation as a "progressive Tory" by his interest, concern, and expertise relating to poverty and the operation of the poor laws.

Steel-Maitland, rather than Bonar Law, formed the last link in the CO chain of command so far as the EAP was concerned. With little knowledge or experience of colonial questions, Steel-Maitland left most matters to be dealt with by the permanent officials, and he almost always took their advice. The one significant exception during his tenure had to do with the soldier settlement scheme. As will be seen, he took a position very favorable to the settlers, and the colonial state acting on their behalf, on that occasion. On the whole, nevertheless, the involvement of the CO's political heads in EAP affairs was light during Bonar Law's tenure as S of S. This gave an even more crucial role to the permanent officials in such affairs.

This, therefore, made even more significant the change in leadership that took place in 1916. In March of that year, Sir John Anderson stepped down as parliamentary under-secretary to become governor of Ceylon. This was certainly a most unusual move, but it was at least partly the result of Anderson's declining health. Anderson's move had been known to the CO staff since at least November 1915.[40] Sir George Fiddes was elevated to replace him as permanent under-secretary. In many ways, Fiddes was a logical choice; his many years of service had left him thoroughly familiar with the dependent empire and with CO procedures. Harcourt strongly recommended his appointment to Bonar Law.[41]

Fiddes became permanent under-secretary of state at a time when the political leadership was more interested in the war and domestic politics than the empire. This was a situation that would continue until the end of the conflict. Fiddes would have a greater role in shaping policy, especially towards a "lesser" territory like the EAP, than his predecessor. It is of more than a little significance to note that as far as the EAP was concerned, Anderson's departure had a very substantial impact. This and the preceding chapter have provided numerous examples of Anderson's strong views on African rights. On many occasions, he had expressed himself strongly on that subject and in opposition to white supremacy in the EAP. Fiddes was certainly not avidly pro-settler, but he was not as strongly disposed to stand up to them, and the colonial state that invariably took their part, in the years ahead. The impact of this personnel change on the CO loss of direction in EAP affairs was huge, as this and following chapters will demonstrate. The elevation of Fiddes caused other personnel shifts that would have an impact on EAP policy. Read was one of three individuals elevated to the position of assistant under-secretary of state.[42]

The final personnel change of the period occurred in December 1916. With the fall of Asquith's government and formation of the Lloyd George coalition, Bonar Law left the CO to be replaced by his former rival for Conservative party leadership, Walter Long. Steel-Maitland remained as parliamentary under-secretary. If anything, Long, the champion of rural England, was even less interested in EAP affairs than his predecessor. He paid virtually no attention at all to them. So far as the S of S was concerned, the next two years would find the permanent officials in charge of any initiatives relating to the EAP.

The Settlers, Belfield, and the War

If the registration ordinance was one gain for the European settlers that the war slowed down, it was one of very few. As the war in East Africa dragged on through 1915, unsatisfactorily from the British point of view, the settlers were able to considerably expand their influence, both directly and indirectly, with the colonial state, thus putting themselves in a position to obtain political rights they had long sought. This was accomplished not so much over the opposition of the colonial state, as Governor Belfield was supportive of the settler demands. Rather it was the unenergetic and inept leadership of the governor, especially critical in time of war, which put the colonial state and the CO on the defensive to such a degree that they would find it very difficult not to make a place for the settlers as partners in the administration of the EAP.

After the British defeat at Tanga, Governor Belfield showed even less interest in the war than previously. There was now little chance that he would enjoy the expanded responsibility of ruling the northern part of German East

Africa, and the governor became increasingly apathetic, in both actions and words, as far as the war was concerned. On at least one occasion during the conflict's first year, he was quoted as holding the opinion "that this colony has no interest in the present war except so far as its unfortunate geographical position places it in such close proximity to German East Africa."[43] The war notwithstanding, the governor allowed protectorate officials to take leave in the ordinary way.

From the start of the conflict, Belfield spent as little time as possible at Nairobi. He much preferred Mombasa. Away from the seat of government, he could not be contacted quickly by his subordinates or the military leadership in the capital. In Mombasa, according to Robert Meinertzhagen, then serving as an intelligence officer with the British forces, "he was able to indulge in his sea-fishing and at the same time avoid all the worries and responsibilities of a war which he refused to recognize."[44]

The governor spent his time at Mombasa not only because he enjoyed ocean fishing; Belfield had spent much of his official career in the tropical climate of Malaya. As he told Fiddes in a personal letter in early 1914: "I am a tropical creature." He found his stays at Mombasa more pleasant than the capital and felt that they did him "all the good in the world."[45] The governor also found in Mombasa an escape from what had seemingly become a difficult relationship with his wife. The governor evidently found the partially deaf Mrs. Belfield an uninspiring companion. He invariably left her at Nairobi during his sojourns in Mombasa. When his wife fell from a horse and cracked a rib in December 1914, for example, the governor still left her behind to spend time at the coast.[46]

Sir Henry's desire for the warmth and quiet of Mombasa and lack of interest in the war was striking, but the settlers, after the first flush of patriotic fervor, lost enthusiasm for the conflict as well. Meinertzhagen felt that, given the attitude of the European public in mid-1915, one might never suspect that war was being waged in East Africa. Even Lord Delamere had to admit, while in Britain in August 1915, that "a good deal of the blame is at present put on the colonists, and to a certain extent we deserve it."[47]

The attitude of the European public, and indeed even that of the governor, would undergo a change in August and September 1915. The change on the part of the governor was provoked, in the first instance, by a call from the CO for greater participation by the EAP in the war effort.

This concern of the CO was principally with the military situation in East Africa. This was sparked by reports from General Tighe, in charge of troops in the EAP, that reached the CO in early August. Tighe stated that many of his white force were ill with malaria, and his reliable troops were few. This together with reports of increasing German troop strength pointed to the possibility of an attack on the EAP that might endanger the British position there.[48] This report indicated to CO officials a potentially serious situation that might be checked by provision of more white manpower. Since Read had already heard from Lord Delamere that the military position in the EAP was unsatisfactory, the CO organized a meeting that brought Delamere together with Read, parliamentary under-secretary Steel-Maitland, and a representative of the War Office on 11 August. Delamere emphasized that a major problem was a "want of cooperation" between Belfield and Tighe. Delamere felt that the situation required a strong governor since Belfield "gave them [the settlers] to understand that they would be of more use on their farms than in the fighting line." The settler leader thought that his colleagues "ought to have a clear indication of what was expected of them." He favored a maximum effort and would not be opposed to conscription, registration, or anything else that would secure this.[49]

As a result of this and other consultations, the CO decided to press for ways to obtain more European manpower for the East African theatre. One way would be to push for the introduction of white troops from South Africa, but the CO, taking its cue from Delamere, also decided to call for greater efforts from the EAP settler population.[50]

This then was the motivation behind the CO telegram of 14 August 1915. The S of S told Belfield that rumors had reached him that there was "a lack of complete co-operation between the civil and military in the Protectorate," and that the military were dissatisfied with the settlers. The telegram went on to state that the British government attached "the utmost importance" to the success of operations in East Africa. Belfield was left in no doubt that he was to provide "whole-hearted" support to the military.[51]

This CO action had, in Meinertzhagen's words, "an electrical effect and Sir Conway Belfield is now doing what he should have done at the outbreak of the war, namely give us every assistance and show an example of patriotism himself."[52] At the same time as he raised himself to take greater cognizance of the war, Belfield sent a telegram to London in an attempt to "contradict emphatically" the statements made to the CO.[53] The CO merely accepted the governor's statements and saw no need to reply.

The CO's telegram really set the stage for the momentous events of September 1915. This would mark the beginning of a period that would see Belfield and the colonial state not only seek to foster greater efforts to aid the war, but also to literally fall prostrate before almost every economic and political demand made by the settlers. While this would be done in the name of patriotism and maximizing the war effort, some also served to meet long-standing demands of the settler community. One of the first measures that falls into this category was the Native Followers Recruitment Ordinance, passed by the Legco in late August 1915. The ordinance had been under consideration by the government for some time. The Execo had approved the introduction of a short ordinance giving power to ensure that a sufficient number of carriers would be recruited.[54] It gave powers to the district administration to force the recruitment of able bodied men under the age of thirty-five to serve as porters for the military.[55] The bill was warmly applauded by settlers since its purpose was to make "idle and irresponsible" Africans work.[56]

Governor Belfield also had gazette notices published calling for further military enlistment from settlers on 1 September, and at the request of the military authorities, he allowed civil-military discussions to decide how such recruitment could be enhanced. As a result, it was agreed that the European population should be "organized on a war footing."[57]

Civil-military discussions were quickly followed by a mass meeting of Nairobi citizens (European and Indian) on 8 September. Organized by Grogan and Meinertzhagen to shake the protectorate out of its apathy towards the war, it produced a unanimous resolution in favor of organizing the total resources of the protectorate on a war footing. Grogan, now serving with the military as an intelligence officer, made an extremely effective speech that won enthusiastic support from the packed Theatre Royal. The meeting accepted Grogan's call for the extension to all citizens of the principle of universal service already initiated by the Native Carrier's Ordinance.[58] A bill to provide for registration of the European population was quickly introduced at a special session of the Legco, and the governor took steps to appoint "a mixed committee to consider steps to be taken to utilize our population to the utmost for military purposes and to place all classes on a war footing."[59] The governor's telegram expressing the willingness of the Nairobi "public" to accept compulsory service caused gratification to the CO.

By far the most far-reaching innovation to come out of the actions of late August and early September 1915, however, was the formation of a war council. After the passage of the Registration of Persons ordinance, Belfield quickly knuckled under to the demand of Grogan and others for the appointment of a "strong committee" to assist him in "formulating the lines of our future procedure." He appointed four civil officials, two military officers, and three unofficial European representatives to serve on what became known as the Governor's War Council. The government officials included C. C. Bowring, the chief secretary, Benjamin Eastwood, general manager of the Uganda railway, A. C. Macdonald, the director of agriculture, and W. K. Notley, the commissioner of police. The unofficial members were Grogan, another prominent settler, W. Northrup Macmillan, and J. J. Toogood, manager of the Nairobi branch of the Standard Bank of South Africa.[60] Belfield's first request of the war council was to provide advice on how compulsory service could best be organized, but his recognition that the council should advise him "on matters and circumstances arising out of the present war" opened the door for the council to involve itself in all aspects of both civil and military affairs in the EAP.

Moreover, the composition of the war council was quickly altered to give greater voice to European farmers. This change in membership was the result of resolutions passed by settlers in Nakuru and Lumbwa stating that they could not accept the war council as then constituted. They advocated that "three practical farmers," elected by the settlers themselves, be added to it. The settlers went so far as to propose the areas from which the additional members were to be elected. The war council quickly adopted a resolution expressing support for the idea of direct rural representation. Belfield decided to accept "in order that the success of the organization scheme might not be endangered by internal differences of opinion."[61] The governor thus allowed settlers in the three areas designated to select representatives, and he soon went further and encouraged district commissioners to form local committees of settlers so as to help "in securing the loyal co-operation of all members of the community in the task that lies before us."[62]

These actions, in fact, changed the balance of power in the protectorate.[63] It is, therefore, of some interest to note that the CO expressed general approval of the war council's formation, though without great enthusiasm. Since it was a representative body, "it should do a good deal to get the local settlers to take more interest" in the East African campaign. The CO obviously did not anticipate the great impact the war council would have in the months ahead. Belfield's actions were approved with an expression of appreciation for the "loyal co-operation" the settlers were showing in their response to the local government.[64]

The war council certainly concerned itself with issues arising from the war, but these were almost uniformly ones that reflected stances long advocated by the settler community. An example was immediately forthcoming in the war council's action in reducing the pay of those serving in the Carrier Corps. Rates of pay for carriers varied between ten and fifteen rupees per month, generally considerably higher than those offered by settler farmers. The latter had for some time pressed for lower wages, and they viewed the war council's recommendation for a reduction of carrier pay to five rupees per month for the first three months of service and six rupees thereafter as a most beneficial measure. From the government's perspective, the reduction could be justified since it now had the power to compel recruitment. This action was carried out without prior reference to the CO.[65]

Another example of war council action that went far towards meeting long standing demands of the settlers in the area of labor was provided by the amendment of the Masters and Servants ordinance in 1916. Desertion and other employee offenses were made cognizable to the police who could make arrests without warrants.[66]

Settler gains as a result of the growing influence of the war council on Belfield's government were not limited to labor matters. In August 1916, citing the experience of the council to prove his case, the governor renewed his call for the grant of electoral rights to the settler community. In effect, he had already conceded the principle with the acceptance of the three additional settler representatives to the council the year before. That was certainly how the settlers saw it.[67]

In presenting his case to the CO, Belfield found no reason to vary any of the views he had expressed in 1913 and 1914. Moreover, he contended that a strong and consistent public opinion in favor of electoral rights existed in the EAP. Among the major reasons he advanced as making that moment the right time for the acceptance was the absolutely essential need to maintain the better relations and the "complete understanding" that now existed between the colonial state and the settler community. Those improved relations would be jeopardized by a refusal to grant electoral rights, and Belfield wished to avoid a return to "the former attitude of hostility and distrust." The governor continued:

Intimately acquainted as I am with the feeling of the people and earnestly desirous as I am of promoting the best interests of the country, I foresee in the grant of this assurance a germ which will develop into a spreading growth of confidence and good will, while I am equally satisfied that determination to adhere to existing conditions can be attended with nothing but disunity and disaster.[68]

As additional justifications, Belfield cited two other factors he deemed significant. "The people," he stated, "rightly" considered that the part they had played in the war gave them "an even greater claim to sympathetic treatment." Secondly, the system of electing members to the war council had been "productive of the best results." The presence of such representatives assured popular confidence and helped produce good feeling between the state and the settlers.

To these points, the governor added a tactical consideration. Since 1912, four of the five unofficial seats in the Legco had gone unfilled. Belfield was now engaged in negotiations aimed at bringing about a return of such members representing the up-country settlers. As a result of conversations with "gentlemen who are in a position to voice the views of the community," he felt certain they would now return "if it is understood that it is to be temporary only and will be followed at a convenient time by concession of the principle of election."

In all of this, Belfield made no reference to the reservations previously expressed by the CO: the size of the white population and the representation of Indians, Arabs, and Africans in the council. Belfield pushed ahead urging the CO that all that was necessary at the present was "Your willingness to sanction the principle of elective representation." Details of the franchise and constituencies would have to wait until after the war, but it was necessary that he be allowed to announce the S of S's concurrence as soon as possible. He therefore requested a telegraphic reply.

The CO was inclined to view the governor's request with sympathy. Butler accepted Belfield's case without demur. He felt the approval of the principle of elective representation should be given. Relations between the colonial state and the white community had markedly improved, and the settlers had assisted in the war effort. Unlike the governor, however, Butler commented on the previous reservations of the CO. As to the number of whites in the EAP, Butler felt it would certainly be enlarged when the country settled down after the war. On what he termed "the vexed questions" of Indian, Arab, and African representation, Butler felt it was impossible to go into them at that juncture. He did add, however, a somewhat naive rationalization: "The white unofficial members are in a minority on the council, so that the interests of Indians, Arabs, and Natives will always be safe in the hands of the official majority." Moreover, Belfield's proposed administrative restructuring would provide for a CNC who, as ex-officio member of the Legco, would "look after the interests of all of the coloured communities." It could be assumed, he concluded "that in one way or another the interests of all of the coloured communities will be fully safeguarded even if it is ultimately decided that the principle of elective representation can not be extended to them."[69]

Perhaps even more shocking than Butler's rationalizations was the fact that Read agreed with him. The man who had first raised objections to the grant of electoral rights exclusively to whites and who could not have possibly forgotten or overlooked the preference, expressed by Anderson and Harcourt, for an Indian member in the Legco, now tamely went along. Clearly this is one case where Read deserved his derisory nickname, "Broken".[70] With the endorsement of Butler and Read, the CO telegraphed acceptance of the principle of electoral representation for whites on 27 September. Questions of voter qualifications, electoral areas, and the best manner in which the interests of the Indian, Arab, and African communities could be represented would have to be left to the conclusion of the war.[71] The slackening of CO initiative in EAP affairs that had been apparent since the start of the war had now become a loss of control.

However, Indians in the EAP were not prepared to wait. They organized meetings in Nairobi and Mombasa in the latter part of 1916, and in late December, the Mombasa Indians sent a telegram to London supporting the concept of Indian elective representation on the Legco and the nomination of Indian members to the council as a temporary measure.[72] The CO was not moved to take any action on the request other than to ask the governor to inform the Indians that the latter would be making recommendations to the CO on the subject. Thus the Indians would have to wait.[73] The CO does not seem to have appreciated the possible effect of the grant of electoral rights to settlers on the EAP's Indian population. In the years ahead, Indian demands for equal rights would generate huge problems for the CO.

The Settlement of Ex-Soldiers

A final example, on the other hand, of the substantial impact of the war council in matters favorable to the settlers may be seen in the form of proposals for the postwar settlement of veterans in the EAP. The council had passed unanimously a resolution in favor of this concept in early 1916. Belfield endorsed it, and the need for ex-soldier settlement in sending the proposal to the CO. Two points stood out for the governor. The first was the pressing need for an enlargement of the European population at the conclusion of hostilities for "security" reasons. Belfield put it quite bluntly:

> There can be no doubt that the experience of the past eighteen months must have impressed on the African native a sense of his value as fighting material when opposed to Europeans, and, though I do not go so far as to anticipate serious trouble on that account, I am satisfied that the influx of a large additional number of white settlers would materially minimize any risk of native aggression, and should be encouraged on that account irrespective of the advantage which would accrue to the country from a further flow of white immigration."[74]

A second point in favor of such a settlement scheme lay in Belfield's view that after the war there would be a large number of young European men who, having been on active service would be unfit, at the end of the war, "to return to an indoor life and to sedentary occupations." The governor differed from the war council, moreover, in recommending that settlement by such young men be not limited to those Europeans who had fought in East Africa. He urged that veterans of British nationality who had served in the conflict, whatever the theatre, be included in any scheme as well.

The war council proposals, for which the governor expressed general support, called for granting "each British soldier or volunteer" taking part in the East African campaign a block of land not exceeding 320 acres agricultural or 1000 acres pastoral on a 999-year lease at an initial rental of ten cents per acre. The council maintained that there were already a number of farms available "which would only be required to be resurveyed into smaller plots."

The proposal for government action to promote additional, closer European settlement in the EAP provoked little initial enthusiasm at the CO. Bottomley felt it would be best not to give an early reply. T. C. Macnaghten,[75] from the CO's General Department, held that East Africa was quite "unsuited to the ordinary British immigrant." He felt, moreover, that it had not been clearly established whether Europeans would thrive and retain their "vigour" after fifty or one hundred years in the highlands. Macnaghten suggested that Belfield be asked to prepare a memorandum indicating the amount of suitable land in the EAP, and where it was located. Anderson agreed and added that since there were so few roads in the protectorate, the CO should be informed as to details of potential expenditure on roads and railways that would be required to make lands "really available for settlement."[76] In its response, therefore, the CO, while making it clear that the government had not yet made any decision on the question, requested additional information from the governor. The S of S directed Belfield to prepare a memorandum setting out in detail the amount of suitable land, its location, the amount of capital required for purchase and development, the amount of land required for successful cultivation, and the expenditure the government would have to make on roads and railways.[77]

By mid-August 1916, Belfield had sent the requested memorandum, prepared by a committee consisting of the land officer, the director of agriculture, and the director of public works, to London, endorsing the conclusion that "there is a considerable area of unalienated Crown Land which could be made suitable for a closer settlement scheme." There were two factors that the governor felt complicated the idea of soldier settlement. These were, first of all, "the capital required by each settler to enable him to maintain himself and to develop his holding until such time as it becomes a lucrative investment." The committee recommended that each potential settler would require £700 for these purposes. Belfield felt that unless some government assistance was provided, it would probably not be possible to obtain any great number of veterans to take part. "I am bound to come to the conclusion," Belfield wrote, "that, unless financial assistance is provided, the success of any close settlement scheme must necessarily presuppose the possession by the settlers of a small capital."[78]

The second reason for the governor's hesitancy in backing a soldier settlement scheme was "the inaccessibility of the land which it is suggested might be set aside for the project." He estimated that an expenditure of £334,000 on roads alone would be required to render the blocks of land suitable for settlement. This would further entail an annual recurrent expenditure of at least £23,000. Roads were especially vital in the case of the relatively smaller farms contemplated. Even more important, in the governor's view, was the existence of railway connections between the blocks of land and potential markets. Until the government could construct additional railways, "the small land holder would have but a poor chance of making a living." Belfield concluded his lengthy despatch with a request for approval of the appointment of a "local commission" to go into the question of "closer settlement" in detail. Such a commission had been proposed by the war council. He asked to receive instructions as to the terms of reference for such a commission.[79]

At the CO, the permanent officials reacted to the memorandum and the governor's comments with little enthusiasm. Butler concluded that the EAP government could not contemplate expenditure to support potential settlers and to provide needed roads and railways. He felt, therefore, that "we can not look to East Africa as a field for the settlement of ex-servicemen from the United Kingdom or the Empire generally and that any scheme adopted must be confined to men who have actually served in the East African campaign." Despite this pessimistic assessment, Butler felt that the CO must do something for the double purpose of showing some appreciation of the services of "white men who have fought for us" in East Africa and of endeavoring to increase the white population of the EAP "in face of the overwhelming native population." He concluded by recommending approval of a commission that should have unofficial representation, and he went on to suggest a number of principles that could be laid down for the commission's guidance.[80]

Macnaghten was still "very doubtful whether a British population would thrive in British East Africa in the second or third generation." He strongly suspected they would not. He went on:

> It may be that some sort of settlement scheme should be taken up, but from the point of view of advantage to the race, I am all against any EA settlement scheme if the medical view of prospects of colonization of BEA is that British colonists could deteriorate there, I do not see why we should not oppose any settlement scheme and publish our reasons for doing so.[81]

Read agreed that a "big scheme" was clearly out of the question. Moreover, he feared that if a commission was appointed with unofficial members, "we shall raise expectations which we may be unable to satisfy." The protectorate might very well not be self-supporting at the end of the war. Read, for one, was not convinced that a solider settlement scheme was necessary to combat "the native peril." Considerable armed forces would undoubtedly remain in East Africa for some time after the war, the African population had no firearms, and were "for the most part unwarlike." Read urged doing nothing until the end of the war. Permanent under-secretary Fiddes agreed and warned of the likelihood of a shortage of labor.[82]

These views of the most senior civil servants were turned aside by the political leadership of the CO. Steel-Maitland, the parliamentary under-secretary of state who handled most East African questions, ordered acceptance of a local commission. He disagreed with Read that the appointment of a commission would raise expectations. "They are raised already," he wrote. A commission with unofficial representatives would be valuable, moreover, if it concluded that soldier settlement was impractical. Above all, Steel-Maitland feared the CO ran the risk of "being placed in a very false position" if it turned down the governor's request and the papers were later published.[83] Thus a CO despatch to Belfield in early November gave approval for a local commission on which there would presumably be unofficial representation.[84]

Even though the CO despatch laid stress on the fact that there could be no hope of success for any scheme of land settlement unless the potential settlers were "in possession of a considerable amount of capital," nor could there be any prospect of government grants to such settlers, Steel-Maitland's decision practically guaranteed that there would be a postwar soldier settlement scheme. Any possibility that a local commission, on which present settlers were represented, would return a negative recommendation with regard to additional white settlement clearly was absurd. This fact could easily have been appreciated from a perusal of the war council's views on the subject. Accepting a local commission to report on the issue was tantamount to accepting that there would be a soldier settlement scheme. By overruling the permanent officials, Steel-Maitland handed over initiative to the EAP set-

tlers. The proposals for the settlement of veterans in the EAP was thus yet
another way in which the war council served to promote settler demands and
interests. It also represented further slippage of CO control of the protectorate, and it points to the impact of personnel changes within the CO on
EAP policy.

The War and Economic Changes

It is important also to recognize the economic changes that marked the first
two years of World War I. The start of the war and its economic impact,
rather than any policy initiatives of the CO or the colonial state, were responsible for the changes. Nevertheless, the economic trends that began to
emerge in the 1914–16 period would pick up speed during the last two years
of the war, and the changed conditions that resulted would have an extremely
powerful influence on CO thinking with regard to Kenya after the war.

As Table 3.1 illustrates, there was a precipitous drop in exports from
the EAP in 1914 and 1915. More significant was the rising share in the protectorate's exports provided by European settler production. From approximately 14 per cent of the total in 1913, this rose to at least 42 per cent in
1915.

Items of African origin still held the largest share of the protectorate's exports in 1916, but these had dwindled. After 1916, the dominance of African
production in Kenya's exports disappeared. The most powerful reasons,
though certainly not the only ones, for the shift shown in Table 3.1 was the
effect of the war and the policies adopted by the colonial state during the
period under review.

African production was greatly effected by two crises, manpower and financial, with which the colonial state had to cope throughout the war. The manpower crisis was the result not so much of a demand for fighting men as for
porters to serve the military. African men were recruited, at first voluntarily
and later by direct coercion, into the Carrier Corps. More than 69,000 men
were recruited for the Carrier Corps down to the end of March 1916 with
Nyanza province providing the overwhelming majority (42,300).[85] The forced
export from African areas could not help but have a disruptive effect on production there. An indirect result of this forced recruitment was the exodus of
African manpower from their farms during the war. Because of the poor conditions and the high mortality rates attending Carrier Corps service, work on
settler farms now became a more attractive alternative. Squatting was especially popular.[86] As noted earlier in the discussion of the Native Followers
Recruitment Ordinance, the colonial state gave a high priority to obtaining
African labor, and the CO accepted, with little question, the necessity of
exploiting African manpower for the benefit of the war effort in East Africa.

Likewise, the financial crisis that followed in the wake of the start of the

Table 3.1 Percentage Value of Agricultural Exports, 1913–16

	1913	1914	1915	1916
African				
Hides and Skins	37	44	40	33
Beans and Peas	5	2	1	4
Sim Sim	20	8	8	12
Oil Seeds	*	1	*	*
Cotton	1	1	1	*
Groundnuts	2	*	*	*
Ghee	1	*	2	1
Potatoes	2	2	1	3
% of total	68	58	53	53
Settler				
Coffee	5	6	9	9
Sisal	2	12	27	27
Other Fibre	2	2	1	1
Plantation Rubber	1	1	1	*
Wool	2	4	4	3
% of total	12	25	42	40
Miscellaneous				
Coconuts/copra	7	9	4	5
Gum copal	1	*	*	*
Bees wax	2	4	1	1
Wild animal skins	1	1	*	*
Wild rubber	1	*	*	*
% of total	12	14	5	6
Mixed				
Maize	8	3	*	1
% of total	8	3	*	1
Total Value (rupees)	5,811,990	3,353,625	4,239,584	5,936,022

Source: East Africa Protectorate, *Department of Agriculture British East Africa Annual Report 1916-17* (Nairobi: Government Printer, 1918), 27.

war would cause the colonial state to more fully exploit African resources. The need for heavy expenditure to support the military effort and a drop in revenue from customs duties and railway earnings quickly plunged the EAP into a financial crisis. From early November 1914, the colonial state and the CO sought, by a variety of means, to stave off bankruptcy.[87] Expenditure was reduced across the board, but the EAP government was unable to balance its budgets without increases in revenue as well. The primary means that it sought to do so was by raising the rate of African hut and poll tax.

The colonial state seriously considered such action when framing the financial estimates for 1915–16. Belfield directed John Ainsworth to make a study

of the question in anticipation of a raise in such taxes being implemented for
the financial year beginning 1 April 1916.[88] By the end of May 1915, the
governor sent Ainsworth's report to the CO, endorsing its recommendation
for a raise in the rate of hut and poll tax to five rupees. Belfield supported
this, but he disagreed with Ainsworth's suggestion that a definite percentage
of the taxes collected from Africans should be devoted to improvements in
the reserves. While concluding that the African population could pay the increased rate without hardship, Ainsworth had argued that the government
must return a definite portion to them in services, but the governor felt that
"it would be indiscreet to fetter the discretion of Government by giving any
such undertaking."[89]

The CO accepted the governor's view. Financial necessity made increasing
taxes for the African population acceptable. Provided the increased taxes
would provoke no unrest, legislation could be introduced to effect that end.
Anderson insisted, however, that the increase must be fully explained to the
Africans. "I wish it could be deferred til after the war," he minuted, "but we
are badly in need of money."[90] In informing Belfield of its approval, the CO
added, at Read's suggestion, that while a definite commitment to devote a
percentage of tax receipts to improvements in the reserves was "not desirable," the governor should, when submitting each year's estimates, furnish a
statement of suggested improvements in the reserves.[91]

While placing heavy burdens on African production in the form of increased taxation and forced recruitment for the carrier corps, the colonial
state undertook little in the way of stimulating peasant production during the
war years. Administrative officers had been responsible for most government
assistance to the peasant sector before the war, but during the conflict, most
of their efforts were directed toward labor recruitment. Shipping difficulties
and loss of markets caused by the war also served to discourage production
for export. So too did a fall in prices for most export crops produced by
Africans.

In at least one case during the war, the colonial state did attempt to intervene on behalf of the prices offered to African farmers. By early 1915, cotton
prices had fallen by 25 per cent from their previous level, and Belfield urgently telegraphed the CO asking for assistance. If prices remained at that level,
he held, cotton cultivation in Nyanza province would probably cease. He
urged that cotton purchasers be approached with a request that they make an
effort to offer higher prices.[92] The CO did not even bother to contact any
textile manufacturer before rejecting Belfield's request out of hand. "Nyanza
cotton is relatively unimportant," concluded Bottomley. It was negligible
compared to Uganda's exports. The CO quickly informed the governor that
the buying price of cotton had to be fixed "according to commercial values
alone." Government action, the CO went on, "should be confined to warning
growers that prices lower than usual must be expected. . . ."[93] Value of cotton sales fell, not surprisingly, by 56 per cent from 1915 to 1916. Cotton grow-

ing in Nyanza was not important enough in 1915 to cause the CO to step in with special assistance.

The colonial state did intervene, on the other hand, to block African cultivation of what was becoming an increasingly valuable cash crop: coffee. Belfield considered the question of African coffee-growing, at the urging of the director of agriculture, in May 1916. As one might expect, Belfield's pro-settler orientation made him strongly opposed to peasant cultivation of coffee. In his despatch informing the CO of his decision on 1 June, he put forward a series of rationalizations for opposition that would regularly emanate from settlers over the next three decades. Africans would not be able to manage the crop, African-grown coffee would be extremely susceptible to disease, African coffee would be of inferior quality, and African coffee growing would lead to increases in thefts from settler coffee estates. In the governor's assessment, however, these factors were much less important than other, more general, racist myths. He maintained:

> The native is not at the present time sufficiently educated or sufficiently industrious to warrant any assumption that he could embark on an adventure of this nature with any prospect of success, while on the other hand, there are many products from which he can, and does, reap a good and steady return.[94]

The CO accepted the governor's position on the issue without demur. Fiddes noted that the governor was probably right in his assessment. As Belfield had not asked for approval, Fiddes ordered that the EAP despatch be filed with no reply necessary.[95] Thus the CO let stand a prohibition that would remain government policy, and provoke considerable African opposition, until 1933.[96] With little encouragement from the colonial state and the CO, African production for export was declining. The decline would become a disastrous fall after 1916.

In production for the domestic market, however, peasants did not fare nearly as badly as in the export. Production of grain, vegetables, and other foodstuffs received a spur from the demand created by the military forces stationed in the protectorate. Internal prices for grain were quite high, and producers in Nyanza and Kenia (later Central) provinces expanded output to meet it. Production among the Kikuyu of Kenia province rose as a result of the military demand and the growing size of Nairobi's population during the war. Increasing amounts of livestock were sold to meet military demands. At least until the end of 1916, African production for internal markets offset the fall in production for export.[97]

Settler producers were able to capitalize on the same trends, but the real gain for the settler sector came in the export area, especially the plantation crops, coffee and sisal. The increase in sisal exports was astounding: more than 2400 per cent in value between 1912 and 1916. Coffee also prospered as large prewar plantings came into bearing in 1915 and 1916.[98] John Overton has convincingly demonstrated how the settler sector was able to capitalize and thrive in the war conditions.[99] They were actually helped, as noted earlier, to obtain sufficient labor by the wartime circumstances. The colonial state gave much assistance to the settler sector in the provision of transportation and in sustaining its export markets. The result was that in the first two years of the war, the settler economy was well on the way to becoming more productive and profitable. In short, it was on the threshold of establishing its dominance, at least in the export sector, over peasant production.[100] This would be accomplished in the succeeding three years. The dominant position that the settlers would then come to occupy in the export sector was also the result of the fact that much of the previous African exports consisted of food crops. During the war, these were directed to internal, rather than external, markets. Nevertheless, the settler export dominance would have immense influence on the attitude of CO officials toward Kenya.

This trend coincided with important gains made by the settlers in issues such as registration, the land ordinance, the lowering of African wages, electoral representation, and the consideration of a soldier settlement scheme. The changed conditions brought by the war, Belfield's inertia and sympathy with the settler demands, Harcourt's illness, the absence of interest in, or protests about, EAP from such groups in the metropole as the ASAPS or from financiers or merchants, and changes in the permanent and political leadership of the CO all played a part in the latter losing control in the EAP. Nor would the CO be able to reassert the initiative it had lost to the settlers and the colonial state in the remaining years of the war.

4
The Continued Lack of CO Direction,
1917–18

The last two years of the First World War witnessed further impetus to the strengthening of the European settler position, both economically and politically, within the EAP. The trend toward settler supremacy speeded up with little in the way of checks provided by the colonial state or the CO. Just as in the initial period of the war, the CO was little troubled by protests from metropolitan financiers or merchants, nor by humanitarian and missionary criticism either in or out of parliament. The absence of such concerns was significant as both before and after the war, the CO was forced to take note, and more often then not to take some action, as a result of the concerns of these interests in Britain. The movement towards settler supremacy thus produced little struggle in this period. Lack of direction from London continued to be the most noteworthy characteristic of these years. By the end of 1918, the settlers position, therefore, was far stronger than it had been before the world conflict began. On most issues that interested them, they either got their way, with little opposition from the CO, or the latter reserved final decision until the EAP situation had been studied, and recommendations forwarded, by a new governor who would not arrive in Nairobi until early 1919.

The War and Its Impact on African and European Production

As described in the preceding chapter, the war in East Africa brought with it new conditions on which the settlers were able to capitalize. They had started to make considerable economic gains in the first two years of the war. In its final two years, that trend accelerated. By the end of 1918, settler producers had clearly established themselves, as John Overton has shown, "the dominant sector of the economy."[1]

Table 4.1 helps to give some indication of the commanding position settler production had assumed, by the end of 1919, in the export sector. During this period, the total share of export value for the settlers' two main export crops, coffee and sisal, rose from 32 per cent to 57 per cent. At the same time, the value of exports of African origin was falling. In 1917, 60 per cent of the value of exports came from African production, but in 1919 that source only provided 30 per cent.

Table 4.1 Percentage Value of Agricultural Exports, 1917–19

	1917	1918	1919
African			
Hides/skins	42	36	22
Beans/peas	3	*	3
Sim Sim	12	4	4
Oil seeds	–	–	*
Other grain	*	*	*
Groundnuts	1^	–	–
Potatoes	2	3	1
% Total	60	43	30
Settler			
Coffee	8	18	34
Sisal	24	33	22
Flax	*	1	2
Wool	2	2	4
% Total	34	54	62
Miscellaneous			
Coconut/copra	5	3	5
Mixed			
Maize	1	*	3
Total value £s	546,853	618,503	725,000

1^ Groundnuts and other grain exports equal 1% of total.
* Exports less than 1% of total
– No exports

Sources: East Africa Protectorate, *Annual Report for the Year 1919–20 by F. W. Major Chief of Customs* (Nairobi: Government Printer, 1921) and Colony and Protectorate of Kenya, *Department of Agriculture Report 1924* (Nairobi: Government Printer, 1925), insert.

Settler production was able to withstand the setbacks and take advantage of the opportunities the war brought in its wake more successfully than African production for export. Exports of sisal and coffee increased, and "a new phase of settler ascendancy in the export trade was begun."[2] Not only successful in the export sector, the settlers, able to obtain adequate labor during the war, had by the end of 1918 established themselves as important suppliers of grain for the domestic market.[3] Nevertheless, it was plantation agriculture that made the most headway during the war. This was partly the result of the settler sector capitalizing on the coming into production of much pre-1914 planting (especially coffee and sisal), and plantation agriculture expanding during the war as it proved, "for the first time, to be highly dynamic and readily responsive to new market and labour opportunities."[4]

To a considerable degree, this success was the result of assistance from the colonial state. Through help in labor recruitment, the securing of export markets, and assistance with the development of new crops, the colonial state, dragging the CO with it, helped insure the dominance of the settler sector. Some examples will serve to illustrate this point.

The colonial state and the CO sought to protect the settler sector from additional military call ups after the start of 1917. In asking for guidance on how to respond to a military request for an additional two hundred Europeans and the possibility of additional demands in the future, Governor Belfield maintained, in February 1917, that the production of sisal, hides, and so on might have greater importance to the war effort than the small number of Europeans who would be conscripted.[5] CO officials agreed with the governor's assessment of the potential negative consequences of the manpower demands. C. J. Jeffries, who had only just joined the CO, argued that if the loss of two hundred men caused plantations to close down, "it would attack the general revenue and finances of the protectorate and the production of sisal and hides to which the W[ar] O[ffice] at present attach the greatest importance for military purposes."[6] As a result of this line of reasoning, the CO sent a strong note to the War Office urging the necessity, on economic grounds (the need for sisal and hides in Britain), not to draw away manpower that would cause the plantations to close down unless there was extremely strong justification.[7]

Even clearer examples of the colonial state and the CO attempting to alter wartime regulations so as to bring greater benefit to European settler production occurred in the coffee industry. Unlike sisal, coffee was not considered to be essential to the British war effort. In fact, for most of the war, the supply of coffee in the United Kingdom far exceeded demand. Small wonder then that the War Office and the Board of Trade would consider banning the shipping of coffee so as to give preference to raw materials more essential to the allied war effort. Thus on 23 February 1917, the British government placed an embargo on coffee imports into Britain. Even before protests and calls for assistance from European settlers were heard in London, the CO intervened with the Board of Trade to soften "drastic enforcement" of the coffee embargo. As a result, the board relented to a degree in April; it agreed to treat "as in transit and therefore to admit into the United Kingdom coffee which was already in route to the port of shipment at the date of prohibition" as long as the amount shipped did not exceed fifteen hundred tons.[8]

This concession, won through the representations of the CO, left the settlers far from satisfied. At the end of May, a Legco motion was moved and supported by settler unofficial members, who had decided to end their boycott of the council earlier in the year, to the effect that the colonial state provide a subsidy to coffee planters to tide them over the current crisis. After some study, the Legco went on record as recommending that the EAP government should provide advances to coffee planters for coffee stored with the government since banks in the EAP were unwilling to make advances against the crop. C. C. Bowring, acting as governor with Belfield absent in Britain on what would be his retirement leave, strongly advocated providing financial assistance so that "many valuable plantations" would not be ruined. He put the total amount required at £50,000 for one year, an amount the EAP could afford.[9]

Bowring urged this course because of the damage the embargo would cause to the future of the coffee industry. It would be "little short of a calamity" if the coffee industry collapsed for want of financial assistance which in normal times would come from banks. In his despatch, the governor added the need to uphold white prestige to economic arguments:

> The effect on the Natives of large areas of land at present cultivated by Europeans being abandoned would be very bad, as most tribes have prophesies to the effect that sooner or later the Europeans will leave the country. Further it would be extremely difficult to reestablish the coffee industry if it were given up.[10]

The CO had already pressured the Board of Trade for some relief, and the latter relented at the end of June when it was agreed to allow importation of coffee under special licensing arrangements.[11] Although Fiddes found it hard to understand "how advances on cured crop help maintain plantations," the CO, in August, authorized the acting governor to advance up to £12,500 for relief of coffee planters.[12]

A final example illustrates the colonial state's willingness to restrict African production to protect that of the white settlers. As noted in the preceding chapter, the colonial state had decided to restrict coffee planting to European-owned plantations in 1916, and in the following year, it took a stand against pig raising by Africans and Indians. The acting governor raised this issue in September 1917 because he had been informed that a "negligible" number of pigs were being kept by Indians and Africans. He wished to protect the "valuable asset to the country" that was in the process of development by Europeans. If Africans were allowed to raise pigs, he maintained, disease would spread among the animals raised by settlers and heavy mortality "must inevitably occur." Bowring therefore directed the administrative staff to discourage African and Indian pig raising "as much as possible," leaving the field for European enterprise.[13]

These examples illustrate that the CO was willing to exert itself to assist and protect settler production during the last years of the war. It should be noted, however, that the CO's willingness to fall into line with settlers demands had limits. When faced with criticism of the EAP administration and demands for strong government direction of the economy from two prominent settlers in April 1918, the CO refused to go along. Lord Cranworth and H. F. Ward had an interview with W. A. S. Hewins, who had replaced Steel-Maitland as parliamentary under-secretary in September 1917. They were critical of the economic policies of the colonial state and advocated "proper" organization and direction of the colonial economy so as to make the EAP not only "self supporting", but also to supply an exportable surplus of products such as sisal and flax. Bottomley, who sat in during the meeting, felt the CO and colonial state should do what they could to meet practical demands "of the local agitators without being led astray by their red herrings of a military governorship and direct access to the War Cabinet."[14] The CO took the only sensible line in the difficult circumstances of early 1918 by urging the EAP government to encourage production, primarily of commodities required to make the protectorate independent of imports, and foodstuffs needed by the war effort; but sisal and flax could not be neglected.[15]

Although the settler section suffered some setbacks, it emerged from the war far stronger than before. However, there remained potential limits on further advances. One of considerable importance was raised by Hewins in his interview with Cranworth and Ward. This was the availability of adequate labor supplies. By the end of 1918, both government and settler employers were experiencing difficulty in obtaining labor. As will be seen below, this was not surprising given the military situation, the 1918 drought, and the spread of disease, but labor shortage would emerge in 1919 as a major limiting factor on settler agricultural expansion.[16]

Despite potential labor shortages, settler production ended the war years in far better shape than did African. The years 1917 and 1918 may well have been the most disastrous for Kenya's African population of any similar period of the twentieth century. Huge demands were made on African resources, combined with large scale crop failures and epidemic disease, to cause not just drops in African production, but severe social dislocation and considerable loss of life in these two years.

With the shift of military operations to the southern portion of German East Africa in 1917 came an increased demand for men to serve in the Carrier Corps there. The demand fell very heavily on the EAP. To help meet this requirement, the military authorities obtained the services of Ainsworth as military commissioner for labor in March. He was to arrange the recruitment of the thousands of additional men needed. The protectorate government tried not "to interfere more than was necessary in the existing labour requirements" of the EAP. By the end of May, 30,000 men had been recruited as porters.[17] For the last two years of the war, more than 112,000 men were registered as recruits.[18]

The removal of such large numbers of men from the rural areas could not help but have a negative impact on the African production. This negative effect was magnified by the fact that a high proportion of those who were conscripted for service in German East Africa died or were disabled. As Hodges has shown, the death rate for carriers was highest when the carrier corps was at its greatest strength between April and November 1917.[19]

If the negative impact of Carrier Corps recruitment and service was not sufficient to hamper African production during 1917 and 1918, nature added particularly grave hardships. The initial rainy season of 1917 (February to June) was marked by heavy and unseasonable downpours. Approximately half the crops planted during that season were lost. As a result of the wartime demand, almost all surplus grain produced by Africans had been sold, and maize continued to be sent to German East Africa throughout 1917 in anticipation of the harvests that would take place as a result of the short rains (October to December). However, those rains failed completely over almost the whole of the EAP. The result was famine conditions in many districts by the end of 1917. The EAP government was forced to import maize from South Africa to cope with the severe food shortage throughout 1918.[20] So serious was the situation that the colonial state rushed a measure through the Legco in April 1918 to provide "some measure of coercion" to get Africans to work for famine relief and to plant more food.[21]

To the setbacks to peasant production caused by Carrier Corps recruitment and famine was added the impact of epidemic disease in 1918 and 1919. The world wide influenza epidemic hit the EAP particularly hard. People weakened by famine and war service fell ill and a considerable number died. Not only did the disasters of 1917–18 cause a fall in African production, they served to severely reduce the number of able-bodied men available to work for private employers or the government. By the latter half of 1918, this had become a serious concern.[22] A labor shortage would indeed play a very large part in EAP affairs in 1919.

In the face of these disasters, the EAP government struggled to provide food to ward off famine, but not nearly as much was done to restore African production as was done to protect and support settler exports. Nevertheless, it is important to note, in light of future policy, that acting governor Bowring did propose to direct some additional expenditure toward the benefit of African reserves when framing the budget estimates for 1918–19. As a result of prodding from Ainsworth, now holding the position of advisor on native affairs to the acting governor, Bowring called for appropriation of an additional expenditure, not exceeding £20,000, as a way of starting a scheme of expanded expenditure directed toward improvement of the reserves. The increased spending would provide higher salaries for chiefs and headmen in the most productive provinces (Nyanza and Kenia), some road work, and agricultural assistance. A major thrust would be to provide improved medical care through the provision of eight additional medical officers.[23] Although the sum was paltry in contrast to the subsidies provided by the colonial state to support the settler sector, Bowring was willing to commit some resources toward what would later become known as the Dual Policy. The government would encourage peasant production for internal and external markets as a way of complementing settler production. With the inauguration of a new governorship in 1919, however, this policy would be cast aside in favor of total state support for settler production.

In one sense, this would be a logical outcome of the economic experience of 1917–18. African production, "the mainstay of the pre-war colonial economy" had experienced a profound decline. Settler production had come to dominate in the export field, and settler agriculture seemed, to EAP officials and settlers alike, poised to enter a period of continued prosperous growth. This view, nevertheless, was illusory. Settler dominance had developed, in Overton's words, "upon artificial and abnormal economic circumstances."[24] That fact would not be grasped, unfortunately, by London or Nairobi officialdom for at least three years.

Changes in Command

As mentioned in the preceding section, C. C. Bowring took over responsibility for the EAP in 1917 as Belfield went on leave. Since the governor's illness in 1913, the CO had anticipated his coming on home leave with the likelihood that he would not return to the EAP. The start of the war delayed any leave. Belfield decided that he would stay at his post until hostilities came to an end. They dragged on instead, but at the end of 1915, it seemed that Belfield had decided that it was time to leave East Africa. In a private letter to Read of 12 December, he expressed a desire to come to Britain for a vacation. He was feeling the "strain of enormous work," and, he told Read, "my brain is getting a bit fuddled." The governor was also experiencing difficulties, he admitted, with his eyes. Belfield asked, therefore, for a period of home leave so that the CO could "get more value out of me later if I have a change."[25] Although Belfield had written a private letter, he asked for a decision of the S of S as soon as possible.

On 24 January, practically the same moment his letter arrived in London, Belfield telegraphed asking that his letter be cancelled since he had made up his mind to stay on as governor.[26] Despite this disclaimer, CO officials took seriously the possibility of Belfield's retirement. Sir George Fiddes argued, in a lengthy minute, that "the letter gives a good opening for suggesting that he should now retire on grounds of health." It was not only the rumors of Belfield's inaction and lack of leadership in mobilizing the protectorate for the war that had surfaced some six months before that caused Fiddes to take this stand. The CO official expected the East African campaign to end soon, and there would be much work to be done in introducing civil administration in German East Africa. It would be better for a new governor to go out as soon as possible so as to have thoroughly assimilated the local conditions. Fiddes

and Anderson were all the more anxious for Belfield's retirement since they
already had a most suitable man in mind as his successor, Horace Byatt.
Fiddes thus urged on Anderson the sending of a "tactful telegram" to recall
Belfield "putting it on the grounds of our concern for his health."[27]

The "tactful" private and personal telegram was sent to Nairobi on 28 January. The CO expressed appreciation for the governor's desire to stay on the
job, but urged him, in his own interest, to apply to retire on grounds of ill
health not later than the end of February.[28] A prompt reply came back from
Belfield regretting "the misapprehension" created by his letter of 12 December. The letter, he explained, was written "under stress of temporary over
strain," but Belfield maintained he was now in perfect health. He had already
publicly announced his intention to stay on in the protectorate for another
year. "Departure without adequate cause," the governor averred, "at this
vital juncture would be discreditable to myself and disloyal to my people."[29]
This flat refusal to leave the EAP before 1917 drew a rueful "I am afraid we
have been too 'tactful'" from Anderson.[30]

This, of course, ended any chance of an imminent change of governor.
After digesting two further personal letters the governor wrote to Read on 24
and 31 January, CO officials decided not to try to recall him against his will. In
the second of these, Belfield made much of his robust health. Stays at the
coast had refreshed him, and his success in sea fishing, he boasted, demonstrated "that I am not exactly a weakly." In this letter as well, Belfield gave a
clear hint as to what had caused him to wish strongly to stay on; this was the
suggestion of retirement. The governor had only desired to come away on
leave.[31] Sir Horace Byatt would be appointed to administer former German
East Africa, but Fiddes' hope that he would take over Kenya never became
reality.[32]

Belfield would serve out 1916 before renewing the issue of leave. He wrote
to the CO in October to request permission to come home in February 1917.
He pointedly refrained from mentioning retirement, however.[33] With the
agreement of the CO, Belfield actually left the EAP in April 1917.[34] Bowring
assumed control as acting governor for the period of Belfield's leave.

Belfield seems to have made up his mind that he would not return to
Kenya, but he did not wish to retire from the colonial service. The CO, nevertheless, gave him no option. As he painfully told former S of S Harcourt in
October, the CO leadership had decided "to get rid of me as cheaply as possible." He claimed that the amount of the pension was not what bothered him.
"It is the fact that after 33 years of long and strenuous service in our Tropical
dependencies, I am flung aside, without a word of thanks . . . as a husk to be
disposed of as expeditiously and as economically as possible."[35] The CO decided not to appoint a new governor until the end of Sir Henry's leave. This
expired on 31 December 1917. At this point, it was hoped to defer an appointment of a new governor until the end of the war. This turned out to be longer
than anyone at the CO had anticipated. Bowring would act as governor until
February 1919.[36]

Bowring acted as chief executive of the EAP during very difficult times. The calls for manpower, the famine, the rising tide of settler political demands, among other issues, placed heavy burdens on the acting governor. In the midst of his term, he had the misfortune to suffer a broken leg. In the view of CO officials, he handled a difficult task with reasonable efficiency. Both Belfield and Northey gave Bowring very favorable reports.[37] Bowring had been, for a long period, at the center of affairs in the EAP; he was thus familiar with all issues and personalities. He was particularly respected for his grasp of the protectorate's finances.

Like Belfield, Bowring did not enjoy much respect from the European settlers. He was, at one time or another, accused of being lazy, out of touch with "public" opinion, and pro-African.[38] In truth, however, Bowring, like Belfield before him, would prove very susceptible to pressure from the settlers and acceptive of their demands. Removed from such pressure, Bowring was capable of hostile judgments on settler political tactics and economic prospects while at the same time pushing measures that might be beneficial to the African population. He certainly did not take as bigoted a view of the Indian population, for example, as did Belfield or Northey. Yet when forced to work closely with leading settler politicians, Bowring more often than not fell into line with, and became a strong advocate of, their way of thinking. His role on the prewar NLC and the later Economic and Finance Committee provide stark examples of this tendency. In short, the acting governor would not be the man to halt the drift of policy in favor of settler agriculture and their political demands.

Neither would the political leadership of the CO be disposed to adopt such a stance. Walter Long held office as S of S for all of 1917 and 1918, but as noted in the previous chapter, he took little interest or part in EAP affairs. Long's biographer contended that the former's administrative ability "was never more conspicuous than during the two years he was at the Colonial Office."[39] As far as the EAP was concerned, however, it was totally inconspicuous. What was perhaps Long's longest minute on an EAP matter consisted of his penning two lines after reading Bowring's account of Ainsworth's efforts to recruit porters in 1917.[40] At any rate, Long had never been much interested in the African colonies; this did not change during his tenure as S of S.

By contrast, W. S. A. Hewins, who became parliamentary under-secretary of state in September 1917, was by training an economist and by inclination much drawn to colonial questions through his strong advocacy of tariff reform (i.e., he wished to see Britain adopt protective tariffs). Yet he too took relatively little interest in East Africa during his period of office. Perhaps this was because his appointment was not so much the result of his qualifications winning him the post as it was an attempt by Lloyd George and the leaders of the cabinet to co-opt him into the government to keep him quiet and from causing potential embarrassment to them from the back benches.

Hewins had been the first director of the London School of Economics, but he left that post to direct Joseph Chamberlain's unofficial campaign for protective tariffs. Elected to parliament in 1912, Hewins proved a thorn in the side of both the Asquith and Lloyd George governments. When in August 1917 an antigovernment amendment pushed by Hewins was only narrowly defeated, he was quickly offered the post at the CO left open by the decision to transfer Steel-Maitland to the new joint department of the Board of Trade and the Foreign Office.[41] At the CO, Hewins' main interest was in chairing a subcommittee whose task he directed toward constructing a system of preferential tariffs.[42] He had little time or interest to meddle in EAP affairs.

This left policy where it had previously been, with the permanent officials. They were no more willing to check the drift of policy in the direction desired by the EAP settlers than in the first two years of the war. Their usual response to most crucial issues, putting off a decision until the end of the war or the arrival of the new governor, did relatively little to reestablish control. The European settlers would continue to hold the initiative in the most crucial matters.

At the start of 1917, F. G. A. Butler headed the EAD. He had served as Bonar Law's private secretary during the period the latter headed the CO. Long made other arrangements, and Butler returned to head the EAD. As the succeeding pages will show, he was deeply involved in the consideration of several important issues, but his tenure at the EAD was relatively short. In December 1917, Butler followed Steel-Maitland to the new joint department of the Board of Trade and the Foreign Office as Director of the Overseas Division.[43] W. C. Bottomley assumed the position as head of the EAD. He would occupy a very crucial post with regard to EAP affairs through 1923.

Settlers and Political Representation

One matter of concern to the EAD was the political demands pushed by the settlers during Bowring's stewardship. The settlers wished to move to the implementation of a system of electoral representation that had been conceded by the CO in 1916. Parallel to this, settlers put forward calls for unofficial representation on the protectorate's Execo. Finally, the settlers generated considerable heat, during the first half of 1918 especially, in their calls for the appointment of a new governor.

The push to implement a system of elective representation for unofficial members of the Legco actually was as much an initiative of the administration as the settlers. Following the acceptance of the principle by the S of S, settler politicians, as they had earlier intimated to Belfield, accepted nomination to the Legco in February 1917. The four vacant unofficial seats were now filled by Lord Delamere, A. C. Hoey, W. C. Hunter, and W. McLellan Wilson. It is perhaps significant to note that three of the four were, at the time of their appointment, "elected" members of the war council.[44] With the return of the settler members, Belfield quickly moved to set up a special committee of the Legco to report on the steps to be taken to provide for the election of European non-officials, including voter and candidate qualifications and electoral areas, and how the African, Arab, and Indian communities were to be represented on the council.

Belfield appointed the attorney general, J. W. Barth, as chair, but he and the three other officials named to the committee were outnumbered by the five unofficial European members of the Legco. This virtually insured that the committee's recommendations would reflect the views of the settler leaders. The committee submitted its report to the acting governor on 19 June. Bowring took almost two months to complete his own analysis of the report, sending it, together with a lengthy commentary, via confidential despatch on 14 August 1917.[45]

The committee, first of all, tackled the question of voter and candidate qualifications. It mirrored the position set forth by settlers in their past demands for the franchise: any adult British male resident continuously in the protectorate for twelve months would have the right to vote. Bowring endorsed this rejection of property or educational qualifications. He also supported the additional requirements for council membership of two years residence and English literacy. Bowring agreed with the proposal for a three-year term of election, and he urged that there should therefore be regular "general elections" every three years.[46]

Bowring also found himself in agreement with the number and distribution of electoral areas. The committee proposed ten constituencies, and the acting governor went to great lengths in an attempt to justify this number as warranted "by the special circumstances" of the EAP, although at first sight the total European population would not appear to justify so many representatives. Describing each electoral area in detail, Bowring's main point in justification was that all the various settler interests (plantation, mixed farm, pastoral, and merchant) would be represented under the proposed system. Population as a basis for the electoral districts was thus disregarded. The largest number of potential voters for any of the constituencies were in Nairobi (935) and the smallest in the West Kenia-Nyeri and Laikipia area (49). Only four of the ten areas had more than three hundred voters.[47] Thus was put forward what would for long be a characteristic of European elections in Kenya; there would be little relation between population numbers and the configuration of constituencies. Rural areas would always be overwhelmingly over-represented at the expense of Nairobi.

Bowring then turned to the potential thorny questions of Indian, Arab, and African representation under a system of European elections. The committee recommended that Indian interests be represented by "the nomination of two members by the Governor." The Arab community should be represented by the Resident Magistrate at Mombasa, and the Africans by the CNC who would soon be appointed. The committee felt that any extension of the franchise to Indians "for election of their own representatives or otherwise" should be considered after the Legco had been reconstituted through the election of European members.[48] This was, in effect, saying that there would be no election of Indians as the ten white elected members would be unwilling, as events were to show, to support the principle. Bowring strongly concurred:

> I am in entire agreement that it would be undesirable to extend the franchise to Asiatics and Natives. In the special circumstances affecting this protectorate, it is in my opinion essential that each race shall be separately represented and that any general scheme of franchise embracing all British subjects would be most unsuitable because of the complete difference in the education, mental development, standard of living, local interests, and in fact the whole social fabric of the various races which constitute the local community of British subjects and British protected subjects.[49]

Bowring admitted that this point of view had not proved popular with Indian opinion. He had already received protests from the Mombasa and Nairobi Indian associations. They demanded that Indians have the right of election also. Nevertheless, Bowring held to the committee's suggestion of two nominated Indian members. Just selecting two suitable members would prove difficult, the acting governor maintained. He then put forth an additional rationalization. "There is a risk of a political agitator being imported from India who, with the prestige of a seat on the council at his back, might do a vast amount of harm in sowing discontent and stirring up strife."[50]

Bowring agreed with the committee that African interests on the council should be represented by the CNC, but he differed from them on the question of Arab representation. He felt that community should be represented by one of their own number, the assistant liwali of Mombasa.

Bowring concluded his commentary on the report by calling attention to the fact that official representation on the Legco would have to be increased so as to retain the official majority, if his proposals were accepted, and he mentioned a "fresh controversial matter" that had been introduced into the question since February. That matter was female suffrage. The East African Women's League had been founded in March to press for the right to vote for white females. Bowring was not in favor of the vote for women. He felt that raising the issue now would cause delay in consideration and implementation of the electoral scheme. The whole issue should wait until the new Legco had been constituted.

The arrival of the detailed proposals at the CO was cause for some surprise as the approval of the principle of elective representation had been conditioned by the fact that no final decision could be made before the end of the war. As Butler noted: "The observations and suggestions have come rather earlier than one would have expected. This is, I suppose, the measure of the desire of the Acting Governor and the unofficial community to get the new system started." He therefore decided to "examine and pronounce upon" the recommendations even though the war was far from over and the S of S was under "no obligation" to make any verdict. Any final decision, Butler maintained, should await the selection of a new governor who should have the opportunity to comment.[51]

In his detailed memorandum on the EAP proposals, Butler found himself generally in agreement with Bowring's views. He backed general elections every three years, the deferral of the question of the vote for white women, and no electoral representation for Indians. He felt that the nomination of two Indian members was sufficient. When consulted on the matter, Belfield had strongly opposed any Indian representation in council. He held that "the Indian community of the Protectorate is drawn from a class which is unfitted to participate in legislative procedure."[52] Nevertheless, Butler recognized that the former governor's views were politically impractical. The granting of electoral rights to Europeans would certainly produce an "outcry" from the Indians, and Butler felt that the CO could at least point to the fact that two Indians would represent that community's interests. "The outcry would be very much greater," he went on, "and be very much more difficult to face if the concession were not made."[53]

On the important issue of number of elective seats, Butler's opinion differed from that of the acting governor. The head of the EAD felt that "it was a big jump from the present five unofficial members to the proposed ten;" he therefore suggested combining some of the electoral areas to come up with seven.[54]

Despite Butler's lengthy review of the issue, the CO decided to take no action on the matter. Both Read and Fiddes felt that they must wait for the appointment of the new governor who should have the opportunity of studying the situation before CO decisions were finalized.[55]

This continued to be CO policy for the next several months. In mid-May 1918, however, Bowring reopened the issue of representation in the Legco. The session that had just ended had convinced him that council business would be expedited by an increase in members. He recommended "most strongly" that one official and three unofficials should be added. So strongly did Bowring feel that he requested approval as a temporary measure, if the CO was not prepared to approve of the arrangement as a permanent solution. The acting governor asked endorsement by telegram so he would be able to institute the changes before the next sitting of the council.[56] CO officials were somewhat reluctant to approve the increase. This was mainly because it would narrow the official majority in the Legco to only two (not including the governor). Bottomley doubted that this was sufficient for working purposes, but he decided that Bowring had made a strong enough case for the increase that the S of S should approve.[57] Once the increase in unofficial members to eight was sanctioned, however, there would be no chance of adhering to Butler's proposed seven unofficial members when elections actually were approved.

Some three months later, with the war finally at an end, Bowring transmitted a Legco resolution, moved by the unofficial members, calling for the enactment of legislation to provide for electoral representation. Bowring stated that he was "emphatically of opinion that problems of reorganization and reconstruction which are now before us would be dealt with far more easily and more efficiently if the measure of representation . . . were now to be granted. . . ."[58] Bottomley, now head of the EAD, did not think that such a step could be taken until the new governor, Sir Edward Northey, had had the opportunity to frame his views on "such outstanding points as election or nomination of Indians" on the spot. The CO thus telegraphed that the new governor would give the matter his early attention; only on receipt of his report would the CO act.[59]

As noted above, the introduction of elective representation was not the only political issue of concern to the settlers. They also wished to gain a voice on the protectorate's Execo, and, in fact, much more heat would be generated, and pressure brought to bear, over that issue than elections. Shortly before the completion of the Legco select committee's report on elections and Legco representation, the unofficial members presented Bowring with a request that two unofficial members should be appointed to the Execo. Bowring discussed the matter with the Execo and the unofficial members; he decided to forward a recommendation to London in favor of the appointment of two unofficials without waiting for the report on electoral representation. In his despatch of 23 June 1917, the acting governor strongly expressed the view that the appointment of unofficial representatives to the Execo "would tend to remove a considerable amount of dissatisfaction on the part of the general public and would lead to a better feeling generally and greater confidence in the actions and policy of Government."[60] He asked that if appointment could not be made, to be allowed to announce acceptance in principle.

Bowring's sense of urgency was not shared by officials at the CO. Butler recommended taking the unofficial members at their word and making a response when they replied on the electoral question. "There is," he concluded, "no hurry." The CO thus left the issue in abeyance as no reply was sent to Nairobi.[61]

Bowring was not willing to let the matter lie in abeyance, however. Under pressure from the war and famine, his administration had, by early 1918, come in for unrelenting criticism from settlers and their mouthpieces in the Nairobi press. There were calls for a military governor being heard from the same sources and criticism of many of Bowring's actions (e.g. his appointment of Ainsworth as adviser on native affairs). On 5 February, for example, the CO received a telegram sent on behalf of an "European and Indian mass meeting" that Sir Percy Girouard be appointed military governor to organize the colony's efforts,[62] and a second from Bowring in which he expressed the opinion that the protest movement was organized by "certain prominent local settlers who have long objected to system of crown colony government." They were masking their desire to change the system of government behind a call for a new, dynamic governor. What they also desired, the acting governor held, was "a policy of forced native labour."[63]

The harassed Bowring followed this up on 20 February with a telegram stating his belief that the local position would be "much relieved if two unofficial members of the Executive Council were appointed." He recommended strongly that he be allowed to make an immediate announcement to that effect.[64]

At this point, Bottomley, on behalf of the EAD, undertook to construct a lengthy memorandum for the purposes of decision on this matter, the question of Girouard's suitability to return to the EAP, and to prepare for a question to be raised on the EAP in the House of Lords. Bottomley saw in the agitation of the settlers a desire for more direct control over the protectorate's affairs. Bottomley's extremely perceptive insight is worth quoting at length.

> The settlers are largely from South Africa or are men of position in this country who find themselves cramped by the limitations of administration in a Black Man's country. They have been anxious in the past not only to obtain self government, or as a first step, a system of representative government which would lead at an early stage to the grant of responsible government, but also to secure decisions in such matters as land and labour which would benefit their own interests, irrespective of those of the future European community of the country and irrespective also of the claims of the native population. The herds of cattle belonging to the Masai and the Wakamba and the fertile land in the Kikuyu reserve, adjacent to the Uganda Railway, attract the East African settler, who says, no doubt with truth, that he could make better use of that. Until the Imperial Government is prepared to hand over its responsibilities for the welfare of the Natives to the local European community it is impossible to leave out of consideration the native interests in dealing with the perfectly legitimate aspiration of that community for some voice in the management of their interests.[65]

This very accurate understanding of settler aims and aspirations led Bottomley to the conclusion that the CO should give way to their demands for the two unofficials to be appointed to the Execo. By this he seemed to suggest that a small concession would give them a greater voice in, but not control of, affairs. With this kind of attitude characterizing the CO, it is little wonder that the settlers were able to extend their political influence. Nevertheless, Bottomley would not propose giving way on the appointment of Girouard or anyone else who would seek to organize the EAP for the exclusive benefits of the whites. Bottomley added a very prophetic warning.

> There is a danger lest the emergencies of wartime be made a ground for hasty decisions which, though they might be justified by the exigencies of the time, would be too arbitrary for post-war conditions. If we give way to the unofficials now we should find that we had surrendered native interests to them for all time.[66]

This would form a basic theme in CO thinking for some years to come. They would make concessions to the settlers without allowing them ultimate control of the EAP's affairs. Yet the effect of continued concessions to the settlers would be a loss of CO ability to regain control over the course of events in that dependency.

Despite Bottomley's recommendation that the addition of two unofficial members to the Execo be approved, the CO took no action. After speaking to the S of S, Fiddes advised waiting for a few days.[67] After further discussions between Bottomley and Fiddes, it was decided to refer the matter to the new governor because Fiddes felt that the grant of the concession on his appointment "might smooth his path." Thus the CO decided to wait until discussion could be held with the new appointee, General Sir Edward Northey.[68]

These would not take place until the latter's return from Africa towards the end of the year, but Bowring once again urged that he be allowed to announce the agreement of the CO to the appointing of two unofficials as a way of greatly relieving the local situation in early May. In the just completed Legco session, the unofficial members had been especially obstructive and hostile, primarily on budgetary issues. He sympathized with their demand to have "a larger voice" in the expenditure of public funds and the raising of revenue. Besides his hope that concession of this demand would make government business easier to accomplish, Bowring put forward another argument in favor of it. This was the "attitude of the local press and its effect not only on the public but on the government servant himself." The Nairobi press was losing no opportunity to criticize the present system of government. In the hopes of fostering "a spirit of confidence between local government and the general public," Bowring beseeched the CO for rapid approval.[69] The CO were unmoved, however. Since General Northey was coming to Britain, any decision must await discussion with him.[70]

Bowring waited for almost five months before renewing his concern. He telegraphed in November suggesting that when the draft estimates would shortly be considered in the Execo, the presence of unofficial members "would be advantageous."[71] By the time this telegraph arrived at the CO, Northey had been consulted. He approved the appointment of unofficials to the Execo.[72] CO acceptance was thus now certain, but it was decided to allow Northey to announce the concession after his arrival as it would, in Read's words, "strengthen his position if he starts with the credit of the new arrangements."[73] Clearly the delay of the CO made little difference; the essential point was that the settlers had got their way as the result of the strong pleading from the colonial state.

Indian Protest

European settler political demands and protests were not the only ones requiring attention from the CO in 1917 and 1918. Indians in the EAP also were extremely concerned about representation in the Legco. But this would not be the only cause for Indian complaints directed to the CO. At least two other basic grievances that would come to constitute the postwar Indian question were voiced during the last two years of the war. These were the colonial state's insistence on residential and commercial segregation between Indians and Europeans in urban areas, and the prohibition on Indian land ownership in the white highlands.

Early in 1917, the CO received a series of resolutions passed by meetings of Indians in Nairobi and Mombasa. Sent through the EAP government on this occasion, the resolutions reiterated an earlier demand for elective representation for Indians in the Legco and Nairobi municipal committee.[74] By the end of 1916, the EAP government had agreed to nominate an Indian, whose name would be submitted by the Nairobi Indian Association, to the Nairobi Municipal Committee.[75] Since the EAP government had told the Indians that representation of the Indian community was occupying the attention of both the S of S and the governor, the CO only acknowledged receipt of the resolutions.

In October 1917, Bowring himself raised the question of urban segregation to the CO. He laid down the policy he had adopted to stop the transfers of urban plots from Europeans to Indians in Nairobi. It was the protectorate government's policy to enforce a system of segregation as laid down by Professor W. J. R. Simpson in a 1913 report. Bowring felt that "no person of impartial judgment" could question an arrangement whereby the two races would reside in different areas. This would not be the last time this issue would be raised.[76]

At the height of the settler agitation in January-February 1918, the Indian community in Nairobi sent a telegram to the S of S declaring their nonadherence to the claims made by the settler telegrams to London that Indians supported their demand for the appointment of Girouard as military governor. The Indians depreciated the "attempt being made to revive controversial matters."[77]

The reference to controversial matters caused Bowring to make further inquiries of the Nairobi Indian Association. The reply he received provides a clear picture of Indian concerns in early 1918. These included the introduction and operation of the Crown Lands Ordinance, the veto on land sales from Europeans to Indians in urban areas, the contemplated legislation to prohibit Indians from residing in the Nairobi residential areas of Parklands and the Hill, the nonrepresentation of Indians on the EAP Economic Commission, appointed earlier by Belfield, and on the Land Settlement Commission.[78]

For the remainder of the year, ill feeling between Indians and settlers was of concern to the colonial state. Bowring felt that it was serious enough to call for drastic measures. At the end of October, he suggested to the CO that two Indians should be nominated to the Legco. He was strongly of the opinion that direct representation was "justified by their commercial interests." Not only did Bowring propose appointment, but he was now prepared to suggest the names of two men, one Hindu and one Muslim, to take the seats as soon as permission from the S of S was received. At the same time, he advocated appointing an Arab to represent the interests of that group.[79]

This suggestion surprised officials at the CO. As Bottomley noted, the CO had been repeatedly told by Belfield that there was no suitable Indian to sit in the Legco. Now two had been put forward. The head of the EAD suggested approval of the appointments, but cautioned that appointment of representatives for non-European interests at that time implied similar representation in the future. However, they did not "imply that when elective representation of Europeans is introduced the non-Europeans will necessarily be elected."[80] After study of the issue, Northey was prepared to agree to Bowring's proposal, but Fiddes did not feel that the matter was urgent. It should be left to the new governor to deal with on his arrival.[81]

The CO position on nomination to the Legco remained unchanged after the receipt of a despatch of 25 November describing further Indian complaints against segregation regulations in Mombasa. Bowring again defended the colonial state's actions on the grounds of public health. The acting governor then went on to call for "a more definite expression of policy of the Government with regard to Indians," with a presentation of his own views. The two chief Indian complaints, he held, centered around "the acquisition of land and representation on various councils." Bowring indicated that he had now appointed two Indian members to the Nairobi Municipal Committee, and he felt some increased measure of representation on other bodies might be of utility. As for land acquisition, he urged setting aside areas "in low-country districts" for Indian agricultural activity.[82] One change with regard to segregation had emerged by the time Bowring's despatch was considered in London. This was the possible avoidance of segregating against Indians by name "by the provision of suitable public health legislation." This was Bottomley's idea.[83] Like most other issues, the CO would await the new governor's arrival and recommendations before taking any action on the question of Indian grievances.

Other Issues Deferred

Several other matters of importance relating to the EAP were given some consideration by the colonial state and CO in 1917–18, but final decisions in each case were deferred until the new governor's arrival. In terms of future importance, three issues stand out for brief mention: the soldier settlement scheme, the Uasin Gishu railway, and the annexation of the EAP as a colony.

Serious CO consideration of the possibility of putting into effect a scheme for the settlement of veterans in the EAP awaited, in 1917–18, the report of the local commission approved by London in 1916. Such a land settlement commission was appointed by Belfield in March 1917. The commission, chaired by attorney general Barth, had six unofficial and four official members.[84] It did not complete its report, however, until the close of 1918. Bowring telegraphed a summary of the commission's report at the end of December, but the full report was not available in London until well into 1919.

Bowring's lengthy telegram certainly did not surprise anyone at the CO with its report that the committee advocated a soldier settlement scheme. It did, however, identify several points for serious consideration. The acting governor agreed with the committee, for example, that settlers should possess capital of more than £500. He also concurred that under existing circumstances, the labor supply of the protectorate "is not organized to cope with any large and immediate influx of settlers." Bowring felt that "until organization and control is established labour question must prove an obstacle to any large increase of European settlement and it will take at least two years before reliable estimate of available labour can be formed."[85] Moreover, Bowring did not think it possible that 83,000 acres of land could be found from the Kikuyu reserve for the scheme, as the commission seemed to feel was feasible. Lacking the complete report, the CO could do little but await full particulars from Northey in the new year.

By contrast, Bowring gave far more detailed attention to the need to construct a railway line across the Uasin Gishu plateau for the benefit of the European settlers there. It will be recalled that the proposal to construct such a line had been seriously considered by the CO prior to the war. A survey of the proposed route from the mainline at Nakuru across the plateau to Mumias, a distance of 205 miles, had been completed in 1915. The war had made further consideration impossible, but in early 1918 a strong settler campaign in support of building such a line was revived, largely by the same individual who had been influential in 1913 and 1914, E. S. Grogan. The public demand for a railway actually formed only a part of the "agitation" that Grogan orchestrated in the EAP.[86]

Grogan certainly had strong economic reasons for his advocacy of the railway line. He had been unable to effectively exploit his huge timber concession due to lack of a rail line. Not only did he orchestrate a public campaign to push for consideration of the rail line, Grogan also arranged an interview between A. L. Lawley, a representative of the construction firm Pauling and Co. Ltd, and Bowring in February. Lawley made an offer on behalf of Pauling to construct a railway from Nakuru to Mumias, and Bowring quickly telegraphed it to London with his strong recommendation that the offer be taken up in London with Pauling and the financial house Lawley identified as capable of raising money for the construction, Erlangers.[87] There was no enthusiasm for the offer at the CO, however. Read advised against doing anything because the financial position of the protectorate at the end of the war was very uncertain, rails and rolling stock would not be available due to the war, and it was doubtful there would be adequate African labor. The CO quickly telegraphed that it would be impossible to discuss such a scheme until the end of the war.[88]

This hardly ended consideration of the issue. Lawley's offer appeared in the Nairobi press, and settlers on the Uasin Gishu plateau began to raise a cry for consideration of their transport needs. During February and March, Bowring was pressed by unofficial members in the Legco to provide more information, and they criticized his handling of Lawley's offer.[89] Feeling the heat from a campaign that the acting governor attributed to Grogan, Bowring sent two telegrams to the CO in mid-March urging reconsideration. His second wire spoke of reports of "unrest and strong discontent" on the plateau and asked for the precise objections to the scheme.[90] The CO was still unwilling to commit to a major railway building project "in view of the great uncertainty over the future." In two telegrams of 21 March, the CO suggested that feelings of unrest would be better allayed by "construction at an early date of a good road," and detailed its reasons for refusing to take up the scheme at that time.[91]

Within a month, the issue was pressed on the CO by two M.P.s. Frederick Guest, long a supporter of settler economic interests, wrote to Hewins in April to proclaim great interest in the development of the Uasin Gishu and the need for a railway.[92] H. Page Croft wrote to S of S Long later in the month in response to "a deputation of gentlemen from East Africa" who had recently called on him to complain about "the neglect of the Uasin Gishu." The M.P. held that the lack of adequate transportation was one type of neglect. Uasin Gishu was "likely to become one of the most prosperous agricultural centres of the empire. . . ."[93] Despite these approaches, the CO stood fast in its position that a railway could not seriously be considered until a long time after the war.[94] Though the politicans' intervention was not productive of immediate gains for the settlers, it did little to provoke the CO to reverse the trends in favor of settler aspirations that marked these years.

By the end of April, however, Bowring had completed a visit to the Uasin Gishu plateau. He had seen first hand the great difficulties posed by existing roads, and he was sympathetic to the demands of settlers there for urgent improvements in transport facilities. Bowring urged against building a permanent road from Londiani, on the current Uganda railway, to Eldoret, the district headquarters of Uasin Gishu, since it seemed that it would take as long to construct as a railway. He now proposed the building of a trolley line, constructed with rails from German East Africa, to supplement the existing road.[95] Approximately a week later, the acting governor wrote to further press for the approval of the latter, which he now termed "a tramway." It would cost only £114,070, and Bowring requested that in the event of the CO's agreement that the EAP should act immediately to improve transport proposals, the money for the construction of the tramway could be provided by loan.[96]

The CO was totally uninterested in such a proposal. No reply was made to either of Bowring's May despatches. Nevertheless, in a mid-June confidential despatch, Bowring raised the need for a tram line again. He felt the EAP could afford the interest and redemption charges on the loan, and he added that improved communications in the interior "might prove to be of the greatest value imperially in opening up fresh sources for the supply of raw materials. . . ."[97] This despatch finally moved the CO to consider the proposal. After much discussion, the CO formally approached the Treasury, in early 1919, with the request that the Londiani to Eldoret tram line should be incorporated in the works to be covered by the 1914 loan and that the Nakuru-Eldoret-Mumias railway be included in an expanded future programme of borrowing for the EAP.[98]

By this time, however, Bowring had further investigated the feasibility of constructing and maintaining a tram line. After asking Lawley's advice on the matter, he became convinced "of the inadvisability of constructing a light railway" to the Uasin Gishu plateau. In informing London of his acceptance of Lawley's assessment, Bowring all but admitted that the only viable alternative for meeting the transport needs of the Uasin Gishu and Trans Nzoia settlers was the Nakuru-Eldoret-Mumias railway proposal.[99] This indeed would be the position that Governor Northey would initially press for implementation upon his assumption of office.

Like the Uasin Gishu railway scheme, the possibility of annexing the EAP as a colony also predated the start of World War I. In fact, the idea was closely related to the problems of raising the capital for the construction of such a line. As CO officials studied the possibilities for raising a loan, it became clear to them that as a colony, the territory could obtain loans on much more favorable terms, under the Colonial Stock Act, than as a protectorate. Thus Read remarked in July 1914, "we shall get much better terms if the EAP is annexed and made into a crown colony." He urged turning the protectorate, with the exception of the Sultan of Zanzibar's mainland possessions and the Sultanate of Witu, "into a crown colony forthwith."[100]

The war, of course, postponed any serious consideration of that step. But the war brought to the attention of the CO another potential reason for annexing the EAP as a colony. R. F. Mayer, a German national resident in the EAP since 1899, worked for British army intelligence during the war. Mayer, part proprietor of the *EAS*, desired to be naturalized a British citizen. When the CO examined the legal position, it was found that the naturalization statutes under which he wished to accomplish the change in citizenship applied only to dominions and crown colonies, not protectorates.[101] While this was a much less compelling reason for annexation than the easing of loan terms, it nevertheless provided a second advantage for changing the EAP to a colony.

There were, as Read had noted in his 1914 minute, international complications to be considered in any such annexation. Britain recognized the Sultan of Zanzibar as the owner of the coastal strip ten miles inland. There were also treaty considerations involving France and Germany. The latter, which involved the so-called Sultanate of Witu, were rendered unimportant by the war, but the claims of the Sultan of Zanzibar and France would have to be considered in any annexation. When Bowring was asked for his views in 1918, he returned a rather negative assessment. Read's idea that all the EAP except the coastal strip should be annexed, leaving the sultan's dominion as a protectorate, he judged to be undesirable under existing conditions. It would offer no administrative advantages, and there would likely be difficulties because the sultan's mainland dominions had never been clearly delimited. Neither was Bowring sympathetic towards Mayer's predicament since he regarded the latter as an anti-administration agitator. As he had experienced several months of political opposition from settlers, Bowring was cognizant of another negative effect of annexation. He stated:

> It is true that an annexation would probably be welcomed by the local European community as a sign of progress and as a marked step towards the goal of 'Responsible Government', but I do not attach much importance to this aspect of the proposal because I consider that there are many important matters concerning the administration and constitution of the East Africa Protectorate which will have to be settled before 'Responsible Government', which term is generally used by local politicians to describe government by the European community, can even be discussed.[102]

Other business, rather than the acting governor's negative assessment, kept the CO from returning to the issue until the end of the year. The matter was discussed with General Northey in London in November. He was instructed to consider it on his arrival in the EAP and submit a report on the possibility of annexing to the crown all of the EAP that was not included in the mainland domains of the Sultan of Zanzibar. The problem of accurately delimiting those domains was identified for special investigation by the new governor.[103]

The Appointment of a New Governor

As noted in the preceding pages, most important administrative, political, and economic matters raised during the acting governorship of Bowring were left for decision or recommendation by the new governor. It is important at this point to describe the process by which Sir Edward Northey came to be named the EAP's next governor. As mentioned above, the CO was in no hurry to name a successor to Belfield until the expiry of the latter's leave. The most obvious reason for this course was so as not to have to pay salaries to two governors out of the protectorate's tight wartime revenue. Belfield's period of leave did not expire until the last day of 1917. The CO also preferred not to make a new appointment until the end of the war, at which time it was assumed that there would be a wider choice available.

The EAP's settler politicians were not willing to wait, however. Their demand for the naming of a new governor, in conformity with their views, formed a facet of their political agitation in early 1918. As mentioned earlier, they demanded a man "with special organizing capacity and prestige of past achievements;" specifically they asked for the return of Sir Percy Girouard as a military governor.[104] Bowring had little time for this recommendation; he informed London that certain prominent local settlers were stirring up a furor over the choice of a new governor so as to obtain a governor who would have a freehand "to organize the country for the supply of foodstuffs and war material." This would be accomplished by, among other things, a policy of forced labor.[105]

As described earlier in this chapter, the CO had no intention of sending Girouard back to the EAP. The CO's brief telegraphic response to the settlers' demand stated that "other arrangements are in contemplation."[106] Disappointed, the settlers kept up the pressure for a man who fit their profile. A committee representing settler opinion wired the CO on 7 March stating that they trusted

> that the other arrangements will in conformity with vital principles that Governor's qualifications will be sufficient to secure him delegation of authority to decide locally all matters which have no extra territorial or Imperial significance serious consideration by Imperial Government.[107]

CO officials did not find the telegram amusing. The CO reply emphasized that it would not "be dictated to in the choice of new governor," but promised the settlers full consideration of their views.[108]

Bowring had clearly had enough of the settlers' demands by this time. On 11 March, he sent a lengthy despatch to the S of S in which he scorchingly analyzed the settler agitation. In his opinion, that agitation was caused by people who promoted discord between the rulers and ruled so as to acquire political prominence "and in some case pecuniary profit; it suits them to foster a spirit of antagonism and they do so." In this category he placed the proprietors of the *EAS* and, to a lesser degree, *The Leader of British East Africa* (*LBEA*). The papers, he held, had engaged for some time in a campaign of vilification against the government and his leadership. The stimulus behind the whole uproar over a military governor and other political agitation was, Bowring was sure, E. S. Grogan, in conjunction with Mayer.[109]

Grogan had taken up the issue of "development of the material resources of the Protectorate with the object of assisting the Empire in the prosecution of the War," and he gained a following for the proposition that the colonial state had shown apathy in that subject. He was able to pull most of white public opinion, including several members of the war council, with him for a time; that some unofficial members of the war council would join in the agitation for, as Bowring put it, "their own glorification instead of putting their proposals before me" was a bitter pill for the acting governor to swallow.

Despite the heat that had been generated, Bowring contended that it had by March died down. As he paused to consider the significance of the demands put forward by Grogan and company, the acting governor suspected that there might be something more behind it than "an irresponsible megalomanic and a couple of corrupt newssheets." In an interesting insight for the future, he thought the real issue was forced labor.

> Every planter and every farmer, though he might not willingly admit it, desires forced labour in his heart of hearts and knows that he cannot get it constitutionally. Hence the cry for increased production to help the War and the call for an autocratic Governor in the shape of Sir Percy Girouard. . . .

Although this agitation does not seem to have had a direct impact, the CO now moved relatively quickly to appoint a new governor. Their choice in fact fell on a military man. Within three weeks of the receipt of Bowring's heated despatch, they had decided, having cleared the matter with the War Office, to offer the post to Sir Edward Northey. In many ways, this was an amazing choice. Unfortunately, CO records provide few clear clues for what would be, in many respects, a disastrous selection. Northey had no experience in colonial administration at all. Son of an Anglican clergyman, he was educated at Eton and Sandhurst, and he entered military service in 1890. He served in India, the South African war, and World War I.

At the start of World War I, Northey was a Lieutenant Colonel. He served in France and Belgium in 1914–15, and by March 1915 he was promoted to Brigadier General. In command of an infantry brigade, he was wounded twice. Early in 1916, he was given command of the Nyasaland-Rhodesia Field Force. He was to advance on German East Africa from the south in coordination with the offensive from the EAP. He was promoted to Major General in early 1918.

In the absence of clear indications in CO records that would help determine the reasons for the choice of Northey, it is only possible to speculate. Undoubtedly London officials wanted a strong leader who would act decisively. Northey was certainly such an individual. The military man, it was probably felt, would not be pushed around by the settlers. This hope was certainly fulfilled, though in a different way than the CO had hoped. Northey did not have to be pushed; he became the settlers greatest ally and champion. If this characteristic of the new governor was soon apparent, so too was lack of experience and understanding of economics and government finance. In those areas, Northey would prove himself an utter disaster. Nicholson and Hughes number Northey among the "cuckoos in the nest," colonial governors who owed their position to political patronage.[110] If that was the case, his appointment was certainly an example of trying to find a specific kind of man for a specific political job.[111]

Such a job would not have been easy for any governor. The EAP had many problems, and getting things moving again after the war would have been difficult. Northey seems to have realized that when he accepted the job in early June 1918. He requested permission of the S of S to return from Africa to Britain since it was most important that he personally discuss policy, especially "concerning planters and Indians and such questions as elected members of council" with the CO.[112] While Bottomley and Read felt that Northey should go to Nairobi to take up the government as soon as possible, Fiddes felt that the heavens would not fall if he came home. It would be as well for the new governor to come to Britain before going to the EAP. Long agreed that Northey should have his home leave first.[113] The announcement of Northey's appointment was telegraphed to Bowring on 19 June and made public the following day.[114]

The settlers, for their part, welcomed the appointment. In their telegram to the CO, however, they continued to insist that "the new Governor should be given adequate powers to decide matters locally with no extra-territorial significance. . . ." They also demanded that he have a staff of sufficient experience and capacity to bring about an early termination "of the prevailing administrative and financial chaos."[115] Northey spent a good deal of time in Britain reading correspondence and being briefed at the CO. He presumably came to understand the background of the most outstanding issues that demanded a resolution.

In fact, General Northey faced a daunting agenda when he left for the EAP. He had been given responsibility for formulating policy on practically every outstanding political and administrative issue. The CO had not given him a list of prescriptions to carry out or specific policies to implement. The initiative was left entirely with the new governor, and he would indeed take it. The next two years would see Northey's administration implementing one pro-settler measure after another. The CO, in its appointment of Northey, had given up, in effect, its control of events in the EAP. But this was no more than a logical outcome of the stance the CO had consistently taken throughout 1917 and 1918. It clearly demonstrates the CO's continued loss of direction and control that marked the period since late 1914. And it pointed to a future in which the CO would be on the defensive in the face of Northey's pro-settler onslaught and the struggle for Kenya that it provoked.

5

General Northey on the Offensive, 1919–20

The arrival of Sir Edward Northey to take the governorship of the EAP began a rapid push towards settler primacy. Quickly establishing himself as the settlers' champion, General Northey bulldozed ahead with measure after measure for the benefit of the settlers. Many of the latter's long-standing demands, such as elective representation, registration of African men, and government assistance in labor recruitment, were now brought into effect. For its part, the CO seemed virtually powerless to halt the rush towards white supremacy. Unlike during the war years, it would be groups external to the CO, such as the IO, British humanitarians, and metropolitan financiers, whose protests would touch off the struggle for Kenya in earnest. It was this struggle, which pitted those external groups and African and Indian protest in Kenya on the one hand against the settlers and the colonial state on the other, that would force the CO to slow down the pace of Northey's rush to make the territory he renamed Kenya a settler state.

Changes at the CO

The inauguration of Sir Edward Northey's governorship coincided with new leadership at the CO. In January 1919, a reshuffle of Lloyd George's cabinet brought Lord Alfred Milner and Leopold Amery to the CO as S of S and parliamentary under-secretary. The appointment of these two, who were longtime allies in the Conservative Party, to the CO marked the culmination of a noticeable shift in British politics. Milner and Amery were staunch imperialists; the war had created a situation conducive to the rise to power of Milner's imperialism, previously repudiated by the British electorate. As Bernard Porter has remarked, "It was a remarkable resurrection of a school of imperialism which had been thought to be dead and buried for years, spurned by successive electorates since 1906. . . ."[1] The contrast, so far as East Africa is concerned, between a CO led by Liberals Harcourt and Emmott and one led by the imperialist tariff reformers Milner and Amery is very striking.

In Milner's view, the British empire was supremely consequential. He felt that those of the "British race" in the empire "must continue to control and guide the dependent peoples within their jurisdiction."[2] Milner and his followers felt that the political and strategic requirements of the empire were all important; they should dominate and shape domestic as well as foreign policy.[3] As part of his imperial view, Milner favored the creation of an imperial union and tariff reform.

Milner came to the CO at the end of his public career. He had won both fame and infamy for himself as high commissioner in South Africa before and during the Boer war. After he left South Africa in 1905, Milner's political ambitions suffered a series of setbacks. None of the causes he identified himself with achieved success (e.g. his fight against Irish home rule), but as noted above, World War I changed all that. He joined Lloyd George's small war cabinet after the latter became prime minister in December 1916. Milner remained at the center of events until the end of the conflict, later serving as minister of war. As a result of his new power and influence, Milner secured the appointment of several of his disciples and followers, one of whom was Amery, to influential positions in the war administration of Lloyd George.[4]

In January of 1919, the war now over and an election overwhelmingly won, the prime minister offered Milner the position of S of S for the Colonies. The latter would only accept, however, if Amery could go with him to the CO.[5] Lloyd George agreed, and Milner assumed office on 10 January 1919. His term of office was not particularly distinguished. He made very little progress, for example, with his cherished dream of imperial unity.[6] In fact, he was away from London and the CO for a good portion of his two years as S of S. As a member of the British delegation to the Paris peace conference, Milner spent much of the first half of 1919 in the French capital. A few months after the end of the peace conference, Milner agreed to head a mission to Egypt to enquire into nationalist disturbances there and make recommendations for its future governance. He left for Egypt at the end of November, and he returned in March 1920.[7] Eleven months later he left office.

Even while at his desk at the CO, Milner's interest in and attention to East African issues were limited. He would be forced, rather against his wishes, to become involved in the Indian question and the EAP's labor controversy. Nevertheless, some of his imperial interests would have an impact on Kenya. A noteworthy example was Milner's enthusiasm for the development of the dependent empire. Both he and Amery felt that government funds should be expended for promoting economic development as the colonies could provide important markets for British manufactured goods and raw materials for her industries. It was particularly important, they felt, for the resources of the empire to be used to build the British economy and improve the quality of life in Britain.[8] Milner created a Colonial Economic Development Committee to survey the economic possibilities and resources of the dependent empire in 1919, and that committee would quickly consider a project in the EAP.[9] Two related issues dear to Milner's heart would figure in CO relations with Kenya during his term of office; these were emigration schemes which would send Britons to other parts of the empire and the extension of railway construction to every part of the British domain.[10]

While Milner was not as directly involved in the work of the CO while S of S as he might have been, the same can not be said for Leopold Amery. Amery was very much absorbed in all EAP issues, particularly those relating to the economy, economic development, and finance. While Milner was in Egypt, Amery served as S of S. Though short in stature, Amery was a very forceful personality. After his student days at Oxford, he joined *The Times* as a correspondent during the Boer war. There he came under Milner's influence and became a member of the latter's famous imperialist "kindergarten". Amery thereafter sought to bring about the fruition of his mentor's ideal of building an effective imperial union from the existing British empire. Amery's concept of empire was "much more than a political programme. It was an ideology that constituted a coherent system of thought to which every issue, political, economic, social, cultural, and even moral, could be related. More than that, it was a faith."[11]

Upon entering parliament in 1911, Amery became a champion of protective tariffs and army reform. With Milner's patronage, his influence rose, after 1916, to the point that he served as assistant secretary to the war cabinet. His appointment to the CO marked his first ministerial service, and he was determined that he would play a major role in the work of the CO. The day after assuming office, Milner had a meeting with permanent under-secretary Fiddes to make it clear that Amery's "position in the office would have to be very different from that occupied by Steel-Maitland or Hewins."[12] This would indeed be the case so far as Kenya affairs were concerned. His lengthy minutes, the several memoranda that he authorized, and the numerous occasions he chaired meetings dealing with East African questions all attest to the fact that Amery would be an important player in the CO between January 1919 and April 1921.[13]

Economic Realities

An assessment of the economic circumstances of the EAP at the end of World War I is important since it had a great impact on the evolution of the new governor's policies, and his attempts to implement them, just as it did in determining the CO's position on postwar issues. As noted in the preceding chapter, the war and its aftermath left the African sector of the colonial economy in a very weak position. African production for export suffered a major setback at the end of the war, and as Table 5.1 illustrates, the value of African produce exported fell dramatically during 1920 and 1921. From generating 30 per cent of the value of exports in 1919, peasant production had shrunk to 11 per cent in 1921. While a substantial portion of the maize exported during the latter year came from African growers, maize exports only provided 2 per cent of the total export value. By contrast, settler generated products made up 86 per cent of exports with coffee and sisal leading the way (82 per cent).

As noted earlier, African households had dominated domestic markets and export trade prior to 1914. The impact of the war and the postwar environmental crisis had undermined this preeminence. Yet there is nothing in the agricultural and trade reports of the time to indicate that this was permanent. Every major category of African produce experienced a rise in the quantity exported in 1920 as compared to 1919. With the return of normal rainfall, African producers were able to generate increased production. The quantity of sim sim exports rose by 34 per cent; those of potatoes 18 per cent, grains other than maize by 658 per cent, and beans and peas by 133 per cent.[14] This experience clearly suggests that the peasantry, which had been "captured" before the war, could have been "captured" again. The export figures for 1921 and 1922 indicate, however, that they were not. The most important factors accounting for this relative decline of African export production was the postwar trade depression that gripped the EAP from 1920 until at least the beginning of 1923, and the conscious decision of Sir Edward Northey's administration not to encourage peasant production.

Table 5.1 Percentage Value of Agricultural Exports, 1919–21

	1919	1920	1921
African			
Hides/skins	22	15	6
Beans/peas	3	4	*
Sim sim	4	4	2
Other grain	*	2	1
Groundnuts	–	*	1
Potatoes	1	1	1
Total %	30	26	11
Settler			
Coffee	34	41	53
Sisal	22	16	29
Flax	2	1	2
Wattle	*	1	–
Wool	4	2	2
Total %	62	61	86
Miscellaneous			
Coconuts/copra	5	1	1
Mixed			
Maize	3	12	2
Total value £s	725,000	947,254	709,515

Source: Colony and Protectorate of Kenya, *Department of Agriculture Report 1924* (Nairobi: Government Printer, 1925), insert.

For the new governor, settler production for export had to be the basis of the EAP's future prosperity. It amounted to more than 60 per cent of the total value in 1919 and 1920, and it rose, as noted above, to 86 per cent in 1921. Obviously no governor could overlook this fact. Yet as noted in the preceding chapter, settler dominance of the export markets was the result of the extremely unusual circumstances of wartime. The settler sector would not be strong enough to carry the protectorate on its back without a huge level of support from the colonial state. This would become clear as the depressed trade conditions of 1920–22 hit settler production hard. Kenya would be faced with a continual financial crisis during that period as state revenue fell short of projected expenditures.

It took Northey a long time to grasp the fact of the weakness of the settler sector and the difficulty, indeed impossibility, of building the colonial economy solely on settler production for export. It may well be that Northey was convinced by the dominance the settler sector had attained in the export market at the end of the war to support it to the almost total exclusion of African peasant production. It is quite clear, however, that the new governor brought with him a basic predilection to support the settler sector; in a very real sense, the export figures did not really matter to Northey. He would demonstrate his preference for, and support of, the settlers time and again.

In fact, Northey made clear where he stood in his first speech to the Legco in February 1919. He asked if it was "our duty to allow these Natives to remain in uneducated and unproductive idleness in the so-called reserves?" His answer was, of course, that this could not be allowed to happen, and he went on to assert that the protectorate could only develop its full productive capacity by "the encouragement of the thousands of able bodied natives to work with the European settler for the cultivation of the land and the improvement of stock." The country had a great future before it, he asserted, "but only if a steady flow of Natives out of the Reserves working willingly for a good wage, well housed and fed, under European control and supervision, can be properly organized."[15]

Northey further elaborated this kind of thinking in the policy memoranda he prepared for the CO in October 1919. He maintained that the African could play a large part in the economic development of the protectorate, but that he would need a push from the administration. The push was not to be directed toward production for export, but to getting Africans to leave the reserve to work on settlers farms and estates. In Northey's words:

> There are two points to consider, firstly that native labour is required for proper development of the country, and secondly that we must educate the native to come out of his reserve to work, for his own sake, because nothing can be worse for the young native than to remain, according to his inclination, idle in the reserve. Those that do so are likely to become vicious and effete.[16]

Northey's preference for European settler production would be especially evident in his encouragement of soldier settlement, labor policies, his advocacy of improved transportation to assist the settlers, and his beefing up the department of agriculture to provide greater support to the settlers, but a major constraint on his actions and proposals during 1919 and 1920 was provided by the protectorate's financial position. Northey often found himself banging against a partially closed door of CO and Treasury resistance to his schemes for expanding expenditure to aid the settler sector. Partly this was the result of CO and Treasury lack of enthusiasm for government spending to promote economic development, but it was also the consequence of the financial problems experienced by the EAP and Britain itself in these years. It did not seem that the protectorate could afford to undertake development schemes from its own revenues, nor could it afford to borrow the large sums needed for public works construction. Given its economic problems after the war, the British government was not likely to provide grants or other types of financial assistance for the EAP.[17]

Within a month of his arrival in the EAP, Northey pressed for imperial financial assistance to improve and extend the communications system. In his telegram, the governor contended that "the settlement and development" of the EAP was being "seriously retarded through want of capital expenditure on communications." He asked for what amounted to a loan of £3,000,000; this would include some £1,900,000 that constituted the unissued portion of the 1914 loan and a fresh £1,100,000. He requested additional funds to extend the Thika rail line thirty-two miles to the north and construct the Uasin Gishu railway. In what would become typical of his style of approaching the CO, Northey requested provision of the money without any particulars on his part. He merely promised to send detailed estimates as soon as possible.[18]

At the CO, the key issue was that Northey wanted an additional £1.1 million raised, and how the Treasury would respond to this. The CO had already approached the Treasury to release funds for needed public works in East Africa. This had partly been the result of Bowring's urging the construction of the railway across the Uasin Gishu plateau to Mumias. Prior to receipt of Northey's telegram of 27 February, the CO had received replies from the Treasury indicating that only £500,000 could be issued to the EAP, Uganda, and Nyasaland under the 1914 loan during the 1919–20 financial year.[19] On receipt of Northey's telegram, therefore, Bottomley urged that it be used as a "lever" with the Treasury to press for additional expenditure. The CO thus strongly urged the Treasury, on 20 March, to allow "the extension of the borrowing powers of the protectorate by approximately £1,000,000." The extra amounts would provide for the Uasin Gishu railway and the Thika extension. The CO letter pushed the need to improve communications because the EAP was "a valuable source of raw materials which are needed for imperial purposes, in particular sisal, flax, coffee and all these depend on the provision of proper communications and adequate harbour facilities." In addition, a program of land settlement for veterans was in the offing, and it would not be successful without an improved transportation network.[20] However, the Treasury refused to consider this request until they had received from the CO a program of all development schemes in the colonial empire requiring finance from the metropolitan government.[21]

Northey was not prepared, however, to let the matter rest. In April 1919, he renewed his request for development assistance, asking for an increase of up to £3,000,000 in the amount that would go to the EAP. The money could only come from a loan if development of communications was to go forward, he emphasized, since government revenues were well under estimate. This had forced the governor to delete additional public works from the financial estimates for 1919–20.[22]

CO officials were not extremely pleased about this, but they bowed to what they saw as the pressing need to provide capital for public works in the EAP. Even before they received Northey's despatch, the governor had sent a telegram to London on 28 May asking for a reply to his request for a communications loan. He mentioned specifically the Uasin Gishu railway.[23] Upon reading Northey's despatch in June, Bottomley expressed a preference for providing expenditure on public works out of annual revenue. However, he conceded that there was so much to be done in the EAP that a new loan would have to be raised. The 1914 loan was "definitely ear-marked for improving communications and trade facilities."[24] Before a response could be made to Northey, he telegraphed again in July urging an immediate start to contract negotiations for the Uasin Gishu railway survey and the inauguration of earthworks. He began his telegram: "I presume that loan sure to be granted."[25] On 17 July, the CO responded to Northey's despatch informing him that obtaining another loan would not be easy nor would the terms of such a loan, if approved.[26]

Obtaining Treasury approval would be complicated by, among other things, the growing financial crisis that engulfed the EAP as 1919 wore on. As suggested above, revenue fell short of estimated and actual expenditure. The downturn in trade that marked this and subsequent years was an important factor, and the saddling of the EAP with a portion of the imperial war debt added to the problem. Yet another reason was the rising level of expenditure that marked the start of Northey's administration. To an extent, this was inevitable as there were vacant administrative posts to be filled, raises in salary to be funded, repairs of government buildings to be accomplished, and increased medical and educational services to be provided. In addition to these, Northey pressed for improvements in the agricultural department for the benefit, almost exclusively, of settler agriculture. He arranged, for example, for the appointment of Alexander Holm from South Africa as new director of agriculture at a considerable advance in salary over his predecessor, and he called for the appointments of eight additional specialist agricultural officers, all of whom would serve in settled areas or provide services exclusively to settler endeavors (e.g. an entomologist for coffee and a pig and dairy expert).[27]

The result of all these actions was that by early August, Northey found himself in a rather desperate position. He telegraphed to the CO the unhappy fact that because of a decline in trade, owing to a shortage of shipping, railway and customs revenue had dropped. Because of famine, epidemics, and a shortage of staff, hut tax prospects were also not good . Overall, the present moment, he concluded, was an "unsuitable" time for considering fresh sources of revenue. Since the estimates had originally been prepared, the governor went on, "considerable other expenditure has become essential." Northey regretted that in light of all this "it will be impossible to prepare a budget that would balance." He urged therefore that he might be allowed "to draw on the Treasury for up to £600,000."[28]

Officials at the CO were shocked at this seemingly cavalier demand for an unofficial grant-in-aid of such size. Parkinson felt that if the EAP really tried it could effect large reductions in expenditure since there was no chance of putting the governor's proposal before the Treasury. He went on: "The Governor does not appreciate the Treasury point of view nor yet the financial position in this country." He did not see why fresh sources of revenue could not be considered. "One obvious source," continued Parkinson, "is some kind of income tax."[29]

Permanent under-secretary Fiddes was even more astounded at the governor's request. In what was a very caustic minute, even for him, Fiddes wrote:

> This is a light hearted telegram. Sir E. Northey seems to think that the Treasury have a bottomless purse into which he can dip when he likes. The sooner he is undeceived the more likely we are to avoid very serious trouble.[30]

With the agreement of Amery and Milner, a strong telegram was sent to the EAP. The CO would not take up Northey's request with the Treasury; he was told "it will be necessary for you to cut down expenditure drastically and to discover fresh sources of revenue."[31]

The financial crisis Northey called attention to in July 1919 would remain one of the central economic realities of postwar Kenya. Revenue would continue to fall short of expenditure, necessitating cuts in the latter and the seeking of new sources of the former. In the long run, this reality would be of absolutely fundamental importance in determining CO policy in the 1919–23 period and the outcome of the struggle for Kenya. In the short run, it forced the EAP administration to examine alternatives for raising additional revenue. In doing so, Northy's government would place the additional burdens most heavily on the African population and least heavily on the European settlers. In other words, Northey's revenue policies would fall into line with most of his other initiatives: the African population should underwrite European settlement.

In pursuit of new sources of revenue, Northey turned to the report of a committee set up earlier by Bowring to make proposals for increasing EAP revenues. The committee, which reported in 1918, examined several possible sources of revenue. One was an income tax. The committee agreed that it was fair, but because its collection would need "an expensive trained staff" which the protectorate did not have, the committee felt the imposition of income tax should be delayed. It also recommended against a tax on the unearned increment of land sales. The committee also noted that the possibilities of raising customs rates were very limited by international treaty obligations (to no greater than 10 per cent ad valorem). It urged change in this regard so that customs duties could be raised steeply, especially on luxury items. With regard to African taxation, the committee held that owing to famine and the fact that the rate of tax had recently been raised to five rupees, it was "not opportune" to raise hut and poll tax. The only recommendation of the committee that had so far been implemented was setting a standard fee for all trade licenses. Northey advised waiting until the Legco had been reconstituted following the European elections before passing any new taxation measures.[32]

The seriousness of the revenue situation meant that the issue of new taxes could not be put off for long. As the EAP government considered its options, a raise in the rate of African taxation seemed to be the most promising. Thus in November 1919, the colonial state proposed a raise in the rate of hut and poll tax to rupees 7/50. In a confidential despatch, Sir Charles Bowring, acting as governor, described the existing tax rates and urged the increase as necessary.[33] The CO were concerned lest there be further increases. Read called attention to the fact that in the case of Nyasaland, Milner had decided against any increase in African taxation. Bowring was told that no increase in African taxation should be imposed in the future without the prior approval of the S of S.[34]

It would be well to diverge at this point to make clear why Bowring was again acting governor. The reason was that serious injury had forced Northey to proceed to Britain as soon as possible. Northey's injury occurred while playing polo. His right eye was so badly damaged that it had to be removed on 6 October. The governor's doctor recommended that Northey should go home, at the earliest opportunity, for further treatment. Besides obtaining better medical treatment in Britain, Northey would have the opportunity to discuss many of the crucial issues which had come up during the first eight months of his governorship with CO officials.[35] The S of S quickly approved Northey's return to Britain, and he would remain there until June 1920.[36] He stayed in close touch with the CO during his convalescence. He was at the center of most EAP issues, including the raise in African taxation.

Before receiving the CO instructions not to raise African taxation without prior approval, Bowring had taken steps to initiate an increase. In December 1919, the Execo approved the preparation of a bill that would make provision for an increase in the hut and poll tax rate, and a month later, Bowring requested authority by telegram to introduce a bill in the Legco which would increase the hut tax to 7/50 per dwelling and the poll tax to 10 rupees per individual.[37] CO officials remained cool to the idea. Parkinson spoke for most when he minuted:

> We can not consider this proposal unless absolutely convincing reasons can be given as to the necessity and satisfactory explanation as to the ability of the Natives to pay and the results which may follow politically from this large increase in Native taxation.[38]

As Fiddes agreed that the increase would "require a lot of justification," the CO decided to write Northey to ask his opinion on the issue.[39]

Northey quickly replied from his London residence that the increase was justified. He had "no doubt whatever that the natives can and will pay the higher tax without hardship to themselves and without difficulty to the government." He maintained that the majority of Africans "are rich." This would not be the last time that Sir Edward Northey would demonstrate how utterly ignorant he was of the economic and social systems of the people whom he had been placed over. All the governor understood was that pastoral peoples held land and livestock "out of all proportion to their necessary requirements. . . ." From this assessment it was but a short jump for the governor to arrive at another of his firmly held, and equally preposterous, tenets. A large portion of the able-bodied males in the reserves, he asserted, "remain idle and consequently drunken and vicious." He then revealed that his reasons for advocating the tax increase were not just to enhance revenue. The raising of taxes for members of "agricultural tribes" would have a beneficial effect on the supply of labor for settlers and "will thereby help the productivity of the country."[40] Nowhere did he mention that higher taxes might induce Africans to greater agricultural productivity. This simply did not form part of his thinking. Settler production was all that mattered to him in his calculation of the EAP's present and future prosperity.

CO officials were still hesitant to approve increased taxes, but since the governor had supported the proposition so strongly, they would have to approve it.[41] This would be a common refrain during the Northey era. If the governor strongly advocated a course of action, the CO felt it had to go along with him. Nothing illustrates the CO loss of initiative so clearly. Fiddes was "suspicious of all proposals emanating from the EAP that have as an object the driving of the native into the labour market." He therefore advised Amery, now acting as S of S, that he should only be prepared to approve it on the understanding that measures were in contemplation to impose a corresponding increase in non-African taxes.[42] As a result of Fiddes' stand, the CO sent a telegram to Bowring informing him that before the S of S could make a decision on the proposed tax increase, he would need to know how it compared with additional taxes contemplated for Europeans and Asians in the EAP.[43]

When Bowring received this telegram, he initially decided to exclude both increased African and non-African taxation from the 1920–21 budget. Facing a potential deficit of £350,000, however, he could not do so and prepare a budget that balanced. The government had been forced to undertake additional expenditure (he mentioned the soldier settlment scheme here), and it became clear to Bowring that he would have to bring forward proposals for major increases in revenue. Thus the EAP government focused attention on a revision of customs duties, increased railway rates, a stock tax on both African and European pastoralists, increased hut and poll tax, and "non-native" taxes on land and income. Bowring quickly ruled out any possibility of raising customs duties, and raising rail rates was opposed by the Uganda government and commercial interests. A stock tax bill was proposed but dropped because of difficulties of assessment and collection.[44]

This left the African hut and poll tax and the European and Asian land and income taxes to be seriously taken up. In his late April budget despatch, Bowring strongly maintained that African taxation would only be increased on the understanding that specific sums of money would be set aside for African education, "technical and agricultural training, and medical improvements." In considering the land and income taxes, Bowring reported his conclusion that the two, to be effective, would have to be introduced at the same time. Because of difficulty in "arranging that data could be made available on which income tax could be assessed and collected within a year of the effective date of the taxation," Bowring decided to increase African tax at once while postponing until the next year the imposition of taxation on non-Africans. Bowring also touched on another reason for holding back the income and land tax measures. Any attempt to consider them in Legco "on the eve of the adoption of elective representation would have been bitterly resented."[45]

Therefore, Bowring's government pressed ahead with the hut and poll tax increase in May. Introducing the measure, the CNC, Ainsworth, stated that the increases were justified by financial necessity, but he emphasized the fact that a portion of the money raised would be spent on improvements in the reserves. The measure called for a hut tax of 7/50 and a poll tax of ten rupees. Against the wishes of Ainsworth, however, the bill was amended by Legco; at the instigation of Lord Delamere and other unofficial members, the maximum rate for both taxes was raised to ten rupees. For the settlers, the primary consideration was not revenue but labor; a higher tax would, they anticipated, bring more Africans out to work for them.[46] The CO accepted this increased rate, as Northey and Ainsworth had stated that Africans could afford to pay it, and hut and poll taxes were increased for the 1920–21 financial year. For most of the EAP, however, the maximum rate for both was eight rupees.[47]

The CO accepted, with little difficulty, a dramatic increase in African taxation. The pressing financial necessity was one powerful factor. The strong arguments in favor of the increase by the EAP officials was a second. Ainsworth's advocacy was particularly influential. When the Alliance of Missionary Societies in the EAP, an organization representing the main protestant missions, protested against the increase in May as being too heavy and not likely to provide much benefit to the African population, CO officials were able to console themselves that the missionary complaints were unfounded as a result of lengthy memoranda by Ainsworth.[48] As soon as he was aware of the missionary complaints, Bowring had forwarded these to London. One dealt with the rates and the need to provide services for the taxpayers, and the second dealt in detail, and some hostility, with the points raised by the alliance.[49]

Africans paid higher taxes in 1920–21. European settlers and Indians did not. The income tax ordinance passed its third reading in July. It was not intended to come into operation until the following year.[50] The bill had encountered strong opposition from some settlers in the Legco, moreover, and this together with opposition from the East African section of the London Chamber of Commerce suggested that the ordinance would continue to prove very controversial.[51] When the ordinance was scrutinized at the CO, many doubts and criticisms were raised there as well.[52] These all pointed to future problems with the income tax ordinance, and indeed the colonial state and the CO had not heard the last of the income tax issue.

The land tax bill did not progress even as far as the income tax ordinance. As it was being considered in Legco, it was altered from a tax on land to a tax on undeveloped land. This fact became clear when the governor sent copies of the ordinance, as actually passed by the Legco, in September. As Northey remarked, "it is now by the exemptions granted to beneficially occupied land become in effect a law penalizing non-development and has lost much of its revenue producing character."[53] The governor still backed the bill as a useful piece of legislation for spurring development of idle land or the transfer of land to more enterprising owners, but a new bill would have to be introduced to tax land values.

The CO found much in the bill that was objectionable. Thus the CO telegraphed its opposition to the ordinance in November. The machinery required to collect the tax would entail greater expenditure than the revenue to be obtained. In the CO's view, the bill would not penalize the speculator but would hit the small man. The present, with high costs of production, labor scarcity, and weak markets, was not the time for such a measure.[54] As a result of the CO intervention, the ordinance was scrapped. The settlers had won yet another round in their postwar battle to avoid direct taxation. Michael Redley argues, however, that it was really a victory for the "large men" among the settlers (like Delamere and Grogan) rather than the "small men" among them who had favored the measure. Thus the CO "saved" the large men and left the field clear for continued land speculation.[55] Whatever the outcome implied, Africans had in reality been made to shoulder the greatest burdens in meeting the severe financial crisis. That would be a consistent characteristic of Northey's governorship.

The Soldier Settlement Scheme

Another issue that occupied Governor Northey's attention immediately after his arrival in the EAP on the last day of January was the scheme to settle ex-soldiers in the protectorate. This had been discussed in London, but the report of the Land Settlement Commission, appointed by Belfield, had yet to arrive at the CO. Bowring telegraphed a summary of the results to London at the end of December 1918, but Northey had no time to consider this in light of his imminent departure for East Africa. As 1919 dawned, the CO too was anxious to obtain further details of the commission's recommendations. Having received nothing by mid-February, it telegraphed an inquiry and requested the governor's "considered views" as soon as possible.[56] Four days later, Northey replied that while the report was ready, the evidence was still in press. He would send it as soon as possible.[57] The CO desire for more information remained strong, however. Numerous enquiries were being made about a possible settlement scheme in East Africa, and the officials at the CO were able to give no specific information.[58]

This started a series of telegraphic exchanges that formed the main means of communication between London and Nairobi relating to the issue. Of the entire postwar period, this would be the best example of the "government by telegraph" that characterized Northey's administration. Little information and few crucial decisions would be based on despatches. This is an important point to note since the soldier settlement scheme set a precedent for Northey's pattern of action on other subjects. In this case, and in others, he seized the initiative and drove the CO along with him at great speed. In this way, he would literally force the CO to leave the matter to him. By pressing to move ever faster in setting up the scheme for providing land for European veterans, Northey took not only the initiative, but also the final decisions, out of the hands of the CO. Nor did he place the issue before the EAP Legco. This would be an example of an authoritarian governor forcing the implementation of a substantial settlement scheme in what appears, in retrospect, to be breakneck speed.

Northey's first real comment on the subject and the Land Settlement Committee's report came in a telegram of 22 February. He told London that as he had just received the commission's report, he could not give his final opinion yet. He did maintain that the question rested on two factors: "A. settlers being right type. B. Native labour which at present is not available sufficient numbers to justify rapid introduction of numbers of settlers." Emphasizing that he had not yet had sufficient time to formulate proposals, Northey concluded with a comment that would be very descriptive of his method of operation hereafter. "Feel sure you wish me to go ahead with the details without reference to you."[59]

The receipt of this telegram proved no help to the CO. Under pressure to answer questions from prospective settlers and other interested parties, the CO decided to put its own proposals to Northey as a way of moving the issue forward. The CO sent a telegram to Nairobi on 5 March in which it laid down what it considered to be the most important points for consideration in any scheme for the settlement of veterans. Since selection of candidates would have to be carried out in both London and Nairobi, the CO proposed issuing a public notice as soon as possible setting out the terms. In this regard, the CO asked to know what land would be available; it needed to be identified at once so as to let those interested know and to release the rest for sale by auction. Northey was asked specifically if he would agree to a special scheme for disabled officers "working under cooperative schemes," and he was told to inform the CO how many soldier settlers could be accommodated, that year, the next year, and in subsequent years. The CO was also very interested to learn the size of farms that could be made available.[60] It is significant to note that the war council had recommended farms of 320 acres for agricultural and 1000 for pastoral farming. Belfield's 1916 committee had called for farms of 160 and 240 acres only. The Land Settlement Commission called for much larger farms. Most would range from 320 to 1000 acres although some might be as small as 100 acres.

Nine days after the sending of its 5 March telegraph, the CO got Northey's answer, and it was definitely more than officials there had bargained for. Northey set out a complete scheme by telegram. The governor agreed that a selection board should sit in London, but he felt that allotment could only be made on the arrival of the individual in the EAP. He was not satisfied that the £500 set as minimum by the Land Settlement Commission constituted sufficient capital. Only "exceptional men," especially those with a trade, might get by on so little. Northey recommended that "the man who wishes to settle independently on land should have capital of at least £1000, should be carefully selected of a good class, . . . prepared to work hard and live simply. . . ." The intending settler should be warned that there was at first likely to be a scarcity of labor, agricultural implements, and oxen.[61]

Northey then turned to the question of land purchase, and he emphatically disagreed with the commission that land "should be alienated to ex-soldiers free from upset price." That recommendation, stated the governor, "practically amounts to giving away our only natural asset."Northey proposed an alternative scheme for alienation by establishing two classes. Class A would be for settlers with less than £1000 "who are prepared to work for a wage the first year or two . . . while saving money and gradually developing their own farms." Class B would be for men with a capital of £1000 or more "to whom I would allot farms at a fair valuation on easy payment of upset price." Despite charging charging a higher fee than the commission had anticipated, Northey held that he could sell two million acres within the next two years. As to the method of sale, he rejected auction and wished to put a "rough valuation" on all land well within the present market price.[62]

Northey then moved on to the selection process, stating that he was ready even then to allocate farms. The first men could be selected by 1 July. While Northey had seemed to the CO slow to respond on the scheme in February, he was not hesitant to push for rapid implementation of his plan. He wished to race ahead, he told London, even though a detailed agricultural survey had not yet been made. He urged being allowed to borrow money for railways and roads so that all parts of the country could be linked by the time the farms came into full production. Northey pressed to be allowed to start selection immediately as he could take half the maximum number he set for Class A (500) and half for Class B (800) in 1920.[63]

Northey had dramatically seized the initiative on the settlement scheme. The CO was taken aback, but on the whole officials there were willing to step aside and let the governor run with it. Bottomley observed that "the Governor has completely altered the basis of the scheme suggested by the commission." Land would not be leased free of premium but should be paid for according to a fixed valuation. This deviation was substantial, Bottomley noted, but he urged approval of Northey's proposal because the sum to be realized for the initial lease price, which he estimated might come to £400,000, would be "an important matter" for the EAP already in serious financial straits.[64]

Bottomley went on to reflect on other potential difficulties with Northey's revised proposal. Class A settlers would find it very hard; they would have to have some previous knowledge of agriculture. Northey's rather easygoing call for a loan for improved communications got little sympathy from the head of the EAD. "We are having the greatest difficulty," he noted, "in getting any money at all for extension of our borrowing." The fact that the governor wanted to start on 1 July meant that applicants in Britain would not be able to have any part in the early allotments. On the whole, Bottomley's minute revealed a lack of great enthusiasm for the scheme that had characterized the response of the permanent officials since 1916.[65]

When the governor's scheme was referred to Amery, he sought a compromise on the issue of purchase price. He thought there was "considerable justification that in the interest of E. Africa" there should be a purchase price, but on the other hand "we do want to give something in the nature of a reward to the ex-soldier." Amery urged impressing on Northey that he should "fix the price substantially below the value."[66]

This was one point emphasized in the CO telegram to the governor. The other indicated CO agreement with Northey's proposals as to allotment, but

London asked that allocations to local applicants be limited so as to save land for applicants in Britain.[67]

Before he had received the CO telegram, Northey had raced ahead, still further refining his proposals for rapid implementation. In a telegram of 25 March, the governor recommended three prominent EAP Europeans to serve on the London selection board (one of whom was Grogan). Once again showing his preference for "large" wealthy men, Northey expressed a willingness to arrange large blocks for syndicates. He warned anew of the labor shortage, but proclaimed his readiness to allot up to 288 Class B farms on 1 July. He would also seek to avoid delay by allowing local representatives to select farms for applicants chosen in England. As he did not wish delay to cause men with capital to look elsewhere, Northey proposed closing the application period on 14 June.[68]

Northey wired further "details" of the soldier settlement scheme to London on 6 April. He preferred a lengthy telegram to a despatch as he wished to rush the process forward as quickly as possible. In fact, this rendering of the scheme provided some slight changes from that sent to the CO earlier. The land would be divided into A farms, less than 160 acres and B farms, more than 160 acres. There would be a selection board in Nairobi to divide the applicants for Class A farms, which would be free grants, and Class B farms which would be purchased. This recommendation suggests that Northey had been influenced by the CO telegram of 29 March which called for a lowering of purchase price and the provision of land as a reward for war service. The governor's new proposal seemed to incorporate that idea. Class A applicants could thus be men "with small capital" but would have to satisfy the selection board that they could meet development conditions. Class B applicants should have capital of at least £1,000.[69]

The governor also set out qualifications for acceptance in the scheme. They must be British subjects, "purely European extraction engaged in active service present war" in the armed forces of the United Kingdom, British colonies, or self-governing dominions. There were at present 250 Class A farms and 800 Class B farms available, the governor continued. The potential applicants would then go before the board to be selected for a place in the lottery. Allotment would be made on 1 July.[70]

Northey then went into great detail as to the conditions of issue of title, the prerequisites of the Class A and Class B leases as to payment and residence requirements and transfer regulations. These were particularly welcome as they provided the basis for a CO press release prepared to provide full information on the soldier settlement scheme.[71] In a separate telegram of the same date, Northey sent details of individuals in the EAP who had been selected to act as representatives for applicants in Britain.[72]

The CO found these telegrams acceptable in the detail they provided on the schemes. Officials were ready to move forward even if not as rapidly as Northey desired. After reading a wire sent by the governor on the 14th, officials were satisfied that the arrangement was, in Bottomley's words, "as good as can be desired."[73]

The scheme set forth by telegraph in April would, with but a few exceptions, be that actually utilized for the soldier settler scheme. In a large part, the CO accepted what the governor had laid down. Government by telegram had indeed worked for Northey. The main problem that now remained was the speed with which the allotments could be put into effect. In a telegram of 4 May, Northey asked that Milner "will instruct Home selection board to hustle. We are hustling here to get things done. . . ."[74] Despite Northey's urging, the London selection board only met for the first time on 25 June and did not complete its work until 16 August.[75] An important change did emerge when the protectorate government raised Class A farms to not exceeding 300 acres (rather than 160) and Class B to more than 300 acres. The CO accepted the change.[76]

The implementation of the soldier settlement scheme, therefore, certainly is a clear example of the CO loss of initiative that marked the immediate postwar period. Northey planned and implemented the scheme with little input from the CO. This was a result not only of a loss of control over the direction of policy in the EAP, but it was also due, in this particular episode, to the fact that permanent officials at the CO had never been particularly enthusiastic for the scheme. They went along without eagerness. The political leadership of the CO, Amery in this instance, was, on the other hand, quite ardent for the scheme and prepared to accept practically anything the governor proposed in order that an empire settlement initiative might be implemented. He did, it must be recognized, initiate the only CO change of substance in the system; at Amery's insistence the land was provided on extremely easy terms to the ex-soldiers.[77] As for the permanent officials, their lukewarm attitude was soon reinforced by the lack of success the scheme experienced.

By the end of 1919, even Northey had changed his mind and decided that land settlement must be halted. Consulted while in Britain recuperating from surgery, Northey advised that no further allotments be made under the scheme in 1920. In Parkinson's view, the governor's decision resulted from the fact that he was "nervous as to the labour situation." Bottomley went further: "He is more than nervous about labour—he says definitely that there is not enough for the people who have already got land."[78] Sir George Fiddes saw clearly what this meant to the CO, and he pointedly advised Amery to accept the governor's decision. He wrote: "The decision lends itself to criticism, but I don't think that we should override the Governor under penalty, if we do so, of having the criticism transferred to us later."[79] The CO had followed Northey's lead previously, Fiddes was, in effect, saying, and now that it appeared likely the scheme would be less than a smashing success, the CO could only continue to follow. Nevertheless, the CO could at least blame him for any failure.

Events in 1920 pointed to the wisdom of this stance as the Kenya government was forced to take extreme steps to try to salvage the soldier settlement scheme. The depression, currency problems, and shortage of labor, among other factors, combined to provide huge difficulties for the new settlers. In March, for example, Northey felt forced by complaints from the soldier settlers to postpone payment of rents, purchase prices, and other fees in respect of the new farms.[80] Six months later, the financial conditions of most of these settlers had worsened to such a degree that Northey approved the reduction in purchase price for Class B farms by 33⅓ per cent. He also urged that settlers be allowed to mortgage their farms prior to the fulfillment of occupation conditions.[81]

Not only did the soldier settler scheme run into economic difficulties. By the end of 1920, the CO had cause to realize that the scheme had opened the colonial state and the CO to potential humanitarian criticism in Britain on the question of African land. The CO had warned Northey in 1919 that land was not to be taken from African reserves for any soldier settler farms even though the Land Settlement Commission had recommended taking a portion of the Kikuyu reserve. Bowring had advised against the recommendation, and when Northey was informed of humanitarian concern, the governor responded in July in unequivocal terms. "There has never been any intention on the part of this Government to take away any portion of the Kikuyu or other native reserves for alienation in connection with European or ex-soldier settlement," thundered Northey.[82] By the end of 1920, nevertheless, the governor was seeking to justify to the CO the excision of an area of approximately 100 square miles from the Nandi reserve.[83] While CO officials would, after further detail from the governor, proclaim themselves satisfied with the reasons for his actions, this episode pointed to another of the liabilities of the soldier settlement scheme as far as the CO was concerned. It was a liability the officials themselves had invited by their passing the initiative to the governor on this matter.[84]

Labor Shortage and the Colonial State's Response

As suggested above, labor shortage was also an issue demanding immediate attention from Governor Northey. It had an impact on the soldier settlement scheme without question. The labor question would, in fact, loom as a truly significant issue in Northey's governorship. In many ways, his handling of the labor issue was similar to that of the settlement question. Northey made decisions, without consulting London, that were extremely favorable to the settlers, and he singlemindedly set out to carry them through. In this instance, however, the negative repercussions, for Northey and the CO, would be far greater and more far reaching.

The causes of the shortage of African labor that characterized most of 1919 and 1920 have already been alluded to. The experience of the war, forced recruitment, famine, and disease all helped produce a drop in the number of African men wishing to work away from their homes for wages. At the same time, this period was marked by a large increase in the demand for African labor. The requirements of government increased, as did those of the settlers, as the result of the soldier settlement scheme and the desire of most settlers to take advantage of what they perceived to be the favorable opportunities for expansion of production. They viewed the shortage of labor as an acute obstacle in the way of such expansion. They would thus clamor for government assistance in labor recruitment. This reflected the fundamental weakness of settler agriculture. As Berman noted:

> The Kenya settlers could not have operated within, or indeed have survived, a market in which demand for 'free' labour exercised an upward pressure on real wages. They had to rely on extra-economic coercion to produce forms of semi-servile labour extracted from the peasant sphere at a price below its cost of reproduction.[85]

The experience of the war had demonstrated that forced recruitment could be effective, and many settlers felt that the techniques which had proved effective in war time should be used in peacetime as well. The postwar conditions simply increased the settler determination "to reconstruct their economy around a cheap, steady African labor supply."[86]

However, the colonial state's first concern was with labor for essential government services (e.g. porters for administrators and men for road work). The shortage of labor for government work became so severe by the second half of 1918 that the state decided that compulsory recruitment by chiefs and headmen, used during and prior to the war for works in the reserves, would have to be relied upon. Bowring believed, however, that such a system should be regularized through legislation. In early August, the Execo recommended that a bill be drafted "to provide for compulsory recruitment of labour for urgent Government works" as a matter of urgency.[87] It was decided to make an amendment to the Native Authority Ordinance for the purpose. Administrative officials, including chiefs and headmen, would be given power to compulsorily recruit labor "for government works of urgency." Bowring telegraphed London in October requesting approval of the measure.[88]

The acting governor was surprised when a rapid telegraphic reply from the CO expressed shock at the suggestion of forced labor having been used in the past and now being formally proposed. The CO, holding to its prewar stand on forced labor, refused to approve the measure and called for the "fullest explanation."[89]

Bowring again placed the issue before his Execo, and it recommended another telegram to London. The council urged that the S of S be told that for many years African headmen had "employed compulsory methods in procuring labour required by the government." This should be recognized and regularized, the council felt, so as to provide safeguards for the labor so recruited. Bowring once again telegraphed to the CO for approval of the measure. He stated his firm conviction "that the principle of compulsory labour for state projects should be openly recognized (for without such labour we are unable to carry on)", and the regularization by means of the proposed legislation constituted the most effective way of accomplishing this.[90]

This renewed request found CO officials still unwilling to accept that compulsory labor should be legislated in the EAP. The CO telegraphed its reply on 22 November, expressing its disapproval. The S of S stated:

> I am unable to agree to your proposal for regularizing the compulsory recruitment of native labour for government works. The new governor will be instructed to enquire on his arrival into the matter and put forward his views as to future policy; compulsory labour must however cease for the present.[91]

As a result of this rebuff, Bowring had a circular issued to all administrators on 13 January 1919 calling attention to the S of S's decision. All previous circulars and instructions for procuring labor for government were cancelled. Hereafter, the administrator or head of department requiring labor for the government would have to make "his own arrangements to procure it." District commissioners could only publicize government labor needs; they could take no active part in recruitment.[92]

That was the position as regards government recruitment of labor on Sir Edward Northey's arrival. He found administrators most dissatisfied with the situation. The result was that provincial commissioners were unable to procure sufficient labor for essential works. Northey thus quickly took up the matter again in a private and personal telegram to Milner. He started with the premise "that no Parliament will ever recognize legislation of any kind for what can be termed forced labour." He also maintained that responsibility for the type of action taken previously to compulsorily recruit labor for government works could not "be borne by subordinate officials and I am accepting responsibility myself by instructing provincial and district commissioners to carry on as before." Forced recruitment of this type would be a temporary measure, Northey maintained; therefore he was not asking for CO sanction but merely reporting his action.[93]

CO officials quickly realized that Northey had stolen the initiative from them on the issue of government labor. Bottomley minuted: "The telegram is sent 'p & p' as I suppose so that the S of S may be officially ignorant of the Gov.'s action and disown it when (it may be hoped) it has served its purpose." As things stood, Bottomley concluded, "I think we must adopt the position Sir Edward Northey has chosen for us and leave the question to be raised in Parl. or elsewhere as it will be."[94] Fiddes decided to take no action until Milner himself could consider the issue. The S of S's absence in Paris, however, meant that it was not laid before him until mid-June. At that time,

Fiddes recommended that no action be taken.[95] No reply of any sort was sent in response to Northey's 21 February telegram.

This was a particularly significant action. By it the CO, in effect, allowed the governor to go ahead and institute forced labor for government works for what they hoped would be a temporary period. While legislation to accomplish this end could not be countenanced, it would be acceptable if carried out by executive orders. This position had the further advantage of allowing the CO to make Northey the scapegoat if the action raised criticism in Britain. For Northey, the fact that the CO made no reply to his telegram was obviously very meaningful. The governor assumed that his policy was acceptable in London, and had already gone ahead to implement it. He would make no further reference to the CO.

Northey had a circular issued over the name of the CNC, Ainsworth, on 24 February. In somewhat circumspect language, the circular dealt with the question of labor shortage. Northey assumed that administrative officials wished to go back to the old system by which they had merely ordered chiefs to produce men for government jobs. The S of S vetoed legislation to regularize this, but the circular, in somewhat ambiguous language, suggested that if officials could not get sufficient labor to carry on "the ordinary services" in their districts:

> the position where necessary would be satisfied by means of the personal influence of the particular officer concerned. Under these circumstances the efficient conduct of the local administration is a matter that the local natives must assist in and officers, as far as necessary, will be justified in using reasonable pressure as before in this connection.[96]

The circular concluded with a statement that the governor himself would take responsibility for any necessary action taken by the district administration.

This "temporary" solution was not altogether satisfactory as difficulties with labor for government work continued to manifest themselves. Thus in August Northey telegraphed a request to be allowed to enact legislation, similar to that passed in Uganda, for compulsory paid labor for government work subject to certain limitations. He justified this request by claiming that "without such legislation many natives remain idle and deteriorate through lack of regular work and important government work can not be carried out for lack of labour."[97] The CO replied that it was willing to consider a draft ordinance on the lines of the Uganda act.[98]

Northey sent a draft of the bill to the CO at the end of September. The only variance with the Uganda ordinance was in the time periods set for compulsory labor. The EAP bill called for work for periods of ninety days with a maximum total of six months where the Uganda act provided for sixty days and three months. The EAP bill allowed for exemption if a man had been employed during the preceding twelve months for a period of three months.[99]

While the governor took this approach to the problem of obtaining adequate labor for government needs, the demand for workers from European settlers grew in intensity as 1919 wore on. Northey became increasingly concerned, especially in light of his push to carry out the soldier settlement scheme. One step that he took was the implementation of the registration system. The CO had approved such a system in 1915, but it had been deferred for the duration of the war. In November 1918, a motion was overwhelmingly passed in the Legco supporting the introduction of an identification and pass system as soon as possible. In framing his first budget, Northey included a sum of slightly more than £5,600 to get the system started.[100] It was left to CNC Ainsworth to develop and implement a system of fingerprinting, record-keeping, and the issuing of registration certificates to all African males. The system finally began in a small way in November 1919, but registration and issuance of certificates, better known by the Swahili word *kipande*, did not really begin to effect large numbers until 1920. This was a measure that the settlers had long demanded as a means to better control labor, and Northey viewed it as a contribution to meeting the labor shortage.[101]

The governor also acted to meet settler complaints of labor shortage in a more direct way. By October, he had decided to take decisive action. As discussed earlier in the chapter, he was convinced that Africans had to be made to work for the settlers. As he put it in his comments on the report of the EAP Economic Commission in October, "native labour is required for the proper development of the country." Beyond that, moreover, "the native must be educated to come out of the reserves to work for his own sake for nothing can be worse for the young native than to remain, according to his inclination, idle in the reserve."[102] As with government labor, Northey had a circular to administrative officers issued by the CNC, but this time he did not inform the CO in advance.

Dated 23 October, the "Ainsworth" or "Northey" circular laid down government policy with regard to recruitment of African labor for private employers. From the first, the circular made clear Northey's desire that increasing supplies of labor would result from an "insistent advocacy" of the government's wishes that Africans should leave the reserves to work. To obtain an increased supply of workers for settlers, Northey laid it down that all government officers in charge of African areas "must exercise every possible lawful influence to induce able bodied male natives to go into the labour field." Women and children should be encouraged to go out to work on settler farms if they were close to the reserve. Northey wished it to be understood that African chiefs and elders should at all times render "all lawful assistance" in labor recruitment. Northey's circular had the effect of placing the EAP government in the business of recruitment of labor for settler farms and estates.[103]

Northey deviated in another important respect from his actions with regard to the February circular, however. This time the circular was published in the

Nairobi press. Northey undoubtedly did this to try to quiet the clamor from the settlers and their supporters for assistance in a period of acute labor shortage. This clamor had reached a peak in September and October 1919. By publication, Northey could demonstrate that his government was now prepared to do something for the settlers and at the same time solidify his own standing and popularity with them. Yet the publication of the circular soon called forth criticism of this aspect of labor policy from protestant missionaries in East Africa, and it would lead to controversy in Great Britain which would force the CO to become involved.

Shortly after publication of Northey's circular, CMS bishops Willis of Uganda and Heywood of Mombasa together with the Church of Scotland leader J. W. Arthur met with Bowring and Ainsworth. The missionaries read the two officials a draft memorandum of protest against the circular, and they forwarded a copy to Northey who was indisposed as a result of the injury to his eye.[104] While Bowring and Ainsworth expressed agreement with the missionary concerns over the circular, Northey was adamant in emphasizing the need for the circular.[105]

The missionaries then submitted a formal protest to the EAP government which upon publication on 15 November became known as the Bishops Memorandum. The missionaries were in agreement with much of the circular; they claimed a strong desire to see the African come out to work for wages. They particularly objected, however, to recruitment by chiefs as most Africans, in their view, would not distinguish between government encouragement and government orders. The circular thus held great potential, the memorandum maintained, for African discontent and unrest.[106]

The CO and Northey's Labor Circular

With the publication of the missionary protest, humanitarian and other groups in Britain became aware of the circular, and the focus of protest and concern rapidly turned to the metropole. In these circumstances, the CO was put in the rather embarrassing position of trying to answer questions concerning, and defend, a policy it knew nothing about.

The first indication the CO had about the October circular came in a letter from the London correspondent of the *EAS*. He wrote to Amery in early January 1920 to ask what the CO were going to do about the "considerable controversy" in the EAP "on the new regulations for obtaining labour."[107] Not having received any copy of the circular, the CO could only reply with a description of the proposed Native Authority Amendment Ordinance which provided for compulsory government labor.[108] The same day that a reply was sent to the journalist, the CO received a letter from the ASAPS requesting a copy of a labor circular issued in West Africa "on October 27 last by Colonel Ainsworth." The CO could only reply that it did not have a copy.[109]

Undeterred by the lack of response from the CO, the *EAS* correspondent wrote to Northey in London on 20 February to inform him that "an attack is being organized in the House of Commons" on the governor's labor policy. It was being planned, he intimated, by the ASAPS.[110] Northey sent the information to the CO. Buxton wrote to Amery on 5 March to directly criticize the October circular that the society had now obtained and analyzed. It found the circular and EAP labor policy very objectionable, and the society did not mince words in stating its objections.

> It is the avowed object of both these communications to bring pressure to bear upon the administrative officials, and native chiefs, to augment the supply of labour for private settlers. We beg leave to remind His Majesty's Government that declarations are on record by former Secretaries of State, both of the Colonial and Foreign Offices, that labour secured by force for private profit amounts to slavery.[111]

The society noted that while the word force did not appear in the document, the governor's statement that the African "must be brought out to work" and that "power should be provided by legislation to prevent idleness" approximated "very closely to the principle of compulsory labour."[112]

This would be the first salvo in an extended campaign against the circular by the ASAPS, its members, and sympathizers. Questions would be raised in parliament between February and July, and criticisms of the Kenya labor policy were voiced in the debate on the CO vote in April. Critics felt that Northey's policy was the equivalent of forced labor or slavery, and they voiced worries that Northey's policy would have a negative effect on African production.[113] This would be one of the most important issues around which the struggle for Kenya revolved.

The initial response of CO officials was to discount the critics and to give the governor every opportunity to justify and support his policy. Parkinson remarked after reading Buxton's letter: "A letter of this kind was to be expected from the Society. Obviously the best course would be for Sir E. Northey to meet the Society and tell them exactly what is being done . . . and it would probably do a great deal of good to clear the air."[114] Read sent a copy of the protest letter to Northey and asked him to "take an early opportunity to discuss their letter at this office." He also asked if the governor would be willing to meet with the society.[115]

Northey responded on 26 March. He expressed his willingness to meet representatives of the society as he welcomed the chance to explain "exactly what the policy of the protectorate government is." Northey then went on at great length to dispute the points raised by the society. Strongly maintaining that there was no force involved in his policy, Northey then gave a ringing enunciation of the racist mythology that formed the major justification for his labor policy.

> The whole matter is one of imperial policy. The imperial government has encouraged white settlement and the production of raw materials East Africa can provide; the white settlement is wrong and the idea of increased production is futile unless we

are to do all in our power to bring the Native to the labour market and teach him to work; his work under good European supervision, and with proper training, is many times more productive than it is when left to his own methods, and he improves, physically and mentally, very quickly with regular work and healthy exercise; left to his own resources he does little work, he makes his women and children do it for him; very little effort in turning up the rich soil provides him with food; left alone the majority of adult men in the native reserves live a miserable life of idleness, drunkenness and vice; encouraged and taught to work, he soon sees the advantage of earning money, lives better, becomes more intelligent, and dresses himself more decently.[116]

For the good of the empire, the protectorate, and the African "whom we protect," he went on, "I am convinced we must do all that is justly and legally possible to encourage and induce the idle native to come out to work."

The governor claimed that when he took over the EAP it had "no declared native policy." Now it did; for after study and consultation with Ainsworth, he had "propounded a policy, the publication of which has met with universal acclamation from civil servants and settlers alike, and except in one respect the approval of leading missionaries." Only later would the CO come to realize that this was a gross exaggeration. Northey concluded stridently:

So far from advocating a method by which natives are to be forced to work for unpopular employers in a state of semi-slavery, I intend to induce the native, for his own advancement, to work for a fair wage where he likes, instead of idling.

As the governor had now strongly stated his case, the CO was in a position to respond to humanitarian criticism. Some three weeks later, Bottomley prepared a lengthy memo for his superiors, summarizing the situation with regard to the Northey labor circular. He had finally obtained a copy from Northey even though the CO had still not received one officially from the EAP, and he also had a copy of the so called Bishops Memorandum.[117] Bottomley summarized the position of the governor, the missionaries, and "the agitation on this side." He felt that the humanitarian critics gave the issue a "hard name" (i.e., used the label forced labor when such a term was not warranted) and then condemned it. The government policy was "to stimulate industrious habits on the part of the native", and it had to "take some active form." Bottomley concluded that the circular did not amount to forced labor; in fact there was little new in it. He defended the inclusion of women and children in the circular since their work was of the lightest possible description, and there was "no reason to suppose it will be abused." The real effect of the Northey circular, Bottomley maintained, "is to stimulate the other administrative officers who have taken no interest in this matter" and whose apathy had affected the chiefs and headmen.[118] This last point would also be emphasized by Northey, but it was, in fact, little more than a ploy by the officials to try to give the circular a purpose that was never intended.

While the governor and the CO had seemingly taken up strong positions in defense of Northey's policy, the CO was nevertheless inundated with protests over the next several months. In addition to questions in parliament, letters and protest resolutions were received. These came from the Labour party, the China Inland Mission, the Baptist Missionary Society, the Primitive Methodist Missionary Society, the London Missionary Society, and the Conference of Missionary Societies in Great Britain and Ireland.[119] The latter letter of protest was significant since it marked the official entry into the controversy of J. H. Oldham, secretary to the conference. He played an important part in stirring up and coordinating the protest in Britain, and he would play an increasingly central role in that protest movement as time passed.[120] In addition to condemning "forced labour" for private employers and the encouragement of women and children to work for wages, the conference, like several other protesting bodies, was "gravely disquieted" by the statement in the circular suggesting that endeavours would be made to obtain labor from Tanganyika.

Shortly before the matter was to be raised again in parliament, Northey met with representatives of the ASAPS in an attempt to cool the controversy. The governor was able to do little to change their minds. "Not one of these gentlemen knew anything about the East African native first hand and they were therefore unable to grasp the situation or sympathize with me," Northey reported to Bottomley after the meeting. They had never heard of the protectorate's Masters and Servants Ordinance and had no idea of its provisions for the protection of the African employee. Northey promised to come and discuss the issue at the CO before Amery spoke in the House of Commons on the CO estimates.[121]

Northey's meeting at the CO prior to the Commons debate on the CO vote helped Amery prepare his response to critics. It was agreed that Amery "should, if he found it necessary, say that the Governor would have no objection to issuing a new circular which would remove any ambiguity as to any intention of compulsion in the matter."[122] Amery did, in fact, promise that a new circular would be issued when responding to the debate in the House of Commons.[123]

The new circular was hammered out after discussion between Milner and Northey in May. On 3 May, Northey had forwarded to the CO a revised circular.[124] After studying the draft, Milner was still not satisfied with the new circular. He therefore wrote Northey to express his uneasiness. The new circular did not, in the S of S's opinion, "quite meet the case." Milner continued:

> The feeling in the House is pretty strong on the subject, and I should like to have something which, quoted in parliament, would completely satisfy all reasonable people if the question is raised again, as it probably will be. Moreover, I feel some real doubt whether there is not more danger of abuse of the powers of the chiefs than you think.[125]

The S of S wanted particularly to assuage any potential missionary unease. "I always rather discount the missionary view in such matters," he told Northey, but he felt the government must be extra careful to guard against the evils the missionaries felt might be the result of the EAP policy. Milner showed a far keener appreciation of the importance of missionary opinion in East Africa on the protest in Britain and the need to moderate that protest by rewording the new circular.[126]

Milner then turned to the points he wished to see included in the revised circular. First, women and children were not to be employed away from their homes.[127] Secondly, care had to be taken that chiefs did not make calls for labor "an occasion for favouritism or oppression, and in particular that they do not attempt to put pressure upon men whose labour is wanted for cultivation of their own land." This principle had been conspicuously absent from the original Northey circular. Third, government officials must exercise vigilance to see that the provisions of the Masters and Servants Ordinance as amended in 1919 were fully observed. Milner had had the new circular drafted, including these points, and he sent it to Northey for comment.[128]

The governor replied immediately, accepting all the proposed circular with one exception. His only objection had to do with the reference to women and children working away from home. Northey proposed softening the statement so as not to impede the flow of such labor to coffee estates.[129] This was accepted by the S of S, and the circular would read, when eventually published, as amended by Northey.[130]

It was later decided that the new circular, to be titled Native Labour Required for Non-Native Farms and Other Private Undertakings, should be issued by the governor on his return to the EAP. It consisted of five paragraphs purporting to prevent misconception.[131] CO officials also decided to publish the circulars and other documents relating to EAP labor issues. Fiddes laid great stress on publication of the original and revised circulars together, and Milner endorsed this view.[132] The papers were published, after Northey's issue of the new circular, on 14 July.[133]

CO promises to issue a revised circular did not quiet the British critics of EAP labor policy. The ASAPS returned to the attack on 17 June. It welcomed the new circular, but the society's lengthy letter again criticized the "advice" to be given to chiefs to send young men out to work for private enterprise. While reluctantly accepting compulsory labor for government works in Africa, the society expressed disquiet at the lengthy maximum periods provided for in the Kenya legislation.[134]

Nor did the issue of the new circular by Northey assuage the society's concerns. The ASAPS continued to feel apprehension regarding "the great stress laid by the Governor upon getting the natives to come out of their reserves and work on plantations," and in a lengthy October letter it stated that the best means of "securing the contentment and well being" of the African and "of obtaining maximum production" in Africa was for the "indigenous worker to cultivate his own land and develop it to the utmost of his ability." The society expressed continued concern about the terms of the Native Authority

Amendment ordinance of 1920 which sanctioned compulsory labor for government for up to sixty days.[135] Milner saw no need to alter the policy already laid down. It would not satisfy "people like the writers, who are deliberately calumnious and sophistical. I think a pretty stiff reply is justified by their casuistry and deliberate fault-finding."[136]

Despite this view, protest against Northey's labor policy, with Oldham increasingly active, continued. Some truly "big guns" were now brought into the fray at his instigation. Oldham drew together the leaders of practically every Protestant sect in Great Britain, including the Archbishop of Canterbury and many influential peers and members of parliament from all parties, in support of calls for an alteration in the Kenya policy. Oldham prepared a lengthy statement of policy that was approved by the group.[137] Addressed to Lord Milner, it was titled Labour in Africa and the Principle of Trusteeship. The archbishop now took the lead; he dined with Milner in November and won the S of S's agreement to receive a deputation.[138] Oldham's policy memorandum was thus presented to the S of S, and he received a delegation on 14 December.[139]

Prior to Lord Milner's meeting with what would prove to be a most prestigious delegation, CO officials received a severe jolt. This came as a result of an interview Bottomley had, in late November, with J. A. E. Elliot, district commissioner at Embu, who was in Britain on leave. Elliot expressed strong opposition to all aspects of Northey's labor policy. Compulsory labor for government, Elliot held, was "bad because it takes the native away from his home." According to Bottomley, Elliot stated that "the first stages of cultivation—clearing bush, stumping, breaking the ground—are men's work, only the subsequent tilling being done by the women. If the men are away, the ground is not prepared and crops are not grown." Here was a different picture of the "idle native" than that painted by Sir Edward Northey. The person providing the information could not be dismissed as a "crank" with no experience in Africa. Elliot asserted that the government "ought to content itself with entering the market for voluntary labour." He was equally hostile toward encouragement of labor for settlers. Headmen abused the system by chasing men they were "'down' on", making them go. The negative impact on African cultivation of this part of the labor policy was intensified because of longer absence, and the fact that settlers wanted workers at the same seasons when preparations for cultivation in the reserves were required. Elliot told Bottomley that the number of idle men, "whom the circular was intended to bring out, is small."[140]

Elliot made an extremely strong attack on the circular, and, by implication, its author, the governor. He told Bottomley: "No administrative officer who can afford to resign will carry out the Circular policy, and if the Government wants to get gentlemen to enter its service, it must drop 'forced labour'."[141] Bottomley, who had throughout 1920 been willing to take Northey's word for conditions in Kenya and the need for the governor's labor policy so as to prevent idleness in the reserves, was shaken by Elliot's blunt expression of opposition to the governor's policies. He could only console himself that Elliot's experience of African conditions was "not to be compared with that of Mr. Ainsworth, who has shown no sign of misgiving."[142] Following Ainsworth's retirement, this last pillar holding up Bottomley's hope that Elliot might be wrong would collapse.

Fiddes, who had been somewhat hesitant to enthusiastically jump on Northey's bandwagon as the criticism of the labor circular grew apace, was less shocked. He minuted: "I wish I could feel that Mr. Elliot is quite wrong— but I can't."[143] For Amery as well, the danger signals were clear. "I confess to misgivings about the whole policy—not in theory but in actual working," he wrote.[144]

As Elliot's statement was digested, the seeds of doubt were sown at the CO. Officials would realize, in the months ahead, that they had been much too hasty in their defense of Northey's labor scheme and their adoption of the reasoning that lay behind it. In retrospect, it can be suggested that they did so for a variety of reasons. First and foremost, there was the need to support the man on the spot. As long serving CO official C. J. Jeffries noted, "to overrule the considered and maintained advice of a Governor is a thing which no Secretary of State would do lightly. . . ."[145] Moreover, Northey had been in office only about a year when the storm surrounding the labor circular broke; to question the governor so quickly would suggest to critics that the CO had made an inappropriate choice in the first place. In this and other issues where Northey undertook questionable policies or left himself open to criticism (e.g. on the Indian question), CO officials often fell back on a rationalization that went something like this: "the governor has strongly advocated this line of policy, therefore we must accept it." In addition, until the interview with Elliot, the CO staff believed that the provincial administration was in agreement with the governor and fully supportive of his policy. Another reason for CO support of Northey's position lay in the fact that they too believed the racist characterizations of the governor. Most officials had spent little time in Africa, and those who had experience there (Milner, Amery, and Fiddes) had, like Northey, gained it in South Africa. They accepted, without question, his stereotype of the "lazy, drunken, and vicious" African male. Finally, Northey's policy seemed to make economic sense. European settler production was now the backbone of Kenya's exports, and therefore the settler sector had to be supported and enhanced. This assumption too would later be revealed to be false, but CO officials had yet to open their eyes to this fact by the end of 1920.

Despite the doubts raised by Elliot, Milner went ahead with his meeting with the delegation still prepared to defend Northey's policy and practice. The deputation which waited on Milner on 14 December was headed by the Archbishop of Canterbury. Besides Oldham, it included the Marquess of Salisbury, the Bishop of Westminster, the Reverends A. E. Garvie and

Donald Fraser, Conservative party notable Sir Samuel Hoare, and K. Mac-lennan. The deputation emphasized that the concept of trusteeship must be the key to British policy in East Africa. This meant that Britain had a duty to East Africa to pursue policies which benefitted the whole community, not just the European settlers. All those who spoke expressed disquiet over the Kenya government's policies for procuring labor for government and private enterprise. The deputation also called for the appointment of a Royal Commission. This demand had already been made clear in the memorandum drafted by Oldham and previously submitted to the S of S; the commission would, it was proposed, inquire "into the guiding principles of Imperial policy in the East African Crown Colonies and Protectorates with special reference to the means by which the principle of trusteeship may be applied to existing conditions. . . ." Seven specific matters for investigation were identified. These dealt with other issues than merely labor and included African land tenure, the effect of western civilization on "the tribal system", African taxation, the best means of obtaining expression of African opinion "in matters effecting their interests" and the best means of achieving "the economic and moral advancement" of the African population.[146]

Lord Milner responded to the deputation by stating that "he found little difference between the views of the deputation and his own on questions of principle." The difficulty, he went on, "lay in applying these principles to very varying circumstances." He would not commit himself to a Royal Commission. There were many other problems "that need enquiry into." He still held to Northey's view of "numbers of young men idling in the villages," but stated that the government wished to know more about conditions in Kenya's African areas. Milner defended European settlement as beneficial to the colony's economic development. "Even if no revenue derived from taxation of natives had been devoted to the direct interests of the natives," Milner felt "that the natives would have good value of their money in the peace and prosperity resulting from British rule." Milner then asked to be provided with examples of abuse that had arisen as a result of the labor circulars and Native Authority Ordinance. He concluded his remarks by maintaining that European capital and enterprise was essential for developing East Africa. He went on: "Experience in South Africa showed that employment of natives for limited periods away from their homes was not necessarily incompatible with the happiness and prosperity of the native."[147]

Such a response from the S of S would not please the humanitarians. Protests would continue. In retrospect, however, one of the more significant aspects of the controversy over labor policy in Kenya was the mobilization of a strong body of humanitarian and missionary opinion which would continue to concern itself, for the next few years, with African affairs in Kenya. This concern would be particularly epitomized by the views and activities of J. H. Oldham. He would press on successive governments his concept of trusteeship and how it should effect British policy in Africa. This was well expressed in the memorandum presented to Milner, and Oldham continued to expound on the idea over the next three years.

Trusteeship, in Oldham's view, imposed a clear duty on the British to rule their African colonies in the interests of both Britain and the subject peoples. Specifically, it implied "the duty of hastening in all possible ways the growth of a healthy and independent native life." That included the assurance to the Africans that they would have adequate land with security of tenure, "complete freedom" in the disposal of labor, the furtherance of the Africans' economic development, their education in agriculture and industry, and a definite and progressive policy of training them in responsibility and self government. Oldham's vision of trusteeship accepted peasantization but was very suspicious of proletarianization. The latter process was "not easily reconciled with the healthy growth of village life, the fostering of native agriculture and industries, and a continuous policy of native education." Oldham and those who shared his views were very fearful that extensive demands on Africans for labor would lead "to the destruction of village life."[148] This vision of Africa was paternalistic, but it is important to note that it was radically different than that espoused by Sir Edward Northey.

Settler Political Gains

Just as with the labor question, Northey was quickly confronted with settler political demands upon his arrival in Kenya. The main issues to be dealt with were the implementation of European elections and unofficial representation on the Execo. Within a short time of his arrival, Northey telegraphed the CO recommending the adoption of elective representation without delay. He asked for a telegraphic reply so that he could make a public response. He also called for the appointment of unofficial members to the Execo.[149]

The latter matter was comparatively easily dealt with by the CO. Bottomley recalled that the matter of unofficial members on the Execo had been held over so as to let the new governor take credit for the initiative. Thus on 22 February the CO telegraphed approval.[150] As to elections of European unofficials, this too had been conceded by the CO, and after approval by Milner, Northey was told by telegraph that steps should be taken for introducing a system of elective representation,[151] and Bottomley worked up a draft despatch setting out the CO position on the subject in response to Bowring's August 1918 despatch. Sent to Nairobi approximately a month later, the CO laid down that for the present, electoral representation "must be confined to the European community." The interests of Indians and Africans "must for an indefinite time to come be secured by nominated representation" in the Legco. Two nominated Indians were proposed. Bowring's proposal that general elections should be held every three years was also approved. On the matter of the number of seats, however, the CO diverged from the EAP suggestion of ten constituencies. Six of the proposed ten electoral districts could be combined into three, making the total number of elected seats seven. The CO despatch went on to propose a council of nine unofficial members (seven elected Europeans and two nominated Indians) and at least eleven official members. Finally, London agreed that the question of "women's franchise" should be dealt with by the newly constituted council.[152]

On 2 April, Northey sent to London a draft bill for giving effect to the principle of elective representation in the Legco for the European community. Titled the Legislative Council Ordinance 1919, the bill included all the provisions suggested by the CO with one exception. Ten European elected members were provided for. Northey gave a hint as to the reason for this in his covering despatch; there he asserted that the failure to give effect to elections for whites, though approved in principle in 1916, had been the cause of very general dissatisfaction and had "severely handicapped the local government" since it "kept alive the spirit of distrust and opposition" to the administration.[153]

Just how far Northey was prepared to go in catering to settler views was quickly brought home to the CO. On 17 April, Northey telegraphed changes that had been made in his draft bill by the Legco. These were substantial and far-reaching. Two constituencies had been provided for Nairobi, making a total of eleven seats in all. Only one Indian and one Arab nominated member were to be included in the new council, and European women would be granted the right to vote. Northey concluded his telegram by pressing for a rapid telegraphic approval so that he could assent to the bill on its Third Reading.[154]

At the CO, the governor's new proposals were received with surprise. Bottomley, for example, did "not much like" the increase in European seats to eleven "at the cost of one of the two Indian seats." He predicted that there would certainly be a protest if there were two Indian members prior to approval of the bill who would be reduced to one after its passage. He had no objection to giving the vote to women.[155] Neither did other CO officials, but the proposal to name only a single Indian member was viewed with disquiet. The CO thus sent a telegram to Nairobi on 29 April, agreeing with the amendments, yet again demonstrating its loss of control in the initial months of Northey's governorship. Nevertheless, the S of S expressed "some doubt about the reduction of Indian representation to one member. I should be glad to have the reason for this proposal."[156]

Prior to receipt of this telegram, Governor Northey had despatched a lengthy commentary on 26 April. He informed London that because of the changes in principle adopted as a result of the debate, he had decided to postpone the Third Reading until early June. Northey explained, in more detail, the changes that had been made as a result of the debate in the Legco. He had, the governor told the CO, permitted "the absolute freedom of vote" by official members. He was pleased that the result of the voting on the three issues had "disclosed no cleavages of view between official and unofficial members as such." He had not attempted to use the government majority to dilute or shape the bill, Northey asserted; rather, the outcome indicated the general feeling of all members. He was happy to report that the principle of two members for Nairobi had passed unanimously. The vote on women's suffrage equally divided the council, and Northey had therefore cast the deciding vote in favor. His reason for voting for women's suffrage, the governor stated, was simply "that I was convinced that the feeling of the country as a whole was in favour of female suffrage." Northey added that an amendment had been proposed to give the vote to non-Europeans on an educational test, but this was lost by thirteen votes to three.[157]

On the question of the single Indian member, Northey again fell back on "public" opinion as represented in the council. It had first been claimed in the Legco that if there were two Indians, there must be two Arabs. Those who held this view felt that the Arabs had been in East Africa longer than the Indians and were permanent residents. The Indians were viewed as "merely birds of passage" who remitted the profits derived from their commercial undertakings home to India. After what the governor termed "considerable discussion," the proposal was amended to provide for one Indian and one Arab nominated member. The vote in favor of this proposal was nine to seven. Northey was prepared to accept this with an amazing lack of appreciation of political reality. He explained:

> The only grounds for my original proposition of two Indian members were that Mombasa and Nairobi should each have a representative, but I think it is a matter of little importance. Whether they are represented on the council by one or two nominated members, and I am satisfied that the number as decided by the majority of the council after a very full debate and careful consideration should stand, for the present, with one Arab.[158]

While the CO found it easy to accept the principle of votes for European women and the delimitation of eleven constituencies, the question of Indian representation was far more difficult. The issue of Indian political rights formed part of what, in 1919 and 1920, became a huge concern for the CO, the Indian Question. It would demand much CO time and cause considerable frustration, and it was a key element in the postwar struggle for Kenya. It is best treated here as a separate issue.

The Indian Question Emerges

In addition to Indian representation in the Legco, three other major issues formed a part of the grievances that pitted the protectorate's Indian population against the European settlers and the colonial state in a fierce controversy. These were government edicts providing for segregation of Indians from Europeans in the residential and commercial sections of the principal towns (e.g. Mombasa and Nairobi), the exclusion of Indians from the white highlands under the terms of the Crown Lands Ordinance, and the state's attempt, backed strongly by the settlers, to limit Indian immigration to the EAP. All these had concerned Indians in earlier years, but after the war, Indian protest in the EAP emerged more strongly as a result of growing concern over the gains made by the settler community and the emergence of new and more effective leadership of the Indian protest movement.[159]

So far as the CO was concerned, a new, and rather troublesome element, in the Indian question after the war emerged in the form of the IO. From early 1919, the IO began to take a much greater interest in the status of Indians in the EAP, and the IO became a very important pressure point on the CO so far as the development of policy toward the Indian population of East Africa was concerned. While the CO might dismiss humanitarian and pro-Indian protest in Britain, it could not so easily do so when such criticism and demands for improvement in the status of Indians came from another, cabinet level, department of state. A primary reason for the IO concern about Indians in East Africa was the fact that the government of India itself was anxious over the treatment of Indians in East Africa. Indian nationalists, such as Gandhi, voiced these concerns, and the government of India took the position that the failure to adequately redress grievances in East Africa made it more difficult to control the rising tide of nationalist feeling in India.[160]

However, the concern of the IO, after the war, was the result of more than just this general concern with Indian policy. It stemmed also from the deeply held beliefs of the S of S for India, Edwin Montagu. Montagu was unique among political leaders of the time in believing in true equality for Indians. Unlike most of those in governing circles in Britain, he did not hold that whites must be superior and Indians second-class citizens.

Following his appointment as S of S for India in mid-1917, Montagu took an interest in the position of Indians in East Africa, and, beginning in 1919, he brought his concerns to the attention of the CO. Almost as soon as Milner took up the leadership of the CO, Montagu voiced to him his concern regarding "a marked racial discrimination against Indians" that he felt characterized the EAP government's efforts to enforce Professor Simpson's scheme of segregation in townships. Montagu approached Milner while they were in Paris for the start of the peace conference, and he concluded his complaint to his opposite number with a clear statement of IO concern.

Indian opinion resents, and in my judgement with good reason, measures which by British authorities in any part of the empire conflict with assurances given by H. M.'s Government of full recognition of Indian services in the war. Such measures afford powerful weapons to disaffected, while they perplex and discourage the loyal.[161]

Permanent officials at the CO reacted to Montagu's criticism and call for redress for the Indians with regard to urban segregation with little sympathy and some hostility. Bottomley maintained that Simpson's scheme of segregation had to be supported as the latter had seen the situation on the spot, and as a sanitary expert, the professor had to be believed. Although Simpson's plan that there should be separate areas for Europeans, Indians, and Africans in urban areas, each separated from one another by empty "buffer zones" had not really been applied in the EAP, Bottomley supported the implementation efforts that the EAP government had taken. Fiddes also felt somewhat provoked by the IO's complaints.[162] Nevertheless, Amery was much more aware of political realities than the civil servants. He did not accept the specifics of Montagu's complaints, but the under-secretary wished to see consultation begin with the IO, not only on the issue of segregation but on immigration and potential Indian settlement as well. He urged that "we must get on a friendly working basis with the IO on all these questions as soon as possible."[163]

Soon after Northey's arrival in Nairobi, the new governor noted the heat and "deplorable bad feeling" that was developing between Indians and Europeans there, and this, together with pressure from the IO, forced the CO to take notice of the Indian question. In early March, Northey telegraphed his opposition to the idea of settling Indian ex-soldiers in East Africa. He felt that available land should come under European cultivation as this would bring "greater advantages to the protectorate itself and to the local natives than by importation from another portion of the empire of immigrants of another race."[164]

The idea of restricting Indian immigration and economic opportunities so as to protect the African struck a very responsive chord among CO officials, and would remain a very prominent theme in the responses they developed to the Indian question. Bottomley strongly endorsed the governor's concern for the "development of the African." It would be regrettable, he felt, "if by introducing any large element of Indian immigrants we should restrict the sphere of African development."[165] Amery was not so sure that restricting Indian immigration would do this. He favored consideration of settling "Indian small holders" in East Africa. If CO policy was to be one of "rapid maximum development, based as far as possible on closer settlement and native cultivation, and not mainly on the plantation system," there was good cause, in Amery's view, for "the introduction of Indian agriculturalists." Given his broad imperial view, Amery proposed a review of the whole East and Central African situation and the laying down of a definite policy.[166]

A few weeks later, the CO was forced to tackle the Indian question again upon the receipt of a despatch from Northey that enclosed demands made by the settlers Convention of Associations. The convention called for the refusal of the franchise to Indians, the prohibition of Indians acquiring land "except in townships on short leases, non-employment of Indians by government, and the restriction of Indian immigration." Northey was in agreement with the settlers on most of their resolutions. He was "strongly of opinion" that "anything like universal suffrage to the Asiatic on equality with the European in this Protectorate is out of the question." Most settlers were "of a well-educated and superior class" while the more numerous Indians "include a big proportion of uneducated illiterate Indians of the lower classes." The highlands, Northey felt, should be reserved for European settlement, but the governor believed that Indian demands for land in other areas might be met. He endorsed putting educated Africans into government posts instead of Indians, but he admitted that "at present we cannot replace many of the Asiatics employed in government work." The governor also expressed strong endorsement for restrictions on Indian immigration "as the present unrestricted immigration tends to keep back the Africans."[167]

Bottomley prepared a lengthy minute in reponse to Northey's despatch that illustrates the feelings of the EAD at this time. On the question of common roll elections, Bottomley agreed with the governor that such a thing was "quite out of the question," and though he mentioned the possibilty of Indian communal elections, he felt the Indians would gain "little advantage by elections as against nomination." He endorsed the exclusion of Indians from the highlands, and agreed with Northey that the government could not, at that time, get rid of its Indian employees. The restriction of immigration was, in his view, "a difficult matter." All over East Africa the Indian immigrant was "almost invariably of a type that does no good to the country or to the native," but it was "absolutely impractical" to keep out all Indians.[168] Amery reaffirmed his support for Indian agriculturalists after reading Northey's despatch, and he remarked with regard to the settlers: "I can't help a little suspecting the intense sympathy for the poor African shown in the resolution."[169]

Milner still had not come to any conclusion on the overall policy to be applied to East and Central Africa that Amery had previously urged. He merely ordered an acknowledgement of the governor's despatch, with a statement that the S of S hoped to address the governor more fully on the issue later.[170]

In the midst of considering the settlers' and governor's views on the Indian question, the CO received another communication on the subject from the IO. This enclosed a telegram from the Viceroy of India that described the visit of an Indian delegation from East Africa. The government of India urged sympathetic consideration of the Indian grievances.[171] Montagu followed this up with a note to Milner in which he discussed the convention's resolutions Northey had previously forwarded to London. Montagu rejected the language used by the Europeans as it was bound to embitter relations with the Indians. He asked if the governor could not use his private influence on the whites "to adopt a more restrained attitude in their public declarations."[172]

This was followed within a month by an IO question on Indian representation in the Legco. Since elective representation for Indians was supported for

Legcos in India, Montagu believed that "there are arguments for Indian representation on the local Legislative Council as soon as it is applied to any other class."[173] The IO raised the issue at a difficult time for the CO as, it will be remembered, Northey and the EAP Legco had just approved a resolution calling for only a single Indian nominated member in the new body. While CO officials had no sympathy for the idea of Indian voting rights in East Africa, they recognized that the reduction in Indian representation could not be allowed to stand. Fiddes had "no strong feeling as to whether elected or nominated Indians as I do not expect satisfactory results from either course, but on practical grounds we can not agree to pull an agreed scheme to pieces."[174] Amery felt that the CO should therefore insist on two Indian representatives, and a telegram was sent to Northey informing him of this position.[175]

Northey accepted the CO directive and provision was made for two Indian representatives in the new Legco. In informing the CO of this in mid-June, however, the governor went beyond the issue to delve into the Indian question as a whole in a lengthy telegram. He stated that "bitter feeling" against the Indians had arisen among Europeans as a result of the latter's demands, "including suffrage and rights equal to British white men." This, in Northey's view, was a ridiculous proposition because the number of Indians fit to vote was very few. His telegram read: "Whole agitation caused by few individuals remainder know little and care less about politics."[176]

The governor proceeded to detail his views on the Indian question, which he stated, he had formed after consultation with a committee representing both official and unofficial members of Legco. He supported segregation as recommended by Professor Simpson. He felt that Indians should be excluded from the highlands but might possibly be allowed to acquire a small area of land in the lowlands when soldier settlers had been provided for. Northey strongly endorsed restrictions on Indian immigration. He stated:

At present thousands of Indians of lowest class are pouring into this protectorate. I consider that this should be stopped immediately and that our policy should be to educate African natives so that they can take the place of Indian clerk, artisan, mechanic.[177]

In the meantime, Indian immigration should be strictly controlled. He asked to be allowed to enforce such a policy as he believed "in principle each colony or protectorate should be allowed to control composition of its own population by means of restriction of immigration." Northey concluded his telegram with a plea for a policy to be laid down by the CO, and to "discontinue use of veto behind closed doors."

This request, not surprisingly, called forth a lengthy statement of views from the head of the EAD. He regretted that Northey had offered no details of the Indian agitation. The European comments had "given us difficulty with the IO, and it would have been satisfactory if we had something on the other side to set against it." Bottomley commented on each of the governor's main points relating to the Indian question. He agreed that Simpson's segregation scheme was absolutely essential as a means of preserving European health. However, he felt that provided Indians were prevented from subdividing plots and adequate sanitary arrangements were enforced, "there is no a priori reason why the business premises of Europeans and Asiatics should not exist side by side." Until, however, such sanitary arrangements could be implemented, Bottomley advocated continuing to insist on a policy of commercial segregation. He strongly recommended, moreover, that Lord Elgin's 1908 ruling that Indians not be allowed to hold land in the highlands be continued.[178]

On the other hand, Bottomley disagreed with Northey's demand for a uniform policy throughout East and South Africa. He pointed out that the CO had no responsibility for South Africa. He was in favor of restricting Indian immigration, but rejected Northey's dictum that the EAP should control the composition of its population. The imperial government was responsible for the protectorate, not the local population, and complete restriction of Indian entry would be difficult to sustain under existing international arrangements. Bottomley concluded his minute with an interesting observation:

> The whole question depends on the extent to which it is considered essential to fall in with the feelings of the IO as to placating Indian sentiment. Subject to this, I consider that the Governor's views on the points raised could be accepted as an outline of a definite policy.[179]

Other officials agreed with Bottomley's position, especially the fact that the EAP could not follow a policy of "home rule" with regard to immigration. Fiddes expressed the dilemma CO officials felt in his minute of 30 June. If the CO opposed the settlers, "we shall have a first class row, and sooner or later their view will prevail. On the other hand to support them will mean an equal row with the IO, the Indian Government, and a certain class of public opinion here." Fiddes therefore proposed holding off an immediate restriction of immigration, as the CO would "have all the row we want" over the other matters referred to by Northey.[180] Amery laid great stress on the need, "at as early a date as possible," for "a general policy for the whole area between the Union and Egypt," and to decide now "what type of civilization we mean to establish between the Zambezi and the Nile."[181]

Continued Indian Dissatisfaction and the CO Response

Before action could be taken on Amery's weighty recommendation, the IO once again pressed the claims of the East African Indians on the CO. The government of India had forwarded these to the IO with the strong recommendation that Indian claims to "adequate representation" on the Legco and local government bodies should be "sympathetically considered." The IO specifically endorsed the concept of the franchise for Indians without delay. Since settlers were calling for the "ultimate exclusion" of Indians from the EAP, the position of the Indian community "will clearly be worse under a legislature partly composed of elected Europeans than one entirely composed of nominated official members." The Indians deserved consideration, the IO maintained, for this reason, "the substantial interests of Indians" in the EAP, and their services "in originally developing and recently defending the territory." They were also, like the Europeans, taxed—there appeared no reason why only whites should enjoy voting rights. The IO touched on other Indian grievances as well, but the question of the franchise was given most prominence.[182]

This IO complaint called forth a lengthy, and most significant, response by the EAD. Unlike in June, it was A. C. C. Parkinson who drew it up. Given his recent service in East Africa during the war, Parkinson was able to bring personal insights to the issue involved. Parkinson began by reviewing the Indian grievances and fully detailing the present CO position with regard to them. After this, he attempted to explain the strong European hostility to the Indians. The first reason noted was a racist feeling that Parkinson completely sympathized with. He did not mince words for his superiors: "A natural barrier exists between white and coloured races which no amount of political and religious theorizing will in practice remove so far as the white (dominant) race is concerned." Second was the feeling of Europeans that Indians had made a lot of money, especially during the war, and transferred those profits to India. Noting the missionaries were not any more in favor of the Indians than the settlers, Parkinson turned to what he termed the "native point of view." He wrote:

> To the native the 'Mzungu' [white man] is the master. The native sees the Indian trading and doing the artisans work etc and sees that he is in a lower position than the white man. The native is quick to notice distinctions of this kind, and on the whole he despises the Indian, who is neither one of the ruling race nor of his own race . . . he often realizes that the Indian is making an unfair profit out of him and he resents it.[183]

Parkinson then turned to discuss possible lines of CO action. He rejected both the absolute exclusion of Indians from East Africa and absolute equality between Indians and whites. For the latter, he put forward three major jusifications. First, the whites in the EAP would be swamped and the government would be in the hands of people who were "for the most part uneducated, illiterate, low caste and self seeking." Secondly, there was the government's "first duty" to the African people. Parkinson continued that the influence of the Indian was regarded as harmful to the African by the government officials and missionaries "from the point of view of religion, morality, and industrial development &c, and it is only by the persence of Europeans as the ruling race . . . that this deleterious influence can be kept in check." Thirdly, if the whites were "subordinated in practice to the Indian, they would probably leave the country all together . . . and the agricultural development on which East Africa will largely depend for its prosperity will practically cease. In short, the country will stagnate and ultimately be ruined."

This latter statement clearly represented CO thinking in 1919. Officials believed that settler enterprise was absolutely indispensable. Thus precedence had to be given to their politically and socially exclusive demands. The prominence of settler production in the EAP exports seemed to justify this stand, and it led Parkinson to argue in favor of what he termed a "middle course" in East African policy which ruled out absolute equlity between Indian and European. The government must not attempt, in pursuit of this approach, to oust the Indians who had already gone to British East Africa, and it must make "an honest endeavour" to remedy genuine Indian grievances subject to certain guiding principles. Parkinson defined these as follows:

A The first object of the Government is to safeguard the interests of the natives now and for the future.
B The interests of the natives will outweigh those of the Indian community where there is a conflict of interest between the two just as they will outweigh those of the Europeans if there is a conflict between European and native interests.

Parkinson's suggestion and the justification put forward were of immense significance. The doctrine of African paramountcy he sketched out in this memo would form the fundamental principle in the solution to the Indian question, which the imperial government eventually arrived at in the white paper of 1923. It is important to emphasize this point as it has been the conclusion of some students of the subject that this form of African paramountcy was formulated and presented to the CO by British humanitarians, notably J. H. Oldham, the Archbishop of Canterbury, and C. F. Andrews.[184]

While Fiddes hoped that Parkinson's memo could form the basis of early policy decisions on the Indian question, Milner, after the passage of some time, decided only to send the IO letter to the EAP for comment. In addition to obtaining the acting governor's comments, the subject could also be fully discussed with Northey who was on his way to Britain.[185] The IO was informed of the S of S's decision.[186]

While the CO thus would await further information from the EAP and the arrival and recovery of General Northey, the IO was not prepared to let matters rest. Montagu hoped that discussions with Northey would lead to a solution "of what appears to be the fundamental question in any attempt to deal with Indian grievances, namely the means of securing the representation of the community by elected members on the Legislative Council." To deny the vote to Indians was to assign a "status of inferiority" to British subjects.[187] The CO were not amused by this request from the IO. Parkinson felt the IO letter should be shown to Northey "just to let him realize the sort of attitude the S of S for Colonies has to contend with."[188]

Nothing would thus be done by the CO pending receipt of a response from Bowring and discussion with Northey in London in 1920. Prior to the end of 1919, however, the CO found that it had to contend with another group pressing for Indian rights. This was the Indian Overseas Association (hereafter IOA) which was formed by Henry S.L. Polak and other Indian and British individuals interested in Indians outside India in October 1919.[189] The Aga Khan was chairman of the organization, but Polak, who had worked with Gandhi in South Africa, was, as secretary of the new organization, the driving force behind its advocacy of equal rights for Indians in East Africa. He sent his first letter on behalf of East African Indians to the CO in late Novermber 1919. The association thanked the CO for providing representation for Indians on the Legco, but it urgently requested that the franchise be conferred on Indians on equal terms with the Europeans.[190] The CO, for its part, greeted the new organization with little enthusiasm. "This new association is obviously going to give us trouble," minuted Parkinson. He felt that Indian grievances should be discussed only between the CO and the governor; the CO must adhere strictly to the view that "the S of S is responsible for administration of EAP and that he cannot share his responsibilities with any other individual minister."[191]

Both the IOA and the IO kept the pressure on the CO in January 1920. Polak wrote on 8 January to send resolutions passed by a November meeting of the EAINC. Polak also informed the CO that the EAINC was planning "an influential deputation" to Britain.[192] The CO officials were not pleased with this information. Parkinson did not see what purpose would be served by a deputation from East Africa as the S of S and the governor "will already be in possession of the facts on which to base their discussions." Both Polak and the IO were sent a letter delivering that message, but if the congress decided to send a deputation, no obstacle would be placed in their way by the CO. Since Milner was in Egypt, there would be no opportunity to make firm decisions on the Indian question until his return.

Now in Britain recuperating from his surgery, Northey wrote to the CO on 10 January to provide his views on the Indian question. He maintained that the majority of the settlers, "representing western civilization," despised the Indian and would welcome his total exclusion from the EAP. Northey believed this was going too far. "I believe that the Indian is still necessary," Northey wrote; "the Europeans would be more wise to admit this and devote their attention to the best manner which the two communities can co-exist without friction." European animosity had increased Indian agitation, but Northey went on to maintain his opposition to Indian elections since "90 per cent" of the Indian population of the EAP belonged to "an uneducated class of coolie totally unqualified to express any opinion on public policy" or on municipal matters. Northey would lease no land to Indians in the highlands, but lowland regions might eventually be allotted to Indian farmers. "Where reasonably possible," segregation as proposed by Professor Simpson should be enforced, but, admitted the governor, in established towns such as Nairobi and Mombasa, the principle could not be fully "acted on without expense and offense." Northey now had come to recognize that immigration policy must be controlled by the imperial government, but he advocated restrictions on Indian immigration as the present lack of restrictions "tends to keep back the African and allows thousands of undesirable Indians to flock into the country."[193]

Moreover, when Northey heard, later in the month, that an Indian deputation was planning to come to London, he viewed it as "a foolish waste of time and money on their part." He asserted that the Indians knew that he was "fully cognizant of all their claims. . . ." Northey concluded by stating, absurdly as later events would show, "I am able to put the whole matter quite clearly before Lord Milner without bias or prejudice."[194] The formal call for the reception of the deputation reached the CO in early March as Bowring telegraphed a request of the EAINC. The deputation consisted of three prominent Indians, A. M. Jevanjee, S. T. Thakore (Thakur), and S. Achariar. They would journey to Britain and eventually gain an interview with Milner.

Approximately a week before Milner's meeting with the Indian deputation, the CO received an important despatch from acting governor Bowring. Responding to the CO despatch of 26 November, he transmitted to London his observations on the Indian question. These differed dramatically from those of Northey on the question of elective representation. The scathing and repeated attacks on Indians by European settler leaders seem to have caused Bowring to change his mind. This had also caused an "apparent unanimity which now prevails amongst the various classes and sections of the Indian community on political questions." Moreover, the local situation caused Bowring "some anxiety." Rumors of a general strike by Indian employees were in the air, and this would prove a "serious embarrassment." Thus Bowring agreed with the IO position that Indian representation on the Legco must now be by election rather than nomination. In the past, the acting governor admitted, he had feared elections of one or two Indian members of the Legco "would have resulted in the interests of the most influential sections only being represented, but the unanimity amongst the different sections to which I have alluded above removes that objection." He proposed two Indian elected members, one for the coast and one for the interior. The franchise would be based on age, a knowledge of English, and a "moderate" property or income qualification.[195]

Bowring's change of mind was noted with interest at the CO. It also came at an opportune time; it could be circulated, together with Parkinson's earlier memo, prior to Milner's meeting with Northey and the Indian delegation in mid-April. Bottomley somewhat reluctantly agreed that anti-Indian expressions by the settlers were the cause of much difficulty. He went on:

> It cannot be denied that the great bulk of the Indians in EA were of a low class and their influence on the native (when they are not cheating him) is not good. It is however impossible to label the whole community for the sins of a part, even though a large part, and no amount of invective will get away from the fact that East Africa can not at its present state of development do without the Indians.[196]

Northey met with the S of S on 13 April. He was, at that time, opposed to Bowring's recommendation of elective rights for Indians. The governor strongly held to his previously expressed views, but two days later he wrote to Milner to admit a slight change of heart. He suggested that if it was considered necessary to make some concession to Indian aspirations, it could be made in the form of "a restricted suffrage on an educational qualification for the election of Indians to protectorate and municipal councils." But the governor added a significant proviso: "Whatever electoral powers are given to the Indians must be given to Arabs, Somalis, Kavirondo and other native tribes who all belong to the country and are more entitled to have a say in the Government of the Protectorate than the Indians who are immigrants."[197] Northey's "conversion" was extremely reluctant. He brought the letter in to the CO personally and emphasized his insistence that all voters must have a knowledge of English. Bottomley thought that this was an extremely restrictive position. "We shall get little thanks for a franchise on the basis of an English education," he remarked.[198]

Milner met the Indian deputation from East Africa four days after receipt of Northey's letter. The three man deputation was part of a large delegation which came to meet the S of S on 19 April. Organized by the IOA, the delegation was introduced by Lord Islington, former under-secretary of state at the CO, and it included members of parliament representing the three major parties.[199] The deputation had already prepared a summary of Indian grievances for the S of S's consideration,[200] and Lord Islington and other members of the delegation did not dwell on these in detail. A. M. Jevanjee spoke for the Indians from East Africa. The visitors called for "an independent and impartial enquiry" by a Royal Commission.[201]

In reply, Milner indicated that decisions to the "many big and difficult questions affecting East Africa" had yet to be made. He strongly maintained, moreover, that the responsibility for such decisions lay solely with the CO. Milner would not make any commitment on the question of a Royal Commission, but he hoped it would be practicable to take steps in the immediate future to mitigate, if not remove altogether, the sense of grievance felt by the Indian community in EA.[202]

After the meeting, the CO turned its attention to accomplishing that daunting task. After another lengthy meeting between Northey and Milner, the CO position on the Indian question was formally worked out. It was agreed that there would be no restrictions on Indian immigration in the EAP, and that the existing restrictions that kept Indians from acquiring "agricultural land" in the white highlands should be maintained. The latter point was justified by the fact that this was the only place that Europeans could live, and therefore the restriction had to stand. Other areas would be "marked out as available for Indian agricultural settlement." On segregation, it was agreed to adhere to the Simpson scheme in residential areas of towns, but in the commercial areas segregation would only be adopted "wherever possible."[203]

On the question of elective representation, Northey held out strongly and got his way. According to Bottomley's summary:

It was decided that the attitude towards Indian elective representation should be that the constitution was new and that time should be allowed to see how the present system worked before altering it. The S of S was given to understand that the nominated members representing the Indian community were excellent representatives. It was also pointed out that the number of Indians in EA who would be eligible for the franchise on the same principles as have been approved in India would be extremely small. For those reasons, it seemed better not to adopt the elective principle for representation of the Indian community at present.[204]

These and the other decisions were quickly placed in the form of a secret despatch to Bowring on 21 May. Milner began by stating that "the time has not yet come for basing the representation of Indians in the protectorate on the elective principle." The despatch then went on to detail the other policy decisions Milner had reached following the discussions with Northey. Considerable space was given to justifying "race-segregation" as necessary. The CO concluded by instructing Bowring that the despatch was to be kept secret until the governor's return to the EAP. On his arrival, Northey would make the CO's policy decisions public. Only then could the despatch be published.[205]

Northey's victory proved short-lived. Just over two weeks after sending the despatch to Nairobi, Milner sent a copy to Montagu for information. He recognized that the Indians would not like several of the decisions made, but Milner maintained that he had "done my best to hold the scale evenly between conflicting interests. My own conviction is that there is room for both European and Indian settlements in the country, but that it won't do to mix them."[206] Outraged by what he saw as the failure to provide adequately for Indian grievances, Montagu wrote back immediately to ask for a meeting to discuss the issue. He hoped that there would be no publication of the CO decisions.[207]

The IO pressure forced the CO to agree to suspend the announcement by Northey until the matter could be considered by the cabinet.[208] Thus the CO telegraphed to Bowring on 15 June that no announcement of Indian policy was to be made "pending further instructions" from London.[209]

In June and July 1920, the IO strongly pressed on the CO its view that Indians must be granted electoral rights as this position was being strongly advocated by the government of India. The refusal to provide Indian electoral rights would have a "deplorable effect" in India.[210] Milner refrained from making any specific statement of policy on the Indian question when he spoke in a Lords debate on 14 July as he had not had the opportunity to personally finalize the issue with Montagu.

In the meantime, Northey had returned to Nairobi on 2 July. He made several significant policy announcements when he first addressed the Legco, but he announced that he was not yet in a position to make a statement on the Indian question.[211] However, the governor soon pressed the CO for an early announcement of policy. On 21 July he telegraphed urgently to request "early instruction" on segregation and the franchise. On the latter, he reported that an Indian nominated member, the attorney V. V. Phadke, had introduced a resolution in the Legco calling for an Indian franchise. The bill, which was tabled at Northey's request, provided for property or income or educational qualifications. Northey repeated his opposition to Indian elections in the telegram, but he stated he would accept the S of S's decision in favor of electoral rights provided "Arabs and others with similar qualifications" were given the vote and all enfranchised persons must speak and write English. The principle had to be maintained, the governor believed, that Indian elected members would represent only Indians on council, and he held that there should be only two Indians in the Legco, whether nominated or elected.[212]

The CO recognized Northey's anxiety, but discussions were still going on with the IO. Bottomley agreed that two members were sufficient to represent Indian interests in the Legco, but he regretted Northey's attitude with regard to extending voting rights to Arabs since he knew of no Arab demand for them.[213] In the end, Milner bowed to the wishes of Montagu and agreed that a form of elective representation for Indians had to be granted. The CO saw no objection to Phadke's proposed qualifications, and approved the election of two Indian members.[214] The telegram also expressed doubt as to the wisdom of Northey's adherence to English literacy as a qualification for voting and the enfranchisement of Arabs, which could have been "left over until there is a proved demand for franchise." The principle of segregation was maintained. Northey was instructed to alter the secret despatch of May so as to include the approval of Indian elections.[215] He was then free to announce Milner's decisions on Indian policy publicly, and he did so on 9 August.[216] Although the CO seemed to have laid down a definite policy on all points of the Indian question at long last, it did take one other matter under consideration in August. As a result of a letter from Polak, the CO requested Northey's opinion as to the question of Indian representation in the Execo.[217]

The publication of Milner's decision on the Indian question did not, as events soon demonstrated, provide any end to Indian dissatisfaction. Rather, Indian protest grew stronger and more adamant following the August announcement. The EAINC quickly telegraphed its keen disappointment at the imperial decision, which assigned "inferior status to British Indians" in East Africa. In fact, only the decision regarding Indian immigration was not attacked.[218] The East African Indian deputation, still in Britain at the start of September, registered strong rejection of the CO decisions. The deputation claimed that the policy would keep Indians in an inferior status in every department of life.[219] Later in the month, Jevanjee, the deputation's leader, sought a meeting with the prime minister. The August announcement produced discontent in India also.[220]

As the last months of 1920 rolled by, it became abundantly clear at the CO that the Indian question was far from settled. Not only did the Indian community reject the imperial decisions, but by the end of September Northey seemed ready to make a major departure from the segregation scheme proposed by Professor Simpson for Nairobi. He decided to recommend an expansion of the commercial area to be allotted to Indians because the area provided by Simpson's scheme was "extremely limited and incapable of further expansion." None of the government plots in the capital still available for alienation were open to Indian purchasers. Northey thus proposed increasing the areas of the capital available for Indian commercial establishments. The governor asked the CO to cable approval of these changes so that the sale of town plots could take place soon.[221] In a private letter to Amery, Northey provided additional insight into the thinking that lay behind this recommendation. He hoped to show the Indians and critics in Britain and India that Indians were not removed from favorable areas of the EAP. He also maintained that "it isn't really a question of whom you live or work next to but of *how* they live and what type of house they keep and how they keep it." He hoped, before long, to bring the Kenya European to that point of view.[222]

Officials at the CO were understandably taken aback by the governor's proposal. Bottomley regretted such a radical departure from previous plans, which had envisioned the old bazaar site being depopulated and eventually included in the European area.[223] Fiddes felt that the governor's new attitude represented "a curious development" since accepting Northey's proposal meant "turning our back on sanitary considerations."[224] This would in fact mark the beginning of a retreat on the principle of urban segregation by the colonial state and the CO.

On the question of Indian representation on the Execo, Northey did not soften his position. He strongly opposed the principle on the familiar grounds that there were few qualified Indians; those who might be appointed would likely use their position to provide secret information "to such Indians as might be interested," and an Indian member of the Execo would be looked upon as representing other Indians and not be a free agent, "to advise according to his own personal views."[225]

The CO position was further complicated by the decision of Kenya Indians to pursue a campaign of non-cooperation as part of their protest. One of the

Indian Legco members, A. R. Visram, resigned his seat on 25 November. He did so in compliance with a resolution supported by a meeting of Mombasa Indians that called for Indian members to leave all public bodies. Northey reported this development, with regret, in December, and he further reported to the CO that Indians refused to regard the Legco members as representing them, and that they would not participate in elections until the number of Indian members in the Legco was increased. Indians also refused to discuss the selection of land in lowland regions that might be made available for Indian farms, nor would they discuss "details of the demarcation of residential and commercial areas of townships, for they refuse to accept in any way the principle of segregation." Northey stated the obvious when he informed London that matters were "at a standstill."[226] The end of 1920 found the CO still unable to provide a solution, despite long deliberations and voluminous correspondence, to the dilemmas posed by the Indian question.

The Uasin Gishu Railway Project

Another issue Northey took up on his arrival was the extension of a railway from Nakuru via the Uasin Gishu plateau to Mumias. It was not as contentious as the Indian question, but here, as in other issues, Northey would adopt a position strongly supportive of the views and aspirations of European settlers. Northey quickly examined the proposals for the construction of a trolley line from the main line of the Uganda railway to the plateau that Bowring had earlier proposed; like the latter, he found the idea "impracticable". He wasted no time telegraphing London to that effect on 7 February.[227] In May, with plans for soldier settlement in the Trans Nzoia district north of Uasin Gishu very much on his mind, Northey sent a despatch to London detailing his preference for a railway.[228]

From this time forward, Northey doggedly pressed the CO to agree to build a rail line to the Uasin Gishu plateau financed by an imperial loan. It was part of his policy for assisting and stimulating settler production. He wired the CO again at the end of May, pressing for London's acceptance of the Uasin Gishu railway.[229] Some six weeks later, Northey was even more strident in his advocacy for a railway to the plateau following the line surveyed in 1915. It was, he stated, "absolutely indispensable", and he pressed the CO to give permission for a detailed survey and a start in the construction of earthworks.[230] E. S. Grogan, in Britain in mid-1919, added his voice to that of the governor. Citing hefty potential loss in timber traffic by the railway and, of course, financial loss to himself, he pressed for a commencement of the railroad.[231]

The CO under Milner and Amery was much more willing to accept the need for building a line from Nakuru to Mumias. From the middle of 1919, it was clear that a rail line to the Uasin Gishu plateau would be constructed.

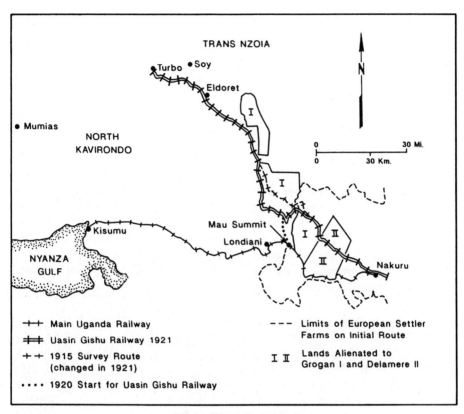

Uasin Gishu Railway

The major concerns of London officials were the exact route to be followed, the raising of a loan to provide capital for construction, and the choice of a contractor.

As it began to seriously consider the latter issues towards the end of 1919, the CO recognized that it was essential to have an estimate of the cost of constructing the railroad along the route surveyed in 1915. London requested Northey to provide such an estimate on 10 November. In its telegram, the CO made a second significant request: "If desirable for financial reasons would it be practicable to stop at Eldoret for the present and what would be the cost?"[232]

By the time the telegram was sent, the CO had begun discussions with two potential contractors. Pauling had revived their earlier offer to construct the railway for a commission of 8 per cent on cost. In mid-August, Sir John Norton-Griffiths, governing director of the construction firm Norton Griffiths & Co. Ltd., met with Amery and Read. A Conservative M.P. and imperialist like Amery, Norton Griffiths maintained that he could build the line more cheaply than the government. Despite the EAP's uncertain financial future, Norton Griffiths stated that he was associated with financial interests that could raise the necessary money for construction and would be satisfied with "a very moderate return on their capital."[233] Little more could be done until estimates of the cost of construction had been received from East Africa.

By the second half of November, these had arrived at the CO. Acting Governor Bowring telegraphed giving an estimate of £2,443,000 for a rail line from Nakuru to Mumias; for a line from Nakuru to Eldoret, the estimate was £1,690,000.[234] Bowring also suggested that Eldoret could be connected to the mainline at Mau Summit at a cost of £480,000 less than his Nakuru estimate, and he asked permission to make a survey of the area between Mau Summit on the main line and the route set by the 1915 survey. Shortly after receipt of the telegram, Fiddes met with a representative of Pauling & Co. and the firm's financial backer. Basing the construction estimate on the 1915 Nakuru to Mumias survey, Pauling put forward a cost of £3,750,000.[235]

This discrepancy in estimates caused CO officials some difficulty. Summarizing the situation on 29 November, Bottomley favored a Nakuru to Mumias route. He did "not much like the Mau alternative" because of the steep gradients that would be involved, and he held out for construction to Mumias which, he wrote, "is a center of active native cultivation."[236] Informed of the situation on 1 December, Milner approved a telegram to Bowring requesting greater detail with regard to his estimates.[237] A week later, Read wrote to Norton Griffiths to inform him of the acting governor's estimate and to request answers to several questions concerning construction costs and finance.[238]

Possible routes, contractors, and finance continued to hold the attention of CO officials in December. When Bowring telegraphed on 16 December that detailed estimates had already been sent by mail, Bottomley still felt little enthusiasm for starting the branch at Mau Summit. At his suggestion, the CO wired Bowring to take no action on the Mau survey.[239] But the following day, the CO telegraphed, ordering that arrangements should be made at once for an economic survey of the Nakuru to Mumias route.[240]

From his residence in Britain, Northey strongly supported following the 1915 route in a letter to Bottomley:

> I consider that it would be shortsighted policy to cut across from Mau Summit on account of less cost. The object of the railway is to develop the country and encourage production. It will therefore be a pity to miss the rich lands from Nakuru northwards.[241]

As a result of Northey's stand, a telegram was sent to Bowring that stated that both Milner and Northey were "anxious that Nakuru-Mumias route should be carried out."[242]

The issue of the Uasin Gishu railway was also considered at the initial meeting of the Colonial Economic Development Committee on 17 December. Chaired by Amery, the committee examined, as its first order of business, the proposal to construct the line. Read provided information on the scheme being considered, but the committee decided that a memorandum should be prepared and circulated for consideration before the next meeting of the committee.[243]

Although no final decision as to construction had yet been taken by the end of 1919, London had expressed a clear preference for the Nakuru to Mumias route. Among the many problems still to be surmounted, the most significant, in addition to finalizing the route, were arriving at an accurate estimate of cost and choice of contractor. In the first months of 1920, extremely important decisions regarding route and contractor were taken. These were made at January meetings of the Uasin Gishu Railway subcommittee of the Colonial Economic Development Committee. The subcommittee was formed at the committee's second meeting on 19 January. It considered a lengthy memo drawn up by P. H. Ezechiel of the Crown Agents for the Colonies, who served as secretary to the committee, and a shorter memo by Sir John Eaglesome, a former director of railways and works in Nigeria. Ezechiel's memo set out in detail the need for the railway and the previous construction proposals. He recommended that it be built through to Mumias and be financed with a loan raised under the terms of the Colonial Stock Act of 1900.[244] Eaglesome's memo dealt more with the route. On the basis of cost, it opposed starting from Nakuru and going to Mumias. Sir John argued that the present time was one of "financial stringency and high prices;" therefore, it would save a great deal in construction costs by running the rail line from Londiani to Eldoret. If the aim of building the railway was "opening out the Kavirondo country," it would be much cheaper to do so by building a line from Kisumu to Mumias.[245] By the time the committee met, Northey had expressed his preference for building the railway from Nakuru to Soy, fifteen miles beyond Eldoret. In a 15 January letter to Bottomley, he recommended that "we estimate in the first place for a line only as far as Soy. . . . Soy is central for the Trans Nzoia people and quite far enough to go until the through line to Uganda is arranged for later."[246] As justification, Northey pointed to reduced costs, the great productive potential of the Uasin Gishu and Trans Nzoia districts, and the plan to move the headquarters of North Kavirondo from Mumias. The Colonial Economic Development Committee considered the case for stopping at Soy, but left the Uasin Gishu Railway subcommittee, that was formed at the 19 January meeting, to make further study.[247]

The subcommittee considered the issue of route, together with that of contractor at its meetings of 27 and 30 January. At the latter meeting, Norton Griffiths had been brought in for discussions concerning construction. He had replied to the CO's request for information by giving an undertaking, on 22 December, to construct the railway on the basis of Bowring's November estimate for a contractor's profit of 5 per cent.[248] As this was considerably cheaper than the offer of Pauling, it was decided to invite Norton Griffiths to the subcommittee's meeting of 30 January. As a result, the subcommittee recommended that a contract be arranged with the latter.[249] On the question of route, Grogan attended the 27 January meeting to press for the 1915 route to be adopted since that would run through his timber concession; Northey, also present at the same meeting, added his voice in favor of a start from Nakuru.[250] After a second meeting on the 30th, the subcommittee recommended that "the suggestions for starting a new line from Londiani or Mau Summit should be dropped, and that a railway following the surveyed route should be built from Nakuru. . . ."[251]

With much less discussion than that surrounding the decision to start from Nakuru, the subcommittee made another, even more momentous, recommendation with regard to route at its 30 January meeting. This was that the rail line should not be built to Mumias, but only as far as Soy, fifteen miles beyond Eldoret.[252] The impact of this decision was huge. As late as November 1919, Bottomley had advocated the importance of opening up North Kavirondo as a means of generating traffic for the line. The concept was now dropped, and a line approved that was to benefit European settler production only.

The completion of the economic survey requested by the CO, moreover, provided strong confirmation for the decision to stop at Soy. The survey was carried out by a four-person committee, chaired by Kenya's new director of agriculture, Alexander Holm. It examined the economic potential of the route from Nakuru to Mumias and the probable traffic. By 11 March, the committee had prepared a summary report that was transmitted to London by telegram. It provided an optimistic picture of present and future prospects of the European settled areas through which the line would run as well as the Trans Nzoia district that would not be directly served by the railway.[253]

The committee made no mention of the productive potential of North Kavirondo in the preliminary report, and its final report, completed on 16 April, made only brief mention of the district. One paragraph of the sixteen-page, forty-one-paragraph report dealt with "the section between Soy and Mumias." Although the committee did not visit North Kavirondo, nor did Holm, who had taken up his Kenya appointment on 1 November 1919, have any firsthand knowledge of the district, it considered that traffic on that section would "for all practical purposes, be confined to Native 'personal' [sic] and that there will be no appreciable production of crops to be carried by rail."[254] With this utterly preposterous statement, the district that had produced the greatest share of the protectorate's exports before 1914 was dismissed as of no significance. This view fit well philosophically with Northey's vision of Kenya's economic development in which the labor of African men on settler farms and estates took precedence over African production of marketable crops. Amazingly, the CO permanent officials accepted this decision as well. Not only does it demonstrate the subordination of peasant production to that of the settlers under Northey, it illustrates the remarkable degree to which the CO had lost control of events in Kenya. It will be recalled that in 1913 and 1914 the CO was only willing to consider the building of a railway across the Uasin Gishu plateau if it were extended to Mumias so that African production could make the line pay; in 1920 the CO completely reversed its attitude and here, as elsewhere, merely fell into line with Northey's pro-settler policy.[255]

The EAP Becomes a Colony

As with railway extension, Northey was expected to examine the potential annexation of the EAP as a colony following his arrival and report his views to the CO. Unlike the situation regarding the Uasin Gishu railway, Northey took some time to form an opinion and to forward it to London. As no word on the subject had come from the governor by the end of May 1919, the CO sent a reminder to Nairobi asking for Northey's views.[256] Northey recognized the advantages of annexing the EAP as a colony in so far as the floating of a loan under the terms of the Colonial Stock Act of 1900 was concerned, but he also appreciated that the status of the Sultan of Zanzibar's claim to the ten-mile coastal strip was a most crucial factor in any such action. Only after he had visited Zanzibar in October was Northey prepared to make his final recommendation.

On Zanzibar, Northey received the response he had hoped for. He discussed the issue of annexation with the acting resident who in turn approached the Sultan. The Sultan agreed to place no obstacle in the way of annexation of the ten-mile coastal strip, technically his domain. The only remaining obstacle to annexation of the whole EAP as a British colony, including the ten-mile strip, was the position of France. In an 1862 treaty, France and Britain had agreed to reciprocally respect the independence of Zanzibar, and in view of this treaty commitment, Northey urged the CO to "consider the possibility of approaching the French Republic."[257] As Northey sent the despatch shortly before his departure for Britain, he asked for the opportunity to discuss the matter with Milner while he was at home.

Upon receipt of Northey's recommendation, CO officials felt that they had nothing to lose by approaching France on the issue even though there was little likelihood of obtaining easy agreement. Fiddes felt that there was no harm in asking the Foreign Office to find out the French position on the matter "if we make it clear we are not prepared to pay through the nose for French acquiescence. I don't think there is the least likelihood of getting the French to agree unless we make it a condition of our doing something that they want."[258] The CO thus wrote to the Foreign Office early in 1920 to request that it approach France.[259] The Foreign Office was willing to seek a formal renunciation of the 1862 treaty, but it replied to the CO that it must have a definite assurance from Amery, then acting S of S, that he wished to go ahead. Amery did so on 21 January 1920 with an interesting observation. He wrote: "I think we might as well try now as later. The French can only agree or else show their hand by asking for the Gambia or something equally absurd."[260]

In the meantime, CO officials became convinced of the need to act as quickly as possible to change the EAP to a colony. Discussions in the Uasin Gishu Railway subcommittee in January pointed to substantial savings on interest if the money for the railway and other development projects could be borrowed under terms of the Colonial Stock Act. Bottomley summed up the situation succinctly on 27 January.

> We can't say how long it will be before we get the French reply and we do not know if it will be satisfactory. If we are to make early progress with Uasin Gishu project then it certainly seems worthwhile to annex the interior and leave the coast strip over for the present.[261]

Read and Fiddes strongly agreed, and the CO took steps to draw up an order-in-council providing for the annexation of the interior only as a colony as Bottomley had urged.[262]

By mid-February, the order-in-council was ready for review by the CO legal adviser. Before the review had been completed, the Foreign Office sent word of the French response to the request to consider the annexation of the coastal strip. The French felt that "the question of Zanzibar should only be discussed with all other African questions pending between the French and British governments." In other words, France would only agree to annexation in exchange for some concession from Britain elsewhere in Africa.[263] This response caused the CO to drop any further contacts with the French and push on with annexation of the interior only.[264] The CO review of the draft order-in-council was rapidly passed on to the law officers of the crown for their opinion on certain difficult issues raised by the CO's legal adviser.

Governor Northey, moreover, had in meetings at the CO proposed a name for the new colony when annexed. It would be Kenya. Northey's choice was taken from Mt. Kenya. As Milner told the king in March, Mt. Kenya was "the most dominating natural feature in the country and its central position makes it well known to the majority of residents and settlers."[265] Northey was particularly concerned, then and later, that the spelling of his choice should be Kenya, not Kenia as the then province was known.[266]

While waiting for a response from the law officers, the CO informed acting governor Bowring that the S of S had decided to pursue annexation of the EAP with the exception of the mainland dominions of the Sultan of Zanzibar.[267] The law officers returned a favorable response to the legal questions outstanding on 22 March, and the CO could now proceed with finalizing the order-in-council as quickly as possible.[268] This was complete by June, and the order was passed on 11 June. Northey was authorized to announce the change on his arrival in Nairobi.[269] Two days after his arrival, the governor made the first public announcement of the impending annexation to the Legco. The order-in-council reached Nairobi later, and it was published in the official gazette on 23 July. From that date, the EAP became known as the Colony and Protectorate of Kenya.[270]

The primary motivation behind the change had been, as Northey told the Legco, that it would be easier to float a loan for development.[271] Milner had made this point in an earlier letter to the chancellor of the exchequer. He wrote: "Our reason for wishing to annex the Protectorate is mainly (though not exclusively) financial. The large railway and other works for which the country is crying out involve the raising of loans, and I consider that the time has come when the Protectorate must float a loan on its own account."[272] Nevertheless, the change to the status of colony was very favorably received by Kenya's European settlers. It seemed to make easier their goal of white minority self-government. To most residents of the new colony, therefore, the change seemed to be a reiteration of the emphasis on European settlers and the pride of place that the colonial state and the CO gave them.[273]

Currency and Exchange

In contrast to the change to colony, General Northey arrived in Kenya with no charge to investigate and report on currency and exchange questions. Nevertheless, he was rapidly struck by the complaints of settlers directed toward the rise in value of the Indian rupee against the pound sterling after the war. Showing an often lamentable lack of economic acumen, Northey persistently advocated what he perceived to be a currency policy in the best interests of the settlers over the next two years. Such advocacy caused considerable friction with the CO, but it showed, as in other issues, that Northey was truly the settlers' champion.

The cause of the currency and exchange crisis that affected Kenya after the war lay in the rise in value, against sterling, of the Indian rupee. Silver-based rupee notes and coins (divisible into 100 cents) formed the unit of exchange. Before the war, the Indian rupee had been valued at one shilling and four pence (1/4) or fifteen rupees to the pound sterling. The war brought in its wake a rise in the price of silver. It began in 1916, and although appreciation was controlled by actions of the United States government in 1917, the withdrawal of American controls in May 1919 opened the way for a more rapid increase. By December the price had risen 186 per cent above that of 1915. Thus the value of the silver-based rupee began to rise rapidly in relation to sterling in 1919. In March its exchange rate stood at Shs 1/6, and it continued to rise throughout the remainder of the year, reaching Shs 2/4 by Christmas.[274]

The rising exchange value of the rupee in relation to sterling posed a threat to the settler producers. Their most important exports, coffee and sisal, went largely to Britain, and they therefore faced diminishing returns while still having to meet expenses (i.e. wages for labor and repayment of locally contracted debts) in rupees. It was the rising exchange rate and a desire for East Africa to be divorced from Indian currency which underlay settler calls for action from the colonial government. The Convention of Associations drew attention to the exchange rate at its January 1919 meeting, and on the arrival of Northey, a month later, the convention passed a resolution calling attention to the unfavorable exchange rate.[275]

The fluctuating rate had an impact on more than just the settlers. Asian merchants were affected as were Africans, both as consumers of imported goods and as employees on settler farms and estates. As in other matters, the EAP government paid little heed to the impact of the currency and exchange problems on these groups; it was the settlers as the producers of the protectorate's most important exports and potential importers of capital from Britain whose plight gained most sympathy from Northey.

The governor lost little time in adopting an attitude most supportive of what he conceived to be settler interests. He took his first step in a private letter to Amery in April. Calling attention to the problems caused by the rise in value of the rupee, Northey maintained that "at present there is a dead loss of 12 to 13 per cent on British capital coming into the country." He called for a gold standard with a "local coin such as a shilling or a local rupee. . . ."[276] It is important to note at this point that both at this time and later Northey took little account of the impact of the changes he was supporting on the Uganda Protectorate that used the same currency.

In this letter, Northey urged that the CO talk to "one of the leading men in the Protectorate" then in Britain, Grogan. While Bowring had little time for

Grogan, Northey found the settler leader most congenial and worked with the latter to promote the interest of the settlers, and more particularly the large landowners like Grogan. The latter maintained to Amery that "capital and interest liabilities of all mortgages and the entire wage bill of the country has been increased by 25 per cent, threatening ruin to the export industries which owing to a lack of shipping and the absence of personnel have been compelled to strain their credit to the limit."[277] Grogan's ultimate solution was to call for the introduction of British gold sovereigns into East Africa, but he maintained to CO officials that the rupee exchange must be immediately brought down to Shs 1/4. Grogan's "administrative solution" was premised on the fact that the East Africa and Uganda Currency Order-in-Council of 1905 had made the sovereign legal tender in East Africa for fifteen rupees. Importing sovereigns would thus bring an end to the use of the rupee and, as Grogan saw it, place East Africa on the gold standard.[278] Such an undertaking by the British government was virtually impossible. Export of gold sovereigns to East Africa had been prohibited both before and during the war; with Britain abandoning the gold standard in March 1919, the government would certainly not alter its stand in that regard.

A month later, Grogan pointed to another reason for concern with the rising rupee exchange rate. Selection of ex-soldiers for the settlement scheme was underway, and a number of applicants intended to transmit sterling to East Africa. They would face the prospect of seeing the value of their capital reduced if the exchange rate continued to rise.[279]

Northey's and Grogan's approaches forced the CO to consider the currency and exchange issue. Officials recognized the problems faced by the settlers, but they also realized that Kenya's Indian merchants trading with India would suffer from the changes proposed. Thus they recommended a conference with the Treasury to try to find a way around the difficulties.[280] Clearly having predominant sympathy with the settlers, the CO officials, after a conference on 1 July and further discussions with the Treasury, sent detailed proposals for "solving" the currency and exchange crisis to the governments of all Britain's East African dependencies in August. These called for the substitution of a new local rupee note, with an exchange value of Shs 1/4, for the Indian rupee. The convertibility of the existing rupee notes in East Africa would be temporarily suspended. The colonial governments were asked to respond as quickly as possible.[281] Yet even as they were despatched, some CO officials were far from certain that they would be beneficial. "I have no enthusiasm for the proposal," wrote Bottomley, "but we have got to do something and I see no alternative course."[282]

After consultation with the chief administrators of Uganda, Tanganyika, and Zanzibar, Northey telegraphed his response some five weeks later. Noting that neither Tanganyika nor Zanzibar favored a change in existing currency arrangements, Northey nevertheless pushed strongly for the adoption of the CO scheme. He did so because it would have the effect of stabilizing the protectorate's currency with sterling as the standard. The governor, neverthe-less, recognized that the proposals would entail "arbitrary and drastic action which will undoubtedly affect adversely some sections of the community temporarily. . . ."[283] In Northey's view, those likely to be hard hit included the EAP's African population as consumers and wage earners, Asian traders, local banks, and European commercial houses while "producers of exports of raw materials" (i.e. the settlers) "that is paid in England will benefit and the new settler will be able to bring his capital without apparent loss."[284]

With the governor's ringing endorsement, the CO was prepared to press on for Treasury approval of the scheme, even while realizing that the change involved both economic and political risks. In a lengthy minute on Northey's telegram, Bottomley admitted that the CO scheme ran the risk of producing higher prices and discontent among Africans, Asians, and European traders; nevertheless, he urged support for the settler producer at almost any cost.

> Personally I am in much the same position as when our telegram was sent, that is to say, I feel we can not foresee the effect of these proposals, that it may be worse than the condition they are intended to remedy, but that the position of the European producer in the E.A.P. and Uganda in particular is at present so serious that we have no option but to make a very hazardous experiment in those protectorates.[285]

The CO thus pressed the Treasury on 30 September for approval and draft-ing of the necessary order-in-council,[286] but a serious obstacle to any scheme of currency stabilization now emerged in the form of opposition of British banks operating in East Africa. These were the National Bank of India, the Standard Bank of South Africa, and the National Bank of South Africa. In response to reports that the banks were uneasy over the exchange situation, Bottomley noted in October: "One does not wonder that the banks are an-xious. . . . Apart from this they are feeling the shortage of money and they are advancing locally only 40 per cent on securities lodged in London."[287] The CO decided that it must now take the bankers "into our confidence." This seemed all the more appropriate as Northey was on his way home following surgery. A final decision on currency arrangements could thus wait for con-sultation with the governor and representatives of the banks.[288]

Consultation with the banks proved that the financiers had many objections to any scheme of stabilization of East African currency that might involve the artificial pegging of the exchange rate well below that of the Indian rupee (for example at Shs 1/4). When contacted in mid-November, none of the three banks endorsed the CO scheme. The strongest opposition came from the National Bank of India, which had the most extensive operations in East Africa.[289] While the bank maintained that the proposals would generate price inflation in Kenya, it also had self-interested reasons for being hostile to the scheme. The bank's general manager noted that it had advanced Indian rupees to settlers over many years, and if the present scheme was proceeded with:

We might be asked to accept payment in paper currency representing a rupee of the declared nominal value of Shs 1/4 instead of British Indian rupees which we had advanced at the present rate of Shs 2/2. You will readily see how serious the loss might be as rupees which have been provided by our Indian branches have eventually to be returned to them.[290]

The other banks agreed with the position of the National Bank of India.

The banks' opposition placed the CO squarely in the middle of a struggle that pitted the colonial state against representatives of metropolitan finance capital. In this dilemma, the CO consulted Sir William Mercer, Crown Agent for the Colonies, and arranged a meeting with the representatives of the three financial institutions.[291] On 12 December the bankers met CO officials, Mercer and P. H. Ezechiel of the Crown Agents, Northey, and Major Humphrey Leggett of the British East Africa Corporation in Amery's office. Although Amery stressed in his opening remarks that in the long run the "interest of the producer is the interest of all, including the banks," any hope that he might have had of bringing the bankers into line with CO thinking was quickly dissipated.[292] The bankers doubted whether any change was necessary, asserted that the loss to settlers was more apparent than real, and reaffirmed that the Indian rupees they had advanced in East Africa must be repaid in the same currency. Moreover, the banks held a strong trump card. Unless they were protected they would call in their advances to settlers.[293] It had been made clear to CO officials even before the meeting that the banks would send instructions to Nairobi for the advances to be called in if they were not satisfied with the outcome of the talks.[294] As CO officials were convinced that the settler producer formed the present and future basis of the EAP's prosperity, their potential ruin by the banks' action interposed a very real brake on any action unacceptable to finance capital.

After considerable discussion, Leggett, whose company was deeply involved in purchasing the Uganda cotton crop among other things, proposed the compromise of stabilizing the rupee at two shillings rather than Shs 1/4, thus greatly reducing the loss to banks. Mercer also thought the proposal to fix the rupee at two shillings was "worthy of very careful consideration."[295] No firm agreement could be reached, nor did Amery's invitation to those present to submit detailed observations in writing provide a way out of the quandary facing the CO. In their written responses after the meeting of the 12th, the bankers maintained their opposition to any scheme of stabilization that would entail loss to them. Both the National Bank of South Africa and the National Bank of India raised the spectre of a run on their East African branches if the CO scheme was carried out.[296]

The banks' opposition presented a dilemma that caused some officials to despair of finding any solution to the Kenya currency problem.[297] Ezechiel, the deputy crown agent, continued to seek an answer through negotiation with Leggett and the general manager of the National Bank of India. By 20 December, he had reached an agreement acceptable to the bank that provided a quite different scheme than previously contemplated. It represented a compromise between the demands of Kenya's settlers and the stand taken by bankers who refused to see their profits compromised to support the former.

In laying out the revised scheme, Ezechiel outlined several factors that necessitated both some alteration in Kenya's present currency and exchange system and stabilizing the exchange with that of Great Britain as soon as possible. A major reason for the scheme was "the desire of the Secretary of State to do something for the settlers, old and new, by meeting their demands to at least some extent, and to do something early so as to restore confidence for the introduction of new capital."[298] Also significant was "the necessity of obtaining for any new scheme that may be introduced the willing co-operation of the banks and in particular the National Bank of India, which . . . has much the most to lose by any reduction in the exchange value of the present rupee. . . ."[299] With the agreement of the latter bank, Ezechiel's compromise seemed to offer hope of early implementation.

The new scheme involved passing an order-in-council after which it would be announced that from a date to be fixed, "the standard unit of value in the EAP and Uganda will no longer be the Indian rupee." A new rupee would be prepared which would have a value of two shillings sterling. An East African Currency Board (hereafter EACB) would be established in London to maintain the rate of exchange with sterling at two shillings or ten to the pound.[300]

These proposals were far from what Northey and the settlers had demanded. The banks had forced considerable modification on the CO, which was left now to push a scheme that, Bottomley resignedly noted at the end of December, "will certainly involve a great amount of trouble and probably please nobody" but was justified by "the necessity for stabilizing exchange in the interests of the settlers."[301] Having persuaded himself that he was assisting the settlers, Amery approved the proposals.[302]

Yet events quickly showed that the settlers were far from happy. Since the "compromise" scheme would not bring the exchange rate back to the Shs 1/4 desired by the settlers, protests from them were soon forthcoming. Northey took the lead on their behalf early in January. The governor wrote to the CO expressing his disagreement with portions of the scheme that he felt was certain to provoke "the strongest local opposition." Northey particularly objected to the fact that the rupee was to be stabilized at a value some 50 per cent above the fifteen rupees to the pound that he termed "the traditional value." While Northey's letter revealed his shaky understanding of the exchange crisis, he made very clear the reason for stabilization at the prewar exchange rate. The settlers' cost of production, particularly wage bills, would otherwise rise by fifty per cent and settler exports "could not hold their own in the world's markets."[303] Grogan also strongly attacked the scheme in a series of letters to, and meetings with, CO officials in January 1920. He wrote of the proposals on 8 January: "Frankly they are appalling—legally unsound and economically NIHILIST."[304] The next day, both Grogan and Northey met Bottomley to express their opposition.[305]

The CO was once again caught in a dilemma. Faced on the one hand with this opposition, for which Bottomley indicated considerable sympathy, and on the other Amery's desire for rapid action, officials decided to place Ezechiel's scheme in abeyance and hold further discussions.[306] On 16 January a meeting at the CO, attended by Amery and Bottomley, O. E. Niemeyer of the Treasury, Mercer, Ezechiel, Northey, and Sir Robert Coryndon, Governor of Uganda, considered whether or not to proceed with Ezechiel's scheme to fix the rupee at Shs 2/-. Amery was committed to making an official statement at an early date, and this, in the words of the notes of the meeting "would appear to rule out any reduction to 1/4 as, even if the banks could be induced not to call in advances all other creditors would do so while they could."[307] Northey continued to hold out for an exchange rate of Shs 1/4, but his was a minority view. Even while not represented at this discussion, the banks position was strongly appreciated. While Amery decided to reserve final decision for further consideration, it was certain that the financial lobby would have the most persuasive voice.

This was made clear on 26 January when Mercer sent a lengthy memorandum to the CO proposing a final form the latter's decision might take. Key features were the introduction of an East African rupee, the establishment of an EACB in London to arrange for the production of the new rupee coins and notes, and stabilization of the new rupee, after a short transitional period, at two shillings or ten to the pound sterling.[308] Mercer made little attempt to hide the real appeal of the scheme.

> But the important consideration is that the National Bank of India is, it is understood, prepared to acquiesce in it. Unless the co-operation of the banks is secured, it is open to them to call up at once the existing advances to settlers and to decline to make any more. If the rate were fixed at a figure which they considered unreasonably low, they would probably do so in self defence before the new currency could be provided. . . .[309]

Following further discussion between Amery, Bottomley, Mercer, and Ezechiel, the latter's original proposal, slightly revised, was finally sent to the Treasury for approval and action on 10 February.[310]

The chancellor of the exchequer gave rapid assent, and, after first explaining it to representatives of the banks, the CO formally announced the new scheme in a press release of 13 February.[311] By the time the press release appeared, the exchange rate between the Indian rupee and sterling had risen to Shs 2/9, adding weight, in officials' minds, to the case for stabilization at Shs 2/-.[312] The announcement contemplated a limited transitional period leading to eventual stabilization at Shs 2/-. On 17 February, the substance of the public announcement made in Britain was telegraphed to Nairobi. The

CO maintained that stabilization at two shillings was being carried out for the relief of British settlers in East Africa but recognized Northey's opposition. The governor, noted the final sentence of the telegram, had been "unable to acquiesce fully in above arrangements as he was anxious that solution more favourable to settlers should be arrived at."[313]

This new policy was, however, the cause of further unhappiness for the settlers. Their protests were quick to emerge. Stabilization at Shs 2/- to the East African rupee would mean, in effect, that "planters will be saddled permanently with an increase of fifty per cent in production costs, and this will mean heavy losses and in some cases the ruin of what have been very prosperous industries."[314] Protests from Asian traders in Kenya both preceded and followed this. Acting Governor Bowring telegraphed his view on 21 February that the new scheme would be deeply resented by Indian merchants "who are very incensed already by rise in exchange with India and increased cost of food supplies caused by recent legislation."[315] No protests were heard from or on behalf of the African population of Kenya. The CO remained unmoved; settler producers and Indian traders could not force a change at this time. The CO replied crossly to Bowring's 21 February telegram with one of its own suggesting the production of food, such as rice, in Kenya rather than continuing importation from India and Burma.[316] Clearly those gaining the most from what proved to be a temporary solution were the British banks operating in East Africa, since stabilization at two shillings would cause them less in the way of losses than the other interest groups involved.

The CO moved quickly, moreover, to scrap the idea of a transitional period and to request that stabilization at two shillings be included in the new order-in-council then under preparation.[317] In the meantime, banks were informed, and it was presumed "they will fix exchange at 2/- at once."[318] The EAP government made a public announcement on 31 March that the S of S "has authorized an assurance being given that the two shilling rate is fixed and permanent."[319]

With this firm pledge by the imperial government, the new currency and exchange scheme seemed well on its way to becoming a reality, but Northey continued to hold out for a system more favorable to the settlers. "I much regret Colonel Amery's decision," he wrote to Bottomley, "to call the (new) coin a rupee. I think that the local administration should have been allowed to decide such a matter, and I know that all, officials and unofficials, would plump for a *florin*."[320] After further discussion, the CO decided to accept the governor's appeal and call the new unit of currency a florin rather than a rupee; at Northey's suggestion, the half rupee coin would be known as a fifty cent piece or one shilling.[321]

Thus when the order-in-council was finally prepared for promulgation in April, it provided for a new florin coinage, linked to sterling, to replace the Indian rupee. The florin was set at two shillings or ten to the pound sterling.[322] The order, approved on 26 April, also established the EACB with

Bottomley, Mercer, and Ezechiel as members. It was brought into force in Kenya and Uganda on 19 July 1920.[323]

Kenya's currency and exchange problems were far from over, but CO officials hoped that the stabilization of 1920 would prove a satisfactory compromise. The settlers, championed by Northey, had succeeded in obtaining a break from the Indian rupee, but they had not been able to bring about the kind of alteration of the rate of exchange that they desired. In this particular question, Northey suffered his first real rebuff from the CO. This was because of the opposition to any such scheme by metropolitan finance. The intervention of the British banks in this case not only caused a dilemma for the CO, but it also illustrated the substantial influence the bankers possessed. This provides an important guide for the future as metropolitan financiers and merchants would exert a not inconsequential influence on CO policy in the struggle for Kenya.

Even so, the years 1919 and 1920 had seen Kenya's settlers make substantial gains. The appointment of Northey as the EAP's governor placed the colonial state more strongly behind the European political and economic demands than ever before. Shortly after his arrival in Nairobi, Northey assumed the offensive, pushing for acceptance of policies he and the settlers favored on a sometimes reluctant CO. The latter had previously lost the initiative in Kenya affairs, and officials in London were pulled along in Northey's wake. On some issues left for the new governor's recommendations, the CO played a significant role in developing solutions, such as the change to colony or currency alterations, but more often than not, the CO gave way before the governor's pleadings, which often took the form of a flurry of telegrams demanding rapid action. Almost supine before Northey's pro-settler onslaught, the CO would find itself caught in the midst of an accelerating struggle over the direction in which Kenya was heading. The result would be to push the CO to intervene decisively. This would come in 1921 and 1922, and it would serve to check Northey's drive to entrench white supremacy. Events in Kenya and forces external to the CO and colonial state would force this intervention by London.

6
The CO Regains the Initiative, 1921–22

During 1921 and 1922, Kenya continued to be the focus of considerable CO concern as the controversies produced by the colony's labor, Indian, and currency policies, to name just a few, continued to burn brightly. As the struggle for Kenya intensified, and the CO sought solutions that would calm or defuse these controversies. At the same time, Kenya's economic situation forced itself powerfully on the attention of CO officials just as it did the colonial state.

Several distinct, yet related, forms of protest converged on the CO in 1921–22. Some represented the continuation of earlier protest movements. Prominent in this regard were the complaints of British humanitarian and church groups. These focused attention on Kenya's labor policies, but the humanitarians also pressed the CO for the adoption of schemes in such areas as education and agricultural development that they felt would be beneficial to Kenya's African population. Indian protest also continued. Indians in Kenya were unhappy with the settlement attempted by Milner, and, supported by the government of India and the IO, they persisted in pressing for rights equal to those granted to the smaller European settler community. The Indian question focused much attention on Kenya, and it was the most difficult and trying issue the CO had to contend with during this period because of the great conflict it generated.

In addition, the CO was compelled to take into account a new type of protest in this period with the emergence of African dissent. Most notably, Harry Thuku's East African Association (EAA) forced itself onto the awareness of London officials. African protest would play a very key part in holding back the colonial state's preference for European settler production and the enshrinement of white supremacy in the colony's economic, political, and social spheres.

Perhaps even more important in bringing about CO action to restrain the colonial state under Northey in its drive towards settler paramountcy was Kenya's continuing financial crisis. Through 1921, Kenya's external trade remained depressed, and the colony was faced with regular budgetary short falls and the need to cut expenditure and raise additional revenue. This situation

led British merchants interested in East Africa, and eventually the colonial
state and the CO, to recognize the need for restoring African production. The
protest of merchant capital, and the economic reality that lay behind it, would
be a most powerful factor in causing the CO to recapture the initiative in
Kenya affairs.

The result of this was that the CO moved, in the end quite dramatically, to
regain the initiative in Kenya affairs it had lost in previous years. The CO
forced significant alteration on Kenya policies in a number of areas, and the
establishment of London's control was graphically demonstrated in mid-1922,
with the recall of Sir Edward Northey.

Changes at the CO

The reestablishment of CO initiative was certainly not unrelated to the fact
that the leadership of the CO changed completely in 1921. The resignation of
Milner in February of that year, and the departure of Amery in April removed the arch-imperialist heads of the CO. Their successors at the political
leadership of the CO, Winston Churchill and E. F. L. Wood, were not wed-
ded to the Milner and Amery brand of imperialism. The new team, particularly Wood, were willing to consider solutions to Kenya issues less favorable
to the settlers. The same approach would be characteristic of Sir James
Masterton-Smith, who succeeded Fiddes as permanent under-secretary of
state at the end of August 1921.

Winston Churchill was no stranger to the CO or to the cabinet. His first
ministerial position, as a Liberal in 1905–8, had been parliamentary under-
secretary of state for the colonies. Churchill had gone from there to hold
several responsible cabinet-level positions prior to World War I, heading the
Board of Trade, the Home Office, and the Admiralty. Churchill's political
fortunes suffered during the war as he was, somewhat unfairly, blamed by the
Conservative Party for naval problems. Demoted as Asquith formed his May
1915 coalition, Churchill resigned six months later, to pursue active service in
the army. His former political ally, Lloyd George, brought Churchill back to
government, though not the cabinet, as minister of munitions in July 1917.
Churchill regained cabinet status in January 1919 when the prime minister
appointed him minister of war. In February 1921, he was transferred to the
CO.

Churchill brought with him an impressive record of political achievement,
and although he was somewhat disappointed at having not obtained a more
prestigious and important office, such as the Exchequer,[1] Churchill threw
himself into his new responsibilities with characteristic decisiveness. East
Africa did not form a major interest for Churchill as S of S. Most of his time

and interest was concentrated on the Middle East. Nevertheless, the ongoing controversies with regard to Kenya's labor policies and Indian question forced him, however briefly, to concentrate his attention on Kenya.[2]

On the whole, therefore, far greater responsibility for dealing with the multiple dilemmas provided by Kenya affairs devolved on Churchill's parliamentary under-secretary, E. F. L. Wood.[3] Wood joined the CO some two months after Churchill's appointment as Amery continued as parliamentary under-secretary to assist in the transition to new leadership. Wood, though also a member of the Conservative Party, came from an entirely different background than his predecessor, and his views on colonial questions proved to be quite different as well. Son of Lord Halifax, Wood was already a member of Oldham's "camp," having been a signatory to the 1920 memorandum. Wood's actions reflected a belief that "trusteeship" should form the basis of British policy towards Kenya, and, unlike Amery, he was prepared to emphasize, at least on some occasions, African interests.

Wood's first ministerial appointment in what would be a long and distinguished political career did not get off to a particularly auspicious start. He learned of his appointment from newspaper reports rather than from Churchill, and for the first several weeks on the job, he had no contact at all with his superior. Wood recalled in his autobiography that he became increasingly uneasy about this state of affairs, and he finally forced his way into Churchill's presence where he unleashed his frustration and demanded to be treated "with reasonable consideration." This broke the ice, and from that day on, Wood recalled, "no one could have been kinder than Churchill was to me."[4]

The other notable change in leadership at the CO took place in August 1921 with the retirement of Sir George Fiddes. Churchill's experience at the CO led him to desire to go outside the office and the colonial service for a new permanent under-secretary. He chose a much younger man with whom he had worked closely on a number of occasions previously. Sir James Masterton-Smith had impressed Churchill as a very able civil servant. Masterton-Smith had served Churchill as private secretary while the latter was First Lord of the Admiralty. As an assistant under-secretary, Masterton-Smith subsequently served under Churchill at the Ministry of Munitions. Although he had only been appointed permanent under-secretary at the Ministry of Labour slightly over a year earlier, Churchill tapped Masterton-Smith for the top civil service post at the CO as soon as he learned of Fiddes' intention to retire.[5] Masterton-Smith's appointment was publicly announced on the day Fiddes left office. This must, however, have been a difficult time for the new permanent under-secretary. A week prior to his appointment, his wife had been tragically killed in an accident.[6]

Masterton-Smith had virtually no experience in colonial affairs, but this would not prove, in every instance, a disadvantage. Unburdened by the prejudices of Fiddes, he was able to view Kenya's problems with more detachment and a willingness to look in new directions. Nevertheless, he listened to and, for the most part, acted on the experience and advice of the EAD.

The Continuing Labor Controversy

The conclusion of 1920 had brought no end to the controversy raging around Kenya's labor policies. Far from settling the issue, the revised Labour Circular of 1920 and the Native Authority Amendment Ordinance had done little to satisfy British humanitarian critics. They continued to find fault with Northey's labor recruitment methods, and they persisted in hammering the CO on the issue.

In early January 1921, the Archbishop of Canterbury forwarded a lengthy document to the CO that Oldham had drawn up in response to Milner's request at the 14 December meeting for specific evidence of labor abuse in Kenya. The document consisted of memoranda by Dr. John Arthur of the Church of Scotland mission at Kikuyu and the Reverend H. D. Hooper of the CMS.[7] Arthur began his memorandum by stating: "Every missionary knows that forced labour has been a fact for years in British East Africa, and that it still goes on today; that this has been not merely for Government, but for private interest." Besides providing several examples of what should have been unlawful compulsory labor, Arthur decried the "enormous depopulation of the Kikuyu Reserves" that was the result of forced labor policies, the rise in African taxation, and the large number of families "emigrating to settlers' farms" as squatters.[8] Hooper also discussed the "emigration" of Kikuyu from their reserve. The causes he identified for this phenomenon were increased taxation "before the need for it has been demonstrated," and the actions of chiefs, who were in the eyes of most Kikuyu "paid labour agents of the Government." Large numbers of young men were being forced out of the reserves for what Hooper viewed as the wrong motives. He was critical of both the encouragement of labor for private enterprise and compulsory labor for state obligations. In his opinion, moreover, government policy was producing growing discontent among the Kikuyu young men.[9]

The CO decided to send the document to Northey for his comments,[10] but in the meantime it received a despatch from the governor describing the working of the circular and the labor problem generally. He also submitted a schedule to illustrate the functioning of the Native Authority Ordinance. This led him to state "unhesitatingly that the Ordinance has been applied with circumspection. . . ."[11] Not surprisingly, Northey contended that the several facets of his labor policy (e.g. registration, the 1919 circular, and so forth) were working well and had produced a steady improvement in the supply of labor.

The CO response to Northey's report was rather cautious. Since Bottomley's interview with Elliot the previous December, the seeds of doubt as to the necessity for, and rightness of, Northey's labor policies had been planted in the minds of the permanent officials. Bottomley, in particular, was suspicious of the governor's attitude though he was not, in March, prepared to give Northey "any occasion to believe there is any suspicion as to the Govt's attitude."[12] The CO merely asked for further detail of labor instructions issued by Northey's government "for the record." Moreover, officials anxiously awaited the governor's response to the memoranda submitted by the Archbishop of Canterbury in January.[13]

Northey finally despatched a lengthy reply to the latter on 21 May. He began by reiterating what he considered "a truth which is obvious to any resident in East Africa." That "truth" was that the administrative officer was not a recruiter of labor for private enterprise; his function in that respect was "to encourage the growth of industrious habits among the natives." From this rather ridiculous misreading of his own policy that encouraged only the industrious habit of working for the settlers, Northey turned to deal with other subjects. He was not convinced that the examples submitted by Arthur and Hooper proved the existence of forced labor. The governor claimed to be alive to the potential abuse involved in the employment of women and in the wrongful application of the Native Authority Ordinance. He also went to considerable length to argue that his administration was not sacrificing African interests to those of whites by suggesting that he planned to use the greater revenue generated from increased African taxation to provide services in the reserves.[14]

By the time the CO received Northey's despatch, events had to a considerable degree passed it by, and there was no reason for officials to take any action on it. It had been decided that Northey would proceed home for consultation with Churchill on several East African issues; labor matters could be raised with him then. Even more important, CO officials had learned, from an absolutely reliable source, that Northey's labor policies were productive of little positive benefit, the labor circulars and the Native Authority Ordinance amendment could easily be dispensed with without causing any labor shortage, and that most administrative officials in Kenya did not support the governor's labor initiative. Armed with this information, the CO was now prepared to decisively intervene in the Kenya labor controversy.

It is important to detail, at this point, how this CO change of attitude had come about. In many scholarly accounts, this CO intervention, and the form it took, has been attributed to humanitarian pressure, and in particular the suggestions of J. H. Oldham.[15] That this was not, in fact, the case can be demonstrated by a reconstruction of CO correspondence and action in the period May to August 1921.

Crucial in this respect was Dr. Norman Leys's criticism of Kenya labor policy that was addressed to Borden Turner M.P. early in May. Leys had served as a medical officer in Kenya and Nyasaland. Now retired in Britain, he was a powerful critic of British policy in Kenya throughout the 1920s.[16] In his letter, Leys stated that it was government policy to induce the African male to leave home to work for the European. The chief factor in this, he asserted, was compulsion. He stated: "The pretense that the system is not compulsory is the most dangerous falsehood." Africans were utterly power-less to resist the pressure of the administration that they go out to work.[17] Leys labelled the defense that those who worked in their own fields would not be compelled to work for whites "preposterous". He maintained that the labor of African men was "being won at the expense of grain stores. . . ."

The only remedy for forced labor, Leys continued, was to treat it as slavery and sweep it away. Leys urged making it plain to every African that whether he lived and worked at home or went away to work for wages "are matters with which no public servant has any concern." Leys's solution to the prob-lem of forced labor was to get the government out of the business of labor re-cruitment and allow the African to decide for himself whether he wished to work in his own land or for wages outside the reserve.

CO officials were not pleased with the charges made by Leys as they were tinged with what was viewed as "pronative fanaticism." Nevertheless, Leys's long residence in Africa meant that his criticisms were, in Parkinson's words, "worth more consideration than most of the anti-slavery people." Parkinson suggested sending a copy of Leys's letter to John Ainsworth, then on retire-ment leave in Britain. The latter's knowledge of Africans was considered to be "far greater than Dr. Leys's;" the late CNC should be asked to comment in detail on Leys's views.[18] Bottomley and Wood enthusiastically agreed with Parkinson's suggestion, and on 27 May Ainsworth was sent Leys's letter with a request that he furnish the S of S with his observations on Dr. Leys's statements.[19]

This request to Ainsworth set in motion a train of events that would lead directly to the CO's decision to significantly alter Northey's labor policy. It will be remembered from the preceding chapter that Ainsworth had repre-sented, at the end of 1920, the main CO hope that Elliot's views regarding Northey's labor policy might be overstated or inaccurate. Ainsworth had served in Kenya since 1892, and Bottomley and the other officials respected his very intimate knowledge of the territory. Ainsworth had, since well before the war, enjoyed a reputation, both among settlers and CO officials, of being the most pro-African of all senior administrators.[20] Rather than wait for Ainsworth's reply to Leys's attack, however, the former CNC was invited to London to meet with Wood on 31 May.

If officials had been aware of no misgivings on Ainsworth's part prior to this time, they now had a chance to hear them first hand. Ainsworth unburdened himself of his long-standing disagreements with Northey's policy. The 1920 Native Authority Amendment, which provided the means to obtain compul-sory labor for government work, had done little good, Ainsworth maintained, and it could just as well be done away with. He also strongly put forward his view that neither district commissioners, chiefs, nor headmen should recruit labor nor should they direct young men to particular employers.[21]

Though astonished by Ainsworth's criticism, Wood and Bottomley quickly realized the implication of the former's statements. With this attack, Northey's labor policy had been blown apart; the suspicions raised by Bottomley's interview with Elliot had now been confirmed. The CO officials realized that they had to move as quickly as possible to bring about a change in Kenya labor policy. Ainsworth was therefore asked to put his views in the form of a draft circular. Ainsworth's rather wordy circular consisted of six paragraphs. Reduced to the bare minimum, the draft document provided for the cancellation of the October 1919 circular together with that of 1920. Likewise, the Native Authority Amendment Ordinance should be abolished.[22] The draft circular also put forward as government policy Ainsworth's long-standing view that there should be a "free labour market" for both government and private employers. Government officials, chiefs, and headmen should do no more than exhort "habits of industry"and discourage laziness among young men. Whether the latter worked on family plots in the reserve or for wages outside made no difference.[23]

When Ainsworth provided, on 7 June, his observations on Leys's charges, moreover, they showed that despite significant disagreement with the former's description of African life, Ainsworth confirmed Leys's view that Northey's labor policy was wrong and in need of considerable alteration. Ainsworth concluded:

> I now incline to the opinion that the Government should step aside as regards all actual activity in connection with native labour and confine itself to a policy of preaching industrious habits among the natives. The Native Authority Ordinance 1920 is, I feel, undesirable; it will continue to make for misunderstandings, while it is of no particular benefit to Government departments.[24]

Armed with Ainsworth's devastating recommendations, Bottomley and Wood decided, so as to "be more courteous to the Governor," to await Northey's arrival in Britain and his report on abuses that had arisen under his system before setting forward Ainsworth's draft circular as the basis of a policy change. In the meantime, Bottomley promised to see if he could revise the draft to improve its language.[25]

In the midst of CO consideration of this change in policy, another memorandum from J. H. Oldham arrived. Titled Memorandum on Native Affairs in the East African Protectorates and dated 17 May, the document questioned "whether the principle of trusteeship in the government of subject peoples is being successfully applied in our East African empire." Oldham was highly critical of labor policy in Kenya, and he renewed his call for the appointment of a Royal Commission to investigate all aspects of British policy in Kenya and the other East African dependencies.[26] Oldham went on to argue that "an honest interpretation" of the principle of trusteeship for Kenya's Africans required adequate land, comprehensive and progressive education, and the improvement of agriculture along with the development of industries. Concluded Oldham: "The policy which leaves the native population no future except as workers on European estates can not be reconciled with the principle of trusteeship nor can it in the long run conduce to the economic prosperity of the East African protectorates."[27]

CO officials were still not keen to see a Royal Commission. Bottomley felt that Ainsworth's circular could form the basis of a new labor policy. In his minute on Oldham's memo, he proposed to make Northey's anticipated reply to allegations of abuse "a peg on which to hang Mr. Ainsworth's new suggestion and we can even now tell the Conference of Missionary Societies that we are exploring a fresh avenue which we hope will lead to a settlement without the delay of a Royal Commission."[28] Bottomley's minute and subsequent CO action clearly illustrate that it was Ainsworth's criticism and advice, not Oldham's, that formed the basis for CO alteration of Kenya labor policy.

In mid-June, Wood followed up his conversation with Ainsworth by submitting the latter's draft circular to Churchill. Wood suggested that if the S of S decided against the appointment of a Royal Commission, "we shall have to try to do something in the direction of a new circular." Ainsworth's draft could be used as the basis for it, "but it will want a good deal of redrafting." Nevertheless, Ainsworth's recommendation that Northey's labor circulars calling for encouragement of labor for private purposes should go and that compulsion for public works was "not necessary and wasteful and could be dispensed with" would form the basis of the new circular.[29]

Churchill decided not to appoint a Royal Commission for East Africa. This left the permanent staff, using Ainsworth's suggested circular as a starting point, to hammer out changes in Kenya labor policy. This was accomplished after extensive discussion with Northey and Coryndon; by the first week of August, it had been concluded. It must have been a painful experience for Northey as the policy he had strongly advocated and defended for the previous year and a half was dramatically altered. At the conclusion of the discussions, it was determined not to issue a new circular. The CO summarized the changes to be made under three headings in an internal memorandum. First, no objection was seen to "traditional unpaid labour by natives in the reserve, for the benefit of the reserve," and no change should be made. Second, the encouragement of labor for private employers by government would have to go. Government officials and chiefs were to "take every opportunity of inculcating among the natives habits of industry, whether inside or outside the reserve, but beyond taking steps to put in touch with one another the employer of labour and the native who wishes to find employment, Government officials should take no part in recruiting labour for private employment."[30] Third, compulsory paid labor for government was not completely scrapped. The CO hoped that it would not be necessary, but as a result of Northey's pleadings, local legislation that empowered the government to make Africans work for public purposes "should remain on the statute book in an amended form." With the exception of paid porters for government servants on tour or the transport of urgent government stores, the government would have to obtain prior authority of the S of S "to utilize the powers of compulsion conferred by the local legislation."[31]

This memorandum became the basis for a despatch to be sent to acting governor Bowring announcing the change in policy. Before sending the despatch to Kenya, however, Wood approached Oldham and the Archbishop of Canterbury to seek their support for the draft despatch that had been drawn up. After hurried consultation with several Kenya missionaries then in Britain, Oldham replied to Wood on 15 August. He and the missionaries were "in complete agreement" with the general spirit and intention of the new policy, but there were two points upon which Oldham was not completely satisfied. The first dealt with unpaid labor in the reserves. The Kenya missionaries felt that this held considerable potential for abuse, and that many young men resented the use of such powers by the chiefs.[32]

The second point of difficulty for Oldham related to labor for private employers. He and the missionaries "heartily welcome the statement that government officials will in future take no part in recruiting labour for private employment," but they feared the qualifying words that immediately preceded that statement in Wood's draft might "leave the door open to some of the evils to which attention has been directed in some of our previous memoranda."[33]

Wood quickly replied to Oldham's criticism. He refused to contemplate doing away with "traditional unpaid labour" by Africans in the reserves, but the official was prepared to make some alteration in the despatch with regard to the encouragement of labor for private employers. Even though the undersecretary asserted that the government "is right in doing what it can to let the employer and employee know the wants of each other," he was prepared to vary the despatch's wording. The sentence to which Oldham objected was altered to read:

> But beyond taking steps to place at the disposal of natives any information which they may possess as to where labour is required and at the disposal of employers information as to sources of labour available, the Government officials will in future take no part in recruiting labour for private employment.[34]

This latter change proved satisfactory to Oldham, and the CO decided to go ahead with the final preparation of its despatch to Bowring. Oldham telegraphed on 23 August that he and the missionary bodies he represented were "entirely satisfied with the main lines of the proposed policy," and that they greatly preferred Wood's rewording.[35] While ordering the preparation of the despatch for Kenya to be taken in hand, Wood sent Northey a copy of Oldham's letters. He hoped the governor would agree "that we have reached a satisfactory solution of this question, in which we may hope to have the missionary societies and their friends with us instead of against us. . . ."[36] The despatch was sent to Bowring on 5 September.[37]

The changes of policy laid down in the S of S's despatch were published as a parliamentary paper. They had the desired effect in dousing the fire of humanitarian protest in Britain. Not only were Oldham and his friends satisfied; the ASAPS let the CO know, in October, their appreciation "of the steps which are being taken to remove the objectionable features of the present labour system."[38] It would be foolish, and historically inaccurate, on the other hand, to suggest that the new CO policy put an end to abuses in labor recruitment in Kenya. Compulsion would continue to play a prominent part in recruiting for both government and private employers as a number of scholars have demonstrated.[39] CO acquiescence in "traditional unpaid labour" in the reserves, moreover, was based upon a completely fallacious view of the traditional history of Kenya's peoples. Labor for needed public works had not been ordered out by chiefs; rather it was the result of cooperative action among neighboring people who were usually related to one another by ties of kin.

Rather the significance of the changes mandated by the CO lie in a different direction. They represented an important reassertion of imperial initiative and control in Kenya affairs. Since early in World War I, the CO had allowed Kenya's governors an increasingly free hand in developing policy initiatives on a number of important issues. The CO intervention represented what would be the first of several attempts in the 1921–22 period to regain the initiative over Kenya policy. That this was the result of strong humanitarian protest and pressure in Britain there can be no doubt.[40] Nevertheless, the CO was not prepared to move decisively in the issue of labor until officials had obtained a clear indication that Northey's labor policy was based on false assumptions of the African way of life, that it represented the total subordination of African production to that of European settlers, that it was ill-advised and unnecessary, and, far from having the support of European administrators, that it had been devised largely to please the settlers and reduce their complaints. These facts were finally brought home to the CO, not by missionaries and "cranks" in Britain, but by men on the spot, such as Elliot and Ainsworth.

Currency and Exchange

Like Milner's attempt to solve the labor controversy, the CO's currency stabilization of 1920 had not ended the controversy surrounding the currency and exchange system in Kenya. It was very unpopular with the settlers, and by the middle of that year, CO officials were faced with an additional difficulty that cast considerable doubt on the wisdom of stabilization at two shillings to the rupee. By July, the exchange rate had fallen below two shillings, and on 19 July, the import of Indian rupees into East Africa had to be prohibited.[41] The necessity for these restrictions pointed clearly to future problems, the chief of which would be continued settler unhappiness with the currency settlement.

The exchange rate for the Indian rupee remained below two shillings for the rest of the year, and the prohibition of imports of rupee coins and notes did not solve the problem as smuggling, in particular of one rupee notes, had reached large proportions by the end of 1920. This placed the EACB in danger of sustaining great losses, largely as a result of having to redeem the one rupee and larger notes at two shillings in Kenya while obtaining only Shs 1/6 for them in India; by the end of December, the board had incurred a loss of over £500,000 on such transactions.[42] This circumstance provided the settlers with a very powerful ally in their continued insistence on stabilization below the two shilling rate. Indeed, the EACB met Amery on 29 December 1920 and urged the need for quick action to avoid the board amassing even greater liabilities. The board's chairman, Mercer, pressed for demonetization of the one rupee note without notice so that the board's liability to redeem them at two shillings should cease. Rupee coins, on the other hand, could not be demonetized immediately as there was, as yet, no florin coinage to replace them.[43]

Faced with this new dilemma, the CO quickly telegraphed to the governors of Kenya and Uganda that it was satisfied that rupee notes must cease to be legal tender forthwith, but it sought their views on the fate of the rupee coins.[44] Northey replied recommending immediate demonetization of one rupee notes after a week's notice. He reported that Coryndon concurred with this advice and the fact that rupee coins could not, at that juncture, be replaced.[45]

To the governor's call for urgent action was added further pleas from settlers. Representatives of Kenya and Uganda producers addressed a particularly strong demand for reduction of the rate of exchange to Mercer early in January. While noting that the settler farmers had been affected by the worldwide depression, Associated Producers of East Africa and Uganda complained bitterly that they "are debarred from the relief which they might otherwise have obtained from the fall in the price of silver and the rupee", thus making their competitive position impossible.[46]

Having thus heard from the governors and representatives of the producers, Mercer set out at length for Amery the board's recommendations for further action. The Indian rupee would be demonetized with at most a week's notice, thus removing the danger that the currency board would incur further huge losses. The florin would remain at two shillings, "and both the small subsidiary coins and old EAP government notes of five rupees and upwards must, we think, be left on the basis of the florin."[47] Mercer justified the plan by stating that it would benefit both the board (and therefore the imperial government) and Kenya settlers. Assuming that florin coins would be available in Kenya in late April or early May, it would result in the eventual disappearance of the rupee from Kenya and a saving to the board. Moreover, he argued, a reduction "in the sterling value of wages seems practically certain to ensue. . . ."[48]

Amery accepted the whole of the currency board's plan, and on 19 January it was telegraphed to Northey for his approval. The Indian rupee was to be demonetized without notice, and prohibitions on import and export of such rupees would be removed. In transmitting these and the other recommendations, the CO concluded with the justification that they "appear to be best in interest of Board and settlers. . . ."[49]

Northey's response must have shocked the board and CO officials who thought that they had averted the crisis that had loomed at the end of the year. The governor telegraphed on 23 January totally rejecting the currency board's scheme, and setting out detailed proposals of his own. These called for the immediate demonetization of the Indian rupee without notice and the equally immediate reduction of the florin exchange rate to sixteen pence (Shs 1/4). The two shilling florin, maintained the governor, was "ruining the country and I have received from every side urgent appeals praying for reconsideration with a view to decreasing the cost of production inflated by action taken last year and once again rendering local enterprise financially remunerative."[50] He went on to assert that Coryndon supported the urgent need to revert to the Shs 1/4 florin, and that Kenya and Uganda must eventually adopt the English pound and shilling as their currency.

Northey made clear that his motive was again to call for an exchange rate that would lower the settlers' production costs. The governor had met settler elected members of the Legco on 19 January, and had promised to support an exchange rate of Shs 1/4.[51] Allying the colonial government fully with the settlers as in 1919, he called for a reduction in the exchange rate so that the colony might avoid bankruptcy. As a result of his experience a year earlier, moreover, the governor deprecated "any discussion with banks or houses financially interested" and called for London's approval of his plan "as soon as possible."[52]

The CO and the EACB were surprised by the governor's telegram, but were at first prepared to accept his plan as he had strongly asserted that it had the support of all classes in Kenya and the government of Uganda. The EACB's position was "that in view of the Governor's attitude we must give way."[53] Thus the CO telegraphed a cautious reply on 26 January. While reminding the governor that many of the settlers' economic difficulties were the result of the world depression, the CO omitted only two portions of Northey's plan from further consideration (withholding all florin coins and fifty cent pieces from circulation and introducing as soon as possible the English one shilling coin). No objection was raised to reducing the exchange rate to Shs 1/4, but the CO reply expressed its reluctance to act without first consulting the three banks.[54] Northey replied quickly, reemphasizing the need to adopt a Shs 1/4 rate of exchange. The governor supported this demand by asserting that there was a great deal of uncertainty in Kenya, making a settlement daily more urgent, and he asked for early action on his proposals.[55]

Yet implementing Northey's salvation of the producers proved extremely difficult. These ideas were no more palatable to financiers in 1921 than they had been a year earlier. The bankers still held the trump cards and were prepared to use them to keep the exchange rate at two shillings. This time their position was also shared by both Asian and European merchants in East Africa.

On 2 February, the EACB met representatives of the banks together with O. E. Niemeyer of the Treasury. The banks were extremely hostile to any alteration of the exchange rate. Convinced that the economic hardships of the settlers were due to the depression, not the currency system, they doubted that a change in the exchange rate would really reduce the settler's production costs because the purchasing power of the local currency would fall and higher wages would be demanded. The banks further complained that the scheme involved "arbitrary interference by Government with existing contracts," which could prove disastrous for them.[56] They stood to lose the difference between the Shs 2/- and 1/4 rates of exchange, and were most unwilling to countenance such a bailing-out of the white farmers.

The banks followed up their opposition to the governor's scheme with very belligerent letters in succeeding days. The National Bank of South Africa, for example, laid great stress upon the fact that the S of S for the Colonies had given an assurance the year before that the two shilling exchange value was fixed. It asserted that if the government made arbitrary changes in the currency of East Africa, there would be a lack of confidence, and "the banks, in their own interests, will have to consider the advisability of restricting facilities to settlers. . . ."[57] The National Bank of India strongly agreed.[58] The banks were in a position, moreover, to do more than merely protest. They acted to protect themselves and put pressure on the colonial and imperial governments by agreeing to suspend all currency transfers from Kenya and Uganda to Britain, stopping the purchase of bills from East African shippers, and refusing to increase their holdings in East African currency.[59]

Niemeyer also found Northey's plan unacceptable. Both at the meeting of 2 February and in a later memo, the Treasury representative strongly opposed any change to fifteen rupees (or florins) to the pound.[60] He well represented the Treasury's strong postwar opposition to what were seen as inflationary schemes.[61] The CO could thus expect little sympathy from the Treasury for Northey's plan.

At the same time, Northey's proposals to change the exchange rate were encountering opposition in Kenya itself. The European community was far from united behind the champion of the settler producers. The Nairobi Chamber of Commerce, made up largely of European merchants, protested at the proposed reversion to Shs 1/4 as likely to create a feeling of insecurity.[62] Nairobi bank managers also vehemently protested against any alteration in the Shs 2/- rate, arguing that it would probably produce serious failure among the Kenya commercial community.[63]

Despite this dissent, Northey continued to press London to adopt his scheme. He assured the CO that the producers of Kenya were solidly behind him. As he was accustomed to telling London officials, it was a matter of thinking largely in these matters of empire building. Kenya settlers, not merchants, would play a vital part in that exercise through the production of raw materials required by the empire. Thus Northey continued to support what he simplistically saw as their interests in the name of developing the empire.

Governor Northey was undoubtedly aware, nevertheless, that there would be opposition to his plan, not only from commercial interests in Kenya but from the British banks. He therefore resolved on an audacious gamble to ensure that his view prevailed. He decided on 7 February to summon the Legco in emergency session; it would consider proposals for "solving" the currency crisis, and official members would "be free to exercise their discretion as to how they vote."[64] The governor informed the CO on the same day, and stated that he would telegraph "their decision to London which he "presumed" must be subject to the S of S's approval.[65]

The CO reacted quickly to Northey's manoeuvre. A curt telegram was hastily despatched to the governor in which the S of S laid it down that "it should be clearly understood that there is no question of decision of Legislative Council."[66] The CO was "anxious to have their views" but would take responsibility for the final decision. The wire from London voiced the hardening opinion of officials and currency board that "results of your proposals would not justify departure from the policy of a stable florin at 2/- which on the strength of statements made here and East Africa has been regarded as permanent."[67] The governor was warned that the special session should not limit itself to debating the pros and cons of his proposals but should consider fully other alternatives.

Before receiving this telegram, however, Northey had gone ahead with his brash scheme. At his urging, the Execo agreed that the acting treasurer would place a single motion before the Legco when it met the following day, calling for alteration of the standard coin to its prewar rate of fifteen to the pound sterling.[68] Northey enthusiastically endorsed the Execo's unanimous recommendation, expecting that the motion would also find total support among the settler elected members of the Legco.

In his haste to present London with a strong resolution in favor of his proposals, Northey seriously miscalculated the amount of support he could obtain from the Legco. He undoubtedly had the backing of the large concessionaire land owners, such as Grogan and Lord Delamere, but the interests of settlers such as these were not heavily represented in the council. The first European elections in 1920 had, in fact, produced a victory for the "small men" and those tied to commercial interests in Nairobi and Mombasa; the "large men" won only three of the eleven seats.[69] Neither Grogan nor Delamere were members of the Legco that voted on Northey's February proposals, and the Nairobi Chamber of Commerce was able to obtain more than sufficient support among European elected members, who were in any event leaderless and "in disarray", to secure the downfall of Northey's plan.[70]

The ground thus caved in under the settlers' champion on 10 February. The motion engineered by Northey was heavily defeated as only one settler voted for it.[71] An alternative motion supporting the continuation of the exchange rate at Shs 2/- and calling for appointment of a committee "to devise ways and means of introducing such currency on a sterling basis, at the earliest date, as will make the shilling, or coin of similar denomination, the standard coin" was unanimously adopted.[72] In the end there was no question of Northey's ploy defeating the CO and the London bankers. Northey could not even take the settlers with him. W. M. Ross's description of the governor captures well his shock and perplexity at what was an unexpected defeat.[73]

Northey lost little time in trying to put the best possible face upon his failure to unite the settlers behind his scheme. Having received the CO telegram of 9 February which favored maintaining the pledge to keep the exchange rate at Shs 2/-, he reported the Legco's action to London by telegraph later on the 10th. The governor adopted a triumphant and knowing tone, posing as the real mover of his motion's defeat! While this was unlikely to fool the CO, Northey stated that unofficial members of the Legco had been "brought to see that Your Lordship's pledge of stability of florin fixation must stand good."[74]

After receiving Northey's telegram, the CO rapidly announced its decision to retain the two shilling rate. A brief statement that it had been decided to keep the florin at its present rate of exchange with sterling was sent to London newspapers on 13 February.[75] The banks thus clearly emerged victorious in this round of the currency crisis. They had accepted the two shilling rate of exchange with some reluctance in 1920, but had stood firm against any change early in 1921, thus bringing about the demise of Northey's devaluation scheme aimed at assisting the settler producer at the expense of the bankers and merchants.[76]

The Failure of the Shilling Swindle

The defeat of Northey's scheme to return the rate of exchange to Shs 1/4 did not bring to an end the efforts of the colonial state to help the settlers lower their costs and improve their competitive advantage in the world market in this time of depressed trade. If financiers could not be brought to provide the assistance, then Kenya's African population would be made to fill that role.

Even before the Legco meeting of 10 February, such an alternative was being spoken of in the Kenyan press.[77] With much fanfare, the *EAS* put forward just such a scheme. It urged that florins be withheld from circulation while the government introduced sterling currency (pounds, shillings, and pence). Sterling and the Indian rupee would thus circulate in the colony at unequal values. This could work to the benefit of the settler. "The employer of labour will be able to reduce his wages openly and to continue to pay his natives in Indian Rupees as long as his natives demand them, instead of their equivalent in Sterling. The employer will be able to purchase them at the world's market value."[78] It will be recalled that the rupee had, by this time, sunk below the florin value of two shillings. The *EAS* presumed that Africans would continue to demand to be paid in rupees and thus unwittingly aid in lowering the settlers' cost of production.

When the committee established by the Legco, consisting of six producers, two European merchants, two Indian merchants, one chartered accountant, and four official members of council, made its report, it came up with a scheme similar to this in many respects. Its recommendations were telegraphed to London on 19 February. The committee advocated that "as soon as possible an East African shilling of value 1/20th of pound should be introduced and be coin of general circulation."[79] The Indian rupee coins should be removed from Kenya as soon as possible, and the existing cents were to be adopted as 1/100th of a shilling rather than a florin.

These recommendation called for the tying of Kenya's currency directly to sterling, a persistent demand of the settlers and Northey for the past two years. This met no opposition from the EACB or the banks. What was new in the committee's plan was the introduction of an East African shilling as the standard coin. The committee's call for the use of existing 50-, 25-, five- and one-cent coins with the new shilling, moreover, represented a new way to benefit the settler producer at the expense of the African wage-earner rather than the banks. By paying the same number of such coins to workers once the transfer from rupees to shillings was complete, the settler stood to halve his wage bill.

Surprisingly, the reaction at the CO and the currency board to the latter aspect of the Kenya plan was largely positive. The CO quickly replied to Northey, altering only minor aspects of the new scheme and asking for a full statement of his views. The CO and the EACB had no objection to the immediate demonetization of rupee coins by florin notes, but felt that such redemption must take place within one month. They also suggested an alteration to the proposal to reduce the value of cents to those of a shilling. "It seems necessary that one cent, five cent, and ten cent pieces should be reduced to corresponding fractions of shilling without compensation, but that twenty-five cent and fifty-cent pieces should be redeemable at florin value."[80]

The CO and the EACB do not seem to have fully appreciated the negative impact on Africans, who held the bulk of the ten-, five-, and one-cent coins. They were thus willing to consider favorably the introduction of a new East African shilling while reducing the value of those subsidiary coins. The

EACB discussed the committee proposals again on 2 March, and the board reaffirmed its view that steps should be taken to mint an East African shilling "midway in size" between the existing shilling and florin. Existing one-, five- and ten-cent pieces "should be marked down to one hundredths of a shilling without notice or compensation."[81]

While making this recommendation, the EACB expressed skepticism about the results of the shilling policy. Members felt that the prospect of obtaining a reduction in production costs was very small as they felt that Africans would, despite the differing size of the coins, quickly recognize that the shilling was worth only half a rupee. Thus since the board foresaw that no disadvantage could result from the adoption of what it termed "the shilling policy", it considered "that in deference to the strong local body of opinion, it should be adopted."[82]

Once again, the imperial authorities were willing to accept a questionable policy because it was advocated by Northey and the Kenya settlers rather than on its merits. It promised to work what W. M. Ross correctly described as a "shilling swindle" on Kenya's and Uganda's African populations.[83] Nevertheless, it could also save the currency board the cost of minting new subsidiary coins immediately, and the London officials hoped that this would finally provide a solution to what had been a most intractable problem.

On 19 March, the CO telegraphed its final decisions in the matter to Northey. It approved the minting of an East African shilling, and an order-in-council would be prepared making it the standard coin and legal tender. The order would provide that "existing one cent, five cent, and ten cent pieces will be marked down to cents of shilling."[84]

Though he had personally taken little part in the currency decisions since assuming office in February, S of S Churchill finally made the new policy public in a statement to the House of Commons at the end of May.[85] He announced that the CO had decided to maintain the original scheme in its essential features but with the substitution of a shilling for a florin.[86] In response to supplementary questions, Churchill stated that the decision had been to "retain the existing exchange value of the rupee at two shillings as against saying that it should be dropped to the prewar value."[87]

Although Churchill made no mention of the reduction in value of the ten-, five-, and one-cent pieces, criticism of that part of the new scheme was already being voiced in Britain and Uganda, and was increasingly heard in and out of parliament. As with the labor question, it came from missionary and humanitarian quarters in Britain. Here also, Oldham was active in pressing opposition to policies which he felt were disadvantageous to the African population. At his urging, the Archbishop of Canterbury came to the CO in early May to protest the reduction in value of the coins. The latter felt the measure would have a negative impact on Africans, and he read a letter from East Africa that stated that there were 108,000,000 such coins in the hands of Africans.[88] Of particular significance were those held by African cotton growers in Uganda, to whom payment was normally made in cents.

After the archbishop's visit, Bottomley set about estimating the value of coins in circulation with the help of the Kenya Blue Book of statistics. He arrived at a value of 1,074,327 rupees; assuming that all were in the hands of Africans, Bottomley, applying his genius for mathematics, came up with "an average of 18 cents for each of the six million natives of Kenya and Uganda, or say two shillings for a family of six, which under the proposal complained of would therefore incur a loss of one shilling."[89] This together with the expense, inconvenience and delay involved in minting a new subsidiary coinage of cents provided the CO's major justification for holding to this scheme in the face of continued criticism. "We can at least claim", concluded Bottomley, "that by cheating the native of his twopence once for all we are saving him from continued frauds by the petty trader. . . ."[90]

However, public attacks on the scheme soon followed. Within a week of the archbishop's visit, criticism appeared in *The New Statesman*.[91] The following month, critical questions were raised in parliament. On 8 June, for example, W. Ormsby-Gore questioned the decision and Earl Winterton called for the deferral of the scheme until the House of Commons had the opportunity of debating the issue.[92] Nevertheless, the CO maintained its support of the initiative as "the lesser evil," and Bottomley's calculation of a loss of one shilling per family had already been made part of the Common's record.[93]

Nevertheless, further criticism of the Kenya administration in Britain and protests from Kenya missionaries and the Uganda administration caused the currency board and the CO yet again to reconsider the issue. The mid-July debate on the CO vote in the Committee of Supply sparked strong attacks on policy in Kenya from both Conservative and Labour members.[94] In late July, the Alliance of Protestant Missionary Societies in Kenya presented a formal protest over the proposed reduction in value of cents to the Kenya government.[95]

The CO first reconsidered the matter in September when deciding the date on which the Kenya and Uganda (Currency) Order-in-Council, embodying the new scheme, should come into effect in East Africa. The real question, as Bottomley noted, was who was going to pay for the reduction: the African population, the banks in East Africa, the East African governments, or the EACB? As a member of the latter, Bottomley was certain that the board, already deeply in debt, should not be required to do so. Thus he concluded: "In the circumstances I think we should maintain the position that this small [average] loss must fall on the [African] holder."[96] Nor did Bottomley believe that the reduction would serve to discourage African cotton-growing in Uganda.

Before making a final decision, Wood consulted Sir James Stevenson, personal commercial adviser to Churchill. Stevenson could see "no reason for reversing the decision to mark down the value of the small coins without compensation to the holders."[97]

Thus Churchill ordered that the order-in-council should be proclaimed on 1 November, or as soon afterwards as possible, without compensation to the holders of the coins.[98] The following day, a telegram to the acting governor of Uganda specifically rejected his earlier plea for compensation to be given to the holders of the coins, "owing to the heavy financial burden which would be imposed on either the currency board or the local governments if any form of compensation were granted."[99]

This decision, which the CO hoped would end the long conflict and seemed to slam the door on any alteration of the scheme to devalue the ten-, five-, and one-cent coins at the expense of the Africans, produced instead even more dramatic complaint. Acting Governor E. D. Jarvis, recognizing that previous Uganda objections had failed to move the CO, despatched a powerful protest to London. Jarvis maintained that he had consulted official and unofficial opinion in the protectorate, and they were unanimously opposed to the scheme. He bluntly stated that his Execo "have advised me unanimously to represent to you their undisguised feeling of the injustice to the native and the possible danger that might result in marking down the cent without the opportunity of redemption."[100] He felt that "the natives' reliance on British justice will be inevitably undermined and I urge that the present value of the cent should remain unchanged at 50 to one shilling and 100 to a florin."[101] The potential adverse economic impact on the African cotton grower was huge, and Jarvis sought to bring the gravity of the situation home to London. Although the order-in-council had already been signed, he took the most unusual step of asking that the king be made aware of his opposition in order that His Majesty could revoke the order before it arrived in East Africa.

This shocked London officials, and finally awoke them to the need to reconsider this "shilling swindle". Bottomley noted the force of the protest, but he felt that Uganda must be "overestimating" the hardship the new scheme would cause and "the effect on the native mind."[102] Nevertheless, he sent a copy of the telegram to Sir Robert Coryndon, on leave in Britain, for comment, and he discussed the issue with Sir James Masterton-Smith. In his reply, Coryndon supported Jarvis's position, taking exception to the CO defence of the scheme as likely to cause little average loss to African holders. "I do not think you can properly estimate the effect of a measure of this sort by a calculation of average loss per head," he stated.[103]

By 18 October, CO officials felt they would have to give way and scrap the plan to devalue. "We cannot ignore," concluded Masterton-Smith, "urgent representations that are being made to us by Uganda and I incline to the view that we should hold off our original decision."[104] Once again Stevenson was consulted, but this time he advised the S of S to postpone the proclamation of the order-in-council for another month and that "an undertaking be given to redeem the small coins at their original value. . . ."[105] The EACB would have to bear the cost of this redemption when new coinage came into circulation, but Stevenson no longer saw this as an overwhelming obstacle. The board could expect a fairly equal settlement between profits made on the new paper money and any loss incurred in redeeming the coins at their original value.

Churchill telegraphed Jarvis on 20 October informing him of the decision to postpone introduction of the order until 1 December. "Public assurances will be given," Churchill's telegram went on "that ten, five, and one cent pieces will remain at florin values until their redemption by new coins when these are available at two cents to the shilling and one cent of a florin."[106] Churchill made the decision public four days later in response to a parliamentary question.[107] The "shilling swindle" had finally collapsed. The CO had known all along that the scheme concocted by Kenya for the benefit of the settler producer would amount to "cheating the native of his twopence;" only when Uganda's protests had invoked the question of British justice and foretold dire political and economic consequences did the London officials give way. Nevertheless, the CO did, in the end, intervene to block an initiative that promised to benefit the settlers at the expense of the African population. This would be a pattern that would be repeated on several occasions in 1921–22.

African Protest

Although currency issues continued to trouble and take up time of CO officials, they had, in 1921–22, for the first time to take note of organized African protest. The initial protest movement to come to the notice of the CO was led by Harry Thuku. It sought, in particular, a redress of African grievances from the CO. Although reflective of African discontent with the lack of economic opportunities and depressed conditions that characterized these years, many of the grievances articulated by Thuku's East African Association (EAA) clearly reflected African unhappiness with settler paramountcy and the measures Northey's government took to support the settler producer. Raises in African taxation, registration and pass-carrying, and the compulsion of African labor provide examples of such measures of the colonial state that were particularly disliked by Africans. These conditions spawned varied types of protest in the 1919–22 period. For example, the Young Kavirondo Association emerged in Central Kavirondo district of Nyanza province. Its protests centered around many of the same issues as the EAA, including opposition to the change of the territory from protectorate to crown colony in 1920. In South Kavirondo, in particular, the politico-religious movement known as Mumbo (or Mumboism) drew support from those discontented with conditions in postwar Kenya. Likewise, the millenial movement led by Ndonye wa Kauti among the Kamba of Machakos represented protest to the political and economic difficulties faced by Africans.[108]

More than the other protest movements, that led by Thuku, like those of the Indians and the British humanitarians, forced the CO to look at the situation in Kenya, more particularly to become aware of African grievances and eventually to recognize the necessity of dealing with what were identified as the causes of African discontent.[109] Yet initially CO officials held little sympathy for African complaints. At first, they saw the African protest as an outgrowth of the Indian question; it emerged, they convinced themselves, with Indian assistance and direction. This can be discerned from their reaction to the colonial state's treatment of the Thuku protest.

Harry Thuku first came to the attention of the CO in July 1921. Thuku sent a telegram direct to the S of S, describing a mass meeting of Africans held in Nairobi on 10 July. Thuku prefaced his list of complaints by the statement that "next to missionaries Indians are our best friends."[110] Thuku demanded the repeal of the registration ordinance, an end to the compulsory taking of girls and married women for plantation work, and the rescinding of the increase in hut and poll tax. He also requested that African revenues should be used solely for their benefit, especially education. The telegram scored the settlers for "cutting down our already low wages," and identified Kenya's only solution as giving the franchise to "all educated British subjects." Thuku's wire closed by authorizing the Indian deputation on its way to Britain and J. C. Wedgwood M.P. to represent African interests to the CO.[111]

CO officials were far from pleased with the Thuku telegram. They had the Indian question very much on their minds as another Indian deputation was expected to call on the CO, and Northey was also expected in London. Bottomley felt that it was "going altogether too far to accept the Indians as the spokesmen of the natives," and he attributed "this new development" to the settler dominated Economic Commission report that had portrayed the Indian as the enemy of the African. This had led the Indians to court the favor of Africans "or of the probably small section of natives which thinks it has grievances."[112] Officials decided to await discussion with Northey before taking any further action.

The telegram was shown to Northey on 2 August; he dismissed this protest as utterly insignificant. It did not represent the views of "responsible" Africans, and in the governor's view "this particular business is clearly engineered by Indians." Thuku, he guessed, was "an educated or part educated Kikuyu." Both Northey and Bottomley strongly maintained that the Indian deputation, which was to meet Churchill on 9 August, should not be allowed to speak for African grievances.[113] Following the S of S's meeting with the Indians, a telegram was sent to Nairobi asking for "full information about Mr. Harry Thuku."[114]

The CO received a reply to this request in mid-September with the arrival of a lengthy confidential despatch from Nairobi. Acting governor W. K. Notley dismissed the EAA as of little consequence. It could not claim to represent East Africa, nor could the EAA be "considered as representative of the most highly educated natives of the colony." Notley regarded it as a mushroom growth induced by several coincident causes, particularly the recent increase in taxation, the still more recent combination of European employers of labour with the object of reducing native wages by one third, and the unreasonable resentment which the application of native registration has caused among a few malcontents. I have no reason to doubt not only that this association will wither as quickly as it has sprung up, but also this alliance between a certain class of natives and the Indian agitators is illusory and impermanent, being due mainly to an attempt by each to use the other for his own ends.[115]

Notley also provided enclosures, notably from the Ganda publication *Sekanyola*, in an attempt to show that not all Africans regarded the Indians as friends.

CO officials found the despatch interesting in that it confirmed the opinions they already held. Parkinson continued to hold his view that the African "speaking generally distinguishes sharply between the white man and the Indian, and that he puts the latter in a much lower category."[116] Bottomley also viewed Thuku's movement in the context of the Indian collecting "testimonials to show that he is the native's best friend."[117]

After his return to Kenya, Northey, perhaps embarrassed by the fact that he had known so little about Thuku and the EAA while in London, provided further detail on the grievances voiced by the EAA. As might be expected, the governor found little to sympathize with in the EAA complaints. The registration of Africans was "working harmoniously as a whole;" although taxes had been raised, the governor proclaimed his "clear intention" to devote a considerable portion of the revenue derived to the benefit of Africans. Northey admitted that settlers had combined to cut wages, but he expressed uncertainty over whether they could in fact be held down while emphasizing to the CO that his government had taken no part in the movement to reduce pay. He was particularly contemptuous in rejecting the idea that any African should have the right to vote.[118]

Northey then turned from the grievances as noted in Thuku's July telegram to describe the protest leader himself. He had now gathered considerable information on Thuku whom he described as "an intelligent Kikuyu who is employed in Nairobi as a telephone exchange clerk in a Government office." In Northey's view, "he had gotten into touch with Indian agitators" who had induced him to act as a propagandist for their claims. There was reason to believe, Northey went on, that Thuku was financed from Indian sources. Here was the real problem with Thuku; in the governor's view, he was being used by the Indians. Thuku's activities in the African rural areas were viewed as ineffective. Concluded Northey: "it is not anticipated that they will lead to any definite results."[119]

Given this assessment by the governor, CO officials were truly astounded to learn in March of the following year that the colonial state viewed Thuku's activities in rural Kikuyuland with considerable alarm. Bowring sent a despatch to London which provided this assessment in late January. The despatch contained a translation of a letter by Thuku seeking to bring all Kikuyu, particularly the rival Kikuyu Association, into alliance with the EAA. In the letter, Thuku identified the chiefs and European administrators as the enemy, and revealed that he had been in contact with Luo in western Kenya who, unhappy with conditions in the colony, seemed ready to link up with the EAA.[120] It was not surprising that the colonial state should be concerned. Thuku not only was gaining great support amongst the Kikuyu, he seemed to be trying to undermine the chiefs and likely to forge a truly panethnic protest movement. These latter two possibilities could not be viewed lightly by the colonial state. The alliance with the government appointed chiefs formed a major pillar of colonial rule; another fundamental pillar of colonial rule in Kenya was the policy of divide and rule.

Despite their shock, officials at the CO were quick to recognize the danger. Any sympathy they might have had with the grievances the EAA had voiced were thrust aside, and the need to counter this threat to colonial rule was uppermost in their minds. Upon reading the despatch, Bottomley minuted: "There is a distinct element of sedition about this, and if these feelings are not yet widespread, there is all the more reason for early dramatic action—before punishment becomes martyrdom."[121] Read recommended strongly "nipping this sort of thing in bud;" the most effective way to deal with "native agitators," he held, was by deportation.[122] Bottomley and Read quickly got Wood's permission to send a strong telegram to Nairobi. Drafted by Bottomley, it read:

> Are you satisfied that you have all the powers you require for dealing if necessary with combinations having a seditious tendency? Do not understand why a native who expresses these views is retained in government service.[123]

The CO telegram brought a prompt response. Within a week, Thuku had been arrested, but that action produced consequences quite unforseen by the London officials. A telegram from Bowring (Northey was at the coast during this episode) of 16 March brought not only news of Thuku's arrest, but also of the protest that followed. Police opened fire on those demonstrating for Thuku's release, killing, according to the telegram, "fifteen of the mob."[124] CO officials realized that their telegram had triggered this tragedy, but their minutes expressed no regrets at the loss of life. Bottomley convinced himself: "We may be quite confident that Thuku and the town mob will have no support among the tribes."[125] Both Read and Bottomley recommended telegraphing the governor the S of S's "full support" in taking "measures necessary for the safety and order of the colony." Churchill had the political sense to veto this.[126] Thuku was subsequently deported to Kismayu.[127]

The officials found no reason to alter their favorable view of the affair when they received, in late May, Northey's detailed account of the colonial state's violent dispersion of the demonstrators who were demanding Thuku's release. This can only be regarded as at least startling since Northey's account revealed that the police had opened fire on the demonstrators without any order being given.[128] Bottomley felt that Northey made a good case for his government's action, and he prepared a spirited defense for potential parliamentary critics.[129] Read felt that "the action of the local authorities in this affair has been quite correct."[130] Thus the CO sent Northey a lengthy despatch on 31 May which, while regretting the loss of life that occurred, strongly approved of the action taken in suppressing the Nairobi demonstrators and deporting Thuku.[131]

At first glance, it seems difficult to conclude that African protest was a very influential factor in bringing about a reassertion of CO initiative in Kenya affairs that slowed down the colonial state's push to bring about settler paramountcy in Kenya. In the short term, it had been the CO which urged decisive action to deal with the "agitator" Thuku, and the CO was quick to approve the brutal suppression of the demonstration which spontaneously occurred. This CO intervention did little to immediately weaken Northey's pro-settler policies or to force change in those policies that had done most to stir African protest. Yet as the next two months went by, the reality of what had happened in Nairobi in March, and why, dawned on CO officials. They realized that there could not be violent suppression of African protest of this sort again. Therefore, the need to avoid the rise of protest movements such as Thuku's became a very significant factor underlying the CO decision, by May of 1922, to intervene in Kenya affairs to push towards a change in policy.

The Continued Problem of Indian Demands

Indian protest remained a concern for the CO, and in the eyes of officials, it was the cause for greater worry than African protest. The Indian question grew more intense in 1921 as the CO grappled with the competing claims of Kenya's Indians and European settlers. This was all the more a CO issue since the colonial state, just as in prewar years, proved incapable of engineering a satisfactory solution to the problem.

By the end of 1920, it was clear that Milner's decisions on the various issues involved had failed to "solve" the Indian question in Kenya. Indeed, Indians there had escalated their protest by refusing nomination to the Legco. Indian grievances that prompted the rejection by Indian opinion, both in East African and India, of Milner's proposals were eloquently set out by the government of India in October 1920. In considerable detail, the latter showed clearly that British policy had not been to 'mete out even handed justice between the races" in Kenya as Milner had maintained. The question of representation in the Legco and the franchise provided a good example, maintained the Indian government, since it did not appear even-handed that Europeans had the vote and Indians did not; that there were to be eleven European members in the Legco and two Indians was not even. The only "reliable safeguard for Indian interests" was adequate representation on the Legco. This would best be accomplished by a common electoral roll and a common franchise on a reasonable property plus an educational test, the government of India maintained.[132]

The despatch went on to show that Indians "bitterly resented" Milner's decision to retain residential segregation in towns and, where practicable, in commercial areas also and to reserve the highlands for whites. Overall, the government of India, like Indians in East Africa, was unable to accept Milner's decisions as a final settlement.

The first months of 1921 saw little new emerge with the Indian question so far as the CO was concerned. It was a period of marking time; the new team of Churchill and Wood were settling in at the CO, and until April, little would be done in the way of seriously tackling the problem of Indian grievances in Kenya. In January, Northey raised the issue of segregation. He proposed expanding the area set aside for Indians in Nairobi so as to give them three-quarters of the commercial plots in the capital.[133] After consulting Professor Simpson, however, officials were not prepared to approve the alterations in commercial segregation that the governor proposed as this would mean the abandonment of "the whole policy of reserved areas" proposed by Simpson.[134]

It was hoped in London, moreover, that a "roundtable conference" between Indians and Europeans could be held in Kenya as a way of facilitating a settlement. This was first suggested as a possibility by Northey in January, but it did not prove feasible to get representatives of the two groups together until May.[135] This formed another reason for marking time in regard to general policy.[136] As an interested party, the IO raised no objections to the policy of marking time; Montagu welcomed the lull as providing additional time to bring the Indian question before the cabinet and putting pressure on the CO to alter the Milner policies.[137]

As well as marking time with regard to the Indian question, the first months of 1921 also witnessed a tightening of consultation between the CO and the IO. The change in leadership of the CO facilitated this, but it was actually the IO that initiated the process with a call by Lord Lytton, new parliamentary under-secretary at the IO, for a closer consultation and sharing of correspondence they received from Kenya and India.[138] Permanent officials at the CO were not very enthusiastic about Lytton's proposal as they feared that the IO was seeking not just consultation but to have a hand in decision making for Kenya. As Parkinson argued, the S of S for the Colonies had "undivided responsibility for the administration of the E. African dependencies."[139] Churchill felt, however, that the IO should be kept fully informed of action taken by the CO.[140] The S of S wrote to Montagu to recommend discussions between the parliamentary under-secretaries of both offices as a means to promoting free interchange and the settlement of items in dispute.[141] This marked the start of much closer consultation, though not necessarily agreement, between the CO and the IO.

The policy of marking time did not, however, sit well with Northey. He telegraphed the CO on 23 April: "Respectfully submit impossible to go on marking time. We must have a policy clearly laid down. . . ."[142] Northey felt that the round table conference due to take place in early May would be "useless if we only mark time." The points that had to be settled, in his view, were the number of Indian members of councils, segregation in towns and land in the highlands. The governor pushed again for dropping segregation in commercial areas.[143]

This strong plea from Kenya forced the CO to move from marking time to a more serious consideration of the Indian question. Of the three issues for decision raised by Northey, Bottomley felt that the Indian demand for a common electoral roll presented the most difficulty. His view was based upon a vision of the future: "There isn't a European settler in Kenya who does not look forward to self-government—either in his own time or his sons—and the prospect of an equal or predominant Indian element will completely alter his outlook." The common roll would make the country less attractive to the European and more attractive to the Indian.[144] Fiddes, on the other hand, held that "the most serious matter is that of the highlands."[145] In the end, the CO sent a conciliatory telegraphic reply to Northey. Regretting any delay in tackling the problem, the S of S told the governor that he expected to discuss the question "in all its bearings" with the S of S for India. In the meantime, Northey was given latitude in his discussions with the Indian and European representatives at the upcoming conference to depart, if he felt it necessary, from the policy laid down by Milner the previous year.[146]

The roundtable conference in Nairobi during the first week of May produced little agreement. There was disagreement over immigration as the Europeans desired a stricter law to limit Indian entry into Kenya. Both sides agreed to abolish segregation in commerce, but Europeans felt that the minimal legal barriers to residential segregation desired by the Indians could not be accepted. Indians demanded either a common roll with educational and property qualifications or the right to elect eleven representatives on a communal franchise. Europeans found neither alternative acceptable and could agree to no more than three Indians elected to the Legco on a comunal basis. Indians demanded the right to acquire land in the highlands while the Europeans maintained that the "present policy of reserving the highlands exclusively for settlement of Europeans must be regarded as a pledge given by Lord Elgin and confirmed by subsequent Secretaries of State."[147]

This pledge would be reiterated by the settlers in the months ahead. The CO's initial reaction was to doubt that Elgin's decision in 1908 had constituted a pledge. On reading Northey's telegram of 5 May, for example, Bottomley minuted: "I do not understand the reference to a pledge about agricultural land in the highlands."[148] Yet by August the CO had come around to the settler position that Elgin's decision did consitute a pledge that the highlands would be reserved for whites only.

In his telegram of 7 May and a more lengthy despatch on 14 May, Northey put forward his own recommendations for a solution. The governor had little sympathy with the Indian demands. This was especially true of the franchise question. Since the "preponderating majority of the non-European section of the population of Kenya is illiterate and totally incapable of making intelligent use of a vote or taking part in the government of the country," Northey rejected a common roll. He also dismissed the Indian demand for equal representation with the Europeans on a communal franchise as unreasonable. He suggested five Indian members of Legco to be elected on a communal franchise.[149]

On the other major problem area, the governor recommended that it was "of the utmost importance" to maintain the ban on Indian acquisition of land in the white highlands. The British government had pledged its word to keep the highlands white, and "any reversal of policy will be regarded as a breach of faith." Northey was more favorable to Indian aspirations in recommending no change in the existing immigration policies and the abolition of segregation in the commercial areas of townships. On residential segregation, however, he urged continuing to bar Indians from the European residential areas of towns.[150]

Northey clearly demonstrated where his sympathies lay in the matter in his secret despatch of 14 May. He concluded with an outspoken statement of his personal feelings.

> The Indian Question as a whole can be summed up in one word, predominance to which all the issues now under discussion are . . . subsidiary. The Indians demand a share in the Government of the country, and they look on the embodiment of Kenya in the Indian Empire as their ultimate goal. Any concessions to their demands on the side issues can only tend to strengthen their aspirations, and I am convinced that their demands must be resisted to the uttermost where any suspicion of equality would be implied by conceding them. . . . While I am anxious to provide justice, fairness and sympathetic treatment to the Indian community here, I consider that they are demanding more than that and must, in consequence, expect to get less than they demand.[151]

At the same time that the Nairobi discussions that called forth Northey's strong anti-Indian feelings were going on, the initial discussions between officials of the CO and the IO, authorized by Churchill and Montagu, went forward. These took place at the IO on 3 May. Wood and Bottomley represented the CO, the IO by Lord Lytton and C. Walton. The IO took as its stand the principle that all British subjects should have equal rights in all parts of the empire. The CO accepted this in theory, but Wood stated that "its application must depend on the circumstances of each colony and that the conclusions that would follow from it must be examined in light of those circumstances." The discussion identified the issues of the highlands and the franchise as likely to be the most difficult. This was especially so with the latter as Bottomley again emphasized the European hostility to the principle based upon a future expectation of responsible government among the settlers.[152]

Upon receipt of Northey's telegram of 7 May describing the end of the Nairobi discussions without agreement and a brief summary of Northey's recommendations, CO officials prepared to follow up the question with the IO. Bottomley felt that they would get IO support for separate representation. "It is merely a question of the number of seats," he went on, and "it will be interesting to see how the IO take the demand for absolute equality."[153] Wood undertook further discussions with Lytton.[154]

Wood then conferred with Churchill on 12 May. After examining the issues in dispute, Churchill made several decisions on principle, and he drew up a telegram to be sent to Northey. He was not disposed at present to go beyond five Indian representatives in the Legco. Land in the highlands had been reserved for the whites, and "we are virtually pledged to the settlers on this subject." While there could be no shift in position there, Churchill suggested that having given up commercial segregation, it would be necessary to soften the colonial state's position on residential segregation. However, this telegram was never sent.[155]

The reason it was never sent was that following further discussion with Lord Lytton, Wood convinced Churchill on the following morning to let him draft another telegram. This telegram placed greatest emphasis on reaching a settlement with regard to the franchise question as that was the point emphasized by the IO. Any possibility of a settlement would turn mainly on it. Since Wood had learned that the IO regarded five Indian representatives as inadequate, that was dropped from the new telegram. It stated: "If agreement is to be reached, choice lies between communal basis franchise with equal number of Europeans and Indians on the one hand and on the other a common roll with a high standard of qualifications which would in effect give Indians fewer members than you propose." Churchill and Wood made no reference to segregation or the highlands until they had Northey's reply which might indicate whether or not there was any possibility of securing agreement with the government of India on the question of representation.[156] Within a week, Churchill decided to send the revised telegram to Nairobi.[157] The IO had thus gained a significant concession in getting the government of India's point of view so seriously considered by the CO.

Prior to receiving a reply from the governor, Bottomley and Wood held further discussions with representatives of the IO on 28 May. The focus of this lengthy dialogue was land in the highlands. The two sides sought to agree on a formula that would give Indians the right to buy land in the white highlands while limiting the likelihood that such transactions would take place. Bottomley confessed: "I fear I cannot suggest any simple way out of the difficulty. We must pass on the conundrum to the Governor. . . ."[158] At the conclusion of the meeting with the IO, he went onto express grave misgivings, obviously felt by others at the CO, as "to whether the concessions of form, which are all the IO presses for (and they assure us they mean no sacrifice of substance) will be likely to have the desired effect." Perhaps, Bottomley suggested, Indians in Kenya would be satisfied with theoretical equality, but it was reasonable to "suppose that a matter that is in the hands of a few agitators will not be so lightly disposed of, and that the more we give, the more will be demanded."[159] Read felt the CO must stick to the line taken in the draft telegram not sent: "that we are virtually pledged to the European settlers to reserve the highlands for them."[160]

Northey's reply to the CO telegram of 20 May provided, of course, no answer to that dilemma, but it did show that the governor was willing to accept one of the alternatives posed on the franchise question. He preferred a "common franchise" rather than giving the Indians eleven seats in the Legco, but he urged that it should be given to all, irrespective of race, on a high qualification standard (English language and property/income). If the common roll was approved, Northey intended to keep Indian members of the Legco to a minimum. He proposed adding three new constituencies, bringing the total to fourteen. The three additional seats (Mombasa North, Nairobi East, and West Nyanza) would be expected to return an Indian. That would give the Indians only three seats, but they might soon take the coast seat from the Europeans.[161]

CO officials appreciated the "helpful" spirit shown by the governor. They followed his reply up with a telegram dealing with the issues of segregation and the highlands. On the former, the CO sent the section relating to the issue that had been set out in the draft telegram of 12 May not sent to Nairobi. On the highlands, the CO asserted that Lord Elgin's decision of 1908 "can hardly be regarded as a pledge on question of principle." The IO view, the telegram concluded, was that the real danger was not that Indians would take over farming in the highlands, but that they would engage in "speculative buying there."[162]

The CO had now gone too far for Governor Northey. He telegraphed three days later manifesting his total refusal to see any change in the white highlands. He maintained that he had agreed to a "common franchise" in order to help the S of S, but the reversal of the highlands and residential segregation policies that he thought the CO was proposing, "must tend to encourage and assist Indians toward predominance in both the municipal and legislative councils." Northey was unable to consider "any proposal that the Kenya highlands should not remain as at present European." Like the settlers, Northey regarded any alteration as a breach of faith. Northey came very near to offering his resignation, but he stated "if by the cabinet's decision," the S of S ordered him to overturn the highlands policy, he would loyally carry it out. However, the governor went on, "I consider that it is my duty to point out that I anticipate the gravest situation will certainly arise from the attitude of the European population."[163]

Four days later, Northey telegraphed again with a request that he come home for discussions. The CO agreed; Kenya's serious financial position was the major reason for the governor's trip to Britain, but the Indian and labor questions provided other justifications.[164] Before leaving for Britain, Northey urged the CO not to make any decisions reversing Milner's policy until he had seen the S of S or Churchill had the opportunity to visit Kenya.[165]

This fact meant that Churchill's meeting with Montagu and IO officials on 14 June did not produce any conclusive outcome. Northey's telegram clearly hardened the attitude of Churchill and his colleagues on the highland issue. Churchill embraced the concept that a pledge had been given to European settlers. This was altogether too much for Montagu. The CO attitude made his heart "full" and "heavy". He therefore addressed a strong personal appeal to Churchill in the hope that the latter might alter the CO's racist stance. Montagu was willing to accept the fact that Indians would not have much of a share in the Legco, but he could not defend a position of affairs where Indians, no matter how wealthy or responsible, could not buy land in the Kenya highlands merely because they were Indians. Europeans did not have to sell to Indians, Montagu concluded, but he would strongly oppose any regulation that did not provide equal rights for Indians.[166]

Seeking a New Policy

With the confirmation of Northey's visit to Britain, the EAINC decided to send another delegation to London. The deputation, which consisted of A. M. Jeevanjee and B. S. Varma, left on 5 July, and in Britain would seek meetings with the S of S for the Colonies and for India.[167] When learning of the Indian intention, Parkinson of the EAD exploded: "This is really foolishness. No deputation is warranted." He agreed with Northey that the "object of all this agitation was predominance of Indians in E. Africa."[168] Despite Parkinson's tirade, Churchill agreed to meet the delegation.[169]

Churchill met the Indian delegation, accompanied by Polak, Labour M.P. Wedgwood, and others on 9 August. The Indian cause had received a huge boost as a result of the decision of the recently concluded imperial conference. The conference reaffirmed a 1918 resolution of the Imperial War Conference that each community in the British Commonwealth "should enjoy complete control of the composition of its own population by means of restrictions on immigration," but it recognized that there was "an incongruity" between the position of India as an equal member of the empire and the existence of disabilities relating to British Indians living in other parts of the empire. The conference, therefore, expressed the opinion that it was desirable that the rights of such Indians to citizenship should be recognized.[170] The

Indian deputation and its supporters thus based their pleas on the concept of equal rights for all British subjects. Supporting their demands also with generally inaccurate historical examples, Jeevanjee and Varma pushed for common roll elections, even if that gave them fewer representatives in the Legco than under a communal system. Churchill was least sympathetic on the question of the highlands, but the deputation had its say.[171] The deputation reiterated its demands, especially the right to acquire land in the highlands, in a letter two days after the meeting. In that message, they were also at particular pains to argue that Africans sympathized with the Indian position and supported the demand for equality.[172]

The visit of the Indian deputation spurred concern from European settlers in London and Nairobi. Those in London, notably K. H. Rodwell, Northrup Macmillan, and E. S. Grogan, wrote to Northey to protest any change of policy regarding Indian rights and to place themselves at Northey's disposal "in so far as we can assist to maintain the policy to which you have been committed."[173] A week later, Macmillan wrote to the CO to request a meeting with the S of S. Churchill agreed, and he met Macmillan and his colleagues immediately after the Indian deputation left his office on 9 August.[174] Lest these meetings raise hopes, or fears, of a settlement, the CO informed the acting governor that "no decision whatever had been made on Indian policy," and it certainly would not be before Northey had returned to Kenya.[175]

Having, in effect, heard from both sides, officials now met with Northey, as on other Kenya issues, to try to hammer out a formula for solution to the Indian question. By 26 August, the broad outlines of a new policy had emerged. It represented a dramatic departure from Milner's Indian policy. On one point only did the CO hold to the latter; that was the question of the highlands. Read outlined the new initiative for Northey in a confidential letter prior to the latter's departure for Kenya. He told the governor, partly to soothe the latter's feelings, that imperial interests had had to overide local in this case, but that the S of S had "every confidence" that Northey would do his utmost "to give effect to the decisions of H.M.G."[176]

Northey was instructed on his return "to consult the leaders of all parties with a view to arranging a settlement on the lines indicated in the memorandum." The proposals were to be kept confidential, and no hasty decision was to be taken. After Northey had fully explored the terms with the settler and Indian leaders in Kenya, he was instructed to make his final recommendations by despatch so as to reach the S of S early in December. In the meantime, the CO instructed Northey to nominate one Indian to the Execo and four Indian members to the Legco.[177]

The Wood/Churchill plans placed in Northey's hands represented, in its departure from the Milner position of a year earlier, a considerable victory for the IO. The general basis for the policy was Cecil Rhodes's so-called dictum of "equal rights for civilized men." Following from this, there would be a common electoral roll for Indians and Europeans. For voters there would be property/income qualifications (£1,000 property or £150 annual income) as well as the ability to write and speak English. Any British subject or protected person who met these qualifications could vote, and it was intended thereby to provide an Indian electorate of roughly two thousand. Constituencies would be revised so that there would be eight; it was anticipated that five would return European members and three Indian. This reservation of seats would, the memorandum suggested, be good for both the Europeans and Indians. European voters already on the register would not be disenfranchised, and the new system would not be introduced until the end of 1922 or early 1923, when new elections to the Legco would be due.[178]

Less detail was given to other issues in the dispute. Immigration regulations for Indians were to be the same as for Europeans. There would be no commercial segregation. With regard to residential segregation, the document provided for an interesting innovation. There would be no segregation of persons on the common electoral roll but "lower class" Indians would be excluded from the European residential area. The highlands would continue to be reserved for Europeans only. This policy was "quite definite"; neither grants of land nor transfers to Indians in the highlands would be permitted. An area suitable for Indian settlement would be set aside for Indian ownership "roughly in the area lying between Voi and the Yatta Plains."[179]

As a result of IO concerns, Northey's instructions were altered slightly. The IO wished the qualifications to be such that 10 per cent of the Indians, rather than two thousand, would receive the franchise since that was what the Indians themselves asked for.[180] On the other hand, the CO did not feel that it should meet the IO's desire by insisting that Northey should telegraph his final recommendations instead of sending them by despatch. The CO also held firm to its position on the white highlands despite adamant objection from Montagu. Churchill refused even to accept Montagu's compromise proposal that although there could be no grants of land in the highlands to Indians, that transfers be allowed between willing purchasers and willing vendors.[181]

The new policy that Northey took back to Nairobi with him at the end of August represented a striking assertion of imperial initiative in Kenya affairs. It took the CO far beyond what had been advocated as acceptable by the governor and the settlers, and it was, largely for those reasons, doomed from the start. Northey's previous expression of view should have left no doubt in anyone's mind that he was not the man to implement this kind of scheme in Kenya. He would do everything in his power to see that it did not become official policy. While CO officials would come to recognize this fact within the next ten months, they do not seem, at that moment, to have appreciated the depth of the governor's pro-settler sympathies. It is, of course, possible that CO officials did not wish a policy of this sort to be implemented, and thus gave the task of implementation to Northey with every assurance that he would sabotage it. While some of the permanent officials may have felt this way, there is every indication that Wood and Churchill were sincere in their belief that they had formulated a policy that would end the controversy by offering concessions on all sides. In this regard, it must be remembered that Northey had other important tasks to accomplish on his return, such as implementing the new labor policy, and the financial crisis alone was sufficient reason for the CO not to wish to dispense with his services at this juncture. In addition to Northey's hostility, the other reason for the failure of the new policy was the adamant opposition of the settler community.

In the second half of 1921, the settlers grabbed the protest initiative as their agitation against the Indian demands for equality pushed the Indians on the defensive. At the end of June, the Convention of Associations met and adopted, unanimously, a set of resolutions that became known as its "irreducible minimum" on the Indian question. These called for "strictly controlled Indian immigration" at present with a view to the "ultimate prohibition" of such immigration, two nominated, not elected, Indian members to Legco, segregation to be maintained in residential areas, and "whenever practicable" in commercial areas, no further alienation of land in the uplands areas, and, as a seeming concession to Indian feeling, the convention urged "full recognition of existing Asiatic rights in property" and security of tenure.[182]

The convention followed this up with a campaign designed to maintain the status quo so far as the settlers' privileged position was concerned. The campaign had a three-pronged focus. The settlers strongly emphasized the pledge the highlands would remain forever under European administration.[183] Secondly, they argued that settler supremacy was necessary for the well-being of the African. A Kenya controlled by the Indians, the settlers alleged, would be bad for Africans "spiritually morally intellectually physically or naturally."[184] They particularly emphasized the bad economic effect that they felt the Indians had on Africans. Finally, the settlers presented themselves as defenders of "western civilization" against the alleged evil and immoral civilization of India. In August, for example, European women in Kenya sent a telegram to be forwarded to the queen imploring her for assistance in protecting them and their children against the "terrible Asiatic menace" that threatened to overwhelm them.[185]

The depth of this sort of settler advocacy was reached with the publication, in September, of a short pamphlet titled *Memorandum on the Case Against the Claims of Indians in Kenya*. Besides stating the settler case that "Milner Policy" was no longer adequate for the protection of their political and economic privileges, the pamphlet maintained that Indian demands for equality did not emanate from the masses but from Indian agitators. If Indians continued to flood into Kenya, the effect on the African would be disastrous the pamphlet alleged. It went on to charge that the "views of the bulk of the local Indians on sanitation and hygiene are worse than primitive," and it raised the awful prospect of Indian children "who are in all probability married and initiated into the mysteries of sex" seated side by side in class rooms with European children.[186]

In November, a petition signed by slightly over three thousand "European subjects" in Kenya was sent to King George V. If Indian claims to equality were granted, it said, a grave injustice would be done to the settlers and the African "whose future welfare has, we believe, been entrusted to our British race by divine providence." The settlers went on to appeal to the king as defender of the faith not to allow the growth of "other eastern religions" in Kenya that might wreck the work done in the past by Christian missionaries.[187]

This strong European stance and Northey's pro-settler bias made it inevitable that the CO proposals of August could not form the basis of a settlement. The governor held meetings with both Indian and settler representatives in October. He urged on both sides the need for compromise, but the process went slowly as both parties took time to consult their constituencies.[188] By the end of November, Northey telegraphed that "agreement by compromise has proved impossible."[189]

In his telegram, Northey summarized both the Indian and settler positions before putting forward his own advice. He called for a retreat from the common roll. Indians would receive five seats on a communal franchise and the Europeans ten in the governor's proposal. Exclusive rights to land in the white highlands would be retained by Europeans, immigration laws would remain unchanged, and there would be no commercial segregation, though residential segregation would stand. Northey also introduced a new element in the dispute by informing the CO that a European delegation, led by Lord Delamere, would arrive in Britain in early January; the governor urged that Churchill postpone any decision until he saw the deputation. Northey ended his telegram on a very ominous note by stating: "Finally, I must impress on you once again the very serious position which I am satisfied will occur if the demands of the Indians are acceded in toto. Europeans have organization complete for resistance as last resort."[190]

In a lengthy despatch providing more detail on the failure to reach a settlement that he completed two weeks later, Northey made clear his strong sympathies with the settlers. He tried to explain his failure to reach agreement by stating that the leaders of both communities had "hardened their hearts against any sort of compromise." He continued:

> The more the Indians are given, the more they will demand. The Europeans, more afraid than ever of eventual domination by the Indians, have organized themselves, with the determination to resist to the last any giving way to the Indian demands.[191]

Still Northey held out the hope that if the CO could agree the substitute communal for common franchise, the remaining proposals in the August memorandum might be accepted.

The CO Tries Again

Northey's telegram set two immediate problems for the CO in dealing with the IO. Officials had to decide whether to wait for the arrival of a European deputation before taking further action, and if they should accede to the governor's request to publish the CO terms since rather complete accounts had appeared in press reports in Rhodesia and India. Bottomley and Masterton-Smith felt there was no choice but to approve publication. The latter was also "quite clear" that Churchill should receive the delegation, and no decision should be taken until he had seen the Delamere deputation.[192] Masterton-Smith advised Churchill, moreover, that he should write to Montagu to personally inform the S of S for India what he planned to do so that the IO would have no procedural cause to complain. Churchill thus addressed a private letter to Montagu on 7 December setting out what he proposed to do and enclosing a copy of Northey's telegram of 29 November.[193]

Montagu was not exactly thrilled with the further delay. He argued that he had done all he could to restrain the Indians, and felt that they had been more forbearing than the Europeans. He pointedly referred to the fact that the Europeans had established an organization for resistance, and he wondered why Northey had not warned them that the government would not be influenced by threats of force.[194] Nevertheless, Churchill went ahead and informed Northey by telegram that he would receive the European delegation.[195]

As the European delegation was on its way to Britain, the CO received word of a softening of the Indian position. The EAINC telegraphed on 24 December their willingness to accept interim representation in the Legco. However, they asked for five seats rather than the four proposed in the August memorandum.[196] After seeking Northey's opinion, which concurred with that of CO officials that four seats were sufficient, the CO telegraphed its approval of four Indian nominated members in the Legco.[197]

By the second week in January, the European deputation, consisting of Lord Delamere and G. W. C. Griffiths, a soldier settler from New Zealand, had begun discussions with first Bottomley and Masterton-Smith and then Churchill.[198] The deputation had a separate interview with Montagu. They later reported to Bottomley that the S of S for India had recognized the principle that Kenya was "to be predominantly European in its Government."[199]

The European deputation, now reinforced by W. M. Crowdy, put forward its own proposals, after further discussions with Bottomley and Masterton-Smith, on 19 January. It requested a completely new initiative, a considerable departure from the Convention of Associations' "irreducible minimum," and raised requests that had not been mentioned in earlier discussions at the CO.[200] Proceeding from the premise that it was intended that Kenya in the future should be dominated by a European government based on Western ideals, the deputation called for "an elected unofficial majority" in the Legco as "the only safeguard the European community would accept." The settlers went on to justify this demand by their alleged payment of "enormous sums in taxation" in a colony that had paid its way for years. "It means," the document went on "that the whole community which pays is governed by the people to whom the money is largely paid. Under these circumstances economy in administration is impossible." Although Delamere and his colleagues agreed that there should be continued government control over African affairs, past agreements with civil servants should be honored, and the governor's veto should still apply, they urged that an unofficial European majority in the Legco would "give the necessary confidence to those we represent in Kenya, to enable them to agree to a policy of citizenship for Indian members of the community."[201]

In addition to the "bombshell"of an unofficial European majority, the settler delegation accepted a common electoral roll with property/income and written and spoken English qualifications, but this was balanced by their insistence on the reservation of seats by race. The eleven European constituencies would remain and three would be added for Indians. They agreed to the possibility of an Indian being nominated to the Execo. They went on to strongly assert that Europeans would not agree to "giving rights of citizenship to domiciled Indians in Kenya unless real control of immigration, amounting practically to prohibition," were given to the settlers. They maintained that this stand was put forward with a view to protecting the interests of Africans. Specifically, they suggested adopting portions of a 1914 Rhodesian immigrants ordinance so as to keep out "low class" Indian immigrants. They advocated commercial segregation "where possible," but insisted on segregation in residential areas. On the highlands, the deputation were "very glad" that Churchill had confirmed their belief that reservation of the highlands was a closed issue.[202]

The permanent officials at the CO quickly recognized the enormity of the deputation's proposals. The settlers had made some concessions, but the most important point, Bottomley maintained in a memo on behalf of the EAD, was the question of an unofficial European majority in the Legco. He did not think that it was "possible to hand over government to the European community while their relations with the Indian community are as they are at present." There was not the slightest chance of the IO agreeing to such a step. Moreover, Bottomley went on to recount several other obstacles to such a concession to the whites. These included African interests, the new loan, official salaries and pensions, and the railway administration. All things considered, plus the fact that an Indian deputation to the CO had now been officially named and would seek an interview with the S of S in February, led

Bottomley to conclude that it was impossible to give an affirmative answer on the question of an unofficial majority.[203]

On the other "new" initiative, that of immigration, Bottomley saw no prospect of a settlement on the lines proposed in the settlers' memorandum. As Bottomley correctly discerned, on this issue the basic position of the deputation was the nonacceptance of the principle of equal rights for civilized men which Churchill had made the cornerstone of CO policy.[204] Nevertheless, the Europeans seem to have had an impact on Churchill on this point for the latter was, after discussion with Masterton-Smith, to significantly alter the CO's stand on Indian immigration.[205]

The settlers as well as the new Indian delegation consisting of Jeevanjee, Wedgwood, and Polak, had seen Montagu by the end of January, but the S of S for India was, in contrast to the CO, not willing to alter his stance on any of the main issues. He made this clear in a long private letter to Churchill dated 28 January. Significantly, he could not agree to an exclusion of Indian immigrants, but Montagu indicated that he might accept immigration restrictions that "did not imply discrimination between the two races." Overall, Montagu was concerned to urge Churchill that "settlement ought not to be postponed any longer." He therefore proposed another interview with Delamere so as to ask them to give up "their prejudices against racial equality in return for some restriction on immigration. . . ."[206]

The European delegation had made a greater impact on Churchill than Montagu had realized. This was made shockingly clear to the latter by a speech made by Churchill at an East African dinner on 27 January. In the presence of the settler deputation, Churchill outlined the principles upon which CO policy in the Indian question would be based. The highlands would be reserved for Europeans, and those who conformed to Rhodes's principle of equal rights for all civilized men would not be denied political and civic rights. Churchill went on to state that in the interests of the settlers and Africans, Indian immigration should be "strictly regulated." While this must have pleased the settlers, Churchill's conclusion that the British government did not contemplate any system that would prevent Kenya from becoming "a characteristically and distinctively British colony, looking forward in full fruition of time to responsible self-government" certainly gladdened the settlers.[207]

The statement caused shock to the government of India and the Indian deputation, and it called forth a very strong disclaimer from a most unhappy Montagu.[208] Montagu accused Churchill "of a grave breach of the ordinary conventions of political life between colleagues and members of the same Government." He complained, in particular, that Churchill had made pronouncements on two subjects without giving him any indication of what he was to say. The first was the issue of the highlands, and the second was the restriction of immigration. Montagu had understood that both issues had not been decided definitely, and that he would be able to take them to the cabinet for final decision.[209]

Churchill replied to Montagu's strong protest on 1 February. He felt that the IO had no cause for complaint. He went on: "My personal friendship for you has led me to the extreme limit about the Indians in Kenya, and I am not at all sure we have not gone too far. Anyway I shall go no farther—not an inch."[210]

The following day, Churchill met the European delegation, and on 4 February he sent a copy of the European proposal to Montagu. He felt bound to tell his colleague "that my mind is working very much on the same lines." Churchill attached considerable importance to some form of immigration control.[211] Montagu replied that he "could not possibly agree" to the European proposals. He observed, quite correctly, that Lord Delamere and his friends "seem to think that they are the population of the colony." Montagu did not agree, and he maintained his strong support for the concept that no disability should be put in the way of Indians merely because they were Indians. He suggested that a decision on the issues in dispute between the IO and the CO by the cabinet seemed to be the only way out of the present impasse.[212]

Montagu did raise the Indian question in the cabinet on 13 February. No decision on the problem was taken, but it did provide the occasion for Churchill to put forward his point of view. He did so in characteristically blunt terms:

> The demands of Indians as regards their treatment in East Africa were unreasonable, and if they were conceded, they would throw the whole of British East Africa into confusion. We had no force there to coerce the white population, who felt strongly on this question, and any repudiation of the statement he made might lead to them ejecting the Indians from East Africa. The Indian population of East Africa mainly consisted of labourers, about 20,000 in number, who had been brought to East Africa for the construction of the Uganda Railway.[213]

In the end, the cabinet decided that Montagu would be allowed to tell the House of Commons that "the matter was under consideration of the cabinet."[214]

The day following the cabinet discussion, Bottomley summarized the position of the CO in the Indian question as a result of the events of the preceding six weeks. These had produced some significant changes in the CO position. This was most momentous with regard to immigration where the CO position had, as a result of the European deputation's pleading, hardened. In this regard, the CO were now inclined to accept Delamere's interpretation of the 1921 Imperial Conference resolution that if Indians were to have citizenship rights, the Kenya "community" had the right to determine its own composition. In his 27 January speech, Churchill had emphasized that "present residents" had to be consulted. Thus the CO was now committed to an effective form of immigration restriction to be applied to Indians. The electoral system left much room for discussion, but the CO had come down in favor of reservation of seats.[215]

On 18 February, Churchill had his final meeting with Delamere and Griffiths. He reaffirmed his position on the highlands, and he emphasized the acceptance of the principle of "some immigration control, without racial discrimination, in which the existing inhabitants would be consulted." He also considered it would be necessary to maintain the principle of residential segregation. Beyond stating that he accepted "the principle of Kenya being a characteristically British colony," Churchill would not agree that there should be an immediate unofficial European majority. Churchill told the delegation that "it was useless to remain longer in England." A decision would not likely be forthcoming for several months.[216]

Two days after the meeting with Churchill, Delamere wrote to formally withdraw the deputation's proposals laid before the CO in January. While defending the demand for an unofficial majority as the only way to gain settler acceptance for the principal of "equal rights for civilized men," Delamere lamented the fact that the S of S had found himself "unable to introduce our proposals in your policy." The settlers would have to be satisfied with what can only be considered a successful visit, since Churchill had laid the "foundation for a future self-governing colony" in the face of very great opposition.[217]

Three days later, Bottomley used Lord Delamere's letter as a springboard for suggesting a new CO policy on the question. On the issue of the franchise, he felt, as a result of the European opposition to the common roll, that it would have to be communal with five seats for Indians. If the communal franchise was not acceptable to them, then four nominated seats should be provided for on an interim basis. As to immigration, Bottomley suggested that all immigrants into Kenya should possess £100 cash on arrival and be able to read and write "in an appropriate language."[218] He would have liked to make the language English, but this would likely exclude immigrants from other parts of Europe and South African Boers. One Indian would be added to the Execo, the highlands would remain for whites only, and the CO would continue to maintain residential segregation in the towns. This then was the CO position prior to meeting the Indian deputation in early March. As Masterton-Smith told Churchill, "presumably the next move rests with the Indian delegation. . . ."[219]

The Indian delegation, led by Jeevanjee, met Churchill on the morning of 7 March. Their reception was hardly warm. When Polak raised the question of land in the white highlands, Churchill curtly replied that "the highlands question is closed." The S of S then expressed his opinion that "the Indians would be better advised to be content with special areas than to thrust themselves in where they were not wanted." In response to complaints that Indians should not be treated as second class citizens, Churchill maintained that he was anxious to improve the position of the Indians in Kenya, but at the same time Europeans must not be swamped. Churchill went on to further observe that "the position might arise that a settlement from here being impossible, an unoffical majority might have to be conceded."[220]

Following the meeting with the two deputations, there seemed little hope of reaching an agreement that both would accept. Bottomley summed up the position on 28 March by stating that the meeting with the Indian deputation "was conclusive only as to the utter impossibility of settlement by agreement."[221] Wood had reached a similar conclusion after a long talk with Polak on the 23rd. According to Wood's account, he put it to Polak that at the present time "no satisfactory solution was possible." It had been rendered more difficult because the CO were now aware of the "recent strength of feelings of white settlers." Wood's conclusion that "no action, whether by Royal Commission or anything else held out any promise of settlement at this time" brought reluctant agreement from Polak.[222]

The most suitable option for the CO seemed to be to take no new policy initiative and to wait on events.[223] At the request of Masterton-Smith, Bottomley did examine again the proposition, evidently favored by Churchill, that an unofficial majority in the Legco should be acceded at once. Bottomley felt "that it is not yet time to do this." It would have, he rightly predicted, a "bad effect so far as Indian opinion is concerned." Moreover, so many subjects would have to be "reserved" that there would be little for such a council to govern.[224]

The CO decision to do nothing as far as the Indian question was concerned had been boosted in early March as a result of changes at the IO. Montagu's sympathies for the Indian point of view in the row caused by the Treaty of Sevres with Turkey finally drove him from office on 10 March.[225] The new team at the IO, Viscount Peel as S of S and Earl Winterton[226] as undersecretary, took time to familiarize themselves with Kenya issues.

Continued unhappiness in India with the position of Indians in Kenya and the lack of progress toward a settlement of Indian grievances there meant that Peel would not let the matter lie for a long time.[227] Great pressure from India caused the IO to press the CO for movement towards a settlement. By early May, as a result, discussions got underway once more between the IO and CO as both sides sought common ground on which to press a settlement on Kenya's Indians and settlers. The principals this time were Wood and Winterton. The clear intention was that both offices would this time seek agreement between themselves before going forward and involving the Kenya and Indian governments. They began by attempting to frame a settlement on the franchise and segregation questions. By mid-July agreement had been reached. Known as the Wood-Winterton plan or proposal, it was submitted to both S of Ss.[228]

Well before that time, however, the likelihood of agreement with the IO had led the CO to consider the best means of achieving acceptance of these terms in Kenya. Based upon past events, it was quite clear that Sir Edward Northey was not the man to accomplish this task. Thus Northey's recall on 29 June 1922 was in part a result of the CO feeling that a new governor, not so closely tied to the settlers and supportive of their demands, would be better able to bring about settlement by agreement. As can be seen from the preceding pages, Northey played little part in the Indian question in 1922. This was not, of course, the only reason for Northey's recall.[229]

Kenya's Continuing Economic Difficulties

Nineteen twenty-one witnessed no abatement of Kenya's financial crisis. A major factor in the colonial state's continuing budgetary difficulties was the depression that had begun to squeeze the colony in the preceding year. Trade continued to decline in 1921 as world prices for Kenya's major exports slid. With no improvement in the depressed conditions of trade, the value of Kenya's agricultural exports fell by 25 per cent from 1920, and government revenues declined. The state's financial position worsened during the year as a result of a number of other factors. It was decided to alter the colony's financial year so as to begin on 1 January as from 1922; this meant that the 1921 financial year began on 1 April and ended on 31 December (nine months). Among other things, this left a shorter period for collection of hut and poll tax with the result that collections did not meet estimates. Measures intended to produce additional revenue, such as the proposed land and income taxes, had not been implemented as of 31 March 1921. The land tax was never approved by the Legco, and Northey telegraphed the CO in March to confess that the income tax could not be collected at all in 1921. The CO agreed that collection was impossible until the end of the year.[230] Kenya was also saddled with payments to the War Office to cover a portion of the imperial war debt. Although the exact amount of Kenya's responsibility for the war debt took a long time to be settled, payments to the War Office proved a drain on Kenya's revenues.[231] The currency changes of 1920 had, moreover, necessitated the awarding of a "local allowance" to European civil servants so as to avoid a reduction in the value of their salaries. This added some £300,000 a year to Kenya's expenditure.

The colonial state's financial position thus steadily worsened as 1921 wore on. By June Governor Northey recognized that the situation with regard to government revenue was extremely serious. There would be no contribution from income tax, and customs revenue looked likely to fall short of the estimate by at least 30 per cent. All this produced a situation in which the governor projected a budget deficit of £300,000 by the end of the year and an overdraft with the Crown Agents for the Colonies of more than £1,000,000.[232] The estimated budget deficit was further revised in the following days at £635,857.[233]

Northey reacted to this worsening crisis by characteristically asking the CO to bail him out. He maintained that he had cut expenditure to the bone by leaving vacant posts unfilled. "In looking round for means of meeting these difficulties," he wrote to the CO on 13 June, "it becomes abundantly clear that no further departmental instructions in addition to those already issued regarding economy in public services can have an appreciable effect."[234] Neither did taxation provide any hope since raising taxes would "add to the general financial distress of the colony under which industry and business is suffering." Northey's conclusion was, therefore:

> A solution of the financial difficulties is, I feel, not in my hands, and I have to ask whether any assistance can be obtained in the form of a grant-in-aid from the Imperial Government without which the present functions carried out by local Government can not be maintained.[235]

No such grant-in-aid was forthcoming. Northey was told to make every effort to bring about further reductions in expenditure. It was also decided that he should come to Britain so as to fully discuss the financial crisis. On 1 July, Northey reported that "by drastic pruning and suspension of unfilled posts," he had reduced the estimated budget deficit to £416,000.[236] Northey suggested raising customs duties as one means of closing the gap between revenue and expenditure, and by the time of his arrival in Britain, this had been accepted.[237] Previously, the CO and Kenyan government had felt bound by international treaty obligations which set Kenya's maximum customs duties at 10 per cent ad valorem. The treaties were abrogated in mid-1921, and the Kenya administration was now free to raise customs duties. Legislation to this effect was passed in August 1921. It was also decided while Northey was in Britain that the local allowance of European officials should be reduced by half.

Another positive item in Kenya's otherwise dreary financial picture was provided by Treasury approval, during Northey's stay in Britain, of a loan for development of transportation. While this demonstrated the imperial government's faith in the future prosperity of Kenya, the actual issue of the loan included a substantial sum to cover a portion of war expenditure, thus reducing somewhat the drain on Kenya's expenditure.[238]

Northey thus returned to Kenya armed with what the CO hoped would be the means and the determination to balance the budget for 1922. He initiated an increase in customs duties aiming to bring in an additional £241,000 and undertook measures to produce a reduction of expenditure of £184,485 (£79,700 of this was to be obtained by halving the local allowance as from 1 April 1922).[239] By these and other measures, the governor was able to achieve what "appeared at first to be beyond the bounds of possibility if the functions of government were to be maintained." In addition to the measures mentioned above, sixty-one European appointments had been left unfilled.[240]

Questioning Settler Paramountcy

Despite this paper balancing of the colony's budget, Kenya's financial position remained critical as 1922 dawned. In light of this and complaints from outside the CO, officials there were forced to examine more closely the reasons for the colony's difficulties. In the course of several examinations in the first half of 1922, they were driven to the inescapable conclusion that Kenya's expenditures were extremely large in comparison to other colonial territories, and the colony's revenue had suffered gravely from an over-emphasis on settler production and the virtual ignoring of African production for export.

The first serious questioning of Northey's pro-settler policies came from a voice representing merchant capital in Britain, Sir Humphrey Leggett, managing director of the British East Africa Corporation and chairman of the East African section to the London Chamber of Commerce that had been established in 1919. He directed a long memo to Masterton-Smith late in January 1922 in which he maintained that "there is much anxiety among financial and business men as to the future of Kenya. . . ."[241] The cause of Kenya's financial difficulties, Leggett asserted, was that too great an emphasis was being placed on European settler production, specifically the fact that special services had to be provided for Kenya's whites, and the fact that settlers had too much political influence. Leggett provided a fiscal analysis that suggested European settlement cost the colony about a million pounds per annum. This had to come from "the native producers."[242]

Leggett went on to propose a solution to the problem. Opposing a drastic increase in African taxation, the merchant capitalist called attention to the fact that African production "in the great Reserve areas, which in 1913/14 yielded a substantial export surplus, is reduced, and has now little or no export surplus." This was at least partly due, Leggett perceptively continued, "to the local policy of 1919 which laid it down that the place of the native is primarily as a wage earner under European farmers." The result of the latter was that African buying power was reduced, a matter of some significance to Leggett and his merchant friends. To deal with this difficulty, Leggett made several suggestions. First and foremost there was "the grave need to stimulate native production on their own land (maize, beans, sim sim etc.)."[243]

The reaction of CO officials to this strong criticism of Kenya economic policy was to dismiss Leggett as a critic whose self interest had caused him to overstate his case. Bottomley noted that Leggett's British East Africa Corporation had posted a hefty loss for the preceding financial year. His criticisms were not taken very seriously initially.[244]

Yet Leggett's criticism was soon followed by another, this time the settler leader Lord Delamere. This forced the first serious CO examination of Kenya's finances of 1922 in early February. Lord Delamere, heading the European deputation to the CO, suggested to Bottomley that "the administration of Kenya is extravagant."[245] As a result of Delamere's observation, Bottomley set out to carefully study Kenya's expenditure. He compared it with that of other colonies of similar size "or more or less similar conditions": Uganda, Nigeria, and the Gold Coast. Bottomley recognized, of course, that Kenya differed from the other three dependencies by having large European and Indian populations. Unlike the West African colonies, both Kenya and Uganda employed Indian or Goan clerks and this pushed administrative costs up.[246] Nevertheless, he proceeded to closely compare Kenya's expenditure with that of Nigeria.

The result of his comparison was most striking. Bottomley found Kenya's system of African administration far more expensive than Nigeria's. So too were legal, educational, medical, and postal expenditure as well as the land, public works, and police departments. The sectors where Kenya's expenditure was most out of line with Nigeria's were agricultural and veterinary. The Kenya department of agriculture employed thirty-seven specialist European officers at a cost of almost £44,000.[247] What was striking also was that these officers were almost exclusively employed in support of European agriculture. In fact, in every head of expenditure where Kenya far surpassed Nigeria, the obvious answer was the presence of European settlers in Kenya.[248]

Bottomley was clearly struck by the extravagance of Kenya's expenditure. He circulated the memo to his superiors at the CO with the recommendation that further cuts in expenditure should be undertaken. At Masterton-Smith's request, he drew up a draft despatch to Northey. Approved by Churchill, the despatch, dated 14 February, urged the governor to take advantage "of all possible economies" to avoid a budget deficit. It was essential also to be able to tell the Treasury "with complete confidence that the Colony is spending no money unnecessarily."[249]

The CO set out several principles that must guide a comprehensive search for economy. In such a examination, the most useful vehicle would be a "small committee, largely composed of unofficial gentlemen, who would examine the expenditure and report to you on possible reductions."[250] Since this would put any such committee strongly under the influence of European settlers, it is perhaps important to note the reason the CO made this recommendation. Officials felt that heads of departments in Kenya could "hardly be expected to be impartial" in an exercise that might very well lead to their budgets being slashed. Thus the suggestion of an unofficial majority was made. The chairman of the committee should be, on the other hand, "an official whose seniority and standing will enable him to hold an independent view." The CO suggested Sir Charles Bowring.[251] This provided the impetus for the establishment of Kenya's Economic and Finance committee, the so-called Bowring Committee.

At about the same time that the CO despatch was drafted in London, the Kenya government was considering a similar initiative. A proposal to set up a super-committee on the lines of the Geddes Committee in Britain was defeated in the Legco on 3 January.[252] The matter was not dropped, however. The Execo recommended on 23 February that a committee be appointed to inquire into and report on "the means wherein production and exports may be fostered," the costs of imports and government expenditure decreased, and "the present amount and incidence of taxation." For this task, the council recommended a committee with an official majority. Only bankers and traders would be represented in addition to the officials; the council explicitly recommended "that no representative of the producing interests of the colony be appointed other than the Acting Director of Agriculture."[253] Such a committee, to be chaired by J. W. Barth, was announced shortly thereafter.[254] The Execo revisited the subject on 9 March, however, as the governor had received strong pleas, especially from the Convention of Associations, to include at least three producers on the committee.[255]

The matter was only settled with the receipt of the S of S's despatch. A new committee was constituted and announced at a special session of the Legco. Headed by Bowring, the Economic and Finance Committee would have two government nominees, two members representing the associated chambers of commerce, three settlers, and one Indian member. Its membership was complete and ready to start work on 31 March. It is of more than passing interest that two of the settler members were Grogan, recently returned to Kenya from Britain, and Delamere.[256] The committee did not confine itself to only those subjects suggested by the CO. It took as its first charge that it examine and recommend the means whereby production for export could be expanded. Its recommendations on this subject would bring it to the attention of the CO, but in the meantime, the CO was once again forced to make its own examination of Kenya's finances.

The initial impetus for such an examination came, once again, from Delamere. He addressed a note to Masterton-Smith on his way back to Kenya enclosing a memo on income tax. Long an opponent of the income tax ordinance, Delamere tried to argue that it should be scrapped as a way to solve the colony's financial problems.[257]

Delamere's memo caused the CO staff to once again look at Kenya revenue and expenditure. Both Batterbee, now back in the EAD, and Bottomley felt that Kenya wanted all the revenue it could get because, in Batterbee's words, the "present small export trade of Kenya can not indefinitely carry the present Government expenditure. . . ." Even taking into account internal trade, Batterbee concluded that there could be no doubt that Kenya's expenses were "too great for the present trade to carry."[258] He found further confirmation for this view in the chart he drew up comparing Kenya's revenue, expenditure, exports, and imports with those of seven other British dependencies. Kenya's expenditure exceeded all except two of the colonies to which it was compared. These were Ceylon and Nigeria, and in the case of the former, the value of its exports was almost eight times that of Kenya while Nigeria's exports were more than four times those of Kenya. Particularly striking was

Batterbee's comparison with the Gold Coast. Its revenue, unlike Kenya, exceeded expenditure; though Kenya's expenditure was higher than that of the Gold Coast, the latter's exports exceeded those of both Kenya and Uganda in value by some £7,680,000.[259] Although not overly impressed by Delamere's arguments, the officials were agreed on the need for further cuts in expenditure. They awaited proposals from Northey with some anticipation.[260]

Before they received anything like that, however, CO officials were jolted by further exceedingly strong criticism of Kenya's pro-settler economic policies from Sir Humphrey Leggett, which reached the CO via Labour M.P. Josiah Wedgwood in late March. Wedgwood brought Leggett's criticism to the attention of Wood on 29 March, and expressed his own opinion that "you are helpless in the hands of the Kenya Whites, who live (and borrow) on the taxation of the natives."[261] In Leggett's letter to Wedgwood, dated a day earlier, he asked again that some attention be paid to "excessive native taxation—and its killing consequences—in East Africa . . . more especially in Kenya." Leggett lamented that he got repeated reports from his managers in East Africa about the higher taxes levied on Africans which was "deadening their industry and setting them back in every way." In most districts of Kenya, the rate was Shs 16/-, and Leggett argued that this represented no less than two full months' wages for the average African worker.[262]

Leggett did not stop with criticism of African direct taxation. He complained of the rise in customs duties (from 10 to 20 per cent) on imported goods purchased by Africans. So much was taken from the African in taxation, Leggett maintained, that the inducement to work was gone; for the taxes raised from the African probably not even one quarter was applied to African welfare by the government. Leggett called attention to the shortage of maize that existed in some African districts. "It is a disgrace to the local Government that there should *ever* be a famine in Kenya," wrote Leggett. He concluded his letter: "What a travesty upon all the humbug talk about 'Trusteeship for the native'!"[263]

The CO could no longer ignore the powerful attack on economic policy in Kenya by a prominent merchant capitalist. Lord Hindlip, formerly a Kenya settler and now a board member of the British East Africa Corporation, had also indicated that he would raise a question in the House of Lords on the issue, and officials at the CO naturally felt that Leggett was behind that initiative as well. Assessing Leggett's criticism, they decided to call Colonel O. Watkins for his observations. Watkins, former acting CNC and wartime head of the Carrier Corps, was in Britain on leave. In the meantime, both Batterbee and Bottomley continued to question Leggett's motives. He was a trader, stated Batterbee, and "like traders in this and every other country, he is out to reduce all forms of taxation."[264] Bottomley felt that in light of representation from the British East Africa Corporation alone among the companies operating in East Africa "it is material to look at the corporation's annual report."[265]

By the time Batterbee had had the opportunity to obtain Watkins's views, another letter from Leggett critical of economic policy in Kenya had appeared in the *Daily Express*. With the issue soon to be voiced in the House of Lords, Batterbee went right to the heart of the matter in his detailed minute. He admitted that far more was spent on European education and agriculture than on African. The picture was not so black as painted by critics such as Leggett, he argued, but "until we spend considerably more than is spent at present on native education and agriculture and industrial training, we can not have a clear conscience in the matter." He went on: "The policy of native education and development means turning the native into a producer such as he is in Uganda (cotton) and the Gold Coast (cocoa), whereas the settler in Kenya wants to keep him as a wage earner."[266]

Batterbee went on from there to pose the most fundamental of questions regarding British rule in Kenya: was the African to be denied the right to become a producer in his own right because of the presence of European settlers in the country? "If the native becomes a producer himself will there be enough left to go out to work on the settlers' estates?" "Are we in Kenya primarily for the settler or for the native?"[267] Batterbee provided no answer, but he had raised the most crucial of questions and in the weeks ahead the CO would try to work out a satisfactory answer.

This was important as critics continued to press the CO to reassess its policy in Kenya. W. Ormsby-Gore wrote to Wood on 25 March, for example, to raise the question of African taxation. Ormsby-Gore, son of Lord Harlech, had entered the House of Commons in 1910 after schooling at Eton and Oxford. The Conservative M.P. had developed an active interest in African issues, and he had, on numerous occasions, expressed preference for the West African, or peasant producer, economic model in Africa. He enclosed a letter from a missionary in Kenya that sought to explain the African unrest characterized by Thuku's EAA. Ormsby-Gore went on to remark: "I am afraid the Indian row has rather overshadowed the much bigger and more fundamental problem of the future of the African native in that country."[268] He urged the CO to set up a departmental committee to study African trade and taxation.

CO officials had only to examine Kenya's export figures to see the stark result of Northey's policy. As Table 6.1 illustrates, not only did 1921 witness a dramatic fall in the value of Kenya's exports. It marked the high point of the dominance of settler production in Kenya's exports; 86 per cent of exports for that year were of European origin while only 11 per cent came from peasant production. The ascendancy of settler production was marked, but it was accompanied by a dramatic drop in over all export value. The need to re-establish African production for export was clearly grasped by CO officials; it eventually dawned even on the Bowring Committee and, perhaps astonishingly, on Northey himself. As a result, 1922 and 1923 showed a rising share of African production in the colony's exports.[269]

Table 6.1 Percentage Share of Value of Agricultural Exports

	1921	1922	1923
African			
Hides and Skins	6	7	9
Beans/peas	*	1	2
Maize			9
Sim sim	2	1	3
Other grain	1	*	*
Groundnuts	1	2	2
Cotton		*	*
Potatoes	1	1	1
Total	11	12	26
Settler			
Coffee	53	31	38
Sisal	29	28	18
Flax	2	8	4
Wattle		*	*
Wool	2	3	2
Maize			11
Wheat		*	*
Total	86	70	73
Miscellaneous			
Coconut/copra	1	2	1
Mixed			
Maize	2	16	
Total value £	709,515	915,939	1,298,334

Source: Colony and Protectorate of Kenya, *Department of Agriculture Report for 1924* (Nairobi: Government Printer, 1925), Table 1.

As Table 6.2 demonstrates, although African exports declined after the war, African production was not strangled. Even in 1920-21, it, excluding hides and skins, formed a significant share of total agricultural production.[270] It was on this base that increased exports from the peasant sector would be built.

Table 6.2 Percentage Value of Total Estimated Production 1 July 1920 to 30 June 1921

Crop	European	African	£Total
Maize	17	83	656,346
Wheat	100	0	17,375
Oats	100	0	1,547

Cont'd Table 6.2

Crop	European	African	£Total
Rice/Millet	0	100	386,559
Barley	100	0	2,298
Simsim	0	100	63,765
Miscell. Grain	0	100	364,761
Beans/peas	1	99	118,268
Pulses	0	100	65,369
Potatoes	1	99	94,010
Sisal	100	0	179,539
Flax	100	0	281,515
Coffee	100	0	296,604
Cassava	0	100	10,512
Copra	19	81	3,400
Cotton	0	100	22,512
Wattle	100	0	4,512
Wool	100	0	8,817
Coconuts	12	88	8,770
Dairy Produce	100	0.	50,772
Bacon/Pork	100	0	16,221
Bananas	0	100	262,508
Total	34%	66%	£2,957,959

Source: Colony and Protectorate of Kenya, *Economic and Financial Committee
Report of Proceedings During 1922* (Nairobi: Government Printer, 1923),
38–39.

As officials were preparing for the Lords debate that Lord Hindlip had
given notice he would initiate in May, they were gratified to receive a telegram from Northey recommending reducing African taxation from Shs 16/- to
Shs 12/-.[271] The initiative came at a particularly opportune moment, and the
CO rapidly approved,despite the loss of revenue.[272] In preparing a reply for
the Lords debate, however, Bottomley proposed to take the CO in an entirely
different direction than that which had been advocated since 1919 by Governor Northey. He stated:

> The development of Kenya, especially since the war, has largely gone on the lines of
> the employment of natives by European settlers—due in great measure to the fact
> that there is no staple industry for the natives. Much of the present difficulty is due
> to the fact that only few native labourers are required and for these high wages can
> not be afforded. That is a matter of depression in world trade. Wages will have to
> rise later, but native production will be encouraged provided marketable commod-
> ities can be found for him to grow. This need not mean any serious subtraction from
> European labour supply.[273]

Thus the head of the EAD expressed the need for a change of direction in
Kenya. African production was to be raised from the dust bin to which it had

been consigned by Northey to a role complementary to that of settler production. Kenya needed the exports of both. Bottomley had summarized what would later be officially enshrined as the Dual Policy. What is particularly significant is that the CO had come to this conclusion on largely economic grounds. Once this reality had been accepted at the CO, it would not be long before it would be decided to scrap not only the previous policy, but the policymaker as well.

Leggett returned to his attack on Kenya policy in a letter to Bottomley on 27 April. He called for stimulating African production by spending more on the reserves while reducing African taxation. This would increase African purchasing power, a matter of more than a little importance to Leggett and his merchant friends in London. He admitted that the British East Africa Corporation had lost nearly half a million pounds during the preceding year, and Leggett saw little hope of improvement for his company "until the native gets his stimulus to produce." Heavy taxes and the policy advocated by settlers of openly discouraging the Africans from working in the reserves "have drained the black man white."[274]

Batterbee's memo of 27 April indicates that the CO had already accepted much of this thinking. Thus by the time Lord Hindlip's motion was debated in the Lords on 10 May,[275] the CO was ready to announce a reassessment and change of policy in Kenya. African production would be "assigned a definite place in Kenya's future economic development."[276]

Following the Lords debate, Wood asked Batterbee to draw up a despatch summarizing the issues that the CO had been considering for the past two months. The purpose was to inform Northey of CO thinking and to suggest a new direction for Kenya's African policy.[277] Not only did the Lords debate mark the CO's acknowledgement of the need for policy reassessment, recent events in Kenya pointed in the same direction. The despatch, completed by Batterbee on 30 May, called attention to reports "from many quarters" that there "has been rising in Kenya an increasing wave of Native unrest [an obvious reference to the missionary letter forwarded by Ormsby-Gore] of which the recent disturbances connected with the arrest of Harry Thuku are a symptom." The unrest had not yet reached "dangerous proportions," but "unless steps are taken to remedy such grievances as exist, the state of affairs may become serious."[278] Harry Thuku might be consigned to remote Kismayu, but the implications of the protest movement he led, and the colonial state's violent reaction, had not been forgotten.[279]

What was now required, the draft despatch continued, was for the Kenya government to see that the African received "full value for his taxation." Specifically this meant that more had to done for African education, agriculture, and industry. The CO had to be able to show critics in Britain and Africans in Kenya "that the revenue contributed by the natives is spent in the natives interest." After emphasizing the need to do more for African education, the despatch went to the crux of the matter, the fostering of African agriculture. Thus it was essential, not only to the welfare of the Africans themselves, but "of the Colony as a whole, that all steps possible should be taken to make the native a producer on his own account as he is in other parts of Tropical Africa." Kenya had "lagged behind in this respect," but the CO was convinced "that the time has now come when this problem should be taken seriously in hand." What was essential was "a carefully thought-out programme laid down and approved by Government, adapted to the varying requirements of the different Reserves and capable of being developed as larger funds can be devoted to the purpose."[280]

This draft despatch clearly reflected a change in CO thinking and a determination, on the part of Wood and the EAD, to bring about a change in policy in Kenya. African production must be resuscitated. The despatch was not sent to Kenya at this time, however. This did not reflect a change of mind or lack of determination on the part of the CO. In fact Wood informed the House of Commons on 4 July of the CO's determination "to explore more fully the possibilities of the development of native production in Kenya."[281] Rather by the time the draft was considered for mailing in June, the CO had concluded that no change of policy could be effective with Sir Edward Northey at the head of the Kenya government. The despatch was thus held back during the summer recess of parliament.[282] In addition to considerations involved with the Indian question and Northey's continued inability to put right the colony's finances, as described earlier, events in May and June 1922 finally convinced the CO that Northey had to go.

Northey's Last Battle

The CO's last battle with Northey stemmed from his advocacy of certain of the recommendations of the Bowring Committee. The latter had begun its work in March with an emphasis on reviewing ways in which Kenya's exports might be spurred and imports controlled. The committee's first recommendation was thus that the colony foster, with the least possible delay "an export trade in some easily produced local bulk commodity for which there is a steady and virtually unlimited demand in the markets of the world." In the comittee's view, such a commodity was maize.[283] Action to spur the export of maize was certainly acceptable to the CO, but the committee's proposals aimed toward spurring the wheat and wheat flour industries in Kenya were another matter.

Northey began the "battle of wheat" with the CO on 10 May. In his struggle to win support for the Bowring Committee's recommendations, Northey adopted the tactics that he had utilized with other issues he had portrayed to the CO as particularly important and pressing: lengthy telegrams calling for rapid action to solve what the governor characterized as a serious crisis, the request for rapid telegraphic approval of his proposals, the threat of dire financial outcomes if his advice was not followed, and his assurance to the CO that "public opinion", as expressed in the Legco at least, was solidly behind his recommendations. Northey initiated the battle with a telegram in which he recommended quick approval for the committee's proposal to increase the import duty on wheat to 50 per cent and on wheat flour to 100 per cent. The purpose of this gigantic rise in duty was not revenue but protectionism. It would, said Northey, "promote local industry and restrict importation of an essential commodity which readily can be produced locally." The increase in the price of bread during the "interim period until sufficient local flour available" would not exceed one and a half pence per loaf. Northey agreed that "Kenya can not afford to drain its financial resources by importing wheat which can be grown locally in sufficient quantity and of suitable quality." Since the committee recommendation had been published, the need for approval was urgent for large imports of wheat flour were on their way to Mombasa from India; this would mean a loss of revenue if the duty was not raised before its arrival.[284]

At the CO, on the other hand, there was little enthusiasm for Northey's recommendation. Batterbee began his minute with the remark, "Protection with a vengeance." Upon receipt of Northey's wire, officials called in Colonel Franklin, Trade Commissioner for Eastern Africa and Alexander Holm, Kenya's Director of Agriculture for consultations as both were in Britain at the time. Neither could see any justification for the huge rise in duty on wheat imports. In light of their observations, Batterbee recommended approval of an increase of no more than 25 per cent. Holm had reported that there was only "one big mill" working in Kenya; thus the milling capacity to meet local demand from local sources was just not available. To this practical problem, Batterbee added a political one. Most of the wheat came from India, and Indians were big consumers of wheat flour. The CO did not need another Indian grievance to contend with.[285]

In light of Batterbee's remarks, the CO telegraphed Northey on 15 May expressing "very serious doubt" as to his proposals "which practically amount to prohibition." The telegram went on to raise a series of questions and doubts for the governor's consideration. These included the CO's apprehension that there were adequate local supplies of wheat or milling capacity, the Indian question, and the possibility of monopolistic control of the market. The CO telegram concluded with the suggestion that it might be possible to approve a "moderate increase to say 20 or even 25 per cent."[286]

This telegram brought an immediate, vintage response from Northey. He began by stating that his purpose was indeed the prohibition of wheat imports to "prevent export of wealth not benefit wheat growers." The governor admitted that local flour was not popular with consumers, but he contended that his proposals were necessary to overcome "prejudice" against it. Large areas would be put under wheat immediately, but, good economist that he was, Northey argued that the intention was to increase demand; then supply would follow. Just as wheat would be quickly sown, Northey contended that mills could be quickly constructed. Even though he admitted that the Ugandan government did not approve of his scheme, Northey concluded with the classic observation that "fuller argument is difficult to telegraph." He now urged approval of the principle of the tariff increase, leaving the Legco to determine the exact amount of duty.[287]

CO officials were no more convinced by this telegram than they had been by the initial request. Batterbee began his analysis by an observation: "The Governor appears to be a believer in the mercantile theory, a fallacy which I thought was exploded long ago." It was clear to the official that however Northey tried to argue the case, the effect of his proposal must be to benefit the settler wheat growers. Relying on information from Holm,[288] Batterbee went on to point to several difficulties with Northey's reasoning: domestic wheat supplied very little of the Kenya demand, consumers did not like bread made from Kenya flour, the governors's proposal would raise the price of bread, and Northey was overly optimistic in not expecting political trouble from Indians if the duty was raised.[289]

Moreover, the governor's reference to further import duties contemplated by the Bowring Committee touched a nerve with Batterbee. He suspected that the committee and the governor meant to profit not just Kenya, but certain individual settlers who were members of the committee. He wrote: "It now appears that the committee proposes similar protection in favour of local timber. This means putting large sums in the pocket of Major Grogan, just as wheat proposals mean large profits for the wheat growers." The latter reference was to another member of the committee, Lord Delamere.[290] The CO received confirmation of this view a week later from a Mr. Franklin of the chamber of commerce and manufacturers in Glasgow. In a personal letter to Read, he said that as local flour was cheaper in Nairobi than imported flour to start with, "this looks like a Delamere-Unga ramp. . . ."[291]

Batterbee's continued opposition to Northey's proposal formed the basis for the CO response. In a telegram of 24 May, the S of S told Northey that he could not approve the proposals for a 50 per cent and 100 per cent rise in duty though he was prepared to approve a moderate increase. The brief telegram promised a despatch setting out the CO objections in detail.[292]

Governor Northey did not wait for the CO reply before taking action to further his aims. Following the path he had taken to force his currency proposals on the CO more than a year earlier, Northey prepared a bill for introduction to the Legco that would raise the duty on wheat imports by 50 per cent and wheat flour by 100 per cent. He would allow a free vote to official members on the measure. In order to avoid the embarrassment of 1921, Northey would tell members of the Legco that unless the higher customs duties were enacted there would be insufficient revenue to allow for the repeal of the income tax ordinance.[293] With the promise of the repeal of income tax, there was no chance the settler members of the Legco would desert him as in

1921. To make extra sure of the success of his pressure tactic, Northey did not, as previously, inform London of his intentions before acting.[294]

The Legco this time did as the governor desired. On 25 May, Northey telegraphed London to announce the Legco's action on wheat and wheat flour. The legislation would give the government power to control prices to allow sufficient wheat to be imported at 25 per cent duty to insure there would be no immediate shortage. Northey triumphantly told the CO that the bill had passed by a vote of 22 to 3.[295] The CO was not overawed by Northey's huge consensus for the measure. Bottomley remarked: "I do not know whether it was more undesirable that this measure should have been put to the Legco before, or after, the receipt of the reply. . . . it would have been better if Sir E. Northey had waited for our telegram or having received it had telegraphed back before taking action."[296] If it had been Northey's intention, moreover, to force the CO to accept the overwhelming verdict of the Legco since his own arguments had failed, he was soon gravely disappointed. The CO telegraphed the governor on 31 May insisting on a maximum 30 per cent duty on wheat and flour.[297]

Even upon receipt of this telegram, Northey did not give up his struggle on behalf of the settler wheat producers. He sent an eight-page despatch to the CO on 15 June setting out in detail his reasons for favoring the huge increase in import duties on wheat and wheat flour. He pleaded with the CO to allow the use of other means to prohibit the import of wheat.[298] CO officials found no reason to reply to the governor's despatch.

Northey's action in once more trying to force the hand of the S of S by questionable maneuvers that would make him look heroic in settler eyes, even if he failed to accomplish his goals, proved to be the veritable last nail in his coffin. Prior to the receipt of Northey's long despatch, the CO had sent its detailed reasons for rejecting the increased rates on 29 June. Moreover, Churchill had approved another despatch to Governor Northey that was mailed to Nairobi on the same day. It informed Sir Edward of his recall as governor.[299]

The Exit of a Governor

The news of his sacking reached Northey in late July; he immediately sent a plaintive telegram to Churchill. He began:

> These instructions with no previous warning are heart breaking. I have slaved to help this country through difficulties for three and a half years and I find it very hard to be told to go now just as we are beginning to see day-light.[300]

The governor maintained that he was never in better health, and that "my sudden dismissal from the Governorship must count against me" in any attempt to find reemployment with the army. Northey concluded by stating that he would not be able to wind up his affairs in Kenya in less than a month and by asking for authority to publish the CO despatch "as I cannot explain my sudden departure any other way."[301]

The CO reply was quick. Sir James Masterton-Smith personally placed the concerns raised by Northey before Churchill. The main issue was when to announce the appointment of a successor. Masterton-Smith recognized that since Northey was owed eighty-three days leave in Britain, the usual practice dictated that Bowring should act as governor until the end of the year so that the revenues of Kenya would not have to meet the "double charge" of the salaries of Northey and the new governor. He rejected this line in favor of an immediate takeover by Northey's successor. The main reason for this recommendation was that "the present state of discussions upon the Indian question requires that Sir Edward Northey's successor should get into the saddle with as little delay as possible."[302]

Churchill approved this recommendation with rapidity. On 28 July, a telegram was sent to Northey approving of his leaving for Britain in a month's time. Following Masterton-Smith's advice, the wire sought to salve Northey's feelings to some degree. The S of S told the outgoing governor:

> you will I trust not regard the ending of seven years of high civil and military employment in East Africa as open, with the slightest degree, to the interpretation of dismissal which you place upon it.[303]

The S of S concluded by stating that while he had no objection to the publication of his despatch recalling Northey, the latter must wait until "I inform you of consequential arrangements in a few days."

What the latter phrase meant was the announcement of Northey's successor. The choice had already been made, Sir Robert Coryndon, Governor of Uganda.[304] Nevertheless, Coryndon had not been formally offered the post; now that it had been decided that he should assume office in Nairobi as soon as possible, a telegram was hastily send to Uganda's capital with the offer on 1 August.[305] Following a slight delay caused by Coryndon's absence from Entebbe, the latter telegraphed his acceptance to London on 6 August.[306]

While this was going on, Northey played one last card in an attempt to stay on as governor. On 1 August he transmitted three telegrams to London that called for his retention in light of the important budgetary decisions then under way. These came from the executive of the Convention of Associations, the Economic and Finance Committee, and the elected members of the Legco. All mentioned rumors of Northey's recall, but in fact he had told them of it.[307] Unhurried by the Northey-inspired telegrams, the CO had already given permission to publish its despatch of 29 June when it replied on 15 August with a curt telegram. Northey was asked to "inform the senders that I am confident that their apprehensions are unfounded and that the economy campaign which you have initiated will be maintained by your successor."[308]

The news of Northey's sacking was then made public and the CO despatch published at the end of the second week of August. The CO despatch had been framed expressly for this purpose; it maintained that Northey's recall was the result of changed conditions in Kenya. He had been appointed as a military governor, but the S of S continued:

the circumstances which required the services of a Military Governor no longer obtain, and that the restoration of peace conditions in the Colony has reached a definite stage at which the altered requirements should be reflected in the appointment of a Governor well versed in purely civil administration. I therefore feel it my duty to advise the king to appoint to the Governorship of Kenya a man who possesses the administrative experience that will enable him to take up the task which you have begun and to bring to it the benefit of the knowledge that he has acquired in the development of new countries.[309]

Although settlers and their friends made many unhappy noises at Northey's firing,[310] the CO had no intention of turning back the clock.[311]

The Northey era was over. Never again would Kenya have so inexperienced and so pro-settler a governor. The first half of 1922 had finally convinced the CO that Northey was taking it down the wrong path in Kenya. Northey had alienated the Indian community, caused alarm in India by his favoritism for the settlers, and his stance had brought continuing protests from the IO. Northey had placed all the resources of the colonial state behind settler production and had done nothing to stimulate peasant production for export. This policy had brought troublesome protests from British missionaries, humanitarians, and merchants, and the refusal of metropolitan bankers to give way to the pro-settler currency schemes of the colonial state had forced the CO to block Nairobi's most extreme demands. More significant, it had stirred African protest, not only in Nairobi, but in other parts of the colony, such as Nyanza province and Machakos district, as well. The CO realized that a change of course had to be made to avoid an escalation of further protest. Most important of all, Northey's reliance on settler production had, in economic terms, led the colony to the brink of bankruptcy. The events of the first half of 1922 convinced the CO that African production had to be stimulated to complement that of the settlers, a process that would later be dignified by being called the Dual Policy. By contrast, the CO had little doubt that the man announced as Northey's successor at the time of his removal, Sir Robert Coryndon, would support the expansion of African production, and they at least hoped that he could secure the acceptance of the new proposals the CO would soon send to Kenya for bringing an end to the Indian controversy.

It was thus highly ironic that just prior to his removal, Northey himself had come, very late in the day, to the conclusion that his government must take active steps to encourage African production for export. Northey informed the CO of his change of heart in a confidential despatch dated 10 July. Pressured by the Bowring Committee, he had come to agree that Kenya's financial difficulties required a greater contribution towards exports from peasant producers. The government was now taking measures, Northey reported, to stimulate peasant production. It would concentrate on the Kikuyu, Luo, and Luyia areas in encouraging production of cotton, rice, simsim, groundnuts, maize, and beans. "Native cultivation," he concluded, "with its lower overhead charges and costs of production is in an extremely favourable position in this respect."[312] The man who had begun his governorship maintaining that the African's only economic role in Kenya was as laborer on settler estates and farms had finally grasped this basic fact. It came too late, however, to save him from the ignominy that his one-sided policies deserved.

In its resistance to the labor, currency, and economic policies advocated by Northey in 1921 and 1922, as in its refusal to accept completely the governor's solution to the Indian question, the CO had responded to the struggle for Kenya by taking important steps to regain the initiative in the direction of policy. The sacking of Northey completed that process, and the term of his successor would begin with the CO clearly holding the initiative at the very start of the new governor's administration.

7

The CO Takes Control, 1922–23

During the period of approximately a year that intervened between the recall of Sir Edward Northey as Kenya's governor and the enunciation of imperial policy in the white paper of July 1923, the struggle for Kenya reached a climax. The CO completed the reestablishment of control over Kenya affairs it had largely given up during the war years. With the firing of Northey, the CO intervened to halt the colonial state's exclusive emphasis on settler production. African production for export, within the framework of what would come to be termed a Dual Policy, would be stimulated, and the official doctrine of African paramountcy would form the means for the CO and the imperial government to stamp their control on Kenya. The form that this took removed any chance that Kenya would ever become a settler-state. It was, however, an economic decision.

African paramuntcy as a doctrine grew out of Parkinson's 1919 memo, which argued that African interests had to predominate in the face of the conflicting claims of either Europeans or Asians, but it also reflected the CO view of Kenya's economic realities. For the colony to avoid the financial and trade difficulties of the preceding two years, African peasant production, settler production, and Indian commerce all had to contribute and be given scope for growth. It is important to recognize also, as a means to understanding future developments in Kenya, that African paramountcy also served to get the CO out of the dilemma it faced in the Indian question. It provided a convenient way to justify a final settlement of the controversy that pleased neither the settlers nor the Indians completely. The doctrine could thus provide an escape for the CO, and, as an added bonus, it appealed strongly to the missionary and humanitarian groups in Britain that had been highly critical of British policy in Kenya during the Northey years.

Kenya's New Governor

In removing General Northey, the CO moved quickly to appoint Sir Robert Coryndon, then Governor of Uganda, to take his place. Coryndon, who assumed office on 1 September 1922,[1] was everything that Northey was not. Coryndon's entire career had been spent in African administration; few men in the colonial service could match his extensive and diverse record. As Governor of Uganda he was very familiar with practically every issue that he had to contend with in Kenya. He would need no convincing, moreover, as to the necessity for stimulating African production for export.[2] He had become a strong adherent of that strategy while in Uganda. Given his long administrative experience, which had included dealing with white settlers, the CO also had every reason to hope that he would be able to implement its new solution to the Indian question. It is thus not difficult to discern the reasons for the CO's choice.

Unlike all previous governors, Coryndon was African-born and had spent many years in the administration of territories there. Born in Cape colony, South Africa, Coryndon first rose to prominence as a protege of Cecil Rhodes. His eventful career took him from the service of the British South Africa Company to that of the British government in what is today Zambia, Swaziland, and Zimbabwe.[3] His proconsular occupation brought him to Uganda in early 1918. He had already served four years there when the call to Kenya came. Coryndon thus was very familiar with most of the political and economic issues he would encounter in Kenya. This was a definite advantage from the CO perspective as was the fact that Coryndon had been a far from fervent supporter of a number of Northey's initiatives.[4] Leaving for Nairobi, he is said to have told a friend: "Have accepted Governorship of Kenya; no more peace."[5]

Coryndon's view of his appointment can be seen from a private letter he composed to Churchill shortly after his arrival. He told the S of S:

> I believe I shall be able to handle the settlers; largely by laughing at them a little and by getting them to use a sense of proportion in their outlook. I shall push native development and native crops. I am confident as to the future on the whole.[6]

These were certainly the expectations of the CO in appointing Coryndon to Kenya. Unlike Northey, who was left to undertake policy initiatives and recommendations after local study, the CO would provide Coryndon with a specific formula for reaching a solution to the CO's greatest dilemma in mid-1922, the Indian question. CO officials hoped that Coryndon could bring about agreement on the basis of the Wood-Winterton plan; on that subject, however, he would prove a huge disappointment.

Seeking a Solution to the Indian Question

The first major issue that Coryndon had to deal with in Nairobi was thus the renewed attempt of the CO to end the controversy swirling around the Indian question by implementing what became known as the Wood-Winterton proposals for a settlement. These had taken shape in June and July 1922 as the result of continued discussions between the IO and the CO. Although the settlers had forced a more sympathetic line from Churchill as the result of the Delamere deputation's visit to London in early 1922, the IO and the government of India continued to put strong pressure on the CO. They pressed for a policy which would go a considerable way towards at least meeting the Indian claims for political rights similar to those enjoyed by the European settlers. They urged that a settlement had to be rapidly reached as opinion in India was highly charged on the issue. The other factor that pushed the CO to adopt a new initiative—more favorable to Indian claims than Churchill had seemed ready to accept earlier in the year—was the CO recognition that African production for export must be stimulated. Indian merchants were, in the CO view, the only vehicle through which this end might be attained. The Indian presence was thus essential to any rise in African production; Indian demands would thus have to be met to some degree.[7] It needs to be recognized, however, that the CO willingness to meet the IO demands did not represent a change of attitude on the part of permanent officials. They remained vehemently anti-Indian.

By 14 July, discussions between Wood and Earl Winterton had reached the point where they were able to submit a summary of the conclusions to Churchill and the S of S for India, Lord Peel.[8] Their conclusion was not so much a final, polished document but rather a summary of where the two departments agreed and disagreed.

The Wood-Winterton proposals were summarized in the 14 July document under several headings. Under elections, the recommendations provided for "a common electoral roll for all British subjects and protected persons."[9] It was agreed that qualifications for electors should be so framed that ten per cent of the Indian population would get the franchise. The two offices concurred that the governor should carry out a test census of that population before the final qualifications for the vote were set. Both agreed that there should be educational and property/income qualifications, but all Europeans on existing voter rolls would retain the franchise.

As to the number of constituencies, two alternatives were proposed. In one, seven constituencies would be created; three would return one member each and the others two members each. In the three single-seat constituencies, European candidates only would be qualified for election, and in the other four, one seat would be reserved for an Indian and one for an European. Thus there would be seven European unofficials and four Indians. The second possibility, advocated by the IO, proposed the creation of four large constituencies, returning three members each. In each, a single seat would be reserved for an Indian. This would provide eight European unofficials and four Indian. Indians were also to be given "adequate representation on an elective basis" on municipal councils. Detailed arrangements would be worked out later.

Far less space was given to the other issues in dispute. The plan called for one Indian unofficial on the Execo, no commercial or residential segregation on racial lines, no change in the existing immigration regulations, and the maintenance of the status quo with regard to the highlands. For the latter, the two offices had agreed on language to express their disagreement.

> The Colonial Office can not contemplate any change in the existing law and practice having regard to past policy and commitments. The India Office take note of this view but are unable to accept it and reserve the right to reopen the question, if need be, at some future date.

Upon review of the Wood-Winterton report, Churchill called for a change in the area of immigration. As he had expressed earlier in the year, the S of S felt that there should be an alteration in the immigration laws to make it more difficult for Indians to enter Kenya. As previously, he proposed that this be done by establishing "an equality" between the regulations governing entry for Indians and British immigrants. He asked Wood to take up this point with Winterton.[10]

Wood had further discussions with Winterton and his IO advisers, but he failed to convince them of the need for Churchill's suggested immigration controls. Winterton held strongly "that any attempt to revise the regulations on such a basis would be likely to wreck the chance of agreement being accepted in India." The IO representative further called attention to the concessions he had already made.[11] After his discussion with Winterton, therefore, Wood recommended making no change in the immigration policy recommended. The reason for this was that, after reviewing statistics on Indian immigration for the past two years, the CO representatives at the talks had been forced to recognize that there was no "flood" of Indians entering the colony.[12] Moreover, Wood felt that "if the settlement breaks down on this point the onus for this will rest entirely on us."[13]

Churchill accepted Wood's recommendation, but before giving final approval to the Wood-Winterton plan, he asked to be assured that the proposals did not depart from the promises he had made in his January speech before the settlers and their allies. Wood maintained that the CO had no obligation to consult the settlers over the details of the proposals. Their representative in Britain, Major Crowdy, could merely be informed that "a provisional agreement on the lines of your speech had been reached."[14]

Churchill accepted this assurance the following day, and he approved placing the Wood-Winterton plan in a draft despatch. He minuted to Wood: "This is a good piece of work and justifies all the trouble you have taken. But it is useless and even dangerous to put it to the outgoing governor. Explain this to the IO."[15] A draft telegram was thus immediately prepared, but it would be sent when Coryndon had taken over. At the same time the IO would send a copy of the proposals to the government of India.[16]

The CO now had to wait for the rest of the month so that Northey might vacate office. This time was used to make some small modifications of detail in response to correspondence with the IO.[17] The IO sent a copy of the proposals to the Viceroy on 31 August; the CO hesitated as they awaited official confirmation of Coryndon's takeover. Such did not arrive on 1 September, but by 4 September, telegrams had arrived in London signed Coryndon. There seemed no reason why the telegram prepared on 4 August should not now go to Nairobi.[18]

Thus on 5 September the Wood-Winterton plan was telegraphed to Coryndon. It was prefaced with a statement that it would form the substance of a policy announcement at a later date. Coryndon was told: "Please consult Executive Council confidentially and send your observations by telegram as soon as possible, bearing in mind that the proposals represent a nicely balanced agreement between the two Secretaries of State."[19]

The CO was forced to wait almost three weeks for Coryndon's reply. In the meantime, the reactions of the Indian government were quickly passed on by the IO. The viceroy objected to the reservation of seats "which would largely nullify advantages of common electoral roll" and "perpetuate racial antagonism." If reservation was unavoidable, the Indian government favoured the IO alternative for delimiting constituencies with the number of Indian seats raised to five. The viceroy's other objection, predictably, dealt with the issue of the white highlands; he wished to reserve the right to reopen this question in the future.[20]

Coryndon wired the result of his conversation with the Execo on 21 September. He reported that only the Indian member of the council felt that the proposals formed a suitable basis for a settlement. The rest of the council strongly urged very serious consideration of a number of points before the scheme was published. These were that reservation of the highlands for whites was an issue "upon which no compromise is possible," and that "the common roll creates a grave danger against which no adequate safeguards are provided in your proposals." The Execo majority considered "that unless these two points are settled on lines different to those proposed in your telegram, the only course will be to force the policy on a European population which is bitterly antagonistic."[21]

Coryndon followed the Execo's recommendation with a statement of his own views. He began by confirming the fact that "the whole European population" was immovable as to the sanctity of what they regarded as a pledge to keep the highlands for whites only. The second most important point for the settlers, Coryndon continued, was that there must be "reasonable but effective restriction on immigration." He then went on to describe the motive he perceived behind the European attitude. It was

the fear of Indian political domination not in the remote distance but in a matter of a few years and the arrangement for the constituencies and the limitation of the Indian voters roll now proposed will not operate in practice as an effective bar to Indian domination.

Coryndon confirmed that the only guarantee that the settlers would accept was one from the British cabinet approving the sanctity of the highlands and real restrictions on immigration. He too urged that no public announcement be made of the proposals as, he concluded: "I cannot hold out any prospect of agreement on those lines. I greatly regret the position."

Exactly what the governor meant by the last statement would not become clear to the CO for several months. There is no doubt, however, that he regretted the proposals had been framed with what he viewed as excessive concessions to the Indians. The South African–born Coryndon had no understanding of, or sympathy for, the Indian position. Coryndon had already demonstrated "intense antipathy" towards Indians as Governor of Uganda.[22] During his tenure there, he had, at one time or another, advocated restrictions on Indian immigration, attempted to reduce Indian influence in the colonial economy and bureaucracy, and vigorously opposed Indian demands for equality of representation.[23]

Spurred by the violently racist views of his private seretary Major E. A. T. Dutton, Coryndon was to prove no more capable than Northey of bringing about the settlement desired by the CO and the IO. It was hardly a case of Coryndon coming under the influence of the settlers immediately on arrival, rather his views were, and always had been, those of the settlers. This was clearly apparent from the personal comments he made in the 21 September telegram. He suggested, in complete seriousness it appears, that a genuine fear of the settlers was "that the trusteeship of natives will not in practice be shared but will be handed over to the Indians."[24]

While the CO had not expected an instant settlement, there was obvious disappointment that the new governor's attempt to forge agreement appeared to have brought about a hardening of the European position. It was, Bottomley minuted, "disheartening." He went on: "The fact that the opposition comes entirely from the European side . . . will tell against the Europeans."[25] He saw little chance that the CO could meet the settler objections, and he argued that in light of the small numbers of Indians entering Kenya in 1921 and 1922, immigration restriction simply was not something that the IO and British public opinion would accept. Read also recognized the difficulty of reaching a settlement. He recommended making no reply until the return of Wood, who was away from London.[26]

The day after Read and Bottomley recorded their minutes, the CO received another telegram from Coryndon. This time it was a personal wire to the S of S. The governor reaffirmed his belief that every word of his 21 September telegram was true. He then went on to recommend that "if no guarantee can be given that cabinet will confirm the points of sanctity of the highlands and of restricted immigration then a Royal Commission would probably be wiser than the present basis when neither side will give way." Coryndon asked if Churchill might visit Kenya before deciding on a Royal

Commission. At any rate, Coryndon felt that "a delay in settlement may operate in favour of the European point of view."[27]

In light of the governor's two telegrams, the CO decided to reopen contacts with the IO before pressing Coryndon again. Churchill took Masterton-Smith's advice that when Wood returned to the CO and Winterton returned from India they could reconsider the position in light of the replies received from India and Kenya.[28] A copy of Coryndon's 21 September telegram was forwarded to the IO, and a very brief telegram was sent to Coryndon informing him that it would be necessary for the position to be reviewed at any early date by the CO and the IO.[29]

Review at an early date did not prove possible. At the time Churchill's telegram was sent to Nairobi, the Chanark crisis was already full-blown. Within weeks, Lloyd George's coalition was swept out of office by it. This took Churchill and Wood from the CO to be replaced by the Duke of Devonshire and William Ormsby-Gore in the new Conservative party administration led by Andrew Bonar Law.

New Leadership at the CO

S of S for the Colonies represented the highest office held by Victor C. W. Cavendish, the ninth Duke of Devonshire, during his long political career. After schooling at Eton and Trinity College, Cambridge, he entered parliament as a Liberal Unionist in succession to his father. Like other Liberal Unionists, he was absorbed into the Tory party, and he attained the office of Financial Secretary to the Treasury under the Balfour administration. He succeeded his uncle as Duke in 1908, and he spent the period 1916–21 as Governor-General of Canada. Unlike his two immediate predecessors, Devonshire had neither a wide circle of admirers nor opponents. He was a plodding, pedestrian administrator who had little interest in or experience with African issues. He would rely heavily on the permanent staff, especially Masterton-Smith, for advice and specific policy initiatives.

Unlike the S of S, Ormsby-Gore, had taken an active interest in colonial questions, particularly those pertaining to Africa. Almost twenty years Devonshire's junior, the new under-secretary was a member of the League of Nations Permanent Mandates Commission at the time of his appointment. He had, as noted in preceding chapters, an expressed preference for the peasant producer economic model in Africa. His recent public statements on Kenya had reemphasized this and been anything but sympathetic toward the settlers. Contributing to the Commons debate on the CO vote on 4 July, for example, Ormsby-Gore maintained that current policy in Kenya was "preventing the Africa [sic] native from rising from a proletariat position at all." He went on to express his feelings regarding Kenya very bluntly: "I personally regret the history of that Colony and I would like to have seen the development of Kenya and East Africa proceeding on precisely the same lines as the development of the Gold Coast and Nigeria. . . ." He continued: The "experiment" of white settlement in Kenya "will be an economic failure"; the settlers "are very nearly ruined now, and in five years time they are likely to be absolutely ruined by this policy."[30] He, like Wood, would play a large role in dealing with the Indian question.

Wood-Winterton Once More

Despite the delay caused by the change in government, the CO returned to a serious consideration of how a settlement of the Indian question could best be accomplished in the first week of November. At the request of the new S of S, Bottomley drew up a memorandum titled, interestingly, "Indians in Kenya." It described the development of the dispute and highlighted the major issues and positions taken.[31] This was followed by further discussions with the IO some two weeks later. Winterton, now back from India, and Ormsby-Gore agreed that the Wood-Winterton plan formed the best basis for a speedy settlement that the IO in particular desired. Following Winterton and Ormsby-Gore's meeting, Bottomley and the latter drew up two draft despatches to Coryndon for the S of S's consideration. The second draft contained a threat, included on the order of Ormsby-Gore, that European elective rights could be withdrawn and Kenya returned to a nominated Legco.[32]

As the CO was considering the final form the despatch to Coryndon would take, Lord Peel, who like Winterton had continued at the IO under the new government, sent a lengthy and cogently argued letter to Devonshire in support of the Wood-Winterton terms. Showing himself more conciliatory than Montagu, Peel emphasized the extreme importance of "the Indian point of view" that had been pressed on him by Winterton and the viceroy. Winterton had emphasized the need for a rapid solution to the question as Indian opinions regarded it "as a test of British good faith." Turning to the points in the dispute, Peel maintained that the Wood-Winterton proposals left the highlands situation unchanged. The settlers were not being asked to alter their view; the IO, for political reasons, had only reserved the right to reopen the question. The demand for immigration controls, he felt, was unreasonable since there was no evidence of an influx of Indians. Even more important for the IO was the certainty "that any suggestion to include in the settlement a revision of the existing immigration ordinance would destroy all chance of a settlement being accepted in India." Peel felt that settler complaints against the common roll were unreasonable also, as there existed plenty of safeguards against Indian political domination.[33]

Faced with this powerful plea from the S of S for India, Devonshire held further talks with Masterton-Smith, Ormsby-Gore, and Bottomley.[34] The result of this meeting was that Devonshire authorized the resubmission of the Wood-Winterton plan to Governor Coryndon. In approving a despatch to the governor to impress on him the necessity of acceptance of the settlement terms, however, the S of S ordered the dropping of the threat to return to a nominated council.[35]

First the CO sent its despatch to the IO. Within a day's time, Lord Peel sent his approval of it in a personal letter to Devonshire. He obviously spoke for the CO as well in concluding: "I hope it will have the effect of bringing the people in Kenya to reason."[36]

The following day, therefore, the CO sent two despatches to Coryndon. The first was essentially the initial draft prepared by Bottomley on 22 November. It stated that after further consideration in London, the S of S felt bound to press the governor to make a further attempt to secure settler acceptance of the Wood-Winterton proposals. He assured Coryndon that they would be accepted by the Indian government "as a final settlement of the controversy." The CO went on to argue that the Kenya government should accept them as a compromise final settlement. They were

> intended to meet the legitimate aspirations of the Indians without sacrificing anything really vital in the position of the Europeans and an end could be found to the dispute which has in many ways hampered the progress of Kenya without adding to its reputation in this country. . . . Unless an agreed settlement can be reached in Kenya the question will continue to be an open sore in the relations between India and the rest of the Empire. . . .[37]

This strong plea of imperial necessity was followed by an examination of the Wood-Winterton settlement. Here the CO sought to argue that there was nothing in them "which need be unacceptable to European thought in Kenya." There could be no other basis for a solution, the S of S maintained "other than that of a common electoral roll." Under the scheme proposed, "there should be no danger of Indian predominance in future elections." The CO then went on to specifically rule out Lord Delamere's idea of the grant of an "unofficial European majority in the Legislative Council" as a safeguard.[38] The CO argued that since there was no present indication of any significant Indian immigration into Kenya, no controls could be accepted. These would merely inflame India. As to the highlands, the CO bluntly told Coryndon that though the IO might protest over land reservation, "there need be no misgivings in Kenya as to the possibility of the question being reopened by the present Secretary of State for India, and for practical purposes the position is exactly as if a decision in favour of reservation were given by the Cabinet."[39] Urging Coryndon to press the Execo to accept the scheme, the CO closed by noting the need to extend the life of the existing Legco if a settlement had not been reached before the 1923 elections were due.

In a second, secret, despatch, Devonshire attempted to impress on Coryndon the need to accept the terms. The CO had "given every attention" to the views the governor expressed in September and those of the settlers. Following up on his minute of 8 December, Devonshire told Coryndon:

> The position is however so serious and the importance attached by His Majesty's Government to a settlement on the lines indicated, in broad imperial interests, so great that I must impress upon you the necessity of using your influence, not only to induce your Executive Council to accept the compromise, but also to secure that the unofficial members of that council will make every effort in their power to obtain the acquiescence of the European community when in due course the terms of the settlement are announced.[40]

The Threat of a Settler Rebellion

The CO had now to wait and hope that its strong plea and the more conciliatory attitude of the IO would provide the basis for a settlement. No reply would, in fact, come from Nairobi until almost a month had passed. In the meantime, the CO heard, from more than one source, that the Kenya government was going ahead with European elections and had actually planned to move them up to February.[41] CO officials at first refused to believe that Coryndon would agree to an early election in light of the delicate negotiations. They therefore decided to telegraph the governor that if agreement to the proposals was not likely, he should extend the life of the Legco rather than hold fresh elections.[42] The telegram arrived on the same day as the despatches of 14 December.[43]

Despite the gravity of the issue, Coryndon wasted little time in replying to the CO. He consulted with his Execo, but it appears to have been his private secretary Dutton who had the greatest impact on the governor's rapid reply. Dutton made two essential points in a memo he prepared for his employer on 11 January. The first was that the CO did not really understand or appreciate the absolute correctness of the point of view of the Kenya settlers as did Coryndon and Dutton. Wrote Dutton: "The whole point, the whole issue is in the future. And the S of S appears to have missed it."[44] The second point made by Dutton was that certain phrases in the despatches suggested that the CO wished Coryndon to shoulder the responsibility for getting the terms implemented and for forcing them on the settlers if no agreement was possible. Dutton advised that imposed terms:

> would come better from the Secretary of State than from Your Excellency, since if they come from you the country would be confirmed in its belief that you were sent here to do what General Northey would not do, for the rest of your term you would be regarded as 'the man who let down the country,' 'the man who betrayed the Europeans' and much worse, whereas the shoulders of the Secretary of State are broad enough (and sufficiently out of reach) to accept the responsibility, and by forcing him to take the final step, Your Excellency would still retain the loyal sympathy and assistance of the non-officials in your main task which still lies before you. . . .[45]

These suggestions were both eagerly accepted by the governor. Over the ensuing weeks, therefore, Coryndon moved to distance himself from any attempt to gain a settlement by agreement that did not meet his and the settlers' wishes. If he was not able to do that, he would do everything in his power to force the CO to shoulder the burden for the settlement. In obtaining the latter end, his main tactic would eventually be to convince London that the settlers were plotting a rebellion if they did not get their way. Only when this is understood does Coryndon's behavior over the next two months become explicable.

Coryndon's rapid telegraphic reply thus informed the CO that it was impossible to get the European community to accept the Wood-Winterton proposals unless "I am authorized to consult them." He specifically asked for a free hand to consult settler representatives, in strict confidence, and then propose changes in the CO scheme. Coryndon pressed this strongly on London as the only alternative to forcing the Wood-Winterton plan on the colony's Europeans. He went on: "The effect of this would be a very serious disturbance of public feeling, possibly with some serious violence and the certainty of creating deeply embittered feelings which years would not wipe out."[46] He promised, however, to extend the life of the Legco.

At the CO, it was not so much the governor's request to consult settler leaders that caused consternation as the implication that the terms of the settlement would have to be considerably altered.[47] Read also foresaw that the IO would not agree to further changes and would urge the CO to bring the Kenya government into line. He concluded: "There would seem therefore nothing for it but to announce the terms of the settlement and intimate to both Europeans and Indians that they have got to accept them."[48] Such a step would only be taken by the decision of Devonshire and Ormsby-Gore; before they could review the situation, another telegram arrived from Coryndon.

In this telegram of 15 January, Coryndon went to greater lengths to urge the CO to give him a free hand to make changes favorable to the settlers; failing that, he sought to use threats of settler violence to force the S of S to step in and shoulder the burden for a settlement. He raised again the issue of the bad effect the granting of rights to Indians would have on the Africans and buttressed this by the observation that there was every reason "to suspect Indian stimulus to Thuku riots in 1922." The governor went on to inform the CO for the first time that "vigilance committees" had been formed by settlers and that "responsible leaders" might not be able to restrain them in case of an adverse settlement. The settlers, Coryndon pressed the CO to believe, were prepared to make no compromise on the Indian question. If the Wood-Winterton proposals were forced on them "grave public disturbance" would ensue. As examples, Coryndon suggested hostile demonstrations, boycotts, possible destruction of bazaars, "and at worst the shootings of few Indians in district centers."[49] All these dire forecasts were meant to convince the CO to give him a "free hand" in discussing the proposals and framing alternatives. In addition, the governor did provide one bit of information; for the nine months from April to December 1922, 2,888 more Indians had entered Kenya than had departed.

By this time, moreover, Coryndon had concluded that the London policy was emanating not from Devonshire but from Ormsby-Gore. Only thus could he, and many settlers, come to grips with an understanding of how the CO could push a scheme so disliked by the settlers. Ormsby-Gore's outspoken lack of respect and support for the Kenya settlers made this explanation believable. Thus in the 15 January telegram to the S of S, he referred to the settlers' (and his) feeling that "the present S of S" was "not informed fully of gravity of promises given" by his predecessors.[50] That Coryndon felt the S of S was not involved in the matter was even more clearly indicated by the private and personal telegram he sent Masterton-Smith the same day. By this highly unusual means, he held out the possibility that he might, at the last moment, be able to persuade both sides to make concessions that would be acceptable and avoid the "practical victory of Indian demands." His real motivation was revealed, however, in the final sentence of his telegram. "If you have not already done so," he told Masterton-Smith, "I beg you to bring the question to personal attention of Duke of Devonshire."[51] Three days later, Coryndon composed a letter to Masterton-Smith expressing support for the settlers who were "almost aghast that the destinies of the Colony are so largely in the hands of Ormsby-Gore."[52] As described earlier, Ormsby-Gore did have a considerable part in urging the Wood-Winterton plan on Kenya. Yet Devonshire was involved in all major decisions and had actually toned down the despatch as proposed by Ormsby-Gore.

Following receipt of the two telegrams of the 15th, Devonshire, Ormsby-Gore, Masterton-Smith, Read, and Bottomley met on 16 January to discuss the CO response.[53] Besides deciding on the replies to be sent to Nairobi, the officials were forced by Read to face a fact that would have considerable implications for the future. He wrote in his minute a day later:

> If we eventually decide to enforce the agreement and there is a risk of trouble from the Europeans we must bear in mind that (with the exception of 36 white constables) the rank and file of the police and of the military are Black and that to use them against Europeans would have deplorable consequences. This question does not arise at present, but it is a very important one and must be bourne in mind.[54]

The CO replied to Coryndon on the 18th with two telegrams. In one Masterton-Smith assured the governor that Devonshire "has of course been giving close personal attention to the question ever since he became Secretary of State."[55] In a second telegram, the S of S emphasized the importance of the settlement from the imperial standpoint and informed Coryndon that the acquiescence of the government of India "to any considerable modifications" was highly unlikely. On the other hand, Indian immigration figures for the last nine months of 1922 created "a new factor;" the S of S now felt that "in the native interests, quite apart from the European, some measure of control will be necessary." The governor was authorized to discuss the proposals, in strict secrecy, with European leaders, but he was again instructed to postpone the European elections.[56]

Despite these instructions, Coryndon telegraphed on 23 January to report that "the public" (i.e. the settler politicians) were "strongly opposed to the prolongation of life of present Legislative Council because it embodies a variation of the constitution of the colony." This public were suspicious of any "tampering with the constitution," and postponing the Legco elections would "greatly increase the difficulty" of gaining their agreement to the Wood-Winterton proposals. Coryndon backed this attitude strongly and urged the CO to change its position on the issue.[57]

The CO could hardly accede to the governor's request. Peel sent Masterton-Smith a note on the 25th, urgently requesting a delay in the Kenya Legco elections so as to reduce the difficulties the government of India was facing over the issue.[58] Thus when the CO replied to Coryndon, it turned down his appeal as politely as possible. Not only would holding the elections cause grave difficulties in India, but also it seemed almost certain that holding any election would further delay a settlement since the European leaders would want to await the electoral outcome before making any commitment. In its telegraphic reply, the CO included a statement for release in Kenya.[59]

With the door to this type of concession closed to the settlers, Coryndon now turned increasingly to play up the threat of violent action on the part of the settlers as a means to forcing the CO to take the matter out of his hands and defer a settlement he disliked and opposed.[60] He telegraphed London on the 27th greatly regretting the decision as to prolongation. He prefaced this, however, with vague references to public meetings and strongly worded resolutions on the Indian question all over the colony. Speeches were being made, he reported, which used the phrase "with force of arms."[61] While the governor maintained that he was doing all he could to urge restraint on the settlers, this telegram marked the start of his attempt to derail the proposals while saving himself from the wrath of either the CO or the settlers.[62]

During the last week of January, Coryndon held discussions with some three dozen "leaders of European opinion." On 29 January they submitted to the governor, in the form of letters from the Convention of Associations and the unofficial members of the Legco, their verdict that the Wood-Winterton terms were "so incompatible with the principles which the Europeans of the Colony considered essential to the maintenance of their position of supremacy that it would be useless even to submit to the Colony for consideration."[63] Coryndon telegraphed this verdict to the CO on 1 February. The settler leaders had also protested the prolongation of the Legco, and they urgently called for the passage of an immigration bill at the next session of the Legco. Coryndon detailed the form the settlers desired the bill to take. Among the most crucial points were the requirement of a deposit of Shs 1000/- for all immigrants, and the application of an educational test "to consist of ability to read and write a passage in a European language" to be selected by the immigration officer.[64] The anti-Indian intent of the measure was obvious.

As Coryndon knew that the CO was now willing to consider the tightening of controls on Indian immigration, he attached himself strongly to the need for an amendment of the immigration laws as a means of keeping himself off the hook and avoiding the necessity of using, full force, the threat of violence. In the second half of his telegram, therefore, he strongly urged CO agreement to the immediate passage of a bill on the lines desired by the settlers. He told the S of S:

> I am convinced that your approval will alter the whole complexion of the negotiations. The leaders guarantee to give their earnest consideration to other outstanding points if the stumbling block of the immigration bill is got rid of at once.[65]

Coryndon followed this up the next day with a personal telegram to Masterton-Smith urging immediate enactment of such an immigration bill. It would be, he urged, "a most valuable step forward." He went on: "Delamere, who is really moderate, fully agrees. I can go so far as to say that if this request should be refused the whole of the negotiations may fall to the ground."[66]

CO officials considered this new development on 2 February in a meeting with representatives of the IO. Hampered somewhat by the fact that Peel and Winterton were both away from London at that time, the CO refused to be forced to act hastily. Following the meeting, the CO telegraphed Coryndon, informing him of that fact. Further, the CO asserted that though it accepted the need for "a strengthened immigration law," such a measure as the settlers proposed could only be accepted, after careful consideration with the IO, as part of a general settlement.[67]

Receiving this reply, Coryndon quickly turned to play his last card, the threat of a settler rebellion. He telegraphed the CO on 3 February, raising this possibility, in more graphic terms than before, if the negotiations for a settlement fell through. He reported that the settlers had "complete machinery" prepared to "paralyze the functions of the government." The first actions, he predicted, would be refusal to pay taxes followed by "the most stringent personal and commercial boycott against Indians." This might well be succeeded by the seizure of the Treasury building, armory, the railway, customs, and telegraph offices. A possible future step might be "the wholesale expulsion from Nairobi and Mombasa Island of the Indian population."[68] For this threat of settler direct action, Coryndon professed to have no answer. Very few settlers would come forward to support the administration. Most civil servants and missionaries, he asserted, sympathized with the settlers desire to defend western civilization against the Indian onslaught. African soldiers could not be relied upon to suppress a settlers' rebellion. For good measure, he decried the gravest effect a settler "subversion of government" would have on the African population of East Africa. "The Government's prestige," he maintained, "would inevitably suffer incalculable and lasting damage."[69]

Despite the dire consequences he forecast, Coryndon took pains, at the end of the telegram, to divert any blame from himself. He contended that he was favorably regarded by the settlers personally, but "no individual Governor could in this matter move the whole colony." He believed there was "very little bluff in the attitude of the public" on this matter.[70]

With this telegram, Coryndon finally succeeded in one of his aims in responding to the CO despatch of 14 December; the Wood-Winterton plan was now effectively dead as a basis of settlement of the Indian question. Faced with the governor's account of the threat of settler violence, the CO would reach this conclusion over the succeeding two weeks. On the other hand, Coryndon's personal position was as yet far from secure; he would have had difficulty in explaining why he had not informed London earlier of the threat of rebellion if the plans were indeed as well advanced as he suggested in the 3 February telegram. It would take the next two weeks for the governor to assure the CO that he was not at fault.

The immediate reaction of the CO to the bombastic telegram of 3 February, on the other hand, was to wait for further detail in preparation for submitting an account of the looming crisis to the cabinet. Officials met in the S of S's office on 6 February to discuss the matter, and they decided to be ready to prepare a memo for the cabinet summarizing the whole of the Indian question and the present impasse.[71] Bottomley set to work drawing up the document, and by 8 February he had completed a lengthy draft. The memo to be submitted to the cabinet was again titled "Indians in Kenya". In the initial part, he once more described the background to the present crisis, including a copy of Coryndon's 3 February telegram. The CO envisioned "a breathing space before any positive trouble need be expected," but if the negotiations broke down, the government would have to make a choice between modifying the terms of the settlement "to meet as far as possible whatever views the representatives of the Europeans may ultimately put forward" and taking steps "to combat the action which the Governor anticipates would follow an imposed settlement contrary to their views."[72]

For the CO, the second choice was inconceivable, and the cabinet memo made this very clear. Using African troops in suppressing "organized action on the part of the Europeans" was "unthinkable." This would be "disastrous to the discipline of the troops," "fatal to British prestige throughout Africa," and "it would mean that in the whole of the continent the life of a European would not be safe in any area of native population." Neither was the introduction of sufficient white troops to quell the settlers seen as a viable alternative. It would be "a costly enterprise of a character particularly unedifying to the public in this country and in the Dominions." So too did the CO rule out the

idea of a naval blockade of Kenya. This would wreck the country economically, harm the Indian and African populations, and would have a serious
effect on Uganda.

Devonshire accepted this first part of the memo, but he ordered a more
inclusive historical review "so as to recall to the Cabinet the previous stages of
the controversy."[73] This became Part II of the memo which, with enclosures
(e.g. Churchill's January 1922 speech, the CO telegram of 5 September 1922,
and the resolution of the 1921 Imperial Conference) was finally ready for
submission to the cabinet by 12 February.[74]

In the meantime, the CO received an additional telegram from Coryndon
on 8 February which offered little help. He reported "vigorous unanimous
protests" from settler members of the Legco to the legislation extending its
life. They made plain that "settlement by agreement will become almost impossible unless European elections were held on 21 February." Coryndon
hoped that the S of S could concede the point and allow him to withdraw the
bill providing for extension of the Legco's term.[75] Following a meeting of
Devonshire with Kenyan settlers Major Crowdy and Lord Cranworth, the S
of S, Ormsby-Gore, Masterton-Smith, Read, and Bottomley, met and decided to send two messages to Nairobi.[76] In a telegram addressed to the governor, the CO regretted that the matter could not be reopened because of the
bad impact this would have in India. Moreover, the CO attitude had been
misunderstood. There was "no foundation whatsoever" for the charge that
the CO was disregarding the settlers' political rights.[77]

In a separate, personal and secret, telegram, the S of S took up directly the
threat of a settler rebellion. He stated:

> I cannot believe that European leaders will not realize on reflection that at this stage
> direct action of any kind can only prejudice their case and alienate sympathies of
> Cabinet, Parliament and public here, including those who would be disposed other-
> wise to support them. Do you seriously anticipate such action before the negotia-
> tions break down and before there is any definite prospect of an imposed
> settlement?[78]

In the second part of the telegram, the CO pressed Coryndon further
to state how serious the situation in Kenya really was. It recalled that his
3 February telegram contained the first hint of direct action, and the CO
went on to suggest, in language that Coryndon could not possibly misunder-
stand, that he had been lax in his duty in not, at the very least, giving "a
serious warning of the grave consequences to the prosperity and credit of the
country of such an action." The CO continued: "His Majesty's Government's
imperial and international embarrassments at the moment are sufficiently
grave . . . without their being complicated by Englishmen in a British colony
crying out before they are hurt." While calling for a full report, the CO raised,
for the first time, the possibility of Coryndon coming to Britain "to explain
the situation . . . as you see it."[79]

While awaiting a reply to this telegram, the CO received an additional wire from Coryndon that clearly indicated that the governor had now given over his entire strategy to the threat of violence as the only position which would move the CO in the directions he desired. On 9 February, he telegraphed to report that the settlers would not agree to continue negotiations until some effective check was made on Indian immigration. However, the bulk of the wire dealt with the threat of European direct action. He reported that the officer commanding the Kings African Rifles agreed with him "that it would be quite useless to take counter measures against any concerted action by Europeans and suggests that the facts be brought to the knowledge of the army council." Coryndon professed anxiety that the African population was "closely watching the situation and there is increasing evidence of their hostility to the Indians." These dire predictions formed the basis for Coryndon's appeal to the CO to give way completely to the settlers immediate demands. He continued:

> I believe that one thing only can now relieve the situation and that is prompt and definite decision to accept the principle of the European claims and give it effect at once by agreeing to passage of new immigration bill containing adequate safeguards similar to those stated in my telegram of 21 January. This would be more useful than concession of point as to holding elections on 21 February, but if both points are granted discussions will at once be resumed and there will I believe be fair chance of a settlement.[80]

This telegram did nothing to move the CO. There was no chance that London would change its mind as to postponing the elections and implementing immediately an immigration act. Thus the leadership of the CO decided to wait for a specific reply to their telegram of 9 February.[81] This arrived at the CO on 13 February. Coryndon had been forced to go full force to shock the CO and to ward off any responsibility from himself for not having dealt strongly enough with the settler plans for direct action. He began:

> You will recognize that it is necessary for me to speak quite plainly; the time for anything but the clearest understanding has long past. I thought that in previous telegrams, all of which were carefully worded and contained no exaggeration, I had made the position clear.[82]

He advised the S of S to read again his telegram of 3 February.

He then set out his, and the European, position that they were defending a great imperial cause. This was that the responsibility for the five million Africans in that part of Africa "must remain in European hands and must not be diluted by being shared with Eastern race, alien in spirit, and recognized as being lacking in the genius of government of backward subject races." "No persuasion and no argument," he concluded, "except that of superior force can now compel them to change or abandon that standpoint." Coryndon did not anticipate any direct action until the negotiations have broken down. This would not occur before a meeting of the Convention of Associations on 26 February. However, the governor pulled no punches in detailing the settlers readiness and ability to use violence. He raised again the possibility of Indians in remote stations being shot, and posed the possibility of riots and murders of "Englishmen" in India as a result of such action. He strongly endorsed the idea that he should come to Britain, suggesting he should sail, perhaps with one or two European leaders, by the first steamer leaving after 26 February. The only peaceful avenue now open, concluded Coryndon, was permission to pass his proposed immigration bill through the Legco.[83]

There could now be no doubt in the mind of CO officials that the Wood-Winterton proposals were dead. Before submission of the issue to the cabinet, Devonshire and the others directly concerned at the CO sought to be absolutely sure of the governor's views. The S of S telegraphed to Nairobi on 16 February, confessing his "disappointment" that the Wood-Winterton proposals had been met by a "blank negative" from the settlers with no constructive suggestions of their own. He asked Coryndon for a "definite expression" of his personal view of whether passage of an immigration bill such as he suggested would bring the prospect of solution "appreciably nearer." The S of S pointedly informed Coryndon: "Your deliberate and frank judgement upon this point is essential."[84]

Coryndon's bluff on this point had been effectively called. When he replied to the S of S's blunt query on 19 February, the governor was forced to admit at the outset that the passage of an immigration bill at once "would not secure the acceptance as they stand of the whole of the proposals of September 5th."[85]

He then went on to describe three main difficulties he saw standing in the way of a settlement. These were the reduction of European seats in the Legco from the eleven they insisted they must hold, the retention of the highlands, and immigration restriction. Most important, however, was "the deep rooted fear of the common franchise basis" for in twenty-five or fifty years time the "natural increase" of the Indians "together with education of Africans and Arabs will give large numbers of votes to both and therefore communal franchise basis whatever name it goes by is preferred."[86] The settlers, Coryndon said, could not accept "equal rights of all civilized men" nor were they claiming ultimately a settler unofficial majority or South African–style self-government. What they wanted, nevertheless, was completely at odds with the ideal expressed in Churchill's speech and with that laid down in Devonshire's despatch of 14 December.

Upon receipt of Coryndon's telegram of the 19th that, in addition, included the governor's personal suggestions for ways to overcome settler resistance to the Wood-Winterton proposals, the CO proceeded to initiate discussions aimed at bringing the crisis caused by the governor's reports of threatened violence under control. A meeting was held on 21 February, with representatives of the IO present, to begin that process. Besides the two secretaries of state, the two offices were represented by permanent civil servants. On the CO side, the delegates consisted of Masterton-Smith, Read, and Bottomley.[87]

In an immediate sense, Coryndon had won since both the IO and the CO now accepted that "there is every reason to believe that the fear of direct action was justified to the full." They recognized that "force could in no circumstances be employed against Europeans." It was agreed that in these circumstances, the only thing to be done was to call the governor to Britain. "There would be a valuable gain of time, provided that his departure did not precipitate an outbreak." This was not regarded by the discussants as likely since the call home would be regarded by the settlers as "a good omen," and they would not want to prejudice their case by "direct action."

With the immediate steps to be taken agreed upon, the meeting turned to a consideration of the kind of revisions in the Wood-Winterton plan that would be necessary to obtain the agreement of the settlers and Indians. The conference first considered the proposal for a bill to restrict immigration. The IO held that the kind of bill advocated by Coryndon would "produce deplorable and disastrous results in India." The IO representatives also called attention to the fact that giving in to the settler demands would amount to "the encouragement of non-cooperation." Peel pointed to the bad precedent this would set for India, and he also discounted the signficance of the increase in Indian immigration over the last nine months of 1922. It represented, in the IO view, nothing more than the natural flow back due to the prospects of revived prosperity as the depression began to fade away. No final agreement could be reached on the necessity of an immigration bill, but the CO kept the option of more stringent control of Indian immigration open.

In the course of this discussion, moreover, the conference touched on what would become one of the most crucial factors in the ultimate settlement of the Indian question. This was the economic issue. Both the CO and the colonial state had now committed themselves to measures "for encouraging native agriculture and industry," and this would require the presence of Indians in Kenya. The latter were the trading class who were vitally necessary, in the CO view, if African production for export was to become a reality. There could thus be no question of a complete stoppage of Indian immigration nor could there be a complete denial of Indian claims for equal rights. Economic necessity would thus overcome the lack of sympathy towards the Indians felt by all CO officials.

From immigration and this economic fact, the conference moved to discuss the common roll and the highlands. On the former, the IO agreed to a major concession in that a communal franchise might be accepted by them in return for "the removal of some the most distasteful features of the proposed Immigration Law."[88] On the reservation of the highlands for whites, it was agreed that there was no pressing reason to change the policy of keeping the highlands white. The conferees also concurred that there was no need to alter the Wood-Winterton proposals regarding urban segregation.

In conclusion, the conference considered two possible solutions to the Indian question, though no final decision was made. The first was to give Kenya self-government at once. If this were done, "the embarrassments of the situation would be materially lessened and the strain on Imperial relations modified." The second solution was to reserve the colony "for native interests by restricting European settlement to the areas already granted in the highlands." Indian settlement would also be controlled. The solution would be "consistent with the highest imperial principle," and the conference minutes concluded, "though it would please no one, would provide a complete answer to India." Both these alternatives represented not so much solutions to the problem but ways of removing the CO from it. In other words, they represented avenues of escape from controversy.

In the end, of course, it was only the second of the two alternatives that was possible. As Masterton-Smith minuted on 27 February, it was "altogether out of the question" from the standpoint of larger imperial interests to grant self-government to Kenya at a time when only the settlers had political rights.[89] Thus emphasis on the paramountcy of African interests would form the basis of CO policy until a settlement to the Indian question was announced in July 1923.[90]

With the long-term goal now clearly set in CO thinking, the immediate problem of getting to the point where such a solution could be implemented had to be faced. The CO replied to Coryndon on 23 February with tentative approval for his trip to Britain accompanied by one or two representatives of the settlers. The CO imposed an important condition, however; the governor could leave the colony if he gave a definite assurance that there would be no risk of a disturbance during his absence. The telegram took a highly conciliatory tone, summarizing London's position on the various points in dispute so that Coryndon could place them before the 26 February meeting of the Convention of Associations. On immigration, the CO once again refused to allow the passing of a restrictive measure at present but accepted that "a strengthened immigration law for general application" would form an "absolutely essential" part of any general settlement of the Indian question. On the franchise, the CO told the governor to encourage the settlers to make "any practicable recommendations" they wished on the subject. As to the number of seats, the CO maintained that it was willing to leave the Europeans with eleven. Finally, on the highlands, the S of S reiterated that Lord Peel would not reopen the question.[91]

Coryndon had now got what he wanted. The CO would make the final decision on the matter, and, as he had been invited home as a vital part of the settlement effort, his position was secure. It only remained for him to make sure that the settlers did not fulfill his dire prophecies and take direct action.

This he did by his speech at the 26 February meeting. He made his appeal to the settlers in most unmistakable terms: "I am South African born," he told them.[92] The convention approved a resolution, the wording of which was actually drafted by Dutton, that it "will do all in its power to discourage and prevent direct action" by the settlers while Coryndon was in Britain. Coryndon afterwards gave a "definite assurance" that no disturbances would take place while he was absent from Kenya.[93]

Coryndon concluded his 28 February telegram by informing the CO that Lord Delamere, K. Archer, T. A. Wood, and one missionary would accompany him to Great Britain. Since two of the European delegates were prevented by doctor's orders from leaving Nairobi until the middle of March, he would delay his departure until the end of that month or the first week in April. Coryndon went on to add that Indians in Kenya intended, if possible, to send one or two delegates to London.[94] The CO rapidly approved switching the negotiations to London, and Coryndon and party left Nairobi on 25 March.[95]

Support for African Production

Although Coryndon proved quite incapable of bringing about a settlement of the Indian question, he did not disappoint the CO in his enthusiasm for stimulating African production for export. This, of course, had been the main reason for his appointment. Coryndon's experience in Uganda had made him a convinced advocate of African production.[96] He brought that attitude to Kenya, and, it will be recalled, even Sir Edward Northey had finally been driven, by economic necessity, to advocate increased African production for export. The necessity to cut expenditure and spur production at the same time was, together with the Indian question, the most pressing issue facing the new governor.

At the time of Coryndon's assumption of office, the Economic and Finance Committee was still in full flight. It had turned from considering measures to spur production to ways and means of cutting expenditure. These proved to be immediate priorities demanding the new governor's attention. He had to deal, for example, with proposals to retire Holm as director of agriculture, the abolition of the post of CNC,[97] and the reducing the salaries of all heads of departments.[98]

Nevertheless, Coryndon gave strong support to the initiatives already under consideration for encouraging African production. This may be seen from the report the Kenya government sent to London in November 1922 dealing with the department of agriculture. Its scope and functions, it was reported, "will be modified by the proposals under review in the sense that its energies will be diverted to a large extent from the fostering of European agricultural enterprise towards the encouragement of native production."[99]

As a means to accomplish this, Coryndon's government proposed the abolition of a number of posts and the experimental farm at Naivasha. The measures were justified by "the belief that these institutions, although highly desirable for a country enjoying conditions of prosperity are, so far as European settlement is concerned, a luxury which Kenya can not at present afford." The Kibos experimental station, on the other hand, was being retained since it was essential to the scheme for the promotion of African agriculture. Estimates for the veterinary department also reflected a new desire to foster and protect African livestock since "circumstances no longer warrant such extensive assistance to the non-native agriculture and stock raising industries as has hitherto been provided."[100]

In submitting his 1923 estimates, Coryndon commented further on the measures his government proposed to take to foster African production. Additional staff would be assigned to the reserves to assist with encouragement of "bulk exports" from these regions. Even though the governor felt unable to increase expenditure so as to provide for any expansion of educational and medical facilities in the reserves, he had decided to push forward with the agricultural program.[101]

Coryndon also publicly advocated the benefits of increased African production throughout his governorship.[102] When in London for discussions aimed at settling the Indian question, for example, Coryndon pushed his views on British merchants interested in East Africa. He told Conservative M.P. Sir Sydney Henn[103]:

> But I think you've rather neglected the great potentialities of native production on future finance of Kenya. . . . I hope to build up a big native production of maize particularly and other seeds in Kenya. The native has hitherto been regarded chiefly as a worker on European shambas and a payer of taxes. In Kenya at any rate he's never been considered hitherto either as a big and *cheap* producer of bulk crops and (when prosperous as a result) as a great and increasing contributor to customs revenue. . . . This is a strong factor in my colonial policy—it will mean much to the native himself—better medical service and education being the chief needs.[104]

He expressed similar sentiments a month later at a luncheon for the East African section of the London Chamber of Commerce hosted by Sir Humphrey Leggett. African production, he asserted, "would be the financial salvation of British East Africa."[105]

The most immediate impact of the "new" policy of promoting African agriculture was seen in increasing production of maize for export. Coryndon's government viewed maize cultivation as "an ideal occupation" for Africans, "one eminently suited to his methods of life and social customs." Following the recommendations of the Bowring Committee, the colonial state also pushed settler maize exports. The result of these initiatives was that for the twelve month period from April 1922 to March 1923, 368,770 bags of maize had been exported. This was a huge increase over the previous high in maize exports. Slightly more than half of this export figure (51.5 per cent) came from African producers.[106]

Peasant production had been raised from the dustbin of utter neglect where it had been consigned by Northey, but this would not amount to giving it pride of place in Kenya's colonial economy. This was not Coryndon's intention nor was it the CO's. They viewed African production as complementary to settler. Ormsby-Gore expressed the CO view very clearly in a letter to Coryndon in 1924: "Kenya is a wonderful country with a wonderful future if only the European settler interest and the African interests are not allowed to conflict and both are given fair and reasonable facilities under a strong and impartial Government."[107] Although the Dual Policy advocated by Coryndon and his successors implied corresponding levels of government support for both African and settler agriculture, this was never the case in practice. With the return of prosperity after 1923, the colonial state provided much greater resources for the support of European farmers than it did African.[108] It would be many years before the CO and the colonial state were prepared to give African farmers anything close to support equal to that of the settlers.

The rise of African maize exports and the increased emphasis on African production under Coryndon had great significance nevertheless. It provides clear evidence of the CO's reassertion of initiative in Kenya's affairs that marked 1922 and 1923. The fact that the CO had seized the initiative was clearly brought home by its action in December 1922. The policy memorandum, drafted in May by Batterbee in response to the need to take control in light of growing criticism in Britain of events and trends in Kenya would be used as a vehicle. With Ormsby-Gore's approval, the memorandum, titled "Native Affairs in East Africa," became a full-blown policy statement for Britain's East African dependencies.[109] It reflected the change in CO thinking that had occurred over the preceding nine months, a period that had seen the reestablishment of CO control. In early January, the CO sent the memorandum to East African governors asking them to furnish London with their observations on the policy suggested.[110]

Not only did the action of sending the memorandum to Kenya and the other territories indicate that the CO had re-seized the initiative; the subjects in the comprehensive document clearly indicate that the ball was now in London's court. As far as Kenya was concerned, it set an agenda for the colonial state for the rest of the decade and beyond. It was suggested that the colonial government collect definite information on forms of African land tenure and make sure that reserves were established adequate "for the present and future requirements of the native population."[111]

It was not enough, the memorandum went on, to reserve land to the African; "it is necessary also to take steps to encourage native production on that land." From this strong policy statement, the memo passed on to consider what the African should cultivate and how he could be encouraged to improve his methods of cultivation and marketing. The document concluded that Africans should be encouraged to grow any crops they could rather than, as had previously been the unwritten rule in Kenya, limiting the peasant producer to those crops not grown on European farms. It stated: "there is no reason why with suitable control of agricultural methods, the native should not cultivate them successfully and without detriment to his European neighbours."[112]

The question of African taxation and the services provided from it also received lengthy consideration. It was necessary, the CO held, that some criterion should be fixed as to the proportion of expenditure to be devoted to African areas. Education, medical, and veterinary services were particularly identified as fields for increased spending to benefit the African population. The memo envisioned confining government educational activity to "technical education," leaving "general education" to the mission societies.

Under the heading titled "political," the memorandum laid out suggested initiatives that would lead directly to the formation of Local Native Councils within the next two years. The suggested councils were to be given "as far as practicable some power of local self government in order that the interest of the intelligent members of the tribes may be stimulated by giving them a real share of the management of their own affairs."

By means of this memorandum, therefore, the CO identified the areas and set the tone of policies to be pursued in East Africa for years to come. London would no longer await and react to proposals pushed by Kenya's governors and settlers. That the CO had regained the initiative would be finally and decisively demonstrated in the settlement of the Indian question.

Settlement of the Indian Question

As the Indian controversy wound down towards a solution, the CO likewise strongly seized control of the rudder. With the decision that Coryndon, European, and Indian representatives would come to London for discussions at the CO, the focus of the Indian question moved decidedly to Britain after the end of March 1923. From the time of the arrival of the governor and the European delegation in April, the discussions aimed at reaching a settlement revolved around the CO. As noted earlier in the chapter, the CO's general position, so far as a settlement was concerned, had been worked out at the end of February. The highlands would remain for exclusive European occupation, segregation would be dropped, Indians would be given communal representation in the Legco, and the CO had concluded that there was a need to restrict Indian immigration into Kenya. Overall, the CO solution to the problem was to come down neither completely on the side of the Europeans nor the Indians; rather, African interests would be said to predominate in Kenya. The main issue for the CO, therefore, was not the shape of the settlement but how to achieve its acceptance by the contending parties, the settlers, the Kenya government, the Kenya Indians, public opinion in India, the government of India, and the IO.[113]

The governor and the settler representatives arrived in London in mid-April. The S of S met with Coryndon on 23 April, and the European delegation the following day. The Indian deputation of Jeevanjee, M. A. Desai, B. S. Varma, and H. Virji had their first meeting with Devonshire in May. Before and after the arrival of these parties, the CO had begun to receive suggestions as to the settlement it should attempt to reach. These came from former African administrators, church groups, and capitalists interested in East Africa. The effect of this correspondence was to reinforce the CO decision to base its policy on safeguarding African interests first and foremost.

The CO received letters from John Ainsworth and Lord Lugard, for example, which emphasized the importance of safeguarding future African interests by not granting self-government to Kenya's Europeans. Ainsworth emphasized his view that Kenya "is primarily a Black-man's country and can never become a European colony. . . . "[114] Lugard asserted that it was "contrary to the fundamental traditions of British colonial policy" that the small Kenya settler community should "have political control over large native communities." It was the duty of the imperial government to take direct responsibility for such communities.[115] The Church of Scotland also urged the CO that its main responsibility was the African population.[116] Even Leggett, whose interests were far more commercial than humanitarian or administrative, was also strongly in favor of making it known "that the entire geographical entity now known as Kenya colony is held in trust for its native African population" and that the Imperial Government assumes the position of paramount chief of each and every African tribe therein."[117]

Even more significant than these statements of support for the concept of the paramountcy of African interests was the recognition of the same concept by one of the strongest advocates of Indian equality. Polak wrote to the CO in late April to summarize the Indian demands for "equal citizenship" with the Europeans. He stated, however:

> The Indian community has frankly recognized the paramount claim of the indigenous population over all immigrant communities, but demands equality of citizenship among such communities, with an official majority until the natives are able to manage their own affairs.[118]

If the Indians stood by this claim, moreover, the settlers and Coryndon could not effectively accuse them of desiring supremacy in Kenya.

Nevertheless, this attitude did not solve the basic dilemma that faced the CO throughout May and June. This was how to win at least some acceptance for the settlement they proposed to implement. There could be no question of settlement by agreement. One would have to be enforced, and on most of the points in dispute the CO was prepared to offer far less than what the Indians were demanding. The major problem facing the CO, therefore, was how to win support from those groups in Britain and India who were sympathetic to, and had given active support for, the East African Indian demand for equality. Officials feared that the mere statement of African supremacy might not be enough and that opposition to their proposed settlement would be particularly vociferous and violent in India.

The EAD grappled with this dilemma following receipt of Polak's memo and the settlers first meeting with the S of S in late April. In their meeting with Devonshire, the settler delegation had placed emphasis on restricting Indian immigration and that any settlement arrived at should be regarded as permanent. For CO officials, it seemed difficult to envision the Indians accepting the settler demands for an immigration control measure and a communal franchise that the CO had now adopted as its position.[119]

Bottomley did raise one point, however, in a lengthy minute of 28 April that would become important in framing the final CO decision on the matter of immigration. He called attention to a possible "economic solution" to the immigration issue. By that he meant restricting Indian immigration so that Indians would not take jobs that Africans could be trained to hold.[120] With little thought to the basic contradiction involved in pressing the "economic" sense of curbing Indian immigration on the one hand and the "economic" need for Indian traders in expanding African production on the other, CO officials seized upon the former concept with enthusiasm. It formed a major justification for immigration controls in the July white paper.

When the CO finally received a formal statement of the Indian deputation's claims towards the end of May, officials found little in it to help them out of their dilemma. The Indians declaimed any idea of making Kenya a possession of India, but they maintained their claim to the right to buy land in the highlands. They strongly opposed any immigration law along the lines suggested by the settlers; in fact they maintained, probably correctly, that the latter's real desire was to expel them from East Africa altogether. The deputation echoed Polak's earlier assertion that there should be no responsible government until the African was in a position to "rule over his own country," but they went on to demand "the same rights of franchise . . . as are now enjoyed by Europeans."[121] Bottomley reacted very negatively to the latter demand. "As I have said elsewhere," he minuted, "this explicit demand for adult franchise, serious or not, makes me despair of any *settlement* and there is nothing for it but a *decision* which either party or both will not like."[122] Of course Bottomley knew that it was most likely the Indians who would not like the decisions the CO would impose, and for his part, he would "have nothing more to do with the Kenya Indians."[123]

After talking with Coryndon, however, Bottomley decided that it might be worthwhile to send the Indian demands to V. S. S. Sastri, the unofficial representative of the Indian legislature. After arrival in London, Sastri, a moderate Indian nationalist and supporter of the interests of Indians living overseas, was chosen chief spokesman for the Indian delegation at its initial meeting with Devonshire on 4 May.[124] The CO hope was that Sastri might not strongly endorse the Kenya Indian demands, and that his support, which would help to "sell" the CO proposals in India, might be obtained for a settlement on the lines anticipated by the CO. This path of action was endorsed by both Read and Masterton-Smith, and the CO sent a copy of the Indian demands to Peel with a request that he show them to Sastri.[125]

At the same time the CO sought the help of Sastri, another influential individual entered the Indian question. This was J. H. Oldham; perhaps even more than Sastri, his role was to be very valuable to the CO. It should be emphasized here, however, that Oldham's contribution to the settlement announced in July of 1923 was not, as some have maintained, the maker of a compromise or the provider of a formula, i.e. African paramountcy, by which the CO could cover up the fact that it would endorse the claims of the Europeans rather than the Indians. This has been a popular assertion amongst imperial historians for the last two decades or more, but, as has been demonstrated here, the CO already had decided to clothe its decision in the garb of African supremacy.[126] Oldham's main contribution was rather to sell the CO position, which he assumed, wrongly, was the same as his own, to C. F. Andrews, who had come from India to support the Indian deputation, Polak, and liberal politicians of all parties in Britain.

Oldham had contacts with missionaries, both in Kenya and India. Moreover, he had visited India during the previous two winters, and Oldham was aware of the strong negative impact a settlement that did not meet the Indian demands would have on imperial and missionary interests in India. It was to try to avoid that possibility and a likely conflict between missionaries in Kenya and India, who were already taking opposing sides on the issue, that Oldham felt compelled to approach the CO.[127] In the course of his visits to India, Oldham had come to know and respect Reverend C. F. Andrews, friend of Gandhi and a strong supporter of Indian nationalism.

Oldam's hand in the India question first manifested itself in early May as he and Randall Davidson, the Archbishop of Canterbury, held discussions on the issues in dispute. Oldham then particularly sought out Andrews. Oldham felt that Andrews was a key figure in any potential solution to the Indian question as the latter could, Oldham believed, persuade Indian public opinion to accept a settlement based on the concept of African paramountcy more readily than Sastri.[128] On 9 May, a letter composed by Oldham appeared in *The Times* over the signature of several missionaries. It urged continued imperial responsibility for Kenya and the assertion of African paramountcy. On the same day the archbishop met, at Oldham's prodding, the S of S.[129] Davidson was encouraged by this meeting, but neither Sastri nor Andrews were heartened by the way negotiations with the CO were going. Both suggested to Oldham that they were seriously considering leaving Britain.

Failing to move Andrews from his pessimistic view after a weekend of discussions, Oldham felt that the situation was nearing a crisis. To avoid the possibility of Andrews' withdrawal, Oldham decided to make an urgent and direct appeal to the CO. He drafted a solution to the Indian question, and convinced the archbishop to visit Devonshire on 29 May. In a private and unofficial letter prepared by Oldham, the archbishop urged that the CO declare that Britain's East African territories "shall be administered under the direct authority of the Imperial Government acting as trustee for the native inhabitants and for civilization as a whole, and that as between the different communities inhabiting these territories the interests of the native population are paramount." This phrasing represented a nice way of saying what the CO had all along intended to proclaim. Indeed, the S of S was later to incorporate some of Oldham's terminology in the CO policy statement.[130] The archbishop's letter went on to urge that a Royal Commission be appointed to investigate and make recommendations for implementing this policy in East Africa.[131]

The idea of a Royal Commission was, of course, not new as Oldham and others had urged it on both Milner and Churchill in preceding years. There was little enthusiasm for it in the CO.[132] Eventually, Masterton-Smith was able to persuade Oldham that a Royal Commission "would be worse than useless in the present circumstances."[133] Yet Masterton-Smith, in particular, welcomed Oldham's entry into the controversy and encouraged his efforts to gain support from sources that would prove essential to the settlement that the CO was contemplating.

Oldham plunged more deeply into the fray with a letter to Masterton-Smith on 1 June, a few days after he had met the permanent under-secretary at dinner. He began by setting out the reason for his concern over the Indian question and his fear that Andrews and Sastri might return to India discouraged and disillusioned. Oldham told the permanent under-secretary that the representatives of India (by whom he meant particularly Sastri and Andrews) might well assent to the course proposed in the archbishop's letter.[134]

At the urging of Oldham, moreover, Andrews wrote to Masterton-Smith in early June. Andrews accepted the CO position that Britain alone was responsible, as trustee, for the Africans of Central and East Africa, and he urged Masterton-Smith to build up African production. Nevertheless, Andrews was not optimistic about acceptance in India of any settlement which did not accord the Indians of East Africa equality with settlers.[135]

On 8 June, Masterton-Smith and Devonshire met with Oldham. This was extremely significant for as a result of his first direct contact with the two officials, Oldham now had an awareness of an outline of the settlement the CO proposed. He now knew that the CO would base its policy declaration on its duty to give pride of place to the African population rather than either the settlers or the Indians. He also realized that the CO had decided on a communal franchise rather than a common roll and was leaning towards immigration restriction. These were positions that had long since been decided by the

CO. Most assuredly they were not handed over to Devonshire and Masterton-Smith at this point in the settlement process.

Pleased by the similarity of the CO view to his own, Oldham then set to work to try to convince the Indian supporters to accept the forthcoming policy statement, spending an evening to that effect with Andrews and Polak.[136] Following these discussions, Oldham wrote a lengthy letter to Masterton-Smith on 11 June setting out his belief that it was "possible to avert a break with India" if a settlement along lines he set out could be reached. For the most part, these adhered closely to the positions the CO had already marked out for itself. First and foremost, an announcement would be made that Kenya was essentially an African territory that would be administered under direct authority of the British crown "as trustee for the native population and humanity as a whole and that as between the different communities the interests of the natives are paramount."[137] If there had to be regulation of immigration, Oldham went on, it must be justified "in the proved interest of the native population." India would be willing to "refrain for the present from pressing the claim of land in the highlands." Moreover, there could be no segregation "on purely racial lines." On the crucial issue of the franchise, Oldham argued that "if political control is vested in the Crown the franchise is a subsidiary and unimportant issue."[138]

Oldham went on to make two other suggestions as to the future political shape of Kenya that had not previously formed part of the CO settlement plan. One, that African interests might be represented in the Legco by the appointment of missionaries, was acted upon favorably by the CO in announcing its final decisions. The other, that the Kenya Legco should be turned into a wholly nominated body, was not.[139]

Oldham concluded that he felt the policy under consideration, and the amplifications and modifications he suggested, gave the best hope of acceptance from Andrews and Polak, from the opposition parties in parliament, from the British press, and from the settlers. The only group he left out of the calculation was the Kenya Indian delegation. Not surprisingly, they would indeed be the most disappointed party with the outcome laid down by the CO a month later.

Oldham now set to work with great enthusiasm to win support for the CO's settlement. He talked to officials at the IO and believed they supported the policy he outlined to them. He talked to Sir A. Steel-Maitland in the hope of winning his support, and that of other moderate Tories, and he lunched with J. A. Spender who thought it would not be difficult to get Asquith and the Liberal Party to go along with the settlement. He had induced Andrews, moreover, to write to Ramsay Macdonald, leader of the Labour Party, to see if he might be brought to support the proposed settlement.[140] There can be no doubt of the import of Oldham's efforts; the settlement would be accepted by the overwhelming body of moderate opinion in Britain, and Andrews and Polak would not be diehard opponents. Oldham's role was thus invaluable to the CO in selling the settlement. However, the main points of the latter had already been worked by the CO in February, and they had been foreshadowed in Parkinson's memo of August 1919. They were thus not Oldham's creation.

There remained, nevertheless, the attitude of Sastri to be considered. His strong opposition to the settlement would have a devastating impact on the reaction of India. Oldham had tried to convince him to support the settlement, but Sastri remained doubtful that the imperial government would take seriously any expression of African paramountcy.[141] It was Coryndon who actually seems to have achieved the major breakthrough.[142] The governor lunched with Sastri on 15 July, and he found the Indian leader prepared to accept "the communal system of representation" if he were given adequate concessions to represent the settlement to the people in India as palatable. Sastri was satisfied that the imperial government would retain full responsibility in the "primary interests of the African native population" and that there would be no self-government for Kenya for the foreseeable future.[143] The settlement was now assured some support in India, and the next day Lord Delamere wrote to express his agreement with the idea of imperial trusteeship for the African population.[144] As the major players in the controversy had now been heard from, the CO then went quickly forward to announce its decisions in the Indian question.[145]

The settlement, now formalized, was placed before the cabinet on 23 July. It took the form of a two-part memoradum. Part I provided an historical summary of the question, and Part II a statement of general policy and the decisions made by the CO. This document formed the basis of a white paper titled *Indians in Kenya*.[146] After Lord Peel expressed "the Indian point of view" and warned of the likelihood of "considerable disappointment" in India, the cabinet approved the CO proposals and the publication of a parliamentary paper the following day.[147] The CO telegraphed the substance of the decisions to Bowring on the 24th at the same time it provided the European and Indian delegations with copies.[148]

The policy laid down in what has popularly become known as the Devonshire White Paper was very much in line with what had been laid out by the CO as its policy in February. Part II of the white paper started with these. In its second paragraph, the document stated:

> Primarily, Kenya is an African territory, and His Majesty's Government think it necessary definitely to record their considered opinion that the interests of the African natives must be paramount, and that if, and when, those interests and the interests of the immigrant races should conflict, the former should prevail. Obviously the interests of the other communities, European, Indian or Arab, must severally be safeguarded. . . . But in the administration of Kenya His Majesty's Government regard themselves as exercising a trust on behalf of the African population, and they are unable to delegate or share this trust, the object of which may be defined as the protection and advancement of the native races.[149]

The paper then went on to tackle the tough political issues, and it began with the long-decided corollary to African paramountcy: "His Majesty's Government cannot but regard the grant of responsible self-government as out of the question within any period of time which need now be taken into consideration."[150] So too was an unofficial majority ruled out. Turning then to specific issues, the CO outlined and justified its decision to put into effect a communal franchise, with separate voters lists and constituencies, for Indians and Europeans. As a concession to Indians, the CO were willing to grant a "wide franchise" rather than that contemplated under the Wood-Winterton plan. The Indians were given five seats, Arabs could elect one member to the Legco, and the European electorate retained eleven seats. As noted previously, the white paper approved the principle of a missionary being appointed to the Legco to represent Africans. Representation on the Execo would remain as at present with the governor being given authority to nominate a missionary to advise on "matters affecting Africans."[151] Table 7.1 summarizes these and other decisions of the white paper and contrasts them with the proposed settlements of the past three years.

The white paper then turned to segregation in the highlands and townships. The CO had long since made up its mind on both; residential and commercial segregation could not be accepted. Thus any official policy of segregation "as between Europeans and Asiatics in the townships must be abandoned."[152] Likewise, the CO reaffirmed its long-standing decision on the highlands. After a lengthy review of the history of the reservation of the highlands for whites, the document declared that "the existing practice must be maintained as regards both initial grants and transfers."[153]

The white paper concluded its treatment of the issues under dispute by examining immigration. Though carefully worded so as to give as little offense as possible to Indians, it declared that some immigration control was required. Taking up Bottomley's point of late April, the paper declared that "the consideration which must govern immigration policy in Kenya is purely economic, and strict regard must be paid to the interests of the African." Examined in that light, it was evident "that some further control over immigration in the economic interests of the natives of Kenya is required."[154] As noted earlier, these sentiments were largely to camouflage the real reasons for immigration limitation.

The CO's earnest hope that the decision would help to spur "that spirit of co-operation and good will" so essential for Kenya's welfare and development was never really fulfilled. Although Sastri gave support to the declaration, Indians in Kenya did not. They boycotted the communal seats awarded them for the rest of the 1920s.[155] The Devonshire declaration did put an end to the Indian question so far as the CO was concerned. It formed, moreover, a logical conclusion to the policy changes, begun a year earlier, to enable the CO to recapture the initiative in Kenya it had lost to the settlers and a series of pro-settler governors beginning at the start of World War I. Economic

Table 7.1 CO Indian Policy Initiatives for Kenya, 1920–23

	Milner 1920	Churchill 1921	Wood-Winterton 1922	Devonshire 1923
Highlands	Reservation for Europeans	Reservation for Europeans	Reservation for Europeans	Reservation for Europeans
Urban Segregation	Residential relax commercial	No commercial; no residential for persons on common voters roll	No commercial or residential	No residential or commercial
Franchise	Communal	Common roll	Common roll	Communal
Seats in Legco	11 European 2 Indian	5 European 3 Indian	7 European & 4 Indian OR 8 European & 4 Indian	11 European 5 Indian
Immigration	No Restriction	Restrictions same for Europeans and Indians	No Restrictions	Further controls to be instituted in interests of African

considerations had been most important in forcing the CO into action on behalf of African production. The doctrine of African paramountcy formed a conclusion to the steps taken to promote a revival of African production for export.[156]

It is noteworthy that when the CO sent instructions to Kenya for implementing the white paper's decisions on 9 August, it spelled out the need to promote African development even before turning to the issues that had divided the Indians and the Europeans. The S of S told the acting governor that he was "most anxious that everything possible should be done for the intellectual, moral and economic development of the African population." In drafting the 1924 estimates, Bowring was told to give "very careful attention" to the "allocation of funds on as generous a scale as practicable for appropriate purposes, such as native education, medical work among the natives, and economic development in the native reserves." The CO also requested that beginning with the year 1924, the government of Kenya should prepare a report on African affairs in the colony showing "exactly what progress has been made by the Government during the year with schemes for the advancement of natives."[157]

Students of Kenya's history know that the theory and promise of African paramountcy was not carried out in the years ahead. Relatively little was done by government to stimulate African production and to provide educational and medical services. Thus it is difficult to quarrel with those who see the Devonshire declaration as a cynical and amateurish cover-up aimed at solving a thorny problem by less than inspiring morality.[158] Yet in accepting the truth of such observations, it can not be denied that the declaration had put the CO back in control of Kenya. The doctrine, hollow though it undoubtedly was, would be used by British governments, over the next four decades, to place an insurmountable road block in the path of those in Kenya who wished to see the colony evolve into a settler-state on the South African or Southern Rhodesian model.

8

Conclusion

A major thrust of this study of the struggle for Kenya that took place during the period 1912–23 has been to focus on the evolution of imperial policy. It has sought to describe and account for the loss of imperial control that did much to provoke a struggle and the subsequent reassertion of imperial initiative in the affairs of Britain's East African colony that was the product of that struggle. Although it was clearly in control in 1912, the CO rapidly forfeited, following the outbreak of World War I, the initiative to the Kenya colonial state. The latter moved steadily to initiate and implement policies advocated by Kenya's European settlers or supportive of settler production. After the war, this trend continued, and even accelerated. As a result, white supremacy, on the southern African model, seemed just around the corner for Kenya. The reassertion of CO control in the development and implementation of policy in Kenya checked this trend. Settler interests would still predominate, but the small settler community did not gain total political and economic dominance of Kenya since the CO reestablishment of command took the form of making African paramountcy the basis of future policy in Kenya.

Prior to World War I, the CO still held the initiative in Kenya affairs. It did not rely exclusively on the colonial state for policy proposals as demonstrated by the CO's attempts to frame a new land ordinance in line with what London officials felt would best serve the conditions of settlement in Kenya. London's action in the Cole case was a clear indication that the CO was in control, and this was most graphically indicated by the "retirement" of Governor Sir Percy Girouard.

If intended to reassert CO primacy in Kenya affairs, the appointment of Sir Henry Belfield as Girouard's successor proved to be a huge mistake. Belfield quickly adopted a strongly pro-settler stance. Despite Belfield's favoritism and support for settler political, labor, and land demands, however, the CO held fast in refusing to completely accept the governor's recommendations down to August 1914. For example, the CO resisted elective rights for the whites and easing the terms of the proposed land ordinance so as to please the settlers. This made good sense for many reasons, most particularly economic. By 1914, settler farms and estates had made little contribution to the colonial economy. More than 60 per cent of the protectorate's agricultural exports came from African households.

The advent of World War I dramatically altered this situation, however. As a result of a number of factors, CO direction and control over some very crucial policy decisions relating to Kenya rapidly lapsed. Among the most important of the factors that facilitated this was the rapid removal of the CO from direct involvement in the direction of the war effort in East Africa. Excluded from this crucial area of imperial concern, CO interest in civil issues waned as a result. This situation was magnified by S of S Lewis Harcourt's illness in the fall of 1914 followed by his replacement in 1915 by Andrew Bonar Law. The latter and his successor, Walter Long, took no interest in Kenya's civil administration during the remainder of the war. The 1916 resignation of Sir John Anderson as permanent under-secretary was also crucial. It fostered not so much a loss of control as a weakening of the CO resolve to defend African rights and interests in the face of settler economic demands supported by the colonial state. During the war years, moreover, the CO had to face far less in the way of metropolitan criticisms of EAP policies than in times of peace.

The lack of interest and weakening of commitment to the ideals of trusteeship that resulted from these changes in leadership, together with the "necessity" of war, caused the CO to turn a blind eye to dramatically increased exploitation of Kenya's African population. This took the form of forced labor for the war effort and sharp rises in taxation. This would set a precedent for the postwar period as the colonial state attempted to further exploit African manpower and resources, this time largely for the benefit of the settlers.

In fact, by the end of the conflict, the colony's settlers had made important political and economic gains. These came about not only as a result of the CO loss of control, but of the ineffectual leadership of Governor Belfield. Ill, tired of the war and the responsibility of leadership, the governor, clinging to his position more out of economic necessity and pride than anything else, provided little of the latter after he was successful in obtaining CO approval of the pro-settler changes he proposed in what became the Crown Lands Ordinance of 1915. Aroused briefly from his torpor in 1915 by CO direction that he should give more support to the war effort, Belfield responded by supinely urging the acceptance of any and all demands made by the settlers. The CO accepted most of these as well, and approval was thus given for the registration of African men, the creation of war council dominated by settlers, and the principle of electoral representation for Europeans; in addition, favorable consideration was given for a scheme of ex-soldier settlement after the war.

Belfield's retirement in 1917 made no real difference in the continued loss of CO direction in Kenya affairs. No new measures of significance were approved by London, but practically every issue demanding decision in the

last year and a half of the war was deferred for the recommendation and
action of a new governor. Though settler demands for the immediate approval of railway extension, economic assistance, and implementation of a scheme
of whites-only elections were not sanctioned by the CO, they were merely
postponed until the arrival of the new governor.

Thus when the new governor, Sir Edward Northey, arrived in Nairobi in
January 1919, he quickly moved to make decisions on a number of matters
that had been awaiting his attention. The former general grasped the initiative and bombarded the CO with recommendations on a number of issues.
Pressed for rapid approval, the CO, on the whole, meekly fell into line with
the governor's demands. In every policy recommendation he made, moreover, Northey took a very strong pro-settler line. He gave pride of place to
the settlers' demands and desires for white supremacy as he believed that
settler production for export represented the present and future backbone
of the colony's economy. The only economic role for Africans, in Northey's
view, was the provision of labor on settler farms and estates. He did not
expect Africans to become independent producers. In this stance, Northey
dragged the CO along in his wake.

This was certainly a mistaken, and potentially disastrous, view of Kenya's
economic realities, but Northey could at least find some justification for it
from the predominant position settler production had achieved in Kenya's
exports in the immediate postwar years. Settler products totalled more than
60 per cent of Kenya's exports in 1919, and by 1921 this share had risen to 86
per cent. Yet the predominance of settler-generated exports was very artificial. It was the result, first of all, of the disastrous impact of the war and the
immediate postwar years on African agriculture. Forced labor, death and disability in the Carrier Corps, famine, and epidemic disease set back the latter,
but this would be a temporary condition. Settler exports also benefitted
tremendously from support of the colonial state both during and after the
war. Settler production was protected, assisted, and subsidized, but the postwar depression would expose the uneconomic nature of the state's support.

It was not surprising that Northey never grasped the central economic reality of Kenya's colonial history: that the colonial state could not survive basing
its economic strategy on settler production alone. African agriculture was
vital to the state's survival in terms of revenue for the subsidization of the
settler sector. What is surprising is that CO officials, such as Bottomley,
Read, and Parkinson, did not recognize this fact in light of the importance of
African production in the colony's economy before the war.

The immediate check to Northey's drive to establish settler predominance
in all fields was not economic difficulties, however. It grew out of the postwar
struggle for Kenya. It came in the form of growing criticism from humanitarian and missionary groups directed against the governor's labor policies,
Indian protest, backed by the government of India, the IO, and, most
eloquently, by S of S Montagu against the political privileges granted to

Europeans, and the policies that enforced segregation between Indians and Europeans in urban areas and kept Indians from obtaining land in the white highlands. Northey's proposals to alter British East Africa's currency and exchange system provoked strong opposition from metropolitan banks doing business in East Africa. It was, in fact, the strong 1920 resistance of the bankers that forced the CO to intervene, for the first time in Northey's governorship, to halt the colonial state's headlong drive to establish settler supremacy.

In the following year, continued protests from the Indians, the government of India, and the humanitarian lobby moved the CO to intercede in Kenyan affairs once more so as to significantly alter Northey's labor policies. It also attempted, without much success, to bring about a softening of the anti-Indian stance assumed by the settlers and the colonial state. Moreover, finance capitalists once again, in 1921, refused to swallow currency policies that would have them assist the settler producer at great cost to the banks. Permanent officials at the CO were placed in something of a dilemma by this struggle. Individuals such as Parkinson, Bottomley, and Read shared many of the anti-Indian biases and pro-settler predilections of Northey. Yet the struggle provoked by Northey's drive to enshrine settler supremacy forced these officials to seek modification of the colonial state's position in the direction of that advocated by the IO, humanitarians, British capitalists, and, most significantly, by former colonial servants such as Ainsworth.

It was in 1922 that the struggle turned against Northey and the settlers. The CO finally moved decisively to recapture the initiative in Kenya. The problems raised by the Indian question played a part in this, but the primary reasons for the CO action were the rising African protest that Northey's pro-settler policies had provoked and the colony's serious economic crisis. The tide of African protest that led the colonial state to order the arrest of Harry Thuku and culminated in the shooting of demonstrators demanding his release in March 1922 at first had little impact on CO officials. As the implication of this brutal use of force sunk in at the CO, however, officials there realized that such events could not be allowed to happen again in the near future. Changes in policy had to be undertaken to ameliorate some of the causes of African discontent. To both the civil servants and the political leadership of the CO, this meant the alteration of Northey's policies so as to reduce taxes, provide more education and medical services in African reserves, and, above all, to stimulate African production for export.

An even more powerful factor for the CO's reestablishing its initiative in Kenya was the disastrous economic state the colony found itself in by the end of 1921. Kenya was virtually bankrupt, and Northey could offer no other solution than to beg the imperial government for grants or loans to bail out the colonial state. This situation was the result of the world depression of 1919–22, but it also owed a great deal to the utterly unwise economic policies initiated under Northey. The colonial state placed heavy exactions on the

African population for the benefit of settler agriculture, but the latter was not able to "carry" the colony economically. Kenya's dire economic straits forced the CO, in 1922, to compare and contrast Kenya's revenue and expenditure with Britain's African colonies that had no white settlers. The picture that emerged from this comparison suggested that Kenya's expenditure had been greatly inflated to support European settlement and that African production for export had been underutilized. Pushed by merchant capitalists in Britain, the EAD, in the persons of Bottomley and Batterbee, realized that for the colonial state to survive, a change had to be quickly made to reestablish African production for export so as to complement the exports of the settlers and increase Kenya's potential exports and revenues. Such a dramatic change of direction required that Northey be sacked.

The CO thus acted decisively to attempt to facilitate an increase in African production and to reduce the potential for African dissent. This culminated in the Devonshire white paper of 1923. The doctrine of African paramountcy was a logical conclusion to the CO decision to reemphasize African production for export. It presented the CO with another significant advantage in providing a clever way out of the long-simmering Indian question and bringing a conclusion to the struggle for Kenya. Most significant in the long run, moreover, was the fact that the British government had placed itself squarely in the role of final arbiter in Kenya affairs in categorical terms. The CO had regained control.

A variety of other factors, political, economic, and moral, played a part in this as well. Certainly the missionary and humanitarian lobby marshalled by J. H. Oldham and the ASAPS played a major part in the struggle in Great Britain and brought much pressure to bear on the CO in support of the former's conception of imperial trusteeship and African rights. The CO could not ignore missionary and humanitarian protests critical of Kenya's land, labor, currency, and Indian policies. Yet it would be quite wrong to place significant emphasis on the role of this lobby in bringing about CO intervention to alter the pro-settler stances on these issues adopted by the colonial state in Kenya. It was the Ugandan government's protest, not Oldham and the church groups, that forced the CO to stop the shilling swindle. In addition, it was only when faced with strong criticism of Northey's labor policy by administrators Elliot and Ainsworth that the CO forced an alteration of that policy. As described in the preceding chapter, Oldham did not provide the form of the Devonshire declaration to the CO. Missionary and humanitarian protest kept CO officials on their toes rather than forcing them to undertake, and provide the form of, new policy initiatives for Kenya.

If the effect of the humanitarian and missionary lobby should not be exaggerated, neither should the role of metropolitan capital on the formulation of CO policy towards Kenya during 1912–23. Neither finance nor merchant capital took much interest in, nor had great impact on, the evolution of most British policy toward Kenya. The merchants and bankers were most emphatically not pulling the strings at the CO. In fact, most of the permanent officials there were suspicious of, and hostile to, the few significant economic development schemes, such as the prewar suggestion to build a railway across the Uasin Gishu plateau, that were propounded by British capitalists both before and after the war. If CO officials were cautious, the Treasury was even more so. Throughout the period, nevertheless, metropolitan financiers did wield significant influence on CO action in issues that particularly effected their interests. The 1919–21 currency question provides a clear example of the power the British bankers could bring to bear if they wished. Merchants also helped to convince the CO that Northey's economic policies placing exclusive reliance on settler production were seriously mistaken. These are examples of metropolitan capital making its muscle felt when it saw its interests were at stake, but on the whole, this lobby had relatively little direct impact on CO policy towards the struggle for Kenya. That policy, for the period 1912–23 at least, was the result of the interplay of several forces—personal, institutional, economic, and humanitarian—reflective of various interest groups in Kenya and Britain. Rather than following a guiding light of well-established principles, the CO's policies towards Kenya, greatly complicated by the wartime loss of control, developed by hit-and-miss, largely the result of CO attempts to balance the several competing, and often contradictory, interests involved in the struggle to influence the future direction of that dependency.

Nevertheless, the most crucial result of the 1912–23 period was the reassertion of CO control. This would have a fundamental impact on future relations between the metropole and Kenya. In practice, this meant that the drive towards white supremacy and the creation of a settler state, strongly backed by Northey and the settlers, would never come to pass in Kenya.

Notes

Abbreviations Used in the Notes

ASAPS	Anti-Slavery and Aborigines Protection Society
CNC	Chief Native Commissioner
CO	Colonial Office
diss.	Dissertation
EA	East Africa
EACB	East African Currency Board
EAD	East African Department
EAP	East Africa Protectorate
EAS	*East African Standard*
H.M.G.	His Majesty's Government
HMSO	His Majesty's Stationery Office
IO	India Office
IOA	India Overseas Association
JAH	*Journal of African History*
JICH	*Journal of Imperial and Commonwealth History*
LBEA	*Leader of British East Africa*
Legco	Legislative Council
Legco Deb.	Legislative Council Debates
Parl. Deb.	Parliamentary Debates
PRO	Public Record Office
Ser.	Series
S of S	Secretary of State
USSCO	Under-secretary of State Colonial Office
USSIO	Under-secretary of State India Office

Preface

1. Prior to that date, the territory was known as the East Africa Protectorate. That name is used in the text to refer to the colonial entity between 1912 and 1920.

2. E. S. Atieno Odhiambo, "The Colonial Government, the Settlers and the 'Trust' Principle in Kenya," *Transafrican Journal of History* 2 (1972): 104; E. S. Atieno Odhiambo, *Siasa: Politics and Nationalism in East Africa, 1905–1939* (Nairobi: Kenya Literature Bureau, 1981), 15–16.

3. Particularly George Bennett, "Settlers and Politics in Kenya," in *History of East Africa*, vol. 2, ed. V. Harlow and E. M. Chilver (Oxford: Clarendon Press, 1965), 265–332; and George Bennett, *Kenya A Political History: The Colonial Period* (Oxford: Oxford University Press, 1963).

Chapter 1. The Colonial Office and Kenya

1. Ronald Hyam, "The Colonial Office Mind 1900–1914," *JICH* 8 (1979): 32; Steven Constantine, *The Making of British Colonial Development Policy* (London: Frank Cass, 1984), 17.

2. Sir Charles Jeffries, *The Colonial Office* (London: George Allen & Unwin, 1956), 107.

3. Bruce Berman, *Control & Crisis in Colonial Kenya: The Dialectic of Domination* (Athens: Ohio University Press, 1990), 75–76.

4. Constantine, *The Making*, 17, 18.

5. Ibid., 19.

6. John Lonsdale and Bruce Berman, "Coping With the Contradictions: The Development of the Colonial State in Kenya, 1895–1914," *JAH* 20 (1979): 492.

7. Robert V. Kubicek, *The Administration of Imperialism: Joseph Chamberlain at the Colonial Office* (Durham, N.C.: Duke University Press, 1969), 20; *The Times*, 18 October 1949. In 1912, for example, Read chaired the Colonial Survey Committee, the Colonial Advisory Medical and Sanitary Committee, and the Bureau of Hygiene and Tropical Diseases.

8. Robert Rhodes James, ed., *Memoirs of a Conservative: J. C. C. Davidson, Memoirs and Papers, 1910–37* (London: Weidenfeld & Nicolson, 1969), 11.

9. Cosmo Parkinson, *The Colonial Office From Within* (London: Faber and Faber, 1947), 27. Bottomley concluded his career as Crown Agent for the Colonies.

10. Parkinson was described at the time of his death as a kind and humane man, but many of his minutes on the EAP Indian question gave little hint of such sentiments (*The Times*, 17 August 1967 and 19 August 1967).

11. Parkinson, *The Colonial Office From Within*, 28–29. It was well-established that all correspondence coming from a colonial territory was addressed personally to the S of S. This was true even of routine items that the latter would obviously never see. Likewise, all correspondence from the CO was addressed to the colony's governor.

12. Prior to Harcourt's term as S of S, dates appear to have been given as day and month. According to Parkinson, Harcourt found this unsatisfactory, and he ordered that all minutes must have years in their dates (Parkinson, *The Colonial Office From Within*, 30).

13. Ibid., 31.

14. Ibid., 30. The magic words in this case were "at once," which were normally written by the more senior official after accepting the course of action suggested by the junior.

15. Parkinson, *The Colonial Office From Within*, 30; Kubicek, *The Administration*, 22–23. In 1912 there were two assistant under-secretaries of state in the CO; one was responsible for the dominions and the other for colonies. In 1916, a third assistant under-secretary was added to the establishment in the crown colonies division (Sir William Mercer, et. al, *The Colonial Office List For 1917* [London: Waterlow & Sons, 1917], xv–xvi).

16. *The Times*, 24 December 1936.

17. Kubicek, *The Administration*, 21. See also Sir William Mercer, et. al., *The Colonial Office List For 1921* (London: Waterlow & Sons, 1921), 637.

18. *The Times*, 24 December 1936.

19. Hyam, "Colonial Office Mind," 33. His obituary put it this way: "Officially Sir George was remarkable for his ability to grasp rapidly the essentials of any question which came before him, to summarize them clearly and concisely, and to make sound

suggestions for action which rarely failed to commend themselves to higher authority" (*The Times*, 24 December 1936).

20. Hyam, "Colonial Office Mind," 33.

21. Instances of official brutality or injustice, for example, rarely provoked moral outrage in Fiddes; rather such incidents normally caused him concern only because of the embarrassment they might cause the CO if raised in parliament.

22. Officially, the permanent under-secretary served as the S of S's chief official advisor and "the superior officer of all civil servants" in the CO (Jeffries, *The Colonial Office*, 118).

23. *The Times*, 25 March 1918; I. F. Nicolson and Colin A. Hughes, "A Provenance of Proconsuls: British Colonial Governors, 1900–1960," *JICH* 4 (1975): 94.

24. He told Lewis Harcourt in 1911: "I went abroad seven years ago because I found it was practically impossible for me to do my work whilst I had to live with my wife" (Anderson to Harcourt, private, 19 June 1911, Harcourt Papers, Bodleian Library, Oxford, 442).

25. Ibid. In initially turning down the appointment, Anderson said, "I should only court failure if I were to attempt the work whilst having a miserable home life."

26. Bernard Porter, *Critics of Empire: British Radical Attitudes to Colonialism in Africa, 1895–1914* (London: Macmillan, 1968), 300; 271.

27. As he told Harcourt on accepting the post, Emmott was given a pause at the suggestion he move to the House of Lords. However, he went on, "I hate my present post and after what happened in the past this seems the easiest way of making a change which puts me in the fighting line once more" (Emmott to Harcourt, 19 October 1911, Harcourt Papers, Bodleian Library, Oxford, 466).

28. A. G. Gardiner, *The Life of Sir William Harcourt* (London: Constable, 1923): 2:24.

29. Peter Rowland, *The Last Liberal Governments: The Promised Land, 1905–1910* (New York: Macmillan, 1969), 43.

30. Ibid., 325–26. According to Rowland, the prime minister made the change at the CO because of John Morley's desire to leave the India Office (IO) but remain in the cabinet. Asquith moved Lord Crewe from the CO to the IO and installed Harcourt at the CO.

31. Hyam, "Colonial Office Mind," 38; James, *Memoirs*, 10. J. C. C. Davidson, who served under him at the CO, ranked Harcourt particularly high. "As an administrator, he was really superb, the best Secretary of State I think they ever had. . . ." (James, *Memoirs*, 10).

32. Peter Yearwood, "Great Britain and the Repartition of Africa, 1914–19," *JICH* 18 (1990): 321–22.

33. E. A. Brett, *Colonialism and Underdevelopment in East Africa* (London: Heinemann, 1973), 58–59.

34. Porter, *Critics of Empire*, 295–96; 300.

35. Diana Wylie, "Confrontation Over Kenya: The Colonial Office and Its Critics, 1918–1940," *JAH* 18 (1977): 427–47.

36. Brett, *Colonialism*, 63.

37. Berman, *Control & Crisis*, 140.

38. Ibid., 9.

39. In practice, there was little difference, despite different titles, in the actual working of administrations of protectorates and colonies. Kenya's colonial history provides a clear example (Jeffries, *The Colonial Office*, 29–30).

40. Lonsdale and Berman, "Coping," 487–505.

41. Ibid., 490–91.

42. Berman identifies "the costs of conquest" as a major factor in the increase in the size of the imperial subsidy for the EAP (Berman, *Control & Crisis*, 52).

43. The term Indian is used in this work, as it was at that time, to denote individuals who came to EA from British India, whether Hindu, Muslim, or Sikh.

44. These policy aims applied to all British colonies. Official dogma embodied the idea that access to raw materials in her colonies formed a most important part of Britain's "sacred trust" as an imperial power. Since the cost of defense of the empire fell on the British taxpayer, moreover, it was felt that colonies had a duty to provide a market for British manufacturers. See David Meredith, "The British Government and Colonial Economic Policy, 1919–39," *Economic History Review* 28 (1975): 485.

45. For example *Parl. Deb.* (Commons), 5th Ser., 41 (1912): 1692.

46. John Lonsdale, "The Conquest State, 1895–1905," in *A Modern History of Kenya*, ed. W. R. Ochieng' (Nairobi: Evans Brothers, 1989), 6.

47. Lonsdale and Berman, "Coping," 501; Berman, *Control & Crisis*, 53–54.

48. Wolff's contention, and that of other writers who have based their claims on his work, that the British development program for Kenya created new constraints upon the African population, forcibly diverting them from peasant agriculture to wage labor, thus guaranteeing the "steady disintegration of the traditional African peasant economy" cannot be taken seriously. See Richard Wolff, *The Economics of Colonialism Britain and Kenya 1870–1930* (New Haven: Yale University Press, 1974), 144.

49. John Overton, "The Colonial State and Spatial Differentiation: Kenya, 1895–1920," *Journal of Historical Geography* 13 (1987): 269–71. The severity of the initial land loss was mitigated for many African households, however, by the opportunities offered, as a result of European settlement, for obtaining new land. A major way that this occurred was through the practice of squatting; settlers allowed African families to move on to land granted to the former in exchange for the provision of labor. See Tabitha Kanogo, *Squatters and the Roots of Mau Mau* (Athens: Ohio University Press, 1987), 15–26.

50. Sharon Stichter, *Migrant Labour in Kenya: Capitalism and African Response, 1895–1975* (London: Longman, 1982), 39.

51. Constantine, *The Making*, 14.

52. Ibid., 12–13.

53. Great Britain, *East Africa Protectorate Report for 1912–13* (London: HMSO, 1913); J. D. Overton, "Spatial Differentiation in the Colonial Economy of Kenya: Africans, Settlers and the State 1900–1920" (Ph.D. diss., Cambridge University, 1983), 35. A total of £2.8 million had been provided by the Treasury since 1895.

54. East Africa Protectorate, *Department of Agriculture British East Africa Annual Report 1916–17* (Nairobi: Government Printer, 1918), 27.

55. Girouard to Harcourt, 19 February 1912, PRO: CO 533/102. The total increase in revenue from these three sources amounted to £170,966. After 1905–6, railway revenues had been added to those of the protectorate.

56. *Agriculture Report 1916–17*, 27.

57. R. M. Maxon, *John Ainsworth and the Making of Kenya* (Washington: University Press of America, 1980), 190–92; 217–18.

58. East Africa Protectorate, *Department of Agriculture British East Africa Annual Report 1913–14* (Nairobi: Government Printer, 1915), 19. Because settler-grown maize began to be exported after 1911, the origin of maize exports for the period 1911–13 as mixed (as shown in Table 1.1). Given the available statistics, it is impossible to estimate how large a portion of maize exports came from settler or peasant production.

59. East Africa Protectorate, *Department of Agriculture British East Africa Annual Report 1911–12* (Nairobi: Government Printer, 1913), 7.

60. Overton, "Spatial Differentiation," 138; Berman, *Control & Crisis*, 56–57.

61. John Overton, "War and Economic Development: Settlers in Kenya, 1914–1918," *JAH* 27 (1986): 102.

62. Overton, "Spatial Differentiation," 38.

63. Ibid., 93; Berman, *Control & Crisis*, 67; Tiyambe Zeleza, "The Establishment of Colonial Rule, 1905–1920," in Ochieng', ed., *A Modern History*, 43.

64. Overton, "Spatial Differentiation," 46.

65. E. A. Brett, *Colonialism*, 191–94.

66. See, for example, minute by Read, 9 October 1913, on Ainsworth to Read, 5 October 1913, PRO: CO 533/130; and Hyam, "Colonial Office Mind," 47.

67. Berman, *Control & Crisis*, 56.

68. Minute by Ellis, 1 May 1908, on Sadler to Crewe, confidential, 2 April 1908, PRO: CO 533/43; and Hyam, "Colonial Office Mind," 47.

69. Minute by Ellis, 1 May 1908, on Sadler to Crewe, confidential, 2 April 1908, PRO: CO 533/43..

70. Hyam, "Colonial Office Mind," 47.

71. The term is Berman's. See Berman, *Control & Crisis*, 104.

72. W. C. Bottomley, for example, noted in 1918 that the Kikuyu reserve continued to attract the interests of the settler "who says, no doubt with truth, that he could make better use of it" (Memo by Bottomley, 7 March 1918, PRO: CO 533/193).

73. As it was amongst administrative officers in the protectorate. See Berman, *Control and Crisis*, 66–67.

74. Harry A. Reed, "Cotton-Growing in Central Nyanza Province Kenya, 1901–1939: An Appraisal of African Reactions to Imposed Government Policy" (Ph.D. diss., Michigan State University, 1975), 124–26.

75. Ibid., 65–70; Hugh Fearn, *An African Economy* (London: Oxford University Press, 1961), 70–71.

76. Berman, *Control & Crisis*, 57. Berman perceptively contrasts this with the state's attitude towards the African majority which stemmed from continued power and control over the latter.

77. Overton, "Spatial Differentiation," 33.

78. G. H. Mungeam, *British Rule in Kenya 1895–1912* (London: Oxford University Press, 1966), 196–207.

79. Hyam, "Colonial Office Mind," 47.

80. Ibid. In surveying Girouard's Kenya administration, A. H. M. Kirk-Greene, on the other hand, found it to be on the whole successful for he had "begun to deliver the goods the Colonial Office had wanted. . . ." One of the marks of his success, according to Kirk-Greene, was that "he had won the confidence of the settlers." Such a preposterous view is not supported by the CO records relating to Girouard's administration of the EAP, to which Kirk-Greene's article makes no reference. Hyam's characterization clearly represented the view of the CO staff, both political and permanent. See A. H. M. Kirk-Greene, "Canada in Africa: Sir Percy Girouard, Neglected Colonial Governor," *African Affairs* 83 (1984): 228. See also Robert M. Maxon, "Judgement on a Colonial Governor: Sir Percy Girouard in Kenya," *Transafrican Journal of History* 18 (1989): 90–100.

81. Girouard to Crewe, secret, 25 May 1910, PRO: CO 533/74.

82. Minute by Bottomley, 18 August 1915, on Delamere to Read, private, 17 August 1915, PRO: CO 533/164.

83. Delamere to Read, private, 17 August 1915, PRO: CO 533/164. Lord Cranworth, *Kenya Chronicles* (London: Macmillan, 1939), 61 and 63.

84. Overton, "The Colonial State," 268.

85. Ibid., 271–72.

86. Hyam, "Colonial Office Mind," 46.

87. Eleanor Cole, *Random Recollections of a Pioneer Settler* (Woodbridge, Suffolk: Baron Publishers, 1975), 35.

88. Proceedings Crown vs Galbraith Lowey Egerton Cole, criminal case 94 of

1911, enclosure in Girouard to Harcourt, confidential, 24 June 1911, PRO: CO 533/88.

89. Girouard to Harcourt, telegram, 7 June 1911, PRO: CO 533/88.

90. Minute by Read, 9 June 1911, on Ibid.

91. Minutes by Fiddes, 9 June 1911 and Harcourt, 11 June 1911, on Ibid. Harcourt to Girouard, telegram, 12 June 1911, PRO: CO 533/88.

92. Harcourt to Girouard, telegram, 12 June 1911, PRO: CO 533/88. See also minute by Risley, 9 June 1911, on Girouard to Harcourt, telegram, 7 June 1911, PRO: CO 533/88.

93. Girouard to Harcourt, confidential, 24 June 1911, PRO: CO 533/88.

94. Girouard to Harcourt, private, 25 June 1911, PRO: CO 533/88.

95. Minute by Batterbee, 27 July 1911, on Girouard to Harcourt, confidential, 24 June 1911, PRO:CO 533/88.

96. Minute by Anderson, 27 July 1911, on Girouard to Harcourt, confidential, 24 June 1911, PRO: CO 533/88. Anderson also maintained that if the S of S were asked in parliament why Cole had not been deported "it would be difficult to frame a satisfactory reply."

97. Minute by Harcourt, 28 July 1911, on Girouard to Harcourt, confidential, 24 June 1911, PRO: CO 533/88. Upon learning of Harcourt's decision, Lord Lucas, then parliamentary under-secretary, minuted to Harcourt: "I am glad you have decided for Cole's deportation. This will shew the settlers that we mean business. . . ." (Minute by Lucas, 4 August 1911, PRO: CO 533/88).

98. Harcourt to Girouard, telegram, 28 July 1911, PRO: CO 533/88.

99. Harcourt to Girouard, telegram, 9 August 1911, PRO: CO 533/88.

100. Girouard to Harcourt, telegram, 10 August 1911, PRO: CO 533/89.

101. Minute by Read, 10 August 1911, on Ibid.

102. Harcourt to Girouard, telegram, 10 August 1911, PRO: CO 533/89.

103. Girouard to Harcourt, telegram, 22 August 1911, PRO: CO 533/89.

104. Harcourt to Girouard, telegram, 29 August 1911, PRO: CO 533/89.

105. Girouard to Harcourt, telegram, 5 September 1911, PRO: CO 533/90. As Read noted in his minute on the telegram, the 1906 order created the position of governor and article 3 told the governor to obey instructions issued by the S of S (Minute by Read, 8 September 1911, on Ibid.).

106. Minute by Read, 8 September 1911, on Ibid.

107. Harcourt to Girouard, telegram, 9 September 1911, PRO: CO 533/90.

108. Girouard to Harcourt, telegram, 7 September 1911 and Girouard to Harcourt, confidential, 15 September 1911, PRO: CO 533/90.

109. Minutes by Read, 7 October 1911 and Lucas, 10 October 1911, on Girouard to Harcourt, confidential, 15 September 1911, PRO: CO 533/90.

110. Harcourt to Girouard, private, 24 October 1911, PRO: CO 533/90.

111. Mungeam, *British Rule*, 263–64. See also David Davies, M.P. to Harcourt, 28 September 1911, Harcourt Papers, Bodleian Library, Oxford, 497. Davies enclosed a series of letters from an anonymous correspondent in EA. These strongly intimated that Girouard was misleading the S of S over all aspects of the move.

112. Mungeam, *British Rule*, 265; and Harcourt to Belfield, 21 December 1912, PRO: CO 533/115.

113. *Parl. Deb.*, (Commons), 5th Ser., 37 (1912): 499; and Harcourt to Belfield, 21 December 1912, PRO: CO 533/115.

114. Mungeam, *British Rule*, 266; H. B. Wright [Land Officer] to Chief Secretary, 13 May 1912; and Montgomery to Laikipia land claimants, 18 April 1910, enclosures in Bowring to Harcourt, 29 November 1912, PRO: CO 533/108. As the date of the covering despatch indicates, it was only in November 1912 that the CO obtained written proof of the promises.

115. Mungeam, *British Rule*, 267.

116. Memo by Bottomley, 7 March 1918, PRO: CO 533/193. This memo was written as a rejoinder to a demand from Kenyan settlers that Girouard be sent out as military governor for the rest of the war.

117. Harcourt to Belfield, 21 December 1912, PRO: CO 533/115. Minute by Anderson, 10 December 1912, on Girouard to Butler, 6 December 1912, PRO: CO 533/115. Anderson had advised: "We cannot lock up that reserve indefinitely and . . . the exchange of land in the Southern Reserve for land in Laikipia is a necessary consequence of the move. . . ."

118. Hyam, "Colonial Office Mind," 47.

Chapter 2. Belfield and the CO Before the War

1. Belfield to Fiddes, personal, 4 January 1914, PRO: CO 533/132.
2. M. P. K. Sorrenson, *Origins of European Settlement in Kenya* (Nairobi: Oxford University Press, 1966), 130.
3. Ibid.; Cranworth, *Kenya Chronicles*, 92.
4. Sorrenson, *Origins*, 130.
5. Ibid., 117–31.
6. H. Conway Belfield, "Report on the Legislation Governing the Alienation of Native Lands in the Gold Coast and Ashanti," in *Great Britain and Ghana: Documents of Ghana History, 1807–1957*, ed. G. E. Metcalfe (London: Thomas Nelson & Sons, 1964), 536–40. In his report, Belfield had backed the position, held since 1897 by most Ghanaians, that all unoccupied land in the colony should not be declared crown lands.
7. *EAS* (Weekly), 20 July 1912.
8. Bowring to Harcourt, telegram, 17 July 1912, PRO: CO 533/105.
9. Minute by Butler, 17 July 1912, on Bowring to Harcourt, telegram, 17 July 1912, PRO: CO 533/105.
10. Harcourt to Bowring, telegram, 24 July 1912, PRO: CO 533/105.
11. *EAS* (Weekly), 3 August 1912.
12. Bowring to Harcourt, confidential, 20 July 1912, PRO: CO 533/105.
13. Treasury to Under-secretary of State Colonial Office (USSCO), 2 August 1912, PRO: CO 533/112.
14. Chalmers to Anderson, 10 August 1912, PRO: CO 533/112.
15. Minutes by Harcourt to Anderson, 14 August 1912 and Anderson to Harcourt, 13 August 1912, PRO: CO 533/112.
16. Chalmers to Anderson, 29 August 1912, PRO: CO 533/112.
17. *EAS* (Weekly), 5 October 1912.
18. Mungeam, *British Rule*, 181–83.
19. Girouard to Harcourt, confidential, 19 February 1912, PRO: CO 533/102. When the term of the Indian member, A. M. Jevanjee, expired at the end of 1911, Girouard recommended that he not be reappointed.
20. Ibid.; M. Dilley, *British Policy in Kenya Colony*, 2nd ed. (London: Frank Cass, 1966), 45; Atieno Odhiambo, *Siasa*, 35–36; Petition to Harcourt, 29 July 1913; enclosure in Bowring to Harcourt, confidential, 7 August 1913, PRO: CO 533/121.
21. *EAS* (Weekly), 13 July 1912.
22. *EAS* (Weekly), 7 September 1912.
23. Belfield to Harcourt, confidential, 23 August 1913, PRO: CO 533/121; Bennett, "Settlers and Politics in Kenya," 287.
24. Elspeth Huxley, *White Man's Country* (New York: Praeger, 1967): 1: 276.
25. Belfield to Harcourt, telegram, 22 January 1913, PRO: CO 533/116.
26. Minute by Read, 23 January 1913, on Ibid. Read wrote that Lord Delamere had been on the council two or three times previously and resigned; he went on: "the

sun or the altitude or something has I think affected his mental equilibrium" (Harcourt to Belfield, telegram, 28 January 1913, PRO: CO 533/116).

27. Bennett, "Settlers and Politics," 287.

28. Belfield to Harcourt, confidential, 23 August 1913, PRO: CO 533/121. Only J. H. Wilson of Mombasa remained a nominated member.

29. Petition to Harcourt, 29 July 1913, enclosure in Bowring to Harcourt, confidential, 7 August 1913, PRO: CO 533/121. Subsequent quotes are from this source.

30. Belfield to Harcourt, confidential, 23 August 1913, PRO: CO 533/121.

31. This was a reference to the resignation of all the unofficial members save one, and the refusal of others to accept nomination (Minute by Bottomley, 23 September 1913, on Ibid.).

32. Ibid. Bottomley anticipated that this would cause protest as "the Indians will raise outcry through mouthpieces in India." Ghai and McAuslan suggest that Jeevanjee was not reappointed because of "European pressure." While that may be so, CO officials, as a group very anti-Indian, clearly believed that the Indian leader had added little to the Legco. See Y. P. Ghai and J. P. W. B. McAuslan, *Public Law and Political Change in Kenya* (Nairobi: Oxford University Press, 1970), 47.

33. Minute by Parkinson, 26 September 1913, on Belfield to Harcourt, confidential, 23 September 1913, PRO: CO 533/121.

34. Minute by Read, 30 September 1913, on Belfield to Harcourt, confidential, 23 August 1913, PRO: CO 533/121. Read noted that the total number of registered voters in Southern Rhodesia was almost twice as large as the EAP's white population.

35. Ibid.

36. Minutes by Fiddes, 30 September 1913, Anderson, 30 September 1913, and Harcourt, 1 October 1913, on Belfield to Harcourt, confidential, 23 August 1913, PRO: CO 533/121.

37. Harcourt to Belfield, confidential, 14 October 1913, PRO: CO 533/121.

38. Ibid. The examples given earlier by Read were included in the despatch.

39. Delamere regarded electoral rights as "the second step towards ultimate self-government for the white community." Huxley, *White Man's*, 1: 276; Dilley, *British Policy*, 46.

40. Dilley, *British Policy*, 47–48.

41. G. Williams and S. Donnelly for and on behalf of Convention of Associations to Harcourt, 12 February 1914, enclosure in Bowring to Harcourt, confidential, 16 February 1914, PRO: CO 533/133. The logic of this position was as difficult to follow then as now. In the left margin opposite this assertion, someone at the CO inserted a large question mark.

42. Ibid. Here again, a CO official placed a large question mark in the left margin.

43. Minute by Read, 17 March 1914, on Bowring to Harcourt, confidential, 16 February 1914 and minute by Harcourt to Butler, 18 March 1914, PRO: CO 533/133.

44. Belfield to Harcourt, confidential, 6 March 1914, PRO: CO 533/134. In retrospect, it is clear that the governor's statement provides an excellent description of the working of the European franchise after it was eventually granted.

45. Minutes by Read, 31 March 1914, Fiddes, 1 April 1914, and Harcourt, 2 April 1914, on Belfield to Harcourt, confidential, 6 March 1914, PRO: CO 533/134.

46. Belfield to Harcourt, confidential, 29 June 1914, PRO: CO 533/138.

47. Bowring to Harcourt, 6 April 1912, PRO: CO 533/103.

48. Minute by Batterbee, 10 May 1912, on Bowring to Harcourt, 6 April 1912; see also minute by Bottomley, 23 September 1913, PRO: CO 533/103.

49. Robert G. Gregory, *India and East Africa* (Oxford: Clarendon Press, 1971), 93–94.

50. Ibid., 94; Indian Congress Meeting at Mombasa, enclosure in Belfield to Harcourt, 1 May 1914, PRO: CO 533/136.

51. Belfield to Harcourt, 1 May 1914, PRO: CO 533/136.

52. Minutes by Anderson, 1 April 1914 and Emmott, 2 April 1914, on Belfield to Harcourt, confidential, 6 March 1914, PRO: CO 533/134.

53. Minute by Bottomley, 5 June 1914, on Belfield to Harcourt, 1 May 1914, PRO: CO 533/136.

54. Ibid. Emmott once again came out strongly in favor of an Indian representative in the Legco "if it is found practicable," and so did Harcourt (Minutes by Emmott, 8 June 1914 and Harcourt, 9 June 1914, on Belfield to Harcourt, 1 May 1914, PRO: CO 533/136).

55. Read to Under-secretary of state IO (USSIO), 15 June 1914, PRO: CO 533/136.

56. Harcourt to Belfield, confidential, 10 August 1914, PRO: CO 533/136.

57. Belfield to Harcourt, confidential, 10 October 1914, PRO: CO 533/141.

58. Sorrenson, *Origins*, 95–96.

59. Ibid., 96.

60. Wolff, *The Economics*, 62.

61. Sorrenson, *Origins*, 97–98. As Sorrenson notes, "the concept that the country should be developed by big men" had triumphed.

62. Ibid., 220–22.

63. Ibid., 131–32; A. C. Tannahill, Memorandum No. 1, 2 June 1912, and Memorandum No. 2, 26 June 1912, PRO: CO 533/113.

64. Views of the Committee on Mr. Tannahill's Memorandum, 1 July 1912, PRO: CO 533/113.

65. Memorandum by Sir H. C. Belfield, 27 August 1912, PRO: CO 533/114.

66. Ibid.

67. Sorrenson, *Origins*, 132.

68. Minute by Read, 30 August 1912, on Sir H. C. Belfield's Memorandum, 27 August 1912, PRO: CO 533/114.

69. Minute by Butler, 18 September 1912, on Ibid.

70. Minute by Anderson, 19 September 1912, on Ibid.

71. Minute by Harcourt, 29 September 1912, on Ibid.

72. Report of the Committee on Mr. Belfield's Memorandum, 8 October 1912, PRO: CO 533/113.

73. Ibid. The Committee noted that such a provision had already been included in the revised draft of the land ordinance.

74. Minute by Fiddes, 10 October 1912, on Ibid.

75. Minute by Emmott, 13 October 1912, on Ibid.

76. Minute by Harcourt, 20 October 1912, on Ibid. The underlining was Harcourt's.

77. Harcourt to Belfield, 8 November 1912, PRO: CO 533/113.

78. Belfield to Harcourt, confidential, 27 December 1912, PRO: CO 533/109.

79. Harcourt to Belfield, telegram, 22 January 1913, PRO: CO 533/109.

80. Belfield to Harcourt, telegram, 29 January 1913, PRO: CO 533/116; Sorrenson, *Origins*, 133–35.

81. Belfield to Harcourt, confidential, 7 January 1913, PRO: CO 533/116.

82. Harcourt to Belfield, telegram, 10 February 1913, PRO: CO 533/116.

83. Belfield to Harcourt, confidential, 15 April 1913, PRO: CO 533/117.

84. Ibid.

85. Minute by Bottomley, 12 May 1913, on Ibid. Bottomley had, less than two weeks earlier, prepared a lengthy summary of the situation as regards EAP land (Bottomley, Land, 30 April 1913, Harcourt Papers, Bodleian Library, Oxford, 495).

86. Harcourt to Belfield, confidential, 23 May 1913, PRO: CO 533/117.

87. Sorrenson, *Origins*, 137.

88. Belfield to Harcourt, confidential, 11 July 1913, PRO: CO 533/120.

89. Minute by Bottomley, 10 August 1913, on Ibid.

90. Harcourt to Belfield, confidential, 20 August 1913, PRO: CO 533/120.

91. Sorrenson felt that this showed the CO, "heartily sick of the whole controversy, had given up the struggle to impose legislation on unwilling settlers and officials" (Sorrenson, *Origins*, 138).

92. Belfield to Harcourt, confidential, 18 November 1913, PRO: CO 533/124.

93. Minutes by Bottomley, 30 December 1913 and Read, 31 December 1913, on Ibid.

94. Minute by Harcourt, 2 January 1914, on Ibid; Harcourt to Belfield, confidential, 9 January 1914, PRO: CO 533/124.

95. Belfield to Harcourt, confidential, 8 January 1914, PRO: CO 533/132. See also Harcourt to Belfield, confidential, 23 May 1913, PRO: CO 533/117.

96. Belfield to Harcourt, confidential, 8 January 1914, PRO: CO 533/132.

97. Minute by Bottomley, 6 February 1914, on Ibid.

98. Belfield to Fiddes, private, 4 January 1914, PRO: CO 533/132.

99. "I do not regard the EAP as a White Man's country in the ordinary accepted sense of the term," Read minuted on the despatch (Minute by Read, 9 February 1914, on Belfield to Harcourt, confidential, 8 January 1914, PRO: CO 533/132).

100. Minute by Fiddes, 11 February 1914, on Belfield to Harcourt, confidential, 8 January 1914, PRO: CO 533/132.

101. Minute by Anderson, 11 February 1914, on Belfield to Harcourt, confidential, 8 January 1914, PRO: CO 533/132.

102. Minute by Emmott, 12 February 1914, on Belfield to Harcourt, confidential, 8 January 1914, PRO: CO 533/132.

103. Harcourt to Belfield, private and personal telegram, 17 February 1914, PRO: CO 533/132. Harcourt approved the draft on 16 February, but, surprisingly, no minute by him survives in CO records.

104. Belfield to Harcourt, 28 February 1914, PRO: CO 533/133.

105. Minute by Bottomley, 28 March 1914, on Ibid.

106. Porter, *Critics of Empire*, 303.

107. Harvey to Harcourt, 26 February 1914, PRO: CO 533/149.

108. Minute by Bottomley, 2 March 1914, on Ibid.

109. Minute by Anderson, 3 March 1914, on Ibid; Harcourt to Belfield, confidential, 7 March 1914, PRO: CO 533/149.

110. Belfield to Harcourt, confidential, 11 April 1914, PRO: CO 533/135.

111. Sorrenson, *Origins*, 138.

112. Minute by Anderson, 31 December 1913, on Belfield to Harcourt, confidential, 18 November, 1913, PRO: CO 533/124.

113. Bowring to Harcourt, telegram, 26 August 1913, PRO: CO 533/121 and Bowring to Harcourt, 13 September 1913, PRO: CO 533/122.

114. Bowring to Harcourt, telegram, 28 September 1913, PRO: CO 533/122.

115. Minute by Bottomley, 15 September 1913, on Bowring to Harcourt, telegram, 13 September 1913, PRO: CO 533/122. Significantly, Bottomley felt that Bowring, who acted as governor during Belfield's incapacity, would be able to cope with financial arrangements, but he had no such confidence as to land. Belfield himself had no desire to come to Britain, despite his illness. In a personal letter to Harcourt, he emphasized this and the importance of his getting the land ordinance completed and placed before the Legco (Belfield to Harcourt, 28 November 1913, Harcourt Papers, Bodleian Library, Oxford, 470).

116. Minute by Fiddes, 7 October 1913, on Bowring to Harcourt, telegram, 13 September 1913, PRO: CO 533/122. Read, on the other hand, would later chastise

Belfield for a lack of concern for his health. "The Governor seems to be out of touch with modern developments," wrote Read, "eg. he considered it unnecessary to take the usual precautions against malaria when he went to the EAP. . . ." (Minute by Read, 2 January 1914, on Belfield to Bonar Law, 9 November 1916, PRO: 533/171).

117. Belfield to Harcourt, telegram, 10 April 1913, PRO: CO 533/117 and Belfield to Harcourt, 9 May 1913, PRO: CO 533/118. Here again, the contrast with Girouard was striking. It should be recognized, nevertheless, that Bowring probably deserved most of the credit for organizing and executing the move.

118. Belfield to Harcourt, 30 October 1913, PRO: CO 533/123. Harcourt found it "a very interesting and satisfactory report" (Minute by Harcourt, 22 November 1913).

119. See, for example, Belfield to Harcourt, 29 January 1913 and minute by Harcourt, 28 February 1913 in which he wrote: "Sir P. Girouard *shall* pay—in public refutation!" (PRO: CO 533/116).

120. Upon learning, for the first time, of the difficulties that the advocates for the Maasai were having meeting their clients, Harcourt sent a personal and private telegram to the governor in November 1912 in which he expressed the feeling that the government's action would suggest to people in Britain that "there has been petty obstructionism on the part of local government and unjustifiable interference with freedom of communication between lawyers and clients who may possibly have a case to bring. . . ." (Harcourt to Belfield, personal and private telegram, 7 November 1912, PRO: CO 533/107).

121. See, for example, Morrison to Harcourt, 14 September 1912, PRO: CO 533/115; Bowring to Harcourt, 16 January 1913, PRO: CO 533/116; Morrison to Harcourt, 25 March 1913 PRO: CO 533/131.

122. Belfield to Harcourt, 17 December 1912, PRO: CO 533/109. For Belfield, African opinion did not really count; the government had decided the issue in their best interests, and that was the end of the matter in his view.

123. Minute by Harcourt, 28 January 1913, on memo by C. Tennyson, 23 January 1913, PRO: CO 533/129.

124. Minute by Harcourt, 31 May 1913, on Belfield to Harcourt, telegram, 28 May 1913, PRO: CO 533/118.

125. Minutes by Anderson and Harcourt, 22 July 1913, on Bowring to Harcourt, 27 June 1913, PRO: CO 533/119. CO legal assistant Tennyson's comment was much more perceptive however. He wrote: "This is a most ingenious way of evading a decision on its merits" (Minute by Tennyson, 22 July 1913, on Ibid).

126. Belfield to Harcourt, telegram, 14 May 1914, PRO: CO 533/136.

127. Cranworth, *Kenya Chronicles*, 269.

128. Belfield to Harcourt, confidential, 11 March 1913, PRO: CO 533/117.

129. Minute by Bottomley, 28 March 1914, on Belfield to Harcourt, confidential, 28 February 1914, PRO: CO 533/133.

130. Sir William Mercer, *The Colonial Office List for 1915* (London: Waterlow & Sons, 1915), 492.

131. Minutes of Meeting of the Execo, 10 August 1912 and 9 September 1912, PRO: CO 544/14; Anthony Clayton and Donald C. Savage, *Government and Labour in Kenya, 1895–1963* (London: Frank Cass, 1974), 55.

132. Guest to Harcourt, 2 December 1912 and minute by Harcourt, 8 December 1912, PRO: CO 533/114.

133. Memorandum Representing the Views of Large Interests in British East Africa, enclosure in Guest to Harcourt, 2 December 1912, PRO: CO 533/114.

134. Minutes by Bottomley, 4 December 1912 and 5 December 1912, on Ibid.

135. Minute by Bottomley, 4 December 1912, on Ibid.

136, Minute by Anderson, 6 December 1912, on Guest to Harcourt, 2 December 1912, PRO: CO 533/114.

137. Minutes of Proceedings At a Deputation to the Right Hon. The Secretary of State for the Colonies on the East Africa Labour Question, 16 December 1912, PRO: CO 533/113; Memo by Bottomley, Labour Supply for the East Africa Protectorate, 12 December 1912, PRO: CO 533/114.

138. Leggett had even served briefly as a provisional member of the EAP Legco in 1908. See East Africa Protectorate, *Official Gazette of East Africa and Uganda* 10 (1 April 1908): 186.

139. Minutes of Proceedings . . . , PRO: CO 533/113.

140. Harcourt to Belfield, 23 December 1912, PRO: CO 533/113,

141. Belfield to Harcourt, 9 March 1914, PRO: CO 533/134; East Africa Protectorate, *Native Labour Commission, 1912–13 Evidence and Report* (Nairobi: Government Printer, 1913), 333–36. A good summary of the commission's recommendations is provided by Clayton and Savage, *Government and Labour*, 61–63.

142. Belfield to Harcourt, 9 March 1914, PRO: CO 533/134.

143. Ibid.

144. Minute by Bottomley, 19 April 1914, on Ibid.

145. Minute by Fiddes, 25 April 1914, on Ibid.

146. Memo by Lambert, 30 April 1914, PRO: CO 533/134.

147. Minute by Fiddes, 1 May 1914, on Ibid.

148. Harcourt to Belfield, 20 May 1914, PRO: CO 533/134.

149. Clayton and Savage, *Government and Labour*, 63–64.

150. T. Buxton to Harcourt, 11 June 1914, PRO: CO 533/148. Buxton was secretary of the ASAPS.

151. Buxton to Read, 30 June 1914; and J. Harris to Butler, 14 July 1914, PRO: CO 533/148.

152. Read to Buxton, 9 July 1914, PRO: CO 533/148. In response to the letter of Harris a few days later, Harcourt minuted: "I don't mind his publishing my agreement with his statement re forced labour" (Minute by Harcourt, 15 July 1914, on Harris to Butler, 14 July 1914, PRO: CO 533/148).

153. Overton, "Spatial Differentiation," 83–84.

154. Belfield to Harcourt, 28 December 1912; and minute by Anderson, 25 January 1913, PRO: CO 533/109.

155. Harcourt to Belfield, 30 January 1913, PRO: CO 533/109.

156. Memorandum by His Excellency on the Subject of Compensation to Kyambu Natives for Their Rights on European Farms, enclosure in Belfield to Harcourt, 27 January 1913, PRO: CO 533/116.

157. Minute by Anderson, 4 March 1913, on Ibid.

158. Belfield to Harcourt, 30 May 1913, PRO: CO 533/118.

159. Belfield to Harcourt, 9 March 1914, PRO: CO 533/134. A month later, Belfield strongly restated his opposition to "pernicious pastoral proclivities" (Belfield to Harcourt, 3 April 1914, PRO: CO 533/135).

160. Minute by Anderson, 1 May 1914, on Belfield to Harcourt, 9 March 1914, PRO: CO 533/134. Lord Emmott was also anxious that by limiting the reserves, the government "do injustice" to the African population and cause future trouble (Minute by Emmott, 3 May 1914, on Ibid.).

161. Harcourt to Belfield, 20 May 1914, PRO: CO 533/134.

162. Constantine, *The Making*, 16–17.

163. Sorrenson, *Origins*, 120.

164. Fiddes to Secretary to the Treasury, confidential, 9 July 1913, PRO: CO 533/129.

165. Minute by Harcourt, 25 June 1913, PRO: CO 533/129.

166. Fiddes to Secretary to the Treasury, confidential, 9 July 1913, PRO: 533/129.

167. Ainsworth, Proposal for the Better Development of the Nyanza Province in

the connection with the Grant of Special Funds by the Imperial Government, enclosure in Ainsworth to Read, 8 August 1913, PRO: CO 533/130. Belfield's visit to the province in early 1914 further convinced him of its great productive potential (Belfield to Harcourt, 16 March 1914, PRO: CO 533/134).

168. Constantine, *The Making*, 24–25.

169. Bowring to Harcourt, 19 September 1913, PRO: CO 533/122. It will be recalled that Belfield was sick at this time; Bowring acted as governor during the illness.

170. Belfield to Harcourt, 10 April 1913, PRO: CO 533/117.

171. For a full account, see Robert M. Maxon, "African Production and the Support of European Settlement in Kenya: The Uasin Gishu–Mumias Railway Scheme, 1911–14," *JICH* 14 (1985): 55–56.

172. Fiddes to Lloyd, 15 May 1913, PRO: CO 533/117. See also minute by Fiddes, 9 May 1913, on Belfield to Harcourt, 10 April 1913, PRO: CO 533/117.

173. Lloyd to Harcourt, 28 August 1913, PRO: CO 533/131.

174. Minutes by Fiddes, 3 September 1913 and Harcourt, 4 September 1913, on Ibid.

175. Bottomley, Proposed Nakuru–Eldoret–Uasin Gishu Railway, 13 September 1913, PRO: CO 533/131. Bottomley took notes at the meeting. Any railway connecting the existing line with Mumias via the Uasin Gishu plateau would also, more than likely, pass through Grogan's timber concession.

176. Minute by Fiddes, 16 September 1913, PRO: CO 533/131.

177. Harcourt to Belfield, confidential, 19 September 1913, PRO: CO 533/131.

178. Taylor to chief secretary, 30 July 1913, enclosure in Bowring to Harcourt, 19 September 1913, PRO: CO 533/122.

179. Maxon, "African Production," 52–54.

180. Ainsworth to Read, 5 October 1913, PRO: CO 533/130.

181. Lloyd to Fiddes, 8 October 1913, PRO: CO 533/130.

182. Minute by Read, 9 October 1913, on Ainsworth to Read, 5 October 1913, PRO: CO 533/130.

183. Minute by Fiddes, 10 October 1913, on Ainsworth to Read, 5 October 1913, PRO: CO 533/130.

184. Harcourt to Belfield, confidential, 7 November 1913, PRO: CO 533/122. The Kisumu-Mumias survey had been completed and sent to London in 1912.

185. Belfield to Harcourt, secret, 13 November 1913, PRO: CO 533/124.

186. Taylor to chief secretary, confidential, 7 November 1913, enclosure in Belfield to Harcourt, secret, 13 November 1913, PRO: CO 533/124.

187. Belfield to Harcourt, confidential, 6 January 1914, PRO: CO 533/132.

188. Harcourt to Belfield, telegram, 4 February 1914, PRO: CO 533/132.

189. Bowring to Harcourt, telegram, 19 February 1914, PRO: CO 533/133.

190. Minutes by Bottomley, 21 February 1914 and Fiddes, 23 February 1914, on Ibid; Harcourt to Belfield, confidential, 27 February 1914, PRO: CO 533/133.

191. Minute by Fiddes, 3 July 1912, PRO: CO 533/103.

192. Minute by Butler, 25 October 1912; and Minute by Harcourt to Butler, 26 October 1912, PRO: CO 533/113.

193. Minute by Butler, 18 November 1912, PRO· CO 533/113.

194. Crewe to Harcourt, private, 20 March 1913; and Harcourt to Crewe, private, 21 March 1913, PRO: CO 533/113.

195. Minute by Harcourt to Anderson, 28 March 1913, PRO: CO 533/113.

Chapter 3. The CO Loses Control, 1914–16

1. Belfield to Harcourt, secret, 7 September 1914, PRO: CO 533/140.

2. Paul Guinn, *British Strategy and Politics, 1914 to 1918* (Oxford: Clarendon Press, 1965), 33.

3. Minute by Fiddes, 20 October 1914, on Belfield to Harcourt, secret, 7 September 1914, PRO: CO 533/140.

4. Belfield to Harcourt, telegram, 1 November 1914, PRO: CO 533/141.

5. Anderson called it "an absurd scheme" (Minute by Anderson, 3 November 1914, on Belfield to Harcourt, telegram, 1 November 1914, PRO: CO 533/141). The CO later received more detail from the IO (IO to Read, 3 December 1914, PRO: CO 533/141).

6. Belfield to Harcourt, telegram, 5 November 1914; and minute by Bottomley, 6 November 1914, PRO: CO 533/141.

7. Guinn, *British Strategy*, 33; Richard Meinertzhagen, *War Diary 1899–1926* (Edinburgh: Oliver & Boyd, 1960), 107; Yearwood, "Repartition of Africa," 320.

8. The battle of Tanga, in the CO view, was the responsibility of the IO (Minutes by Bottomley, 7 December 1914 and Read, 8 December 1914, on Belfield to Harcourt, secret, 7 November 1914, PRO: 533/142). See also Harcourt to Belfield, secret, 16 December 1914, PRO: CO 533/142.

9. Minute by Parkinson, 19 September 1914, on Belfield to Harcourt, telegram, 19 September 1914, PRO: CO 533/148.

10. Minutes by Fiddes, 19 September 1914, and Harcourt, 19 September 1919, on Ibid.

11. Harcourt to Belfield, telegram, 21 September 1914, PRO: CO 533/148.

12. Churchill to Harcourt, 10 November 1914, Harcourt Papers, Bodleian Library, Oxford, 444.

13. Earl Buxton to Harcourt, 9 December 1914, Harcourt Papers, Bodleian Library, Oxford, 444; Cameron Hazelhurst, *Politicians at War July 1914 to May 1915* (London: Cape, 1971), 166.

14. James, *Memoirs*, 22.

15. Hazelhurst, *Politicians*, 166–67. Hazelhurst thinks that the reason for Harcourt's strange behavior must have been that "the sombre reality of the world conflict had not begun to penetrate his mind." See also James, *Memoirs*, 22.

16. Wm. Roger Louis, *Great Britain and Germany's Lost Colonies, 1914–1919* (Oxford: Clarendon Press, 1967), 59–60; Yearwoood, "Repartition of Africa," 321.

17. Belfield to Harcourt, confidential, 25 August 1914, PRO: CO 533/139. Subsequent quotes are from this source.

18. The bill tried to effect this without really saying the highlands were reserved for Europeans.

19. Minutes by Bottomley, 25 September 1914, Read, 26 September 1914; and Fiddes, 3 October 1914, on Belfield to Harcourt, confidential, 25 August 1914, PRO: CO 533/139. It will be recalled that the war had brought a large number of Indian troops to EA.

20. Minute by Tennyson, 5 October, on Belfield to Harcourt, confidential, 25 August 1914, PRO: CO 533/139.

21. Minute by Harcourt, 8 October 1914, on Ibid.

22. Harcourt to Belfield, telegram, 9 October 1914, PRO: CO 533/139.

23. Belfield to Harcourt, telegram, 20 October 1914, PRO: CO 533/141.

24. Minute by Bottomley, 21 October 1914, on Ibid.

25. See Minutes by Fiddes, 22 October 1914 and Harcourt, 22 October 1914, on Ibid.

26. Harcourt to Belfield, confidential, 7 November 1914, PRO: CO 533/141. Harcourt took the most unusual step of revising the draft despatch in his own hand. He added the words "so long been felt in the Protectorate."

27. Ibid.

28. The ordinance was finally passed by the Legco on 10 May 1915 and it came into

operation on 1 June 1915 (Belfield to Harcourt, telegram, 11 May 1915, PRO: CO 533/154).

29. Belfield to Harcourt, confidential, 16 February 1915, PRO: CO 533/152.

30. Ghai and McAuslan, *Public Law*, 27–28.

31. Harcourt to Belfield, confidential, 7 November 1914, PRO: CO 533/141.

32. Belfield found this to be a "matter for congratulations" (Belfield to Harcourt, confidential, 16 February 1915, PRO: CO 533/152).

33. The Native Registration Ordinance, 1915, Statement of Objects and Reasons, enclosure in Belfield to Bonar Law, 10 June 1915, PRO: CO 533/154. See also Maxon, *John Ainsworth*, 282–83.

34. Minutes by Read, 30 July 1915 and Risley, 12 August 1915 on Belfield to Bonar Law, 10 June 1915, PRO: CO 533/154.

35. Minute by Anderson to Read, 13 August 1915, PRO: CO 533/154.

36. Minutes by Anderson, 13 August 1915 and Read, 13 August 1915, on Belfield to Bonar Law, 10 June 1915, PRO: CO 533/154.

37. Bonar Law to Belfield, 19 August 1915, PRO: CO 533/154. The CO reiterated this point in a confidential despatch a month later (Bonar Law to Belfield, confidential, 16 September 1915, PRO: CO 533/156).

38. Robert Blake, *The Unknown Prime Minister* (London: Eyre & Spottiswoode, 1955), 251. It also seems clear that the prime minster could not have managed politically to give Bonar Law a ministry more directly concerned with directing the war effort.

39. Ibid., 261.

40. Butler to Harcourt, private, 5 December 1915, Harcourt Papers, Bodleian Library, Oxford, 467.

41. Fiddes to Harcourt, 2 December 1915, Harcourt Papers, Bodleian Library, Oxford, 445.

42. Sir William Mercer, et. al., *The Colonial Office List For 1916* (London: Waterlow & Sons, 1917), xv. At the same time, H. C. Lambert and G. E. A. Grindle were made assistant under-secretaries.

43. Meinertzhagen, *Army Diary*, 110. This opinion came from Meinertzhagen's diary record for January 1915. In should be noted in fairness that Meinertzhagen quickly developed an extremely low opinion of Belfield that is very apparent from his diary entries. The height of Meinertzhagen's frustration was reached in July 1915 when he wrote: "Even Portuguese Colonial Governors are not as bad as Belfield" (146).

44. Ibid., 146.

45. Belfield to Fiddes, personal, 4 January 1914, PRO: CO 533/132.

46. Belfield to Read, private, 5 December 1914, PRO: CO 533/143.

47. Delamere to Read, private, 17 August 1915, PRO: CO 533/164. Delamere, not surprisingly in view of his dislike of the governor, felt Belfield was never "the least interested in the war or anything to do with it."

48. Tighe to War Office, telegram, 2 August 1915, enclosure in War Office to CO, 4 August 1915, PRO: CO 533/161.

49. Minute by Read, 12 August 1915, on War Office to CO, 4 August 1915, PRO: CO 533/161.

50. Minute by Anderson, 12 August 1915, on Ibid.

51. Bonar Law to Belfield, telegram, 14 August 1915, PRO: CO 533/161; Meinertzhagen, *Army Diary*, 149. While Lord Delamere's influence was quite substantial in provoking this CO action, his suggestion, less than a week after his meeting at the CO, that Sir Percy Girouard be appointed military governor met a very cold response. Girouard, Delamere believed, was a "first class Governor" who could bring about the fall of German East Africa with only the troops then available in EA (Delamere to

Read, private, 17 August 1915, PRO: CO 533/164). This suggestion was received with little enthusiasm by CO officials. Bottomley felt Girouard's administration "had left much to be desired." He had gained influence by an "opportunist" policy. "So far as Sir H. Belfield lacks that influence," concluded Bottomley, "it is because he has had to clean up after his predecessor." Fiddes was more blunt: "One does not take Ld Delamere very seriously at any time . . . his letter is simply rubbish" (Minutes by Bottomley, 18 August 1915 and Fiddes, 2 September 1915, on Ibid).

52. Meinertzhagen, *Army Diary*, 149.

53. Belfield to Bonar Law, telegram, 20 August 1915, PRO: CO 533/157.

54. Minutes of the Meeting of the Execo, 21 June 1915, PRO: CO 544/4.

55. Belfield to Bonar Law, 10 September 1915, PRO: CO 533/156. As Clayton and Savage noted, the ordinance gave legal authority for a course of forced recruitment that was already being carried out by chiefs and headmen on orders of district commissioners (Clayton and Savage, *Government and Labour*, 83).

56. *LBEA*, 21 August 1915; and Geoffrey Hodges, *The Carrier Corps: Military Labor in the East African Campaign, 1914–1918* (New York: Greenwood Press, 1986), 73.

57. Belfield to Bonar Law, 10 November 1915, PRO: CO 533/156. It is perhaps significant to note that E. S. Grogan was a participant in those discussions.

58. Belfield to Bonar Law, telegram, 10 September 1915, PRO: CO 533/156; Meinertzhagen, *Army Diary*, 151.

59. Belfield to Bonar Law, telegram, 13 September 1915, PRO: CO 533/156.

60. Belfield to Bonar Law, confidential, 10 November 1915, PRO: CO 533/156.

61. Ibid.

62. Ibid.

63. Clayton and Savage, *Government and Labour*, 92.

64. Bonar Law to Belfield, confidential, 5 January 1916, PRO: CO 533/156.

65. Hodges, *The Carrier Corps*, 73; Clayton and Savage, *Government and Labour*, 92.

66. Clayton and Savage, *Government and Labour*, 92.

67. Bennett, "Settlers and Politics," 289.

68. Belfield to Bonar Law, confidential, 22 August 1916, PRO: CO 533/169. Subsequent quotes are from this source.

69. Minute by Butler, 21 September 1916, on Ibid.

70. Minute by Read, 21 September 1916, on Ibid.

71. Bonar Law to Belfield, telegram, 27 September 1916; and Bonar Law to Belfield, confidential, 29 September 1916, PRO: CO 533/169. The latter despatch, which confirmed the telegram, indicated that the S of S was in no hurry to receive Belfield's observations and suggestions as to the organization of elections and the representation of the non-European community.

72. A. Visram to Long, telegram, 28 December 1916, PRO: CO 533/177.

73. Long to Belfield, 2 February 1917, PRO: CO 533/177. The CO also requested Belfield to inform Visram that his telegram should have been forwarded through the governor. See Gregory, *India and East Africa*, 179–85, for Indian concerns and protests during the war.

74. Belfield to Bonar Law, confidential, 8 January 1916, PRO: CO 533/166. Subsequent quotes are from this source. The war council had also urged the need for increased settlement as a means of providing for the future security of the European colonists.

75. T. C. Macnaghten had served at the CO since 1896. In 1917 he was appointed to a committee for the settlement of ex-servicemen within the British Empire.

76. Read wrote "Very doubtful I shd say" in the margin beside Macnaghten's ex-

pression of uncertainity over whether a British population would thrive in the highlands after fifty or one hundred years. See Minutes by Bottomley, 17 February 1916, Macnaghten, 18 February 1916, Read 21 February 1916, and Anderson, 22 February 1916, on Belfield to Bonar Law, confidential, 8 January 1916, PRO: CO 533/166. This would be one of Anderson's last actions which affected the EAP. Macnaghten was not alone in feeling that Kenya was not fit to be "a permanent home of European races." See Dane Kennedy, *Islands of White: Settler Society and Culture in Kenya and Southern Rhodesia, 1890–1939* (Durham, N.C.: Duke University Press, 1987), 54.

   77. Bonar Law to Belfield, confidential, 2 March 1916, PRO: CO 533/166.
   78. Belfield to Bonar Law, confidential, 16 August 1916, PRO: CO 533/169.
   79. Ibid.
   80. Minute by Butler, 29 September 1916, on Ibid.
   81. Minute by Macnaghten, 3 October 1916, on Ibid.
   82. Minutes by Read, 6 October 1916 and Fiddes, 9 October 1916, on Ibid.
   83. Minute by Steel-Maitland, 25 October 1916, on Ibid.
   84. Bonar Law to Belfield, confidential, 3 November 1916, PRO: CO 533/169. Kennedy notes that this also marked the start of an increasingly selective scheme that would eventually give preference to the wealth and social position of the settlers (Kennedy, *Islands of White*, 54–55).
   85. Hodges, *Carrier Corps*, 207–8.
   86. Overton, "War and Economic Development," 88.
   87. For example: Belfield to Harcourt, telegram, 4 November 1914, PRO: CO 533/141; Belfield to Harcourt, confidential, 12 November 1914; Belfield to Harcourt, telegram, 20 November 1914; Belfield to Harcourt, 21 November 1914 (all PRO: CO 533/142); Belfield to Harcourt, telegram, 15 January 1915; Read to Treasury, secret, 22 January 1915 (both PRO: CO 533/151).
   88. Bowring to Harcourt, confidential, 4 February 1915, PRO: CO 533/151.
   89. Belfield to Harcourt, confidential, 26 May 1915, PRO: CO 533/154.
   90. Minute by Anderson, 31 July 1915, on Ibid.
   91. Minute by Read, 30 July 1915, on Ibid; Bonar Law to Belfield, 10 August 1915, PRO: CO 533/154. The legislation providing for the increases was passed by the Legco in December (Bowring to Bonar Law, 24 December 1915, PRO: CO 533/157).
   92. Belfield to Harcourt, telegram, 28 January 1915, PRO: CO 533/151.
   93. Minute by Bottomley, 29 January 1915, on Ibid; Harcourt to Belfield, telgram, 29 January 1915, PRO: CO 533/151.
   94. Belfield to Bonar Law, 1 June 1916, PRO: CO 533/168.
   95. Minute by Fiddes, 13 July 1916, on Ibid.
   96. At that time coffee-growing by Africans was approved, on orders from London, in three selected areas.
   97. Overton, "Spatial Differentiation," 288–98; Gavin Kitching, *Class and Economic Change in Kenya* (New Haven: Yale University Press, 1980), 28 and 31.
   98. Overton, "War and Economic Development," 94–95. Planting of coffee seedlings continued to expand throughout the war.
   99. Ibid., 79–103.
   100. Ibid., 101.

Chapter 4. The Continued Lack of CO Direction, 1917–18

   1. Overton, "War and Economic Development," 81.
   2. Ibid., 82–84.
   3. Ibid., 90–91.

4. Ibid., 96.

5. Belfield to Long, telegram, 6 February 1917, PRO: CO 533/178.

6. Bottomley agreed that this would be a "big drain on what is left of the planting community" (Minutes by Jeffries, 8 February 1917, and Bottomley, 8 February 1917, on Ibid).

7. Read to Secretary, War Office, 14 February 1917, PRO: CO 533/178.

8. Fountain to USSCO, 26 April 1917; and Long to Belfield, telegram, 3 May 1917, PRO: CO 533/188. See also Overton, "War and Economic Development,"83.

9. Bowring to Long, telegram, 26 June 1917; and Bowring to Long, 26 June 1917, PRO: CO 533/182.

10. Bowring to Long, 26 June 1917, PRO: CO 533/182.

11. Fountain to USSCO, 29 June 1917, PRO: CO 533/188; and Read to Board of Trade, 28 June 1917, PRO: CO 533/182. As Overton points out, the maximum allowed under license, three thousand tons, was far greater than the EAP coffee exports of the preceding year (Overton, "War and Economic Development," 83).

12. Long to Bowring, telegram, 14 August 1917, PRO: CO 533/182.

13. Monson to Long, 1 September 1917, PRO: CO 533/184. W.J. Monson served as acting chief secretary during the period Bowring acted as governor. He sent the despatch to the CO which the acting governor had dictated.

14. Minute by Bottomley, 14 April 1918; Memo on Mr. Hewins' Meeting, 10 April 1918, with Lord Cranworth and Major Ward, PRO: CO 533/202.

15. Long to Bowring, telegram, 17 April 1918, PRO: CO 533/202.

16. Hewins had reacted to Ward's call for total organization of the colony's resources by observing that such a scheme "would apparently involve a degree of control of native labour which the natives would regard as compulsion" (Memo on Mr. Hewins Meeting 10 April 1918 with Lord Cranworth and Major Ward, PRO: CO 533/202).

17. Bowring to Long, 20 June 1917, PRO: CO 533/182; Hodges, *Carrier Corps* , 56–62.

18. Hodges, *Carrier Corps*, 207–8. Forty-four per cent of those recruited in the EAP for that period came from Nyanza province.

19. Ibid., 213. Total deaths for that period, from all of EA not merely the EAP, were in excess of 8,200. For the entire conflict, official statistics point to a death rate of 14.6 per cent for the EAP. Hodges has suggested that the actual figure was more like 22 per cent (Ibid., 111).

20. Bowring to Long, 1 May 1918, PRO: CO 533/195.

21. Bowring to Long, 2 May 1918, PRO: CO 533/195. The ordinance was titled The Native Authority (Famine Relief) Ordinance 1918.

22. Clayton and Savage, *Government and Labour*, 100–101; Minutes of Meeting of the Execo, 22 October 1918 and 3 November 1918, PRO: CO 544/14.

23. Bowring to Long, confidential, 20 March 1918, PRO: CO 533/194.

24. Overton, "War and Economic Development," 101.

25. Belfield to Read, private, 12 December 1915, PRO: CO 533/178. The letter was written from Mombasa.

26. Belfield to Bonar Law, telegram, 24 January 1916; and Belfield to Read, private, 24 January 1916, PRO: CO 533/178.

27. Minute by Fiddes to Anderson, 26 January 1916, PRO: CO 533/178.

28. Bonar Law to Belfield, private and personal telegram, 28 January 1916, PRO: CO 533/178.

29. Belfield to Bonar Law, telegram, 31 January 1916, PRO: CO 533/178.

30. Minute by Anderson, 31 January 1916, on Ibid.

31. Belfield to Read, personal, 31 January 1916, PRO: CO 533/178. Only after his formal retirement more than a year later would CO officials discern the real reason for

Belfield's refusal to consider retirement though his health had indeed been poor. The governor's finances were such that he could not afford to retire on a pension. See Belfield to Bottomley, 6 May 1919, PRO: CO 533/225; Cadman to USSCO, 17 June 1919, and minute by Bottomley, 28 June 1919, PRO: CO 533/223.

32. It is fascinating to speculate, nevertheless, on what Kenya's history might have been had the anti-settler Byatt, not Sir Edward Northey, succeeded Belfield.

33. Belfield to Bonar Law, 9 October 1916, PRO: CO 533/170.

34. Belfield to Long, telegram, 23 February 1917, PRO: CO 533/178; *EAS* 14 April 1917.

35. Belfield to Harcourt, 21 October 1917, Harcourt Papers, Bodleian Library, Oxford, 470. Without mentioning names, Belfield strongly hinted that Fiddes had forced his retirement.

36. Bowring to Read, private, 10 December 1918, PRO: CO 533/195. As will be seen, the CO was forced to name a successor well before the war's conclusion.

37. For example, Belfield to Bonar Law, confidential, 10 January 1916, PRO: CO 533/166; Northey to Milner, confidential, 1 June 1920, PRO: CO 533/253.

38. Memo by Ward, n.d., PRO: CO 533/202.

39. Sir Charles Petrie, *Water Long and His Times* (London: Hutchinson & CO., 1936), 209.

40. He wrote: "This is excellent. Does it not call for some special recognition both for Mr. Ainsworth and the natives" (Minute by Long, 23 September 1917, on Bowring to Long, 20 June 1917, PRO: CO 533/182).

41. Guinn, *British Strategy*, 243; Ian M. Drummond, *British Economic Policy and the Empire, 1919–1939* (London: George Allen and Unwin, 1972), 57.

42. Drummond, *Economic Policy*, 57.

43. *The Times*, 19 December 1917.

44. Bowring to Long, confidential, 14 August 1917, PRO: CO 533/183. The three were Delamere, Hoey, and Wilson.

45. Report of the Select Committee . . . , 19 June 1917, enclosure in Ibid.

46. Bowring to Long, confidential, 14 August 1917, PRO: CO 533/183.

47. Ibid. The committee recommended that Europeans living outside one of the areas should also have the right to vote.

48. Report of the Select Committee . . . , enclosure in Bowring to Long, confidential, 14 August 1917, PRO: CO 533/183.

49. Bowring to Long, confidential, 14 August 1917, PRO: CO 533/183.

50. Ibid.

51. Minute by Butler, 29 October 1917, on Ibid.

52. Notes by Belfield, 24 October 1917, on Bowring to Long, confidential, 14 August 1917, PRO: CO 533/183.

53. Memorandum by Butler, 26 October 1917, PRO: CO 533/183.

54. Ibid.

55. Minutes by Read, 5 November 1917; and Fiddes, 6 November 1917, on Bowring to Long, confidential, 14 August 1917, PRO: CO 533/183.

56. Bowring to Long, confidential, 14 May 1918, PRO: CO 533/195. At the time Bowring wrote, there were ten officials (including the acting governor) and five un-officials in the council.

57. Minute by Bottomley, 14 August 1918, on Bowring to Long, confidential, 14 May 1918, PRO: CO 533/195; Long to Bowring, telegram, 16 August 1918, PRO: CO 533/195.

58. Bowring to Long, telegram, 30 November 1918, PRO: CO 533/198.

59. Minutes by Bottomley, 9 December 1918, and Fiddes, 19 December 1918, on Ibid; Long to Bowring, telegram, 12 December 1918, PRO: CO 533/198.

60. Bowring to Long, confidential, 23 June 1917, PRO: CO 533/182.

61. Minute by Butler, 20 August 1917, on Ibid.

62. Monson to Long, telegram, 5 February 1918, PRO: CO 533/193.

63. Bowring to Long, telegram, 5 February 1918, PRO: CO 533/193.

64. Bowring to Long, telegram, 20 February 1918, PRO: CO 533/193.

65. Memo by Bottomley, 7 March 1918, on Bowring to Long, telegram, 15 February 1918, PRO: CO 533/193.

66. Ibid.

67. Minute by Fiddes, 11 March 1918, on Ibid.

68. Minute by Bottomley, 16 May 1918, on Bowring to Long, telegram, 20 February 1918, PRO: CO 533/193.

69. Bowring to Long, confidential, 8 May 1918, PRO: CO 533/195.

70. Long to Bowring, telegram, 24 June 1918, PRO: CO 533/195.

71. Bowring to Long, telegram, 6 November 1918, PRO: CO 533/198.

72. Minute by Bottomley, 8 November 1918, PRO: CO 533/198.

73. Minute by Read, 6 November 1918; and Long to Bowring, telegram, 11 November 1918, PRO: CO 533/198.

74. Bowring to Long, 2 January 1917, PRO: CO 533/178 transmitted the resolutions.

75. Bowring to Desai, 18 December 1916, enclosure in Bowring to Long, 2 January 1917, PRO: CO 533/178.

76. Gregory, *India and East Africa*, 180–81.

77. Monson to Long, telegram, 6 February 1918, PRO: CO 533/193.

78. President, Nairobi Indian Association to Monson, 15 February 1918, enclosure in Bowring to Long, confidential, 5 March 1918, PRO: CO 533/194.

79. Bowring to Long, telegram, 31 October 1918, PRO: CO 533/198.

80. Minute by Bottomley, 4 November 1918, on Ibid.

81. Minutes by Northey, 5 November 1918, and Fiddes, 6 November 1918, on Ibid; Long to Bowring, telegram, 6 November 1918, PRO: CO 533/198.

82. Bowring to Long, confidential, 25 November 1918, PRO: CO 533/198.

83. Minute by Bottomley, 23 January 1919, on Ibid.

84. EAP, *Land Settlement Commission Report* (Nairobi: Government Printer, 1919), 1. Among others, Lord Delamere, Wilson, and Hoey served on the commission. See Bowring to Long, confidential, 29 June 1917, PRO: CO 533/182.

85. Bowring to Long, telegram, 30 December 1918, PRO: CO 533/199.

86. That, at least, was Bowring's firm opinion. See Bowring to Long, confidential, 15 June 1918, PRO: CO 533/196 and Bowring to Long, confidential, 11 March 1918, PRO: CO 533/194.

87. Bowring to Long, telegram, 23 February 1918, PRO: CO 533/193.

88. Minute by Read, 27 February 1918, on Ibid; Long to Bowring, telegram, 28 February 1918, PRO: CO 533/193.

89. Bowring to Long, 13 May 1918, PRO: CO 533/195.

90. Bowring to Long, telegrams, 15 March 1918 and 16 March 1918, PRO: CO 533/194.

91. Minute by Read, 19 March 1918, on Ibid. Long to Bowring, telegram, 21 March 1918, PRO: CO 533/194.

92. Guest to Hewins, 12 April 1918, PRO: CO 533/194. Guest identified the source of his information about the railway scheme as Trans Nzoia settler and unofficial Legco member A. C. Hoey.

93. Page Croft to Long, 26 April 1918, PRO: CO 533/194.

94. Minute by Bottomley, 16 April 1918, on Guest to Hewins, 12 April 1918, PRO: CO 533/194.

95. Bowring to Long, 13 May 1918, PRO: CO 533/195.
96. Bowring to Long, 21 May 1918, PRO: CO 533/195.
97. Bowring to Long, confidential, 16 August 1918, PRO: CO 533/196.
98. Grindle to Treasury, 4 January 1919, PRO: CO 533/196.
99. Bowring to Milner, 30 January 1919, PRO: CO 533/206.
100. Minute by Read, 27 July 1914, on Antrobus to Fiddes, 21 July 1914, PRO: CO 533/144.
101. Steel-Maitland to Guest, 12 May 1917, minute by Bottomley, 19 March 1917, on Simmons and Simmons, solicitors to USSCO, 14 March 1917, PRO: CO 533/192.
102. Bowring to Long, secret, 12 June 1918, PRO: CO 533/196.
103. Minutes by Bottomley, 23 October 1918 and 14 November 1918, on Ibid. Read to Northey, confidential, 18 November 1918, PRO: CO 533/196.
104. Monson to Long, telegram, 5 February 1918, PRO: CO 533/193.
105. Bowring to Long, telegram, 5 February 1918, PRO: CO 533/193.
106. Long to Bowring, telegram, 15 February 1918, PRO: CO 533/193.
107. Bowring to Long, telegram, 7 March 1918, PRO: CO 533/194.
108. Minute by Bottomley, 8 March 1918, on Ibid; Long to Bowring, telegram, 21 March 1918, PRO: CO 533/194.
109. Bowring to Long, confidential, 11 March 1918, PRO: CO 533/194. Bowring described Grogan as "a man of considerable gifts who combines a colossal egotism with a passion for political intrigue." Subsequent quotes are from this source.
110. Nicholson and Hughes, "A Provenance," 96 and 102.
111. Ibid., 99.
112. Northey to Long, telegram, 17 June 1918, PRO: CO 533/205. Northey also had personal reasons for desiring to come to England. He had had six days leave in five years and had not seen his wife for some time.
113. Minutes by Bottomley, 18 June 1918, Fiddes, 18 June 1918, and Long, 18 June 1918, on Ibid. Fiddes wrote in addition: "It is interesting to see that he already has an inkling of his main problems."
114. Long to Bowring, telegram, 19 June 1918, PRO: CO 533/205. His appointment and pay actually took effect on his arrival in Britain.
115. Bowring to Long, telegram, 2 August 1918, PRO: CO 533/197.

Chapter 5. General Northey on the Offensive, 1919–20

1. Bernard Porter, *The Lion's Share: A Short History of British Imperialism, 1850–1970* (New York: Longman, 1975), 237.
2. Guinn, *British Strategy*, 192. For Milner, the only loyal Briton had to be of "British race", i.e. white and "the only safe non-Briton was a subordinate one" (Porter, *The Lion's Share*, 204).
3. Guinn, *British Strategy*, 193.
4. Ibid., 192; Porter, *The Lion's Share*, 231.
5. John Barnes and David Nicholson, eds., *The Leo Amery Diaries*, vol. I (London: Hutchinson, 1980), 252; John Marlowe, *Milner, Apostle of Empire* (London: Hamish Hamilton, 1976), 321.
6. Marlowe, *Milner*, 323–24.
7. Terence H. O'Brien, *Milner* (London: Constable, 1979), 329 and 345.
8. Constantine, *The Making*, 44–45.
9. The committee was to "enquire into the opportunities of economic development in the colonies and protectorates, to make recommendations as to the principles

and methods to be followed in such development and to examine and report on any particular schemes and suggestions as may be submitted to them" (Minutes of First Meeting of Colonial Economic Development Committee, 17 December 1919, Harcourt Papers, Bodleian Library, Oxford, 518). On the whole, however, Milner and Amery's plans to foster colonial development came to little (Constantine, *The Making*, 47–48; Marlowe, *Milner* 324).

10. A. M. Gollin, *Proconsul in Politics* (London: Anthony Blond, 1964), 586–87.

11. Barnes and Nicholson, eds., *Diaries*, 12.

12. Ibid., 252. The diary entry was dated 11 January 1919.

13. Milner resigned in February 1921, but Amery stayed on, under his successor, for two more months.

14. Colony and Protectorate of Kenya, *Department of Agriculture Report 1924* (Nairobi: GP, 1925), inserted table.

15. *EAS* (Daily), 25 February 1919.

16. Northey, Labour in British East Africa, 21 October 1919, PRO: CO 533/227.

17. Constantine, *The Making*, 64–67.

18. Northey to Milner, telegram, 27 February 1919, PRO: CO 533/207.

19. Constantine, *The Making*, 64. The Treasury asked that no further capital commitments be entered into at that time.

20. Minute by Bottomley, 3 March 1919, on Northey to Milner, telegram, 27 February 1919, PRO: CO 533/207; Grindle to Treasury, 20 March 1919, PRO: CO 533/207; Constantine, *The Making*, 64–65.

21. Constantine, *The Making*, 65. Constantine has provided a detailed and insightful account of the negotiations regarding loan funds between the CO and the Treasury in 1919 and 1920. There is thus little need to recapitulate them here.

22. Northey to Milner, 16 April 1919, PRO: CO 533/209.

23. Northey to Milner, telegram, 28 May 1919, PRO: CO 533/210.

24. Minutes by Bottomley, 14 June 1919 and Parkinson, 11 June 1919, on Northey to Milner, 16 April 1919, PRO: CO 533/209. Parkinson had now rejoined the EAD of the CO after active service in the East African campaign.

25. Northey to Milner, telegram, 10 July 1919, PRO: CO 533/211.

26. Milner to Northey, 17 July 1919, PRO: CO 533/209. In fact, negotiations with the Treasury for the new loan would drag on for some two years (Constantine, *The Making*, 72–83).

27. Northey to Milner, telegram, 26 May 1919, PRO: CO 533/210; Northey to Milner, telegram, 19 June 1919, PRO: CO 533/211. The additional cost of filling the eight vacancies was £2950. This sounds small by late twentieth century standards, but at the time the salary of an entomologist or cereal specialist was £400 per annum.

28. Northey to Milner, telegram, 5 August 1919, PRO: CO 533/212. The revenue for 1917–18 showed a decrease of almost 11 per cent from the previous year. Import duties and hut and poll tax showed the biggest decline. See Bowring to Milner, 17 September 1919, PRO: CO 533/213.

29. Minute by Parkinson, 9 August 1919, on Northey to Milner, telegram, 5 August 1919, PRO: CO 533/212.

30. Minute by Fiddes, 13 August 1919, on Northey to Milner, telegram, 5 August 1919, PRO: CO 533/212.

31. Milner to Northey, telegram, 19 August 1919, PRO: CO 533/212. Amery recognized the need to make real efforts at economy in the EAP as this would increase the chances of the Treasury agreeing to the loan money the CO desired. See Minute by Amery, 15 August 1919, on Northey to Milner, telegram, 5 August 1919, PRO: CO 533/212.

32. Northey to Milner, 29 September 1919, PRO: CO 533/213.

33. Bowring to Milner, confidential, 24 November 1919, PRO: CO 533/215. Bowring received a knighthood in June 1919.

34. Minute by Read, 1 January 1920, on Bowring to Milner, confidential, 24 November 1919, PRO: CO 533/215; Milner to Bowring, 8 January 1920, PRO: CO 533/215.

35. Bowring to Milner, telegrams, 7 October 1919 and 8 October 1919, PRO: CO 533/214.

36. Milner to Northey, telegram, 9 October 1919, PRO: CO 533/214.

37. Bowring to Milner, telegram, 13 January 1920, PRO: CO 533/229; Minutes of the Execo, 13 December 1919, PRO: CO 544/14.

38. Minute by Parkinson, 15 January 1920, on Bowring to Milner, telegram, 13 January 1920, PRO: CO 533/229.

39. Minute by Fiddes, 15 January 1920, on Bowring to Milner, telegram, 13 January 1920, PRO: CO 533/229; Read to Northey, 22 January 1920, PRO: CO 533/229.

40. Northey to USSCO, 23 January 1920, PRO: CO 533/253.

41. Minute by Parkinson, 26 January 1920, on Ibid.

42. Minute by Fiddes to Amery, 26 January 1920, PRO: CO 533/253.

43. Milner to Bowring, telegram, 2 February 1920, PRO: CO 533/253.

44. Bowring to Milner, confidential, 27 April 1920, PRO: CO 533/232; Constantine, *The Making*, 73.

45. Bowring to Milner, confidential, 27 April 1920, PRO: CO 533/232.

46. EAP, *Proceedings of Legco*, 2nd session 1920, 5 May 1920, 48 and 7 May 1920, 52; *EAS* (Weekly), 15 May 1920; Bowring to Milner, telegram, 14 May 1920, PRO: CO 533/233.

47. Milner to Bowring, telegram, 21 May 1920, PRO: CO 533/233; Maxon, *John Ainsworth*, 382–84.

48. Arthur to Milner, 10 May 1920, PRO: CO 533/248. Church of Scotland missionary J. W. Arthur was secretary to the Alliance. The missionaries felt the raise constituted a breach of faith because the African population had been assured when the raise to five rupees had taken place that it would be in force for some time.

49. Bowring to Milner, 30 June 1920 and 30 June 1920, both PRO: CO 533/233.

50. Northey to Milner, 25 August 1920, PRO: CO 533/235.

51. Delamere was strongly opposed (Dilley, *British Policy*, 94–95). See London Chamber of Commerce to USSCO, 14 July 1920, PRO: CO 533/249. The chamber held, among other criticisms, that it would not produce adequate revenue, Indians would avoid paying the tax, and it would serve to hinder development of those great many agricultural enterprises in their early stages, and "prejudice the flow of capital into East Africa."

52. Memo on Kenya Income Tax Ordinance, 1920, 18 October 1920, PRO: CO 533/235.

53. Northey to Milner, 21 September 1920, PRO: CO 533/236; and Northey to Milner, telegram, 26 July 1920, CO 533/234.

54. Milner to Northey, telegram, 4 November 1920, PRO: CO 533/236.

55. M. G. Redley, "The Politics of a Predicament: the White Community in Kenya, 1918–1932," (Ph.D. diss., Cambridge University, 1976), 72–73.

56. Milner to Northey, telegram, 13 February 1919, PRO: CO 533/199.

57. Northey to Milner, telegram, 17 February 1919, PRO: CO 533/207.

58. Milner to Northey, telegram, 22 February 1919, PRO: CO 533/207.

59. Northey to Milner, telegram, 22 February 1919, PRO: CO 533/207.

60. Milner to Northey, telegram, 5 March 1919, PRO: CO 533/207.

61. Northey to Milner, telegram, 14 March 1919, PRO: CO 533/207. He sent, by despatch, the Land Settlement Commission report on the same day. See also Kennedy, *Islands of White*, 55.

62. Northey to Milner, telegram, 14 March 1919, PRO: CO 533/207. Northey was upping the ante considerably with regard to the type of settler who would be welcome in the EAP. No conscripts need apply, only officers of substantial means. Little wonder the Michael Redley has observed that the whole scheme reflected the interests and influence of the "large men" among the Kenya settlers: land concessionaires, speculators, and land agents (Redley, "The Politics," 56–59).

63. Northey to Milner, telegram, 14 March 1919, PRO: CO 533/207. The smallest area allotted, he concluded, would be about three hundred acres.

64. Minute by Bottomley, 24 March 1919, on Ibid.

65. Ibid.

66. Minute by Amery, 28 March 1919, on Northey to Milner, telegram, 14 March 1919, PRO: CO 533/207.

67. Milner to Northey, telegram, 29 March 1919, PRO: CO 533/207.

68. Northey to Milner, telegram, 25 March 1919, PRO: CO 533/208.

69. Northey to Milner, telegram, 6 April 1919, PRO: CO 533/208.

70. Ibid.

71. East Africa Protectorate Land Settlement, April 1919, PRO: CO 533/208.

72. Northey to Milner, telegram, 6 April 1919, PRO: CO 533/208.

73. Northey to Milner, telegram, 14 April 1919, PRO: CO 533/208. Minute by Bottomley, 22 April 1919, on Northey to Milner, telegram, 14 April 1919, PRO: CO 533/208.

74. Northey to Milner, telegram, 4 May 1919, PRO: CO 533/209.

75. Milner to Northey, telegram, 7 May 1919, PRO: CO 533/209; Memorandum by C. Jeffries, 23 September 1919, PRO: CO 533/222. The London selection board consisted of Belfield, Lord Cranworth, and J. Berington of the Overseas Settlement Office in addition to the three individuals suggested by Northey.

76. Northey to Milner, 31 July 1919, and Milner to Northey, 27 September 1919, PRO: CO 533/212.

77. Northey, on the other hand, was never altogether happy about this. He noted, in an October review of the whole settlement exercise, that all participants in the scheme had "been the recipients of largess from the Protectorate Government." Any future allotments of crown land, he maintained, "should be based on principles which place the financial and economic interests of the Protectorate exclusively first" (Northey to Milner, 30 October 1919, PRO: CO 533/214).

78. Minutes by Parkinson, 8 January 1920 and Bottomley, 8 January 1920, on Sandford to Parkinson, n.d., PRO: CO 533/216. G. Sandford was Northey's private secretary.

79. Minute by Fiddes to Amery, 13 January 1920, PRO: CO 533/216.

80. Northey to USSCO, 19 March 1920, PRO: CO 533/253.

81. Northey to Milner, 21 September 1920, PRO: CO 533/236. See also Ghai and McAuslan, *Public Law*, 81.

82. Northey to Milner, 5 July 1919, PRO: CO 533/211.

83. Northey to Milner, 11 December 1920, PRO: CO 533/238.

84. Northey to Churchill, 26 July 1921, and Churchill to Northey, 20 September 1921, PRO: CO 533/. The soldier settlement scheme, nevertheless, was not without an impact on Kenya's history. Kennedy, for example, holds that "the subsequent character of the white population was most deeply influenced by the official soldier settlement scheme" (Kennedy, *Islands of White*, 56).

85. Berman, *Control & Crisis*, 143.

86. Wolff, *The Economics*, 112.

87. Minutes of the Execo, 8 August 1918, PRO: CO 544/14.

88. Bowring to Long, telegram, 30 October 1918, PRO: CO 533/198; Minutes of the Execo, 22 October 1918, PRO: CO 544/14.

89. Long to Bowring, telegram, 4 November 1918, PRO: CO 533/198.

90. Minutes of the Execo, 7 November 1918, PRO: CO 544/14; Bowring to Long, telegram, 8 November 1918, PRO: CO 533/198.

91. Long to Bowring, telegram, 22 November 1918, PRO: CO 533/198.

92. This policy was laid down in Secretariat Circular No. 4, 13 January 1919 (Maxon, *John Ainsworth*, 361–62).

93. Northey to Milner, private and personal telegram, 21 February 1919, PRO: CO 533/207.

94. Minute by Bottomley, 26 February 1919, on Ibid.

95. Minutes by Fiddes, 27 February 1919 and 17 June 1919, on Northey to Milner, personal and private telegram, 21 February 1919, PRO: CO 533/207.

96. Confidential Circular No. 4-/1 Native Labour for Government Requirements, 24 February 1919, enclosure in Bowring to Milner, 8 June 1920, PRO: CO 533/233. As the reference suggests, Northey did not send the circular to London or inform the CO what he was doing at that time. Only as the flames of controversy over EAP labor policy burned brightly in Britain during 1920 was it finally sent to London.

97. Northey to Milner, telegram, 8 August 1919, PRO: CO 533/212.

98. Milner to Northey, telegram, 21 August 1919, PRO: CO 533/212.

99. Northey to Milner, 30 September 1919, PRO: CO 533/213. The CO decided to let the bill go ahead, but the periods laid down in the Uganda ordinance would have to be followed. The bill was finally introduced in the Legco in January of 1920.

100. Northey to Milner, confidential, 10 April 1919. PRO: CO 533/209.

101. Maxon, *John Ainsworth*, 355–56.

102. Northey to Milner, 31 October 1919, PRO: CO 533/214. African production was of no account to Northey!

103. Native Labour Required for Non-Native Farms and Other Private Undertakings, 23 October 1919, *EAS* (Weekly), 1 November 1919. It will be important to remember that Ainsworth did not totally share Northey's views on this matter (Maxon, *John Ainsworth*, 372–76).

104. J. W. Arthur, A Statement with Regard to the Committee Minute on the Labour Question October 1920, Arthur Papers, Edinburgh University Library.

105. Northey to Arthur, confidential, 5 November 1919, Arthur Papers, Edinburgh University Library.

106. *EAS* (Weekly), 15 November 1919.

107. Watney to Amery, 2 January 1920, PRO: CO 533/213.

108. Thornton to Watney, 13 January 1920, PRO: CO 533/213. Thornton was private secretary to the S of S.

109. Buxton to USSCO, 12 January 1920, PRO: CO 533/248. Travers Buxton was secretary of the ASAPS. See also Read to Buxton, 6 February 1920, PRO: CO 533/248.

110. Watney to Northey, private, 20 February 1920, PRO: CO 533/227.

111. Buxton to Amery, 5 March 1920, PRO: CO 533/248.

112. Ibid.

113. Ian R. G. Spencer, "The First World War and the Origins of the Dual Policy of Development in Kenya 1914–1922," *World Development* 9 (1981): 741,

114. Minute by Parkinson, 12 March 1920, on Buxton to Amery, 5 March 1920, PRO: CO 533/248.

115. Read to Northey, 19 March 1920, PRO: CO 533/248.

116. Northey to Amery, 26 March 1920, PRO: CO 533/227. Subsequent quotations are from this source.

117. A copy of the circular finally arrived in early June. Acting Chief Secretary to USSCO, 27 April 1920, PRO: CO 533/232.

118. Bottomley, Native Labour in EA, 12 April 1920, PRO: CO 533/227.

119. Labour Party to Milner, 22 April 1920, PRO: CO 533/248; China Inland Mission to Milner, 8 July 1920; Baptist Missionary Society to Milner, 20 July 1920; Primitive Methodist Missionary Society to Milner, 23 July 1920; London Missionary Society to Milner, 26 July 1920 (at this point, Parkinson minuted: "This is becoming almost ridiculous"; minute by Parkinson, 28 July 1920); all in PRO: CO 533/249; Oldham to Milner, 18 June 1920, PRO: CO 533/248.

120. Clayton and Savage, *Government and Labour*, 115. J. H. Oldham had been attracted to missionary work while a student at Oxford. After a short overseas career in India, he returned to Britain and came to hold the post of one of the secretaries of the Conference of Missionary Societies. He also played an increasingly influential role in the ecumenical movement which led to the founding of the International Missionary Council in 1921. Oldham was the founding editor of *The International Review of Missions*. He was not an "agitator" or a brilliant speaker; he got things done through his talent for organizing. He was able to mold disparate opinions and groups together for purposes of effective protest, and he developed very influential contacts among those in key positions in the ecclesiastical and political hierarchy of Britain. See John W. Cell, ed., *By Kenya Possessed* (Chicago: University of Chicago Press, 1976), 41–42.

121. Northey to Bottomley, 23 April 1920, PRO: CO 533/253.

122. Extract of Sir E. Northey's discussion at the CO, nd. PRO: CO 533/253.

123. *Parl. Deb.* (Commons), 5th Ser., 128 (1920): 955.

124. Northey to Amery, 3 May 1920, PRO: CO 533/253.

125. Milner to Northey, 25 May 1920, PRO: CO 533/253.

126. Ibid. Northey had less sympathy with the critics of his policy in Britain. On 8 May he wrote to Bottomley describing the ASAPS members he had met as "cranks who do not really understand the subject under discussion, narrow minded and bigoted and therefore not likely to be convinced" (Northey to Bottomley, 8 May 1920, PRO: CO 533/253).

127. This had been specifically suggested by Bottomley in a minute of 10 May, PRO: CO 533/253.

128. Milner to Northey, 25 May 1920, PRO: CO 533/253.

129. Northey to Milner, 26 May 1920, PRO: CO 533/253.

130. It read: "It must be distinctly understood that such women and children must return to their homes at night; only when the husband is employed and living on the plantation should families be allowed to remain there at night." See also minute by Bottomley, 4 June 1920, on Acting Chief Secretary to USSCO, 27 April 1920, PRO: CO 533/232.

131. Minute by Bottomley, 5 June 1920, PRO: CO 533/232.

132. Minute by Fiddes to Milner, 7 June 1920 and Minute by Milner, 12 June 1920, PRO: CO 533/232.

133. Great Britain, *Despatches Relating to Native Labour*, Cmd 873 (London: HMSO, 1920).

134. ASAPS to Milner, 17 June 1920, PRO: CO 533/248. All officers of the society signed the letter.

135. Roberts to USSCO, 22 October 1920, PRO: CO 533/249. Charles Roberts, M.P. was president of the ASAPS.

136. Minute by Milner, 29 October 1920, on Roberts on USSCO, 22 October 1920, PRO: CO 533/249. In the end, no reply was sent to the ASAPS.

137. The policy was undoubtedly largely the work of Oldham. See Roland Oliver, *The Missionary Factor in East Africa*, 2nd ed. (London: Longman, 1965), 25–53.

138. Leon P. Spencer, "Christian Missions and African Interests in Kenya, 1905–1924," (Ph.D. diss., Syracuse U., 1974), 296.

139. Labour in Africa and the Principle of Trusteeship, PRO: CO 533/247. The memorandum was signed by such political notables as Arthur Henderson, Sir Samuel

Hoare, E. F. L. Wood, E. Hilton Young, and Lords Emmott, Salisbury, and Islington.

140. Minute by Bottomley, 1 December 1920, PRO: CO 533/247.

141. Ibid.

142. Ibid. Ainsworth had, at the instigation of Northey and Bowring, submitted several memoranda to the CO in 1920 in which he attacked missionary and humanitarian critics and argued the benefits of the state's labor and taxation policies. In these, however, Ainsworth had continued to put forth his long-held view that Africans should be encouraged to develop the reserves. Northey did not subscribe to this (Maxon, *John Ainsworth*, 278–81).

143. Minute by Fiddes, 1 December 1920, PRO: CO 533/247.

144. Minute by Amery, 1 December 1920, PRO: CO 533/247.

145. Jeffries, *The Colonial Office*, 36.

146. Memorandum of a Deputation received by Lord Milner . . . , 14 December 1920, and Labour in Africa and the Priciple of Trusteeship, PRO: CO 533/247.

147. Memorandum of a Deputation . . . , PRO: CO 533/247. This pearl of wisdom would mark, fortunately, one of Lord Milner's last pronouncements on Kenya affairs. He left office in February 1921.

148. African agriculture was preferable to Africans working for settlers (Labour in Africa and the Principle of Trusteeship, PRO: CO 533/247).

149. Northey to Milner, telegram, 8 February 1919, PRO: CO 533/206.

150. Minute by Bottomley, 12 February 1919, on Ibid; Milner to Northey, telegram, 22 February 1919, PRO: CO 533/206.

151. Milner to Northey, telegram, 20 February 1919, PRO: CO 533/206.

152. Milner to Northey, confidential, 17 March 1919, PRO: CO 533/206.

153. Northey to Milner, confidential, 2 April 1919, PRO: CO 533/208.

154. Northey to Milner, telegram, 17 April 1919, PRO: CO 533/209.

155. Minute by Bottomley, 24 April 1919, on Ibid.

156. Milner to Northey, telegram, 29 April 1919, PRO; CO 533/209.

157. Northey to Milner, confidential, 26 April 1919, PRO: CO 533/209.

158. Ibid.

159. Gregory, *India and East Africa*, 171–76, 177–85.

160. Ibid., 186–88, 193–94.

161. Montagu to Milner, 25 January 1919, PRO: CO 533/219.

162. Minutes by Bottomley, 3 February 1919 and Fiddes, 15 February 1919, on Ibid.

163. Minute by Amery, 15 February 1919, on Ibid. Amery indicated that Lord Milner concurred with this view.

164. Northey to Milner, telegrams, 23 February 1919 and 8 March 1919, PRO: CO 533/207.

165. Minute by Bottomley, 11 March 1919, on Northey to Milner, telegram, 8 March 1919, PRO: CO 533/207.

166. Minute by Amery, 18 March 1919, on Northey to Milner, telegram, 8 March 1919, PRO: CO 533/207.

167. Northey to Milner, confidential, 14 March 1919, PRO: CO 533/207. Other demands of the settlers included that they be represented at the coming imperial conference and that former German East African not be made an Indian colony.

168. Minute by Bottomley, 17 April 1919, on Northey to Milner, confidential, 14 March 1919, PRO: CO 533/207.

169. Minute by Amery, 24 April 1919, on Ibid.

170. Minute by Milner, 1 May 1919, on Ibid; and Milner to Northey, confidential, 6 May 1919, PRO: CO 533/207.

171. IO to USSCO, 16 April 1919, PRO: CO 533/219.

172. Montagu to Milner, private, 29 April 1919, PRO: CO 533/219.

173. IO to USSCO, 22 May 1919, PRO: CO 533/219.

174. He was referring to the CO proposal for two nominated Indians in the Legco. See Minutes by Fiddes, 27 May 1919 and Bottomley, 26 May 1919, on Ibid.

175. Minute by Amery, 28 May 1919, on Ibid; Milner to Northey, telegram, 29 May 1919, PRO: CO 533/219.

176. Northey to Milner, telegram, 16 June 1919, PRO: CO 533/211.

177. Ibid.

178. Minute by Bottomley, 26 June 1919, on Ibid.

179. Ibid.

180. Minute by Fiddes, 30 June 1919, on Ibid.

181. Minute by Amery, 3 July 1919, on Ibid.

182. IO to USSCO, 15 August 1919, PRO: CO 533/219.

183. Memo by Parkinson, 25 August 1919, PRO: CO 533/219. Subsequent quotes are from this source.

184. See for example, Gregory, *India and East Africa*, 240; Bennett, "Settlers and Politics," 299; Cell, ed., *By Kenya*, 50.

185. Minute by Fiddes to Milner, 17 September 1919; Minute by Milner, n.d. but probably in November 1919; Milner to Bowring, confidential, 26 November 1919, PRO: CO 533/219.

186. Read to IO, 19 November 1919, PRO: CO 533/219.

187. IO to USSCO, 8 December 1919, PRO: CO 533/219.

188. Minute by Parkinson, 10 December 1919, on Ibid.

189. Gregory, *India and East Africa*, 175.

190. Polak to Milner, 26 November 1919, PRO: CO 533/224.

191. Minute by Parkinson, 28 November 1919, on Ibid.

192. Polak to USSCO, 8 January 1920, PRO: CO 533/248.

193. Northey to USSCO, confidential, 10 January 1920, PRO: CO 533/253.

194. Northey to USSCO, 24 January 1920, PRO: CO 533/253.

195. Bowring to Milner, confidential, 28 February 1920, PRO: CO 533/230. When Bowring learned, in March, that his views were not shared by Northey, he expressed regret, but he held to his conviction that the time for elections had arrived (Bowring to Milner, confidential, 12 March 1920, PRO: CO 533/231).

196. Minute by Bottomley, 12 April 1920, on Bowring to Milner, confidential, 28 February 1920, PRO: CO 533/230.

197. Northey to Milner, 15 April 1920, PRO: CO 533/253.

198. Minute by Bottomley, 15 April 1920, on Ibid.

199. Significantly, W. Ormsby-Gore was the Conservative member.

200. Polak to USSCO, 31 March 1920 and 13 April 1920, PRO: CO 533/248.

201. Parkinson, Summary of Meeting Between S of S and Deputation from Indian Overseas Association, 19 April 1920, PRO: CO 533/249.

202. Ibid.

203. Summary of discussions at CO between Milner and Northey, drawn up by Bottomley, May 1920, PRO: CO 533/245.

204. Ibid.

205. Milner to Bowring, secret, 21 May 1920, PRO: CO 533/245.

206. Milner to Montagu, private, 2 June 1920, PRO: CO 533/245.

207. Montagu to Milner, private, 2 June 1920, PRO: CO 533/248.

208. Minute by Parkinson, 25 June 1920, on Jevanjee to Milner, 22 June 1920, PRO: CO 533/248.

209. Milner to Bowring, telegram, 15 June 1920, PRO: CO 533/245.

210. IO to CO, pressing, 13 July 1920, PRO: CO 533/242. See also Montagu to Milner, private, 5 July 1920, PRO: CO 533/242.

211. *EAS* (Weekly), 10 July 1920.

212. Northey to Milner, telegram, 21 July 1920, PRO: CO 533/234.

213. Minute by Bottomley, 30 July 1920, on Ibid.

214. Milner to Northey, private and personal telegram, 30 July 1920, PRO: CO 533/234. Phadke had proposed giving the vote to those who qualified by either being registered owners of property worth at least three thousand rupees, holders of a degree from an Indian university, or received an annual income of two thousand rupees or more.

215. Milner to Northey, private and personal telegram, 30 July 1920, PRO: CO 533/234.

216. Northey to Milner, 9 August 1920, PRO: CO 533/235; Jevanjee to Milner, 20 August 1920, PRO: CO 533/249.

217. Milner to Northey, confidential, 16 August 1920; and Polak to USSCO, 5 August 1920, PRO: CO 533/249.

218. Virji to Milner, telegram, 23 August 1920, PRO: CO 533/249; and Northey to Milner, telegram, 27 August 1920, PRO: CO 533/235.

219. Jevanjee to Milner, 2 September 1920, PRO: CO 533/249.

220. Thornton to Davies, 30 September 1920; and Memo by Bottomley, 30 September 1920, PRO: CO 533/249; Gregory, *India and East Africa*, 195–97; Polak to USSCO, 16 October 1920, PRO: CO 533/249.

221. Northey to Milner, confidential, 30 September 1920, PRO: CO 533/236.

222. Northey to Amery, private, 25 September 1920, PRO: CO 533/236.

223. Minute by Bottomley, 7 November 1920, on Northey to Milner, confidential, 30 September 1920, PRO: CO 533/236.

224. Minute by Fiddes, 8 November 1920, on Ibid.

225. Northey to Milner, confidential, 12 October 1920, PRO: CO 533/237.

226. Northey to Milner, confidential, 13 December 1920, PRO: CO 533/238. Northey anticipated that Phadke would soon resign his Legco seat as well.

227. Northey to Milner, telegram, 7 February 1919, PRO: CO 533/206.

228. Northey to Milner, 6 May 1919, PRO: CO 533/209.

229. Northey to Milner, telegram, 28 May 1919, PRO: CO 533/210.

230. Northey to Milner, telegram, 10 July 1919, PRO: CO 533/211.

231. Grogan to USSCO, 5 August 1919, PRO: CO 533/226.

232. Milner to Northey, telegram, 10 November 1919, PRO: CO 533/211.

233. Minute by Read, 15 August 1919, on Grogan to USSCO, 5 August 1919, PRO: CO 533/226.

234. Bowring to Milner, priority telegram, 22 November 1919, PRO: CO 533/215.

235. The meeting took place on 25 November. See Minute by Bottomley, 29 November 1919, on Ibid.

236. Ibid.

237. Milner to Bowring, telegram, 3 December 1919, PRO: CO 533/215.

238. Read to Norton Griffiths, 10 December 1919, PRO: CO 533/224.

239. Minute by Bottomley, 20 December 1919, on Bowring to Milner, telegram, 16 December 1919, PRO: CO 533/216; Milner to Bowring, telegram, 23 December 1919, PRO: CO 533/216.

240. Milner to Bowring, telegram, 24 December 1919, PRO: CO 533/216.

241. Northey to Bottomley, private, 30 December 1919, PRO: CO 533/227. As Northey would often demonstrate, his interest in developing the country only extended to European settler agriculture; thus the reference to the rich lands from Nakuru northwards.

242. Milner to Bowring, telegram, 31 December 1919, PRO: CO 533/227.

243. Minutes of the First Meeting of the Colonial Economic Development Committee, 17 December 1919, Harcourt Papers, Bodleian Library, Oxford, 518.

244. Memorandum by the Secretary of the Committee on the Proposed Uasin Gishu Railway from Nakuru to Mumias in the E.A.P., 30 December 1919, PRO: CO 533/270.

245. Eaglesome, Memorandum on Proposed Railway to Uasin Gishu Plateau, 10 January 1920, Harcourt Papers, Bodleian Library, Oxford, 518. Eaglesome included with his memorandum a map which illustrated that the route from Kisumu to Mumias involved traversing an area with less extreme changes in elevation than that of Eldoret to Mumias. Besides being shorter, a rail line from Kisumu would also be less expensive since it would have easier gradients to deal with.

246. Northey to Bottomley, private, 15 January 1920, PRO: CO 533/250.

247. Minutes of the Colonial Economic Development Committee, 19 January 1920, PRO: CO 533/250.

248. Norton Griffiths to CO, 22 December 1919, PRO: CO 533/270.

249. Report of the Uasin Gishu Railway Sub-Committee to the main committee, 19 February 1920, PRO: CO 533/234; also in 533/270. The full committee, chaired by Amery, called Norton Griffiths in also; the latter was told that the S of S was "disposed to give him the contract" (Minutes of the Third Meeting of Colonial Economic Development Committee, 20 February 1920, PRO: CO 533/270). Norton Griffiths was indeed granted the contract, without having to tender a competitive bid, a situation that was clearly scandalous.

250. Grogan, Notes on Alternative Alignments for the Proposed Uasin Gishu Railway, 27 January 1920, PRO: CO 533/234.

251. Report of the Uasin Gishu Railway Sub-committee, 30 January 1920, PRO: CO 533/250. The full committee confirmed this at its meeting of 20 February.

252. Report of the Uasin Gishu Railway Sub-committee to main committee, 19 February 1920, PRO: CO 533/234.

253. After three years, for example, the committee estimated that there would be 66,000 tons of maize exported, and after ten years these exports would expand by 98.8 per cent! See Bowring to Milner, telegram, 11 March 1920, PRO: CO 533/231.

254. Report of the Departmental Committee Appointed to make an Economic Survey of the Proposed Nakuru-Eldoret-Mumias Railway, 16 April 1920, enclosure in Bowring to Milner, 24 April 1920, PRO: CO 533/232.

255. The rail line was actually constructed to Turbo, southwest of Soy. The change was made on the basis of a slightly easier route, and the availability of better water supplies at the former site.

256. Milner to Northey, 27 May 1919, PRO: CO 533/196.

257. Northey to Milner, secret, 31 October 1919, PRO: CO 533/214.

258. Minutes by Fiddes, 30 December 1919, Read, 29 December 1919, and Bottomley, 27 December 1919, on Ibid.

259. Read to USS Foreign Office, urgent and pressing, 3 January 1920, PRO: CO 533/214.

260. Minute by Amery, 21 January 1920, on Foreign Office to USSCO, 12 January 1920, PRO: CO 533/240.

261. Minute by Bottomley, 27 January 1920, PRO: CO 533/240.

262. Minutes by Read and Fiddes, 28 January 1920; and Minute by Read to Risley, 16 February 1920, PRO: CO 533/240.

263. Foreign Office to USSCO, 21 February 1920, PRO: CO 533/240.

264. Read to USS Foreign Office, 3 March 1920, PRO: CO 533/240.

265. Milner to H.M the King, March 1920, PRO: CO 533/244.

266. Minute by Bottomley, 24 February 1920, PRO: CO 533/240. Once the change was actually made, Northey was concerned to make the public in Britain aware of the "correct" spelling and pronunciation of the colony's name. He wrote Bottomley a private letter at the end of August to urge that the latter forward a letter to *The Times* stating that Kenya was spelled with a *y* and was to be pronounced with the *e* long: Kēēnya (Northey to Bottomley, private, 25 August 1920, PRO: CO 533/249). Nevertheless, this spelling did not take into consideration the Bantu pronunciation from which the name was derived (in this case the Kamba language). In most Bantu languages, Northey's choice should have been spelled Kinya.

267. Amery to Bowring, 12 March 1920, PRO: CO 533/240.

268. Law Officers of the Crown to Milner, 22 March 1920, PRO: CO 533/249.

269. Milner to Bowring, telegram, 23 June 1920, PRO: CO 533/245.

270. Northey to Milner, 23 July 1920, PRO: CO 533/234. The coastal strip would be known as Kenya Protectorate, the interior as Kenya Colony.

271. *EAS* (Weekly), 10 July 1920. The *EAS* headline read: "Kenya Colony Sir Edward Northey's Surprise Announcement Yesterday."

272. Milner to A. Chamberlain, 12 April 1920, PRO: CO 533/248. Ghai and McAuslan describe this reason as "difficult to follow." They feel that "it would not have been impossible" to change the Colonial Stock Act "rather than the status of the dependency." CO officials certainly did not see the situation in that light. Amending the act would have meant difficult negotiations with the Treasury that they had no desire for (Ghai and McAuslan, *Public Law*, 50).

273. Gregory, *India and East Africa* 191.

274. D. K. Malhotra, *History and Problems of Indian Currency, 1835–1959*, rev. ed. (Delhi: Minerva Book Shop, 1960), 20–22; and Great Britain, *East Africa Protectorate Annual Report 1919–20* (London: HMSO, 1921), 5.

275. *EAS* (Weekly), 11 January 1919 and 1 February 1919.

276. Northey to Amery, private, 5 April 1919, PRO: CO 533/208.

277. Grogan, Exchange Crisis in East Africa, 29 May 1919, PRO: CO 533/208.

278. Ibid. See also Minute by Bottomley, 17 June 1919, PRO: CO 533/208.

279. Grogan to Amery, 28 June 1919, PRO: CO 533/208.

280. Minutes by Bottomley, 17 June 1919, Fiddes, 26 June 1919; and Amery, 29 June 1919, on Grogan, Exchange Crisis, PRO: CO 533/208.

281. Milner to Northey, 6 August 1919, PRO: CO 533/208.

282. Minute by Bottomley, 3 July 1919, PRO: CO 533/208. See also Read to Treasury, 5 July 1919, PRO: CO 533/208.

283. Northey to Milner, telegram, secret, 11 September 1919, PRO: CO 533/213.

284. Ibid.

285. Minute by Bottomley, 23 September 1919, on Ibid. Fiddes generally agreed with Bottomley (Minute by Fiddes, 24 September 1919, on Ibid).

286. Read to Treasury, 30 September 1919, PRO: CO 533/213.

287. Minute by Bottomley, 24 October 1919, on Northey to Milner, telegram, 23 October 1919, PRO: CO 533/214.

288. Milner to Northey, telegram, 28 October 1919, PRO: CO 533/214.

289. General Manager, National Bank of India to USSCO, private and confidential, 19 November 1919, PRO: CO 533/224.

290. General Manager, National Bank of India to USSCO, 1 December 1919, PRO: CO 533/224. At the existing rate of exchange, the bank faced a loss of about 50 per cent.

291. Minute by Bottomley, 25 November 1919, on Secretary, Standard Bank of South Africa to USSCO, 19 November 1919, PRO: CO 533/224. Bottomley first proposed such a meeting on 25 November.

292. Notes of the East Africa and Uganda Currency Meeting, 12 December 1919, PRO: CO 533/224.

293. Ibid. The National Bank of India had made approximately one hundred overdrafts to settlers by that time (Minute by Bottomley, 1 December 1919, PRO: CO 533/224).

294. Minute by Bottomley, 1 December 1919, PRO: CO 533/224. Bottomley had noted this "threat" after a meeting he and Read had with a representative of the National Bank of India on 28 November.

295. Notes of the East Africa and Uganda Currency Meeting, PRO: CO 533/224.

296. Manager, National Bank of South Africa to USSCO, confidential, 16 December 1919 and General Manager, National Bank of India to USSCO, private and confidential, 15 and 17 December 1919, PRO: CO 533/224.

297. Bottomley confessed after reading the letters from the three banks: "I am not sure that it is worthwhile going on . . . ," (Minute by Bottomley, 23 December 1919, PRO: CO 533/224).

298. Minute by Ezechiel, enclosure in Read to Treasury, confidential and most urgent, 20 December 1919, PRO: CO 533/217.

299. Ibid.

300. Ibid. The establishment of an EACB appealed to the CO since a West African Currency Board had successfully managed the currency of Britain's West African colonies since 1913 (G. L. M. Clauson, "The British Colonial Currency System," *The Economic Journal* 54 [April 1944]: 4–11).

301. Minute by Bottomley, 24 December 1919, PRO: CO 533/217.

302. Minute by Fiddes, 29 December 1919, PRO: CO 533/217.

303. Northey to USSCO, confidential, 7 January 1920, PRO: CO 533/253.

304. Grogan to Amery, personal, 8 January 1920, PRO: CO 533/251.

305. Minute by Bottomley, 10 January 1920, on Ibid.

306. Ibid., and Minute by Amery, 11 January 1920, on Grogan to Amery, personal, 8 January 1920, PRO: CO 533/251.

307. Notes of a discussion held in Colonel Amery's room at the CO, 16 January 1920, PRO: CO 533/251.

308. Mercer, East Africa Protectorate Currency, enclosure in Mercer to Bottomley, 26 January 1920, PRO: CO 533/252. Mercer further supported the new rupee currency with the argument that it would be "a very convenient unit forming with the cents a complete decimal system based on the pound."

309. Ibid.

310. Minute by Bottomley, 12 February 1920, PRO: CO 533/252.

311. *The Times*, 13 February 1920.

312. Minute by Bottomley, 12 February 1920, PRO: CO 533/252.

313. Milner to Bowring, telegram, 17 February 1920, PRO: CO 533/252.

314. *The Times*, 17 February 1920. On the same day that the policy was announced in the United Kingdom, a delegation representing EAP settlers and their supporters in Britain called on Amery to protest.

315. Bowring to Milner, telegrams, 21 Februrary 1920 and 11 February 1920, PRO: CO 533/230.

316. Milner to Bowring, telegram, 26 February 1920, PRO: CO 533/230.

317. Bowring argued that events in Kenya made a transitional period unnecessary. The Shs 2/- to the rupee rate could be adopted immediately. See Bowring to Milner, telegram, 25 February 1920, PRO: CO 533/230.

318. Minute by Jeffries, 4 March 1920, on Ibid.

319. EAP, *Official Gazette of the East Africa Protectorate* 22, 31 March 1920, 283; *EAS* (Weekly), 3 April 1920.

320. Northey to Bottomley, 1 March 1920, PRO: CO 533/253. Northey underlined *florin* in his letter.

321. Minute by Amery, 8 March 1920, on Ibid., PRO: CO 533/253. See also Bottomley to Niemeyer, 8 March 1920 and Niemeyer to Bottomley, 10 March 1920, PRO: CO 533/243.

322. The East Africa and Uganda Currency Order-in-Council (No. 2), 1920, 26 April 1920, PRO: CO 533/270.

323. Great Britain, *Colony and Protectorate of Kenya Report 1920–21* (London: HMSO 1922), 5. The EACB actually took over control of East African currency on 31 July.

Chapter 6. The CO Regains the Initiative, 1921–22

1. Lord Halifax, *Fullness of Days* (New York: Dodd, Mead & Co., 1957), 89.

2. His ability to concentrate all his attention on critical areas or problems, to the exclusion of all others, and bring about decisive action left a strong impression on at least one of those who served under him at the CO. See Ralph Furse, *Aucuparius: Recollections of a Recruiting Officer* (London: Oxford University Press, 1962), 85.

3. Wood was created Baron Irwin in 1925, and he succeeded his father as Viscount Halifax in 1934. Wood is the appellation preferred in this work as that was the name he was known by during his service at the CO.

4. Halifax, *Fullness*, 90.

5. Churchill to Lloyd George, private, 15 August 1921, in Martin Gilbert, ed., *Winston Churchill Companion*, part 3 (London: Heinemann, 1977), 1604. Masterton-Smith clearly admired Churchill as a hard-working public official.

6. *The Times*, 29 August 1921.

7. Archibshop of Canterbury to Milner, 5 January 1921, PRO: CO 533/271.

8. Memorandum by the Rev. John Arthur . . . , December 24, 1920, enclosure in Ibid.

9. Memorandum by the Rev. H. D. Hooper . . . December 27, 1920, enclosure in Archbishop of Canterbury to Milner, 5 January 1920, PRO: CO 533/271.

10. Milner to Northey, 20 January 1921, PRO: CO 533/271.

11. Northey to Milner, 31 January 1921, PRO: CO 533/255.

12. Minute by Bottomley, 14 March 1921, on Ibid.

13. Churchill to Northey, 24 March 1921, PRO: CO 533/255; and Churchill to Northey, telegram, 11 May 1921, PRO: CO 533/271. The latter wire expressed a desire for a reply to the Archbishop "as soon as possible." The CO had begun, in early May, to receive yet another stream of humanitarian protest directed against British policy in Kenya.

14. Northey to Churchill, 21 May 1921, PRO: CO 533/259. Northey's position on this last point did not deal completely with humanitarian criticisms; Oldham, for one, would not likely have been satisfied.

15. Cell, for example, termed it "Oldham's impressive victory" (Cell, *By Kenya*, 42). See also Anne King, "J. W. Arthur and African Interests," in B. E. Kipkorir, ed., *Biographical Essays on Imperialism and Collaboration in Colonial Kenya* (Nairobi: Kenya Literature Bureau, 1980), 91.

16. Cell, *By Kenya*, 17–19; Diana Wylie, "Norman Leys and McGregor Ross: A Case Study in the Conscience of African Empire, 1900–1939, "*JICH* 5 (1977): 294–95.

17. Leys to Turner, 3 May 1921, PRO: CO 533/274. Subsequent quotes are from this source.

18. Minute by Parkinson, 16 May 1921, on Ibid.

19. Minutes by Bottomley, 16 May 1921 and Wood, 23 May 1921, on Ibid; Read to Ainsworth, confidential, 27 May 1921, PRO: CO 533/274.

20. Maxon, *John Ainsworth*, 341 and 344.

21. Minute by Bottomley, PRO: CO 533/273.

22. Draft of Proposed Circular dealing with the Question of Native Labour in the Kenya Colony and Protectorate, PRO: CO 533/273.

23. Ibid; Maxon, *John Ainsworth*, 409–11.

24. Ainsworth to Read, 7 June 1921, PRO: CO 533/273.

25. Minute by Bottomley, 8 June 1921, PRO: CO 533/273.

26. Memorandum on Native Affairs in the East African Protectorates, 17 May 1921, enclosure in Oldham to Wood, 24 May 1921, PRO: CO 533/272. The call for a Royal Commission had been made earlier in the month by Conservative M.P. William Ormsby-Gore. He minced no words in telling Wood that "there is hardly a single aspect of Government in Kenia Colony which has not got into an awful mess during the last two years, and I sincerely hope that radical steps will be taken to clear up the mess" (Ormsby-Gore to Wood, 11 May 1921, PRO: CO 533/274).

27. Oldham to Wood, 24 May 1921, PRO: CO 533/272.

28. Minute by Bottomley, 8 June 1921, on Ibid.

29. Minute by Wood to Churchill, 14 June 1921, PRO: CO 533/273.

30. Native Labour in East Africa, n.d. (the CO stamped this internal memorandum as received on 13 August 1921), PRO: CO 533/270. This second heading clearly reflected Ainsworth's influence.

31. Ibid.

32. Oldham to Wood, 15 August 1921, PRO: CO 533/274.

33. Ibid. Oldham specifically objected to the words: "But beyond taking steps to put in touch with one another the employer and the native who wishes to work. . . ."

34. Wood to Oldham, 19 August 1921, PRO: CO 533/274.

35. Oldham to Wood, telegram, 23 August 1921, PRO: CO 533/274. Oldham telegraphed as he was in Scotland. See also Wood to Oldham, 25 August 1921, PRO: CO 533/274. Two weeks later, Oldham termed the labor situation "encouraging" in a letter to Leys as "the Government seems to me to have gone very much further to meet us than I ever expected they would." See Oldham to Leys, strictly private, 5 September 1921, quoted in Cell, ed., *By Kenya*, 192.

36. Wood to Northey, 25 August 1921, PRO: CO 533/274.

37. Churchill to Bowring, 5 September 1921, PRO: CO 533/274.

38. Travers Buxton and John Harris to Churchill, 10 October 1921, PRO: CO 533/272. The society found "special satisfaction" in the fact that government officials were to be prohibited from taking part in the recruitment of labor for private employment.

39. Stichter, *Migrant Labour*, 36–40; Clayton and Savage, *Government and Labour*, 117.

40. George Bennett's view was that "missionary influence had been of first importance." As detailed here, however, the impact of Elliot and Ainsworth was even more crucial. See George Bennett, *Kenya A Political History: The Colonial Period* (Oxford: Oxford University Press, 1963), 44.

41. Great Britain, *Colony and Protectorate of Kenya Report 1920–21* (London: HMSO, 1922), 5.

42. Minute by Mercer to Amery, 18 January 1921, PRO: CO 533/269.

43. Ibid.

44. Milner to Northey, telegram, secret, 31 December 1920, PRO: CO 533/247. Northey was instructed to relay the telegram to Coryndon in Uganda.

45. Northey to Milner, telegram, 10 January 1921, PRO: CO 533/255.

46. Harold Jowers for Associated Producers to Mercer, 10 January 1921, PRO: CO 533/269. Associated producers has been accurately described by Brett as "a loose British grouping of people with agricultural interests in East Africa" (Brett, *Colonialism*, 64).

47. Minute by Mercer to Amery, 18 January 1921, PRO: CO 533/269.

48. Ibid.

49. Milner to Northey, telegram, 19 January 1921, PRO: CO 533/269.

50. Northey to Milner, telegram, 23 January 1921, PRO: CO 533/255.

51. W. M. Ross, *Kenya From Within* (London: George Allen and Unwin, 1927), 205–6; Colony and Protectorate of Kenya, *Legco Deb.*, 3rd Session, 25 February 1921: 89.

52. Northey to Milner, telegram, 23 January 1921, PRO: CO 533/255.

53. Minute by Bottomley, 26 January 1921, on Ibid.

54. Milner to Northey, telegram, 26 January 1921, PRO: CO 533/255.

55. Northey to Milner, telegram, immediate and confidential, 28 January 1921, PRO: CO 533/255.

56. EACB, Memorandum on an Interview with Representatives of Banks Operating in East Africa, 2 February 1921, PRO: CO 533/269.

57. National Bank of South Africa to EACB, confidential, 3 February 1921, PRO: CO 533/269. The Standard Bank of South Africa stated that it understood that the secretary of state's pledge of stability at ten florins to the pound on 31 March 1920 was permanent. See Standard Bank of South Africa to Secretary, EACB, confidential, 3 February 1921, PRO: CO 533/271.

58. National Bank of India to USSCO, 3 February 1921, PRO: CO 533/269.

59. Ibid; and National Bank of India to EACB, 7 February 1921, PRO: CO 533/269.

60. East African Florin, n.d., PRO: CO 533/269.

61. Constantine, *The Making*, 54.

62. Northey to Milner, telegram, 3 February 1921, PRO: CO 533/255. See also *EAS*, 4 February 1921.

63. Northey to Milner, telegram, 3 February 1921, PRO: CO 533/255. The governor telegraphed at the request of the bankers.

64. *EAS*, 8 February 1921.

65. Northey to Milner, telegram, 7 February 1921, PRO: CO 533/255.

66. Milner to Northey, telegram, 9 February 1921, PRO: CO 533/255.

67. Ibid.

68. Minutes of the Execo, 9 February 1921, PRO: CO 544/14.

69. Redley, "The Politics," 69–70.

70. Ibid., 75; and M. F. Hill, *Permanent Way* (Nairobi: East African Railways and Harbours, 1961), 387. Delamere had been elected to a seat in the Legco in 1920, but, as was his habit, he soon resigned. He returned to the council well before the end of its term.

71. *EAS*, 11 February 1921. The sole supporter was R. B. Cole, a large landowner.

72. *Legco Deb.*, 3rd Session, 10 February 1921: 84.

73. Ross, *Kenya From*, 207. Redley maintains that the currency debacle had a significant impact on European politics in discrediting the current Legco members and thus opening the way for the return of "large men" in subsequent by elections (Redley, "The Politics," 75–76).

74. Northey to Milner, telegram, 10 February 1921, PRO: CO 533/255. Despite this defeat, this would not be the last time Northey would try to force a scheme he

favored on the CO by presenting London with a Legco resolution in support of his policy.

75. CO statement sent to papers, 13 February 1921, PRO: CO 533/255; *The Times*, 14 February 1921.

76. It did not end the attempts of settlers and their friends in Britain to bring about a reduction in the rate of exchange. The latter pressed the CO and banks in March for a return to Shs 1/4 but to no avail. See Jowers to USSCO, 3 March 1921; and Jowers to Bottomley, 11 March 1921, PRO: CO 533/271.

77. Ross, *Kenya From*, 208.

78. *EAS*, 9 February 1921.

79. Northey to Churchill, telegram, 19 February 1921, PRO: CO 533/256.

80. Minute by Jeffries, 22 February 1921, on Ibid; Churchill to Northey, priority telegram, 23 February 1921, PRO: CO 533/256. It is thus important to note that while the Kenya committee proposed reducing the value of cents in circulation, it was the EACB and the CO that actually suggested the form that the proposed "shilling swindle" would take. Ross gives the impression that Northey and Kenya bankers had first recommended this (Ross, *Kenya From*, 209–10).

81. East African Currency, 3 March 1921, PRO: CO 533/257.

82. Ibid.

83. Ross, *Kenva From*, 199.

84. Churchill to Northey, telegram, 19 March 1921, PRO: CO 533/257.

85. In light of the need to present the new scheme to parliament and answer criticism, Churchill called a meeting of those who had been involved for the second week of April. "I want to understand the subject," he minuted in explaining the purpose of the meeting. Minute by Churchill, 13 April 1921. Martin Gilbert, ed., *Winston Churchill Companion*, part 4 (London: Heinemann, 1977): 4: 1437.

86. *Parl. Deb.* (Commons), 5th Ser., 142 (1921): 596.

87. Ibid., 598.

88. Minute by Bottomley, 10 May 1921, PRO: CO 533/268.

89. Ibid.

90. Ibid.

91. Ross, *Kenva From*, 211.

92. *Parl. Deb.* (Commons), 5th Ser., 142 (1921): 1851–53; also 1243.

93. Ibid., 1244–45.

94. *Parl. Deb.* (Commons), 5th Ser., 144 (1921): 1565–69; 1575–76. Northey's labor policy was also strongly criticized.

95. *Parl. Deb.* (Commons), 5th Ser., 147 (1921): 467; Ross, *Kenva From*, 211.

96. Minute by Bottomley, 24 September 1921, on Currency Officer, Mombasa to EACB, telegram, 24 September 1921, PRO: CO 533/270. Obviously sick of the whole business, Bottomley thought that "Kenya has done the whole mischief by pressing for the shilling instead of the florin. . . ."

97. Minute by Stevenson to Wood, 29 September 1921, PRO: CO 533/270.

98. Churchill to Northey, telegram, 4 October 1921, PRO: CO 533/270. Northey was told to send a copy of the wire to Uganda.

99. Churchill to Jarvis, telegram, 5 October 1921, PRO: CO 533/270.

100. Jarvis to Churchill, telegram, 10 October 1921, PRO: CO 536/114.

101. Ibid.

102. Minute by Bottomley, 12 October 1921, on Ibid.

103. Coryndon to Bottomley, private, 15 October 1921, PRO: CO 536/114.

104. Minute by Masterton-Smith, 18 October 1921, on Jarvis to Churchill, telegram, 10 October 1921, PRO: CO 536/114.

105. Minute by Stevenson to Churchill, 18 October 1921, PRO: CO 536/114.

106. Churchill to Jarvis, telegram, 20 October 1921, PRO: CO 533/114.

107. *Parl. Deb.* (Commons), 5th Ser., 147 (1921): 468.

108. A more detailed description of postwar African protest movements is provided in Robert Maxon, "The Years of Revolutionary Advance, 1920–1929," in Ochieng', ed., *A Modern History*, 79–84.

109. No attempt will be made here to extensively examine the emergence of the EAA. An excellent account is provided by Marshall S. Clough. *Fighting Two Sides: Kenyan Chiefs and Politicians, 1918–1940* (Niwot, Col.: University of Colorado Press, 1990), 51–64.

110. Thuku to Churchill, telegram, 13 July 1921, PRO: CO 533/272. The EAA did not follow the "correct" procedure for sending representations to the CO; they were to be sent through the governor.

111. Ibid. Thuku also sent a copy of this telegram to the S of S for India (IO to USSCO, 21 July 1921, PRO: CO 533/267).

112. Minute by Bottomley, 21 July 1921, on IO to USSCO, 21 July 1921, PRO: CO 533/267.

113. Minutes by Parkinson to Bottomley, 2 August 1921, and Bottomley to Wood, 5 August 1921, PRO: CO 533/267.

114. Churchill to Notley, telegram, 12 August 1921, PRO: CO 533/267. W. K. Notley, who had been Acting Chief Secretary and prior to that headed the Kenya Police, acted as governor during Northey's absence. Bowring had gone on leave.

115. Notley to Churchill, confidential, 16 August 1921, PRO: CO 533/262.

116. Minute by Parkinson, 17 September 1921, on Ibid.

117. Minute by Bottomley, 19 September 1921, on Ibid.

118. Northey to Churchill, confidential, 1 October 1921, PRO: CO 533/264.

119. Ibid.

120. Thuku to Mathew Njeroge, 23 December 1921, enclosure in Bowring to Churchill, confidential, 25 January 1922, PRO: CO 533/275.

121. Minute by Bottomley, 6 March 1922, on Ibid.

122. Minute by Read, 6 March 1922, on Ibid.

123. Churchill to Northey, telegram, 8 March 1922, PRO: CO 533/275. The second sentence was added at Read's suggestion. See also Minute by Wood, 6 March 1922, PRO: CO 533/275.

124. Bowring to Churchill, telegram, 16 March 1922, PRO: CO 533/276.

125. Minute by Bottomley, 17 March 1922, on Ibid.

126. Minute by Churchill, 17 March 1922, PRO: CO 533/276.

127. Northey to Churchill, confidential, 27 March 1922, PRO: CO 533/276. Kismayu was then still a part of Kenya; it would later be transferred to Italian Somaliland.

128. Northey to Churchill, confidential, 11 April 1922, PRO: CO 533/276. In addition, several of the governor's justifications for government action must have sounded strange, even then. Northey asserted, for example, that notwithstanding the fact that the police had opened fire without orders, the fact that they ceased firing immediately after the order was given showed they were under control!

129. Minute by Bottomley, 26 May 1922, on Northey to Churchill, confidential, 11 April 1922, PRO: CO 533/276.

130. Minute by Read, 29 May 1922, on Ibid.

131. Churchill to Northey, confidential, 31 May 1922, PRO; CO 533/276.

132. Government of India to Montagu, 21 October 1920, enclosure in IO to USSCO, confidential, 30 April 1921, PRO: CO 533/267. See also Gregory, *India and East Africa*, 197.

133. Northey to Milner, telegram, 17 January 1921, PRO: CO 533/255. As noted in the previous chapter, this was one issue on which Northey sought to make concessions to Indian grievances.

134. Milner to Northey, telegram, 3 February 1921, PRO: CO 533/255.
135. Northey to Milner, telegram, 8 January 1921, PRO: CO 533/255.
136. Read to IO, 22 March 1921, PRO: CO 533/267.
137. Montagu to Amery, 11 March 1921, PRO: CO 533/267.
138. Lytton to Amery, 1 April 1921, PRO: CO 533/267.
139. Minute by Parkinson, 7 April 1921, on Ibid.
140. Minute by Churchill to Fiddes, 21 April 1921, PRO: CO 533/267.
141. Churchill to Montagu, private, 22 April 1921, PRO: CO 533/267.
142. Northey to Churchill, telegram, 23 April 1921, PRO: CO 533/258.
143. Ibid.
144. Minute by Bottomley, 26 April 1921, on Ibid.
145. Minute by Fiddes, 26 April 1921, on Ibid.
146. Churchill to Northey, telegram, secret, 28 April 1921, PRO: CO 533/258.
147. Northey to Churchill, confidential, 14 May 1921; and Northey to Churchill, telegrams, 5 May 1921, and 7 May 1921, PRO: CO 533/259.
148. Minute by Bottomley, 6 May 1921, on Northey to Churchill, telegram, 5 May 1921, PRO: CO 533/259.
149. Northey to Churchill, secret, 14 May 1921, PRO: CO 533/259. This was at least some advance on Northey's advocacy of single Indian member a year before.
150. Ibid. and Northey to Churchill, telegram, 7 May 1921, PRO: CO 533/259.
151. Northey to Churchill, secret, 14 May 1921, PRO: CO 533/259. For obvious reasons, the CO did not sent this account of the Nairobi conference to the IO though it did send the earlier telegrams (Minute by Bottomley, 15 June 1921, on Ibid).
152. Indian Question: Discussion at the IO, 3 May 1921, PRO: CO 533/259.
153. Minute by Bottomley, 9 May 1921, on Northey to Churchill, telegram, 7 May 1921, PRO: CO 533/259.
154. Minute by Wood, 10 May 1921, PRO: CO 533/259.
155. Churchill to Northey, personal and secret, and minute by Wood to Churchill, 13 May 1921, PRO: CO 533/259.
156. Minute by Wood to Churchill, 13 May 1921, PRO: CO 533/259.
157. Minute by Churchill to Wood, 20 May 1921; and Churchill to Northey, telegram, personal and secret, 20 May 1921, PRO: CO 533/259.
158. Bottomley, Indian Affairs in Kenya, 30 May 1291, PRO: CO 533/259.
159. Ibid.
160. Minute by Read, 30 May 1921, PRO: CO 533/259.
161. Northey to Churchill, telegram, secret and personal, 28 May 1921, PRO: CO 533/259.
162. Churchill to Northey, telegram, secret and personal, 6 June 1921, PRO: CO 533/259.
163. Northey to Churchill, telegram, personal and secret, 9 June 1921, PRO: CO 533/260.
164. Northey to Churchill, telegram, 13 June 1921, PRO: CO 533/260. As far as the Indian question was concerned, Northey was later to tell settlers that he had expected to resign over the issue when he left Kenya in July. See Strictly Confidential, Meeting of Legislative Council, Certain Members of Executive Council and Delegates of Convention of Associations with His Excellency, 7 October 1921, Scott Papers, Rhodes House, Oxford, Mss Afr. 578.
165. Northey to Churchill, telegram, 9 July 1921, PRO: CO 533/261. Parkinson reacted strongly to Northey's wire; he saw, and hoped the IO would see that "the real object and danger of this Indian agitation is, as Sir E. Northey has warned us, Indian *predominance* in Kenya. I can imagine nothing more calculated to ruin Kenya and to prejudice the interests of the Arabs and the natives. . . ." (Minute by Parkinson, 11 July 1921, on Northey to Churchill, telegram, 9 July 1921, PRO: CO 533/261).

166. Montagu to Churchill, private, 17 June 1921, in Gilbert, ed., *Companion*, part 3, 1513–16.

167. Indian Congress, Mombasa to Churchill, telegram, 5 July 1921, PRO: CO 533/272; Viceroy to IO, telegram, 7 July 1921, enclosure in IO to USSCO, 21 July 1921, PRO: CO 533/267.

168. Minute by Parkinson, 9 July 1921, on Indian Congress, Mombasa to Churchill, 5 July 1921, PRO: CO 533/272.

169. Read to IO, 27 July 1921, PRO: CO 533/267.

170. Gregory, *India and East Africa*, 181.

171. Proceedings of a Deputation . . . , 9 August 1921, PRO: CO 533/270.

172. Varma and Jeevanjee to Churchill, 11 August 1921, PRO: CO 533/272. Parkinson again strongly dissented from the Indian position. European settlers had understood Elgin's decision as a pledge. He concluded: "I sincerely hope we shall not give way on this point" (Minute by Parkinson, 13 August 1921, on Ibid).

173. Rodwell, Macmillan, and Grogan to Northey, 27 July 1921, PRO: CO 533/274.

174. Macmillan to USSCO, n.d., PRO: CO 533/274; Minute by Churchill, 6 August 1921, PRO: CO 533/274.

175. Notley to Churchill, telegram, 16 August 1921; and Churchill to Notley, telegram, clear the line, 20 August 1921, PRO: CO 533/262.

176. Read to Northey, strictly confidential, 26 August 1921, PRO: CO 533/270.

177. Ibid.

178. Indian Policy in Kenya, enclosure in Read to Northey, strictly confidential, 26 August 1921, PRO: CO 533/270. Northey later took credit for getting Churchill to agree that there should be no change in the franchise during the life of the present Legco (Strictly Confidential Meeting . . . , 7 October 1921, Scott Papers, Rhodes House, Oxford, MSS Afr. 578).

179. Ibid.

180. IO to USSCO, secret, 5 September 1921; and minute by Wood, 8 September 1921, PRO: CO 533/267.

181. Observations of the Secretary of State for India on Indian Policy in Kenya, enclosure in IO to USSCO, secret, 5 September 1921, PRO: CO 533/267.

182. Northey to Churchill, 7 July 1921, PRO: CO 533/261. See also Huxley, *White Man's*, 2: 122.

183. For example, Copy of Cable Received by Major W. M. Crowdy, from Mr. Haslewood, Convention of Associations, left at CO by Northey, 11 August 1921, PRO: CO 533/274.

184. Ibid.

185. Notley to Churchill, telegram, 17 August 1921, PRO: CO 533/262.

186. *Memorandum on the Case Against the Claims of Indians in Kenya* (Nairobi: Swift Press, 1921). Parkinson, not surprisingly given his strong anti-Indian views, felt the pamphlet was "quite a good statement" (Minute by Parkinson, 13 December 1921, PRO: CO 533/271). Bottomley, on the other hand, pointed out many inconsistencies in the document. He was especially doubtful of the Europeans' concern for the African. "There is a large body of opinion here which would ridicule," he wrote in a lengthy minute, "the idea of the Kenya European taking any interest whatsoever in the native except as regards the labour which he can get out of him. European sympathy with the intellectual development of the native is rarely articulate, except when it is a question of countering Indian demands" (Minute by Bottomley, 4 January 1922, PRO: CO 533/271.)

187. Convention of Associations to Lord Stanfordham, 10 November 1921, PRO: CO 533/272.

188. Churchill was obviously growing impatient when in mid-November he won-

dered when the CO was going to hear from Northey (Minute by Churchill to Masterton-Smith, 16 November 1921, PRO: CO 533/264).

189. Northey to Churchill, telegram, 29 November 1921, PRO: CO 533/265.

190. Ibid.

191. Northey to Churchill, confidential, 14 December 1921, PRO; CO 533/265.

192. Minutes by Bottomley, 1 December 1921 and Masterton-Smith, 5 December 1921, on Northey to Churchill, telegram, 29 November 1921, PRO: CO 533/265.

193. Churchill to Montagu, private, 7 December 1921, PRO: CO 533/265.

194. Montagu to Churchill, private, 10 December 1921, PRO: CO 533/265.

195. Churchill to Northey, telegram, 13 December 1921, PRO: CO 533/265.

196. Indian Congress, Nairobi to Churchill, telegram, 24 December 1921, PRO: CO 533/272.

197. Churchill to Northey, telegram, 30 December 1921, PRO: CO 533/272; Northey to Churchill, telegram, 31 December 1921; and Churchill to Northey, telegram, 6 January 1922, PRO: CO 533/265.

198. Minute by Bottomley, 11 January 1922, on IO to USSCO, secret and pressing, 10 January 1922, PRO: CO 533/287; Minute by Masterton-Smith to Bottomley, 12 January 1922, PRO: CO 533/287. One immediate result of the arrival of the European deputation was that the CO decided not to publish the August proposals after all. See Churchill to Northey, telegram, 14 January 1922, PRO: CO 533/287.

199. Memorandum by Bottomley, 20 January 1922, PRO: CO 533/291.

200. Delamere to Churchill, 19 January 1922, PRO: CO 533/291; and minute by Bottomley, 20 January 1922, on Ibid.

201. Indian Policy in Kenya, enclosure in Delamere to Churchill, 19 January 1922, PRO: CO 533/291. A copy of the memo may also be found in Churchill to Montagu, 19 January 1922, PRO: CO 533/288.

202. Ibid. The deputation reluctantly agreed to the provision of land in the Voi-Yatta area for Indian ownership as long as this was not to be "made an excuse for Asiatic immigration."

203. Memo by Bottomley, 20 January 1922, PRO: CO 533/291.

204. Ibid.

205. Minute by Masterton-Smith to Churchill, 23 January 1922, PRO: CO 533/291.

206. Montagu to Churchill, private, 28 January 1922, PRO: CO 533/288.

207. Robert R. James, ed., *Winston S. Churchill His Complete Speeches 1897-1963* (London: Chelsea House Publishers, 1974): 3: 3173. See also Huxley, *White Man's*, 2: 130-31.

208. Viceroy to IO, telegram, 1 February 1922, enclosure in IO to USSCO, 5 February 1922, PRO: CO 533/287; and Jeevanjee to Churchill, 9 February 1922, PRO: CO 533/290.

209. Montagu to Churchill, private, 31 January 1922, in Gilbert, ed., *Companion*, part 3, 1743-47. Churchill's publicly stated reason for going ahead with his announcement without consulting Montagu or the cabinet was rather weak. He told the House of Commons: "An enormous mass of business has to proceed, and decisions have to be taken in every sphere of the administration of the Colonial Office, and cannot be in every case, specifically referred to the cabinet" (*Parl. Deb.* (Commons), 5th Ser., 150 (1922): 798).

210. Churchill to Montagu, private, 1 February 1922, in Gilbert, ed., *Companion*, part 4, 1748. Churchill decided, at the last minute, not to send the lines quoted to Montagu. Yet the fact that he had written them shows the way he was thinking.

211. Churchill to Montagu, private, 2 February 1922, in Gilbert, ed., *Companion*, part 4, 1748; Churchill to Montagu, 4 February 1922, PRO: CO 533/288.

212. Montagu to Churchill, 10 February 1922, PRO: CO 533/288.

213. Cabinet Minutes, 13 February 1922, PRO: CAB 23/29. Churchill's description of the Indian population was hardly true. As Montagu had told him in a private letter the preceding October, this view sounded as if it had come from "an European settler of the most fanatical type" (Montagu to Churchill, private, 12 October 1921, in Gilbert, ed., *Companion*, part 3, 1649).

214. Cabinet Minutes, 13 February 1922, PRO: CAB 23/29.

215. Note by Bottomley, Mr. Montagu's Letter of 28 January, 14 February 1922, PRO: CO 533/288.

216. Minute by Bottomley, 23 February 1922, PRO: CO 533/291.

217. Delamere to Churchill, 20 February 1922, PRO: CO 533/291.

218. Minute by Bottomley, 23 February 1922, PRO: CO 533/291.

219. Minute by Masterton-Smith to Churchill, 24 February 1922, PRO: CO 533/291.

220. Rough Notes of Interview with Indian Delegation, 7 March 1922, PRO: CO 533/290.

221. Minute by Bottomley, 28 March 1922, PRO: CO 533/288.

222. Minute by Wood, 23 March 1922, PRO: CO 533/288.

223. Ibid. Minute by Bottomley, 28 March 1922, PRO: CO 533/288.

224. Minute by Bottomley, 28 March 1922, PRO: CO 533/288. Churchill's reason for favoring the grant of an unofficial majority appears to have been to get the CO off the hook over the Indian question.

225. S. D. Waley, *Edwin Montagu* (New York: Asia Publishing House, 1964), 277. Montagu had put himself in the wrong by authorizing publication of a telegram, without cabinet approval, from the government of India critical of the treaty that had been forced on Turkey.

226. Winterton's was an Irish peerage. Thus he had no seat in the House of Lords, gaining election to the House of Commons instead.

227. For example, IO to CO, 1 May 1922, PRO: CO 533/287.

228. Minute by Wood to Churchill, 14 July 1922, PRO: CO 533/287.

229. As will be seen below, a more important reason had to do with the fact that Kenya's economic crisis had revealed the utter failure of Northey's policy of backing settler production to the total exclusion of that of African peasants.

230. Northey to Churchill, telegram, 10 March 1921; and Churchill to Northey, telegram 16 March 1921, PRO: CO 533/255.

231. Constantine, *The Making*, 73–74.

232. Northey to Churchill, confidential, 13 June 1921, PRO: CO 533/260.

233. Kempe to Northey, 4 July 1921, PRO: CO 533/274. W. A. Kempe was the colony's treasurer.

234. Northey to Churchill, confidential, 13 June 1921, PRO: CO 533/260.

235. Ibid.

236. Northey to Churchill, telegram, 1 July 1921, PRO: CO 533/261.

237. Minute by Batterbee, 6 July 1921, on Ibid.

238. Minute by Batterbee, 1 October 1921, PRO: CO 533/271. The initial interest payments for three years were also met from the loan, thus removing a potential drain on Kenya's revenue.

239. Northey to Churchill, 7 November 1921, PRO: CO 533/264.

240. Northey to Churchill, 15 November 1921, PRO: CO 533/265.

241. Leggett to Masterton-Smith, 26 January 1922, PRO: CO 533/291.

242. Ibid. In Leggett's reckoning, European settlement cost £1,400,00 a year while the settlers' output produced £400,000.

243. Ibid.

244. Minute by Bottomley, 29 January 1922, on Ibid.

245. Minute by Bottomley, 8 February 1922, PRO: CO 533/288.

246. Bottomley, Kenya Expenditure, 8 February 1922, PRO: CO 533/288.

247. Ibid.

248. For example, Kenya employed, because of the sensibilities of the settlers, European postal clerks and police constables. These jobs were held exclusively by Africans in the other colonies.

249. Churchill to Northey, 14 February 1922, PRO: CO 533/288.

250. Ibid.

251. Ibid. The CO also urged that the committee include prominent settlers and traders.

252. *LBEA* (Weekly), 7 January 1922.

253. Minutes of the Execo, 23 February 1922, PRO: CO 544/14.

254. *LBEA* (Weekly), 4 March 1922.

255. Minutes of the Execo, 9 March 1922, PRO: CO 544/14. Though Bennett saw in inclusion of unofficials a victory for the settlers, such was not really the case as the CO advocated unofficial membership (Bennett, *Political History*, 47).

256. *LBEA* (Weekly), 25 March and 1 April 1922.

257. Lord Delamere, Memorandum on Income Tax in Kenya, enclosure in Delamere to Masterton-Smith, 1 March 1922, PRO: CO 533/291. Delamere also called for a reduction in African taxation. It is difficult, and it was for CO officials, to accept the sincerity of this proposal. It seems to have been raised so as to deflect criticism of Delamere's advocacy of income tax abolition. Huxley, in her biography of Delamere, mentions, with approval, Delamere's advocacy of a cut in African taxation, but she does not make clear that Delamere linked this with the abolition, not a reduction in rate, of income tax (Huxley, *White Man's*, 2: 104).

258. Minute by Batterbee, 17 March 1922, on Delamere, Memorandum on Income Tax, PRO: CO 533/291. Batterbee had served as private secretary to S of S Long until the latter left office in early 1919.

259. Ibid.

260. Minutes by Bottomley, 18 March 1922, and Read, 20 March 1922, on Ibid. It can not have escaped the notice of the three officials, moreover, that colonies such as the Gold Coast and Nigeria, where there were no settlers, produced more in the way of exports than Kenya.

261. Wedgwood to Wood, 29 March 1922, PRO: CO 533/291.

262. Leggett to Wedgwood, 28 March 1922, enclosure in Ibid.

263. Ibid. During 1922, another merchant capitalist, Sir Sydney Henn, found during a tour of EA that most European businessmen and bankers there felt that the future lay with the development of African production rather than settler (Brett, *Colonialism*, 179).

264. Minute by Batterbee, 6 April 1922, on Ibid. See also Ian Spencer, "Origins of the Dual Policy," 742.

265. Minute by Bottomley, 7 April 1922, on Leggett to Wedgwood, 28 March 1922, PRO: CO 533/291. As noted above, the company had been unable to turn a profit in 1921–22.

266. Minute by Batterbee, 13 April 1922, PRO: CO 533/291.

267. Ibid.

268. Ormsby-Gore to Wood, 25 March 1922, PRO: CO 533/287.

269. The 12 per cent figure for 1922 does not, of course, include maize. Maize exports shot up in 1922 and 1923 in response to the recommendations of the Bowring Committee; African maize exports undoubtedly amounted to 8 or 9 per cent of total exports, bringing the African share to 20 or 21 per cent rather than 12 per cent.

270. Colony and Protectorate of Kenya, *Economic and Financial Committee Report*

of Proceedings During 1922 (Nairobi: Government Printer, 1923), 38–39. Acting Director of Agriculture E. Harrison prepared a report on European and African agricultural production from mid-1921 to mid-1922 for the committee. Although it provided only an estimate of African production, Harrison's report suggested that at a time when the African share of agricultural exports (not including hides and skins) made up only 18 per cent of the total, African peasants contributed 66 per cent of total production.

271. Northey to Churchill, telegram, 15 April 1922, PRO: CO 533/277.

272. Minute by Bottomley, 18 April 1922, on Ibid; Churchill to Northey, telegram, 25 April 1922, PRO: CO 533/277.

273. Minute by Bottomley, 15 April 1922, PRO: CO 533/287. This line of thought was later incorporated by Batterbee into a memorandum for the House of Lords debate. See Batterbee, Memorandum on House of Lords Debate, 27 April 1922, PRO: CO 533/287.

274. Leggett to Bottomley, 27 April 1922, PRO: CO 533/291. Leggett enclosed a copy of a report on the British East Africa Corporation's annual general meeting where the former had made public his criticism of Kenya policy. See also Ian Spencer, "Origins of the Dual Policy," 742.

275. Lord Hindlip's motion drew the government's attention "to the taxation of the native population and products in the Kenya Colony and in Uganda and to its effect on trade with Great Britain" (*Parl. Deb.* (Lords), 5th Ser., 50 (1922): 354).

276. Ian Spencer, "Origins of the Dual Policy," 743; *Parl. Deb.* (Lords),5th Ser., 50 (1922): 363–69.

277. Christopher Youe's treatment of this draft despatch completely misses the context in which it was prepared. He sees the "raison d'etre" for the memo as "the search for a general native policy in East Africa as a whole." See Christopher P. Youe, *Robert Thorne Coryndon: Proconsular Imperialism in Southern and Eastern Africa, 1897–1925* (Waterloo: Wilfred Laurier University Press, 1986), 193–94.

278. Churchill to Northey, draft despatch, June 1922, PRO: CO 533/287. Nor was the CO alone in recognizing this. A mid-May report from *The Times* correspondent in Nairobi spoke of African unrest and the need for a new African policy (*The Times*, 16 May 1922).

279. It is thus difficult to agree with Diana Wylie's assessment that "until the 1940s officials scarcely referred to the growth of African or Indian nationalism as justification for reform." African protest and Kenya's economic situation were far more important, in fact, than the need to "avoid Parliamentary criticism" (Wylie, "Confrontation Over Kenya," 446).

280. Churchill to Northey, draft despatch, June 1922, PRO: CO 533/287. By the time the memorandum had been prepared, moreover, the CO had received further criticism from British capitalists with interests in EA. The Federation of British Industries criticized taxation in Kenya as being too high. This diminished the purchasing power of the African population "and consequently restricts the demand for British goods" and discouraged African production, thereby running the risk of "permanently impairing the exporting capacity of the colonies." Wood met with a deputation representing the federation on 14 June (Director, Federation of British Industries to Churchill, 1 June 1922, PRO: CO 533/290).

281. *Parl. Deb.* (Commons), 5th Ser., 156 (1922): 230.

282. As Bottomley later explained, Wood "had not finally decided what should be done when the change of Government took place" (Minute by Bottomley, 23 December 1922, PRO: CO 533/289). As will be seen, there would be no need to convince Northey's successor of the need to stimulate African production for export.

283. Resolution #1, Economic and Finance Committee, enclosure in Northey to Churchill, 10 July 1922, PRO: CO 533/279.

284. Northey to Churchill, telegram, urgent, 10 May 1922, PRO: 533/277.

285. Minute by Batterbee, 13 May 1922, on Ibid.

286. Churchill to Northey, telegram, urgent, 15 May 1922, PRO: CO 533/277.

287. Northey to Churchill, telegram, urgent, 17 May 1922, PRO: CO 533/277.

288. Holm's part in this episode would have an interesting postscript. On 29 June Northey wrote to the CO to propose Holm's retirement. Acting on the advise of the Bowring Committee, the governor claimed that Kenya could not afford to pay Holm's high salary. It had also been decided to reallocate some department resources so as to help stimulate African production. Since Holm had not taken part in that readjustment, and would probably oppose it, Northey urged his removal from Kenya on that ground as well (Northey to Churchill, confidential, 29 June 1922, PRO: CO 533/278). The timing of this recommendation, however, makes it difficult not to suspect that the governor's attitude was the result of his feeling that Holm must have given the CO information that had led them to scuttle his wheat import duties. The CO refused to countenance the retirement of Holm, and he returned to head the department of agriculture for the rest of the decade.

289. Minute by Batterbee, 19 May 1922, on Northey to Churchill, telegram, urgent, 17 May 1922, PRO: CO 533/277.

290. Ibid.

291. Lord Delamere was the major shareholder in the Unga Ltd. milling company at this time. See Franklin to Read, personal, 27 May 1922, PRO: CO 533/277; also Huxley, *White Man's*, 2: 106.

292. Churchill to Northey, telegram, urgent, 24 May 1922, PRO: CO 533/277.

293. Minutes of the Execo, 13 May 1922, PRO: CO 544/14.

294. When he telegraphed on 23 May, Northey only told the CO that he was introducing legislation imposing higher customs duties "as proposed equal to estimate of revenue from income tax which will be simultaneously repealed" (Northey to Churchill, telegram, 23 May 1922, PRO: CO 533/277). The CO had already given its approval to the repeal of the income tax ordinance. See Churchill to Northey, telegram, 16 May 1922, PRO: CO 533/277.

295. Northey to Churchill, telegram, 25 May 1922, PRO: CO 533/277. Those who voted against were the two Indian members and W. M. Ross.

296. Minute by Bottomley, 26 May 1922, on Northey to Churchill, telegram, 25 May 1922, PRO: CO 533/277.

297. Churchill to Northey, telegram, clear the line, 31 May 1922, PRO: CO 533/277.

298. Northey to Churchill, 16 June 1922, PRO: CO 533/278.

299. Bruce Berman states, in an endnote, that Northey was dismissed "after it was discovered he had secretly purchased shares in a local sisal plantation" (Berman, *Control & Crisis*, 117–18). No source or supporting documentation is provided for this allegation. While it may indeed have been the case that Northey had made such a purchase, the more likely reasons for his ouster are those given above.

300. Northey to Churchill, telegram, 25 July 1922, PRO: CO 533/280.

301. Ibid.

302. Masterton-Smith to Churchill, secret, 27 July 1922, PRO: CO 533/289.

303. Churchill to Northey, telegram, personal and private, 28 July 1922, PRO: CO 533/280.

304. At the close of his secret minute to Churchill on 27 July, Masterton Smith wrote in hand: "Sir R. Coryndon is just the man to tackle the Indian question and to reduce expenditure" (Masterton-Smith to Churchill, secret, 28 July 1922, PRO: CO 533/289).

305. Minute by Masterton-Smith, 1 August 1922, PRO: CO 533/289; Churchill to Coryndon, telegram, private and personal, 1 August 1922, PRO: CO 533/289.

306. Eliot to Churchill, telegram, clear the line, 6 August 1922, PRO: CO 533/289. Since the telegram of 1 August had been private and personal deputy governor Eliot had not opened it. The CO responded to the delay by ordering him to personally decipher the telegram and transmit its contents to Coryndon (Churchill to Eliot, telegram, confidential, clear the line, 3 August 1922, PRO: CO 533/289).

307. Northey to Churchill, telegrams, 1 August 1922, PRO: CO 533/280.

308. Churchill to Northey, telegram, 15 August 1922, PRO: CO 533/280.

309. *EAS* (Weekly), 15 August 1922.

310. The *EAS* headline read: "EDWARD NORTHEY RE-CALLED. Astounding Action by Colonial Office." Ibid.

311. After Northey's return to Britain in mid-September, Churchill did go to some length to salve the former governor's feelings and, perhaps, keep him quiet. Following a meeting with Northey on 5 October, the S of S recommended that the king promote him to Knight Grand Cross in the Order of Saint Michael and Saint George, and Churchill ordered a letter written to the War Office urging that Northey's "claims for further military employment may receive the full and sympathetic consideration of the Secretary of State for War" (Masterton-Smith to Read, secret, 6 October 1922, PRO: CO 533/289).

312. Northey to Churchill, confidential, 10 July 1922, PRO: CO 533/279.

Chapter 7. The CO Takes Control, 1922–23

1. Colony and Protectorate of Kenya, *Staff List July 1923* (Nairobi: Government Printer, 1923), 1.

2. Youe, *Coryndon*, 140–42.

3. Ibid., 7–121.

4. Ibid., 152–55. In addition to the currency question, which is not mentioned by Youe, Coryndon disagreed with Northey over the administration of the pastoral peoples in northwestern Kenya/northeastern Uganda and, most significantly, over the management of the Uganda Railway.

5. Huxley, *White Man's*, 2: 132.

6. Coryndon to Churchill, draft letter, n.d. but probably composed 6 or 7 September 1922, Coryndon Papers, Rhodes House, Oxford, Mss Afrs 633.

7. There was no thought of utilizing Indians as producers. The CO would therefore not soften its stand on exclusion of Indians from the highlands.

8. Minute by Wood to Churchill thru Masterton-Smith, secret, 14 July 1922, PRO: CO 533/289.

9. Joint Memorandum by Wood and Winterton, 14 July 1922, PRO: CO 533/289. This definition enabled the enfranchisement of Africans. It was intended to keep the qualifications high enough so that not more than a handful would qualify. Subsequent quotes are from this source.

10. Minute by Churchill to Wood, 18 July 1922, PRO: CO 533/289.

11. Minute by Wood to Churchill thru Masterton-Smith, 26 July 1922, PRO: CO 533/289. The concessions were 10 per cent of the Indian population as the size of the electorate, leaving Europeans a majority of the elective seats, and leaving the highlands question alone for the time being.

12. Minute by Bottomley, 22 September 1922, on Coryndon to Churchill, telegram, immediate, confidential, clear the line, 21 September 1922, PRO: CO 533/282.

13. Minute by Wood to Churchill thru Masterton-Smith, 26 July 1922, PRO: CO 533/289.

14. Minute by Wood to Churchill, 3 August 1922, PRO: CO 533/289. When presented with the proposals, the settlers definitely did not see in them the same message as they had read into Churchill's January speech (Huxley, *White Man's*, 2: 132–33).

15. Minute by Churchill to Wood, 4 August 1922, PRO: CO 533/289.

16. Read to Kershaw, secret, 9 August 1922, PRO: CO 533/289. In somewhat of an understatement, Read observed that it was best to wait as Northey "would not be in a mood to handle the matter."

17. For example, Bottomley to Kershaw, secret, 23 August 1922, PRO: CO 533/289.

18. Minute by Batterbee, 4 September 1922, on Kershaw to Bottomley, secret 29 August 1922, PRO: CO 533/287; IO to Viceroy, telegram, 31 August 1922, PRO: CO 533/287.

19. Churchill to Coryndon, telegram, confidential, 5 September 1922, PRO: CO 533/287.

20. Viceroy to Peel, telegram, 11 September 1922, enclosure in Kershaw to Batterbee, September 1922, PRO: CO 533/287.

21. Coryndon to Churchill, telegram, immediate, confidential, clear the line, 21 September 1922, PRO: CO 533/282. Subsequent quotes are from this source.

22. Youe, *Coryndon*, 144.

23. Ibid., 144–45.

24. This grave concern could not have fooled anyone in the CO. Coryndon also mistitled the EAINC in his telegram (Coryndon to Churchill, telegram, immediate, confidential, clear the line, 21 September 1922, PRO: CO 533/282).

25. Minute by Bottomley, 22 September 1922, on Coryndon to Churchill, telegram, immediate, confidential, clear the line, 21 September 1922, PRO: CO 533/282.

26. Minute by Read, 22 September 1922, on Ibid.

27. Coryndon to Churchill, telegram, clear the line, personal, 23 September 1922, PRO: CO 533/282. As to this latter idea, Bottomley minuted: "I venture to think that the difficulty is not so much lack of appreciation here of Europeans' standpoint as the failure locally to realize the difficulty of the question from the Imperial standpoint" (Minute by Bottomley, 25 September 1922).

28. Minute by Masterton-Smith to Churchill, 27 September 1922, PRO: CO 533/282.

29. Churchill to Coryndon, telegram, private and personal, 29 September 1922, and Read to Kershaw, secret, 29 September 1922, PRO: CO 533/282.

30. *Parl.Deb.* (Commons), 5th Ser., 156 (1922): 255.

31. Bottomley, Indians in Kenya, 6 November 1922, PRO: CO 533/289.

32. Minutes by Bottomley, 22 November 1922, and Ormsby-Gore, 23 November 1922, PRO: CO 533/289. The latter recognized that his threat was drastic but that "it would not be without advantages from an African as well as an Indian point of view."

33. Peel to Devonshire, 29 November 1922, PRO: CO 533/289. Peel concluded by contrasting the reluctant willingness of the government of India to accept the Wood-Winterton proposals with the attitude of the Kenya colonial state that "ignoring the substantial safeguards provided, shews little disposition to compromise on essential points and seems indeed to accept as necessarily decisive the foreboding of the anti-Indian party in Kenya."

34. Minute by Masterton-Smith to Devonshire, 2 December 1922, PRO: CO 533/289.

35. Minute by Devonshire, 8 December 1922, PRO: CO 533/289.

36. Masterton-Smith to Winterton, secret, 12 December 1922, PRO: CO 533/289; Peel to Devonshire, personal and secret, 13 December 1922, PRO: CO 533/289.

37. Devonshire to Coryndon, confidential, 14 December 1922, PRO: CO 533/289.

38. Ibid. The despatch stated: "It should definitely be understood that in my opinion the grant of responsible Government to Kenya will in the special circumstances of the Colony be out of the question within any period of time which we need take into consideration." As will be seen, this continued to be the CO line.

39. Devonshire to Coryndon, confidential, 14 December 1922, PRO: CO 533/289,

40. Devonshire to Coryndon, secret, 14 December 1922, PRO: CO 533/289.

41. Polak to USSCO, 9 January 1923, and Indian Congress to Devonshire, telegram, 5 January 1923, PRO: CO 533/305.

42. Devonshire to Coryndon, telegram, 10 January 1923, PRO: CO 533/305; Minutes by Bottomley, 8 January 1923 on Indian Congress to Devonshire, telegram, 5 January 1923 and 10 January 1923, on Polak to USSCO, 9 January 1923, PRO: CO 533/305.

43. The Indian Question During the Governorship of Sir Robert Coryndon, Coryndon Papers, Rhodes House, Mss. Afrs. 633.

44. Memo by E. A. Dutton, 11 January 1923, Coryndon Papers, Rhodes House, Oxford, MSS Afrs 633. The same could certainly be said of Dutton's reading of the despatches. The CO made it very clear that there would be no settler political control in the foreseeable future. Dutton and Coryndon reacted, over the next two months, as if they had not read that part of the despatch.

45. Ibid.

46. Coryndon to Devonshire, telegram, 11 January 1923, PRO: CO 533/292.

47. Minute by Bottomley, 12 January 1923, on Ibid.

48. Minute by Read, 12 January 1923, on Ibid.

49. Coryndon to Devonshire, telegram, 15 January 1923, PRO: CO 533/292.

50. Ibid.

51. Coryndon to Masterton-Smith, telegram, private and personal, 15 January 1923, PRO: CO 533/292.

52. Coryndon to Masterton-Smith, 18 January 1923, Coryndon Papers, Rhodes House, Oxford, Mss Afrs. 633. After a personal meeting, Coryndon recognized that Ormsby-Gore's position on Kenya did not necessarily differ dramatically from his own. Ormsby-Gore, for his part, continued to harbor little respect for the Kenya settlers. He told Coryndon the following year that "your policy of encouraging native production is a new policy as far as Kenya is concerned and the reason why I am unpopular with the white settlers—and must be—is because I advocated such a policy in Northey's time when the settlers had it all their own way with the Colonial Government, and thought that cheap wage labour on European plantations would enable the colony to pay its way. All I said was that such an economic policy in Africa and for Africa is not likely to be successful in the long run" (Ormsby-Gore to Coryndon, 5 May 1924, Coryndon Papers, Rhodes House, Oxford, MSS Afrs 633).

53. Minute by Bottomley, 17 January 1923, on Coryndon to Devonshire, telegram, 15 January 1923, PRO: CO 533/292.

54. Minute by Read, 17 January 1923, on Ibid.

55. Masterton-Smith to Coryndon, telegram, secret, 18 January 1923, PRO: CO 533/292.

56. Devonshire to Coryndon, telegram, 18 January 1923, PRO: CO 533/292.

57. Coryndon to Devonshire, telegram, clear the line, 23 January 1923, PRO: CO 533/292.

58. Peel to Masterton-Smith, 25 January 1923, PRO: CO 533/292.

59. Devonshire to Coryndon, telegram, clear the line, 25 January 1923, PRO: CO 533/292.

60. In his treatment of the issue, for example, Youe lays stress on Coryndon's own great opposition to the Wood-Winterton proposals (Youe, *Coryndon*, 170).

61. Coryndon to Devonshire, telegram, 27 January 1923, PRO: CO 533/292.

62. The initial CO response was not, however, very sympathetic. Bottomley characterized Coryndon's attitude as "an unfortunate position for a Governor to take up" (Minute by Bottomley, 29 January 1923, on Ibid).

63. The Indian Question During the Governorship . . . , Coryndon Papers, Rhodes House, Oxford, MSS Afrs 633.

64. Coryndon to Devonshire, telegram, 1 February 1923, PRO: CO 533/293.

65. Ibid.

66. Coryndon to Masterton-Smith, telegram, personal, 2 February 1923, PRO: CO 533/293. Realizing, no doubt, that the terms the settlers proposed would provoke strong opposition from the IO, Coryndon suggested a modification of one important term. He would allow the immigrant, rather than the immigration officer, to choose the European language in which the individual seeking entry to Kenya would be examined.

67. Devonshire to Coryndon, telegram, 2 February 1923, PRO: CO 533/293.

68. Coryndon to Devonshire, telegram, personal and secret, 3 February 1923, PRO: CO 533/293.

69. Ibid.

70. Ibid. It is Youe's view that by this time the governor had begun "to exaggerate the danger of settler rebellion in his correspondence with Whitehall superiors." See Christopher P. Youe, "The Threat of Settler Rebellion and the Imperial Predicament: The Denial of Indian Rights in Kenya, 1923," *Canadian Journal of History* 12 (1978): 358. The most complete account of the settler plans for rebellion is provided by C. J. D. Duder, "The Settler Response to the Indian Crisis of 1923 in Kenya: Brigadier-General Philip Wheatley and 'Direct Action'," *JICH* 17 (1989) 360–63. Like Duder, Atieno Odhiambo based his account of the settler plans for rebellion on the Wheatley papers, but, unlike the former, concluded that the planned rebellion was a successful bluff (Atieno Odhiambo, *Siasa*, 65–66).

71. Minute by Bottomley, 6 February 1923, on Coryndon to Devonshire, telegram, personal and secret, 3 February 1923, PRO: CO 533/293.

72. Draft memo for cabinet, Indians in Kenya, 8 February 1923, PRO: CO 533/303. Subsequent quotes are from this source.

73. Minute by Devonshire, 10 February 1923, PRO: CO 533/303.

74. Minute by Bottomley to Masterton-Smith, 12 February 1923, PRO: CO 533/303.

75. Coryndon to Devonshire, telegram, clear the line, 8 February 1923, PRO: CO 533/293.

76. Minute by Bottomley, 12 February 1923, on Ibid.

77. Devonshire to Coryndon, telegram, clear the line, 9 February 1923, PRO: CO 533/293.

78. Devonshire to Coryndon, telegram, personal and secret, 9 February, PRO: CO 533/293.

79. Ibid.

80. Coryndon to Devonshire, telegram, 9 February 1923, PRO: CO 533/293.

81. Minute by Masterton-Smith, 12 February 1923, on Ibid.

82. Coryndon to Devonshire, telegram, secret and personal, 12 February 1923, PRO: CO 533/293. Subsequent quotes are from this source.

83. He offered, moreover, the interesting ploy of withholding his assent, once the bill was passed, until a settlement on all issues was reached.

84. Devonshire to Coryndon, telegram, secret and personal, 16 February 1923, PRO: CO 533/293. This demand was prefaced with pointed observations that only H. M.'s Government was charged with "the interests of the natives" and that "Euro-

4 STRUGGLE FOR KENYA

peans in Kenya appear incidentally to be singularly ill informed about the status and political privileges which Indian British subjects in other British colonies . . . possess."

. Coryndon to Devonshire, telegram, 19 February 1923, PRO: CO 533/293.
86. Ibid.
87. Minutes of a Conference on Indian Policy in Kenya held in the S of S's room . . . , February 21, 1923, PRO: CO 533/293. Subsequent quotes are from this source. See also Jidlaph G. Kamoche, *Imperial Trusteeship and Political Evolution in Kenya, 1923–1963* (Washington: University Press of America), 29–30, 34.
88. This is, in fact, what happened some five months later.
89. Minute by Masterton-Smith, 27 February 1923, on Minutes of a Conference . . . , February 21, 1923, PRO: CO 533/293.
90. Those authorities, such as Robinson, Gregory, Bennett, and Cell, who have seen the support for African interests as inspired by J. H. Oldham and the Archbishop of Canterbury, have overlooked this conference and failed to appreciate its impact on subsequent events.
91. Devonshire to Coryndon, telegram, 23 February 1923, PRO: CO 533/293.
92. The Indian Question During the Governorship of Sir Robert Coryndon, Coryndon Papers, Rhodes House, Oxford, MSS Afrs 633; *The Kenya Observer* (Weekly), 3 March 1923. The press was not allowed to record the governor's exact words.
93. Draft Resolution, Coryndon Papers, Rhodes House, Oxford, MSS Afrs 633; Coryndon to Devonshire, telegram, 28 February 1923, PRO: CO 533/293.
94. Coryndon to Devonshire, telegram, 28 February 1923, PRO: CO 533/293.
95. *The Kenya Observer* (Weekly), 31 March 1923. The missionary representative was Dr. J. W. Arthur. The latter was strongly anti-Indian. See B. G. McIntosh, "Kenya 1923: the Political Crisis and the Missionary Dilemma," *Transafrican Journal of History* 1 (1971): 106–8.
96. Youe, *Coryndon*, 174–75.
97. Minutes of the Meeting of the Execo, 14 October 1922, PRO: CO 544/14.
98. Economic and Finance Committee Resolution 117, 9 October 1922, enclosure in Coryndon to Devonshire, confidential, 30 October 1922, PRO: CO 533/283. The proposed reduction would take effect only at the occasion of the post being vacated by its current holder.
99. Bowring to Devonshire, confidential, 23 November 1922, PRO: CO 533/284.
100. Ibid.
101. Coryndon to Devonshire, confidential, 12 December 1922, PRO: CO 533/284.
102. Youe, *Coryndon*, 177.
103. Henn cooperated with Ormsby-Gore in establishing a Joint East Africa Board in 1923. The purpose of the board was to provide a means for British capitalists with interests in EA of approaching the CO on a regular basis. It was only finalized in June 1923, however, and had little impact on the settlement of the Indian question (Brett, *Colonialism*, 63).
104. Coryndon to Henn, 2 May 1923, Coryndon Papers, Rhodes House, Oxford, MSS Afrs 715.
105. Cutting from *The Morning Post*, 15 June 1923, Coryndon Papers, Rhodes House, Oxford, MSS Afrs 633.
106. Forty-eight per cent of all maize exports during the period had their origin in Kisumu (Proceedings of Maize Conference, April 1923, enclosure in Coryndon to Devonshire, 11 September 1923, PRO: CO 533/297).
107. Ormsby-Gore to Coryndon, 5 May 1924, Coryndon Papers, Rhodes House, Oxford, MSS Afrs 633.

108. Maxon, "The Years," 90–92.

109. Minute by Bottomley, 23 December 1922, PRO: CO 533/289.

110. Devonshire to Coryndon, 9 January 1923, PRO: CO 533/289.

111. Native Affairs in East Africa, enclosure in Ibid. Subsequent quotes are from this source.

112. This would not be the policy in Kenya, however, for many years to come.

113. It will be recalled that the IO had given reluctant approval to the CO's scheme for solution to the controversy in February. Detailed accounts of the European and Indian deputations' experiences in Britain have been provided by Elspeth Huxley and Robert Gregory respectively. I have tried, therefore, to concentrate on the CO and its attitudes during the period of negotiations in Britain. This account takes as its starting point the fact that the CO recognized that the Indians and settlers could not be brought to agree on any comprehensive settlement of the issues in dispute. Such a settlement would have to be decided and announced by the CO.

114. Ainsworth to Bottomley, 19 March 1923, PRO: CO 533/306. Ainsworth's proposal was the most liberal of all those who suggested ways out of the controversy to the CO. He advocated "a common franchise devoid of all colour prejudice." This meant giving the vote to Africans who would eventually, and rightly in Ainsworth's view, become the majority of voters. Bottomley felt that this was going way too far (Minute by Bottomley, 21 March 1923, on Ainsworth to Bottomley, 19 March 1923, PRO: CO 533/306). See also Ainsworth to Bottomley, 9 April 1923, PRO: CO 533/306.

115. Lugard to Ormsby-Gore, 27 May 1923, PRO: CO 533/307. Like Ainsworth, Lugard felt that giving the settlers political power would create "the worst form of oligarchy."

116. White and Frazer to Devonshire, 19 March 1923, PRO: CO 533/305.

117. Leggett to Marsh, 1 June 1923, PRO: CO 533/307. E. Marsh had been Churchill's private secretary. He continued to perform that task for Devonshire. Leggett, on economic grounds, favored a federation or at least a common policy for all British dependencies in Eastern Africa.

118. A Short Statement of the Kenya Colony Situation issued by The Indians Overseas Association in Polak to USSCO, 27 April 1923, PRO: CO 533/305. CO officials recognized the importance of this statement by underlining the sentence.

119. Minutes by Parkinson, 26 April 1923 and Bottomley, 26 April 1923, PRO: CO 533/303.

120. Minute by Bottomley, 28 April 1923, PRO: CO 533/303. Bottomley's basic idea that "by training the African and making the Indians supervisors," Indians would eased out of EA. The idea had been suggested to him by officials with long Nyasaland experience.

121. Memorandum on the Kenya Situation by the Kenya Indian Delegation, enclosure in Varma to Devonshire, 22 May 1923, PRO: CO 533/305.

122. Minute by Bottomley, 25 May 1923, on Ibid.

123. Ibid.

124. Gregory, *India and East Africa*, 238.

125. Ibid. See also Minutes by Read, 25 May 1923, and Masterton-Smith, 30 May 1923, on Varma to Devonshire, 22 May 1923, PRO: CO 533/305.

126. This interpretation seems first to have been suggested first by Roland Oliver (Oliver, *Missionary Factor*, 260–62). The first edition of Oliver's book appeared in 1952. George Bennett claimed, in 1960, that Oldham was "the real father of the paramountcy declaration," but he presented no evidence to support that assertion. See George Bennett, "Paramountcy to Partnership: J. H. Oldham and Africa," *Africa* 30 (1960): 357. See also Ronald Robinson, "The Moral Disarmament of African

Empire," *JICH* 8 (1979): 92; Bennett, "Settlers and Politics," 299; Cell, ed., *By Kenya*, 50.

127. Oliver, *Missionary Factor*, 260; Leon P. Spencer, "Christian Missions and African Interests in Kenya, 1905–1924," (Ph. D. diss., Syracuse U., 1974), 455–56.

128. L. Spencer, "Missions," 459–60. Andrews enjoyed the confidence of Gandhi; Sastri was an ally of the nationalist leader on a number of, but not all, political issues.

129. Oldham to Leys, 9 May 1923 in Cell, ed., *By Kenya*, 219; Spencer, "Missions," 461.

130. Spencer, "Missions," 463.

131. Ibid. See also Archbishop of Canterbury to Devonshire, 29 May 1923, PRO: CO 533/305; Oliver, *Missionary Factor*, 261.

132. Minutes by Parkinson, 2 June 1923 and Bottomley, 4 June 1923, on Archbishop of Canterbury to Devonshire, 29 May 1923, PRO: CO 533/305.

133. Minute by Masterton-Smith, 13 June 1923, on Ibid; and Oldham to Masterton-Smith, 11 June 1923, PRO: CO 533/303.

134. Oldham to Masterton-Smith, personal, 1 June 1923, PRO: CO 533/303.

135. Andrews to Masterton-Smith, 6 June 1923, PRO: CO 533/303.

136. Oldham to Masterton-Smith, 11 June 1923, PRO: CO 533/303.

137. Oldham to Masterton-Smith, 11 June 1923, PRO: CO 533/303.

138. Ibid. In this judgment, nevertheless, Oldham appears to have been mistaken to some degree. After the announcement of the settlement, Andrews expressed strong dislike for the grant of superior electoral rights to the settlers. "The mere declaration that native interests are paramount," he told the archbishop, "is of no use in the world if you go and make European interests paramount in practice. . . ." Quoted in L. Spencer, "Missions," 469.

139. Oldham to Masterton-Smith, 11 June 1923, PRO: CO 533/303. Oldham actually suggested that two missionaries should be appointed to the Legco to represent Africans. Oldham's suggestion to go to a nominated Legco suggests yet again that he did not provide the CO with the policy statement or the ideas that lay behind the white paper of July 1923.

140. Oldham to Masterton-Smith, private, 15 June 1923, PRO: CO 533/303.

141. Gregory, *India and East Africa*, 237.

142. This, in a sense, is surprising as Coryndon, aided by Dutton, had "gathered as much anti-Indian material as he could to strengthen the European hand" (Youe, *Coryndon*, 171).

143. Coryndon to Ormsby-Gore, 15 July 1923, Coryndon Papers, Rhodes House, Oxford, MSS Afrs 633. Oldham must be credited, however, with doing much of the initial persuasion so far as Sastri was concerned also.

144. Delamere to Devonshire, 16 July 1923, PRO: CO 533/306. He wrote: "The right of India or anyone else to demand to share that trusteeship can not be admitted." He thus effectively cut the ground from under future settler claims to control of Kenya. Yet Duder maintains that the settlers demonstrated considerable political skills during the 1923 crisis (Duder, "The Settler Response," 369–70).

145. British banks operating in EA were not involved. Despite Brett's assumption that they "no doubt had something to say to H.M.G. before the final decision was made," there are no records of any approaches by the banks in finalizing a solution to the Indian question (Brett, *Colonialism*, 180).

146. The choice of title for the policy announcement was very much in line with previous CO treatment of the issue. In November 1922 and February 1923, it will be recalled, Bottomley had produced memoranda setting out at length the background and dimensions of the controversy. On both occasions, he titled the document *Indians in Kenya*. The 1923 title was thus very much a product of past CO treatment of the

question, just as was the settlement announced rather than being formulated for the CO by Oldham. See Bottomley, Indians in Kenya, 6 November 1922, CO 533/289; Bottomley, Indians in Kenya, draft memorandum for Cabinet, 8 February 1923, CO 533/303.

147. Meeting of Cabinet, 23 July 1923, Cabinet Papers, PRO: CAB 23/46; also in PRO: CO 533/303.

148. Devonshire to Bowring, telegram, 24 July 1923, PRO: CO 533/303. This led to one last bit of drama as almost a week passed before Bowring acknowledged the CO wire. This silence provoked sufficient concern at the CO to cause telegrams to be sent to Tanganyika and Zanzibar to ask "for information regarding events in Kenya since decisions on Indian question were published." Both replied that all was quiet in Kenya. See Devonshire to Byatt and Acting High Commissioner, Zanzibar, telegram, urgent and secret, 27 July 1923, PRO: CO 533/303; and Byatt to Devonshire, telegram, clear the line, 28 July 1923 and Acting High Commissioner to Devonshire, telegram, secret and urgent, 28 July 1923, PRO: CO 533/303.

149. Great Britain, *Indians in Kenya*, Cmd. 1922 (London: HMSO, 1923), 10.

150. Ibid., 11.

151. Ibid., 14.

152. Ibid., 15.

153. Ibid., 17.

154. Ibid., 18.

155. Gregory, *India and East Africa*, 249–58.

156. Atieno Odhiambo ("'Trust' Principle in Kenya," 104) is one of the few scholars to grasp this essential point. See also Atieno Odhiambo, *Siasa*, 18 and 27. The most detailed analysis of the declaration is provided by Kamoche. More concerned with the white paper's impact on future imperial policy, he completely overlooks the economic factors that lay behind the CO's policy declaration (Kamoche, *Imperial Trusteeship*, 49–80).

157. Devonshire to Bowring, 9 August 1923, PRO: CO 533/303.

158. Robinson, "Moral Disarmament," 93; Youe, "The Threat," 360.

Bibliography

Primary Sources

The major source for this study of imperial policy is the CO 533 series located at the Public Record Office in London. Specific references for these files of correspondence may be found in the notes.

Manuscripts and Private Papers

Manuscripts: Great Britain, Public Record Office, Colonial Office Archives, London.
CO 533/100–309, Original Correspondence, Kenya.
CO 544/14, Minutes of the Executive Council 1912–23.
Manuscripts: Rhodes House, Oxford University.
Coryndon Papers Afrs. 633.
Sir Edward Denham's Diaries Mss Brit. Emp. 212.
Girouard Papers Afrs. 1865.
Lord Francis Scott Papers Afr. 578.
McGregor Ross Papers Afrs. 1178.
Manuscripts: Bodleian Library, Oxford.
Papers of Lewis Harcourt 442, 444, 445, 466, 467, 470, 495, 497, 518.

Government publications

COLONY AND PROTECTORATE OF KENYA

Department of Agriculture Report 1924. Nairobi: Government Printer, 1925.
Economic and Financial Committee Report of Proceedings During 1922. Nairobi: Government Printer, 1923.
Land Tenure Commission Report. Nairobi: East African Standard, 1922.
Report of the Labour Bureau Commission 1921. Nairobi: Government Printer, 1921.
Staff List July 1923. Nairobi: Government Printer, 1923.

EAST AFRICA PROTECTORATE

Department of Agriculture British East Africa Annual Report 1911–12. Nairobi: Government Printer, 1913.
Department of Agriculture British East Africa Annual Report 1913–14. Nairobi: Government Printer, 1915.
Department of Agriculture British East Africa Annual Report 1916–17. Nairobi: Government Printer, 1918.
Legislative Council Debates. Second Session 1920 and Third Session 1921.

Native Labour Commission, 1912–13 Evidence and Report. Nairobi: Government Printer, 1913.
Official Gazette of East Africa and Uganda, 10 (1908).
Official Gazette of the East Africa Protectorate, 22 (31 March 1920).
Report of the Land Settlement Commission. Nairobi: Government Printer, 1919.

GREAT BRITAIN

East Africa Protectorate Report 1912–13. London: HMSO, 1913.
East Africa Protectorate Report 1919–20. London: HMSO, 1921.
Colony and Protectorate of Kenya Report 1920–21. London: HMSO, 1922.
Indians in Kenya. Cmd. 1922. London: HMSO, 1923.
Parliamentary Debates (Commons), 5th Series, (1912), 37 and 41; (1921), 142 and 147; (1922), 150 and 156.
Parliamentary Debates (Lords), 5th Series, (1922), 50.

Books

Amery, L. S. *My Political Life.* London: 1953.
Barnes, John, and David Nicholson, eds. *The Leo Amery Diaries.* Vol. 1. London: Hutchinson, 1980.
Furse, Ralph. *Aucuparius: Recollection of a Recruiting Officer.* London: Oxford University Press, 1962.
Gilbert, Martin S., ed. *Winston S. Churchill Companion.* Vol. 4. Parts 1–3. London: Heinemann, 1977.
Halifax, Lord. *Fullness of Days.* New York: Dodd, Mead & Co., 1957.
James, Robert Rhodes, ed. *Memoirs of a Conservative: J. C. C. Davidson's Memoirs and Papers, 1910–37.* London: Weidenfeld & Nicolson, 1969.
———. *Winston S. Churchill His Complete Speeches 1897–1963.* Vol. 3. London: Chelsea House Publishers, 1974.
Long, Viscount of Wraxall. *Memories.* London: Hutchinson & Co., 1923.
Meinertzhagen, Robert. *Army Diary 1899–1926.* Edinburgh: Oliver & Boyd, 1960.
Metcalfe, G. E., ed. *Great Britain and Ghana: Documents of Ghana History, 1807–1957.* London: Thomas Nelson & Sons, 1964.
Thuku, Harry. *Maisha Yangu.* Nairobi: Oxford University Press. 1971.

Secondary Sources

Unpublished Papers

DISSERTATIONS

Overton, John David. "Spatial Differentiation in the Colonial Economy of Kenya's Africans, Settlers and the State, 1900–1920." Ph.D. diss., Cambridge University, 1984.
Reed, Harry A. "Cotton-Growing in Central Nyanza Province Kenya, 1901–1939: An Appraisal of African Reactions to Imposed Government Policy." Ph.D. diss., Michigan State University, 1975.

Redley, Michael Gordon. "The Politics of a Predicament: The White Community in
    Kenya, 1918–32." Ph.D. diss., Cambridge University, 1976.
Spencer, Leon P. "Christian Missions and African Interests in Kenya, 1905–1924."
    Ph.D. diss., Syracuse University, 1974.

Books

Atieno Odhiambo, E. S. *Siasa: Politics and Nationalism in East Africa, 1905–1939.*
    Nairobi: Kenya Literature Bureau, 1981.
Bennett, George. *Kenya A Political History: The Colonial Period.* Oxford: Oxford
    University Press, 1963.
Berman, Bruce. *Control & Crisis in Colonial Kenya: The Dialectic of Domination.*
    Athens: Ohio University Press, 1990.
Blake, Robert. *The Unknown Prime Minister.* London: Eyre & Spottiswoode, 1955.
Blakeley, Brian L. *The Colonial Office, 1868–1892.* Durham, N.C.: Duke University
    Press, 1972.
Brett, E. A. *Colonialism and Underdevelopment in East Africa.* London: Heinemann,
    1973.
Cell, John W., ed. *By Kenya Possessed.* Chicago: University of Chicago Press, 1976.
Clayton, Anthony, and Donald Savage. *Government and Labour in Kenya.* London:
    Frank Cass, 1974.
Clough, Marshall S. *Fighting Two Sides: Kenyan Chiefs and Politicians, 1918–1940.*
    Niwot, Col.: University of Colorado Press, 1990.
Cole, Eleanor. *Random Recollections of a Pioneer Settler.* Woodbridge, Suffolk:
    Baron Publishers, 1975.
Constantine, Stephen. *The Making of British Colonial Development Policy.* London:
    Frank Cass, 1984.
Cranworth, Lord. *Kenya Chronicles.* London: Macmillan, 1939.
———. *Profit and Sport in British East Africa.* London: Macmillan, 1919.
Davis, Lance E. and Robert A. Huttenback. *Mammon and the Pursuit of Empire: The
    Political Economy of British Imperialism, 1860–1914.* New York: Cambridge Uni-
    versity Press, 1986.
Dilley, Marjorie Ruth. *British Policy in Kenya Colony.* 2nd ed. London: Frank Cass,
    1966.
Drummond, Ian M. *British Economic Policy and the Empire, 1919–1939.* London:
    George Allen and Unwin, 1972.
Farrant, Leda. *The Legendary Grogan.* London: Hamish Hamilton, 1981.
Fearn, Hugh. *An African Economy.* London: Oxford University Press, 1961.
Fiddes, George V. *The Dominions and Colonial Offices.* London: G. P. Putnams Sons
    Ltd., 1926.
Gann, L. H., and Peter Duignan, eds. *African Proconsuls.* New York: The Free Press
    and Hoover Institution, 1978.
Gardiner, A. G. *The Life of Sir William Harcourt.* Vols. 1 & 2. London: Constable &
    Co., 1923.
Ghai, Y. P., and J. P. W. B. McAuslan. *Public Law and Political Change in Kenya.*
    Nairobi: Oxford University Press, 1970.
Gollin, A. M. *Proconsul in Politics.* London: Anthony Blond Ltd., 1964.
Gregory, Robert G. *India and East Africa.* Oxford: Clarendon Press, 1971.
Guinn, Paul. *British Strategy and Politics, 1914 to 1918.* Oxford: Clarendon Press,
    1965.
Harlow, Vincent, and E. M. Chilver, eds. *History of East Africa.* Vol. 2. Oxford:
    Clarendon Press, 1965.

Havighurst, Alfred F. *Twentieth Century Britain*. 2nd ed. New York: Harper & Row, 1962.

Hazlehurst, Cameron. *Politicians at War July 1914 to May 1915*. London: Jonathon Cape, 1971.

Hill, M. F. *Permanent Way*. Nairobi: East African Railways and Habours, 1961.

Hillmer, Norman, and Philip Wigley, eds. *The First British Commonwealth*. London: Frank Cass, 1980.

Hobley, C. W. *Kenya From Chartered Company to Crown Colony*. London: 1928.

Hodges, Geoffrey. *The Carrier Corps: Military Labor in the East African Campaign, 1914–1918*. New York: Greenwood Press, 1986.

Huxley, Elspeth. *White Man's Country*. Vol. 1 & 2. New York: Praeger, 1968.

Hyam, Ronald. *Britain's Imperial Century, 1815–1914*. New York: Barnes and Noble Books, 1976.

Jeffries, Sir Charles. *The Colonial Office*. London: George Allen & Unwin, 1956.

Kamoche, Jidlaph G. *Imperial Trusteeship and Political Evolution in Kenya, 1923–1963*. Washington: University Press of America, 1981.

Kanogo, Tabitha. *Squatters and the Roots of Mau Mau*. Athens: Ohio University Press, 1987.

Kennedy, Dane. *Islands of White: Settler Society and Culture in Kenya and Southern Rhodesia, 1890–1939*. Durham, N.C.: Duke University Press, 1987.

Kinnear, Michael. *The Fall of Lloyd George*. London: Macmillan, 1973.

Kipkorir, B. E., ed. *Biographical Essays on Imperialism and Collaboration in Colonial Kenya*. Nairobi: Kenya Literature Bureau, 1980.

Kitching, Gavin. *Class and Economic Change in Kenya*. New Haven: Yale University Press, 1980.

Kubicek, Robert V. *The Administration of Imperialism: Joseph Chamberlain at the Colonial Office*. Durham, N.C.: Duke University Press, 1969.

Leys, Norman. *Kenya*. 4th ed. London: Frank Cass, 1973.

Louis, WM. Roger. *Great Britain and Germany's Lost Colonies, 1914–1919*. Oxford: Clarendon Press, 1967.

Malhotra, D. K. *History and Problems of Indian Currency, 1835–1959*. Revised ed. New Delhi: Minerva Book Shop, 1960.

Marlowe, John. *Milner, Apostle of Empire*. London: Hamish Hamilton, 1976.

Maxon, Robert M. *John Ainsworth and the Making of Kenya*. Washington: University Press of America, 1980.

Memorandum on the Case Against the Claims of Indians in Kenya. Nairobi: Swift Press, 1921.

Mercer, Sir William, et. al. *The Colonial Office List for 1915*. London: Waterlow & Sons, 1915.

———. *The Colonial Office List for 1916*. London: Waterlow & Sons, 1916.

———. *The Colonial Office List for 1917*. London: Waterlow & Sons, 1917.

———. *The Colonial Office List for 1918*. London: Waterlow & Sons, 1918.

———. *The Colonial Office List for 1921*. London: Waterlow & Sons 1921.

———. *The Colonial Office List for 1922*. London: Waterlow & Sons, 1922.

———. *The Colonial Office List for 1923*. London: Waterlow & Sons, 1923.

———. *The Colonial Office List for 1924*. London: Waterlow & Sons, 1924.

Morgan, Kenneth, and Jane Morgan. *Portrait of a Progressive: The Political Career of Christopher, Viscount Addison*. Oxford: Clarendon Press, 1980.

Mosley, Paul. *The Settler Economies: Studies in the Economic History of Kenya and Southern Rhodesia 1900–1963*. Cambridge: Cambridge University Press, 1983.

Mungeam, G. H. *British Rule in Kenya, 1895–1912*. London: Oxford University Press, 1966.

Nabudere, Dan. *Imperialism in East Africa*. Vol. 1. London: Zed Press, 1981.

O'Brien, Terence H. *Milner*. London: Constable, 1979.
Ochieng', William R., ed. *A Modern History of Kenya*. Nairobi and London: Evans Brothers, 1989.
Oliver, Roland. *The Missionary Factor in East Africa*. 2nd ed. London: Longman, 1965.
Parkinson, Cosmo. *The Colonial Office From Within*. London: Faber and Faber, 1947.
Petrie, Sir Charles. *Walter Long and His Times*. London: Hutchinson & Co., 1936.
Porter, Bernard. *Critics of Empire: British Radical Attitudes to Colonialism in Africa, 1895–1914*. London: Macmillan, 1968.
———. *The Lion's Share: A Short History of British Imperialism, 1850–1970*. New York: Longman, 1975.
Ross, W. McGregor. *Kenya from Within*. 1st ed. London: 1927
Rowland, Peter. *The Last Liberal Governments: The Promised Land, 1905–1910*. New York, Macmillan, 1969.
Sorrenson, M. P. K. *Origins of European Settlement in Kenya*. Nairobi: Oxford University Press, 1966.
Stichter, Sharon. *Migrant Labour in Kenya: Capitalism and the African Response, 1895–1975*. London: Longman, 1982.
Strayer, Robert W. *The Making of Mission Communities in East Africa*. London: Heinemann, 1978.
Tignor, Robert. *The Colonial Transformation of Kenya*. Princeton: Princeton University Press, 1976.
van Zwanenberg, R. M. A. *Colonial Capitalism and Labour in Kenya, 1919–1939*. Nairobi: East African Literature Bureau, 1975.
Waley, S. D. *Edwin Montagu*. New York: Asia Publishing House, 1964.
Wolff, Richard D. *The Economics of Colonialism: Britain and Kenya, 1870–1930*. New Haven: Yale University Press, 1974.
Youe, Christopher P. *Robert Thorne Coryndon: Proconsular Imperialism in Southern and Eastern Africa, 1897–1925*. Waterloo, Ontario, Canada: Wilfrid Laurier University Press, 1986.

Articles and Periodicals

Newpapers have been listed by title only. Complete references are found in the notes.

Atieno-Odhiambo, E. S. "The Colonial Government, the Settlers, and the 'Trust' Principle in Kenya." *Transafrican Journal of History* 2 (1972): 94–113.
Bennett, George. "Paramountcy to Partnership: J. H. Oldham and Africa." *Africa* 30 (1960): 356–61.
Clausen, G. L. M. "The British Colonial Currency System." *The Economic Journal* 54 (1944): 1–25.
Cross, J. A. "The Colonial Office and the Dominions." *Journal of Commonwealth Political Studies* 4, no. 2 (July 1966): 138–48.
Darwin, John. "Imperialism in Decline? Tendencies in British Imperial Policy Between the Wars." *The Historical Journal* 23 (1980): 657–79.
Duder, C. J. D. "The Settler Response to the Indian Crisis of 1923 in Kenya: Brigadier-General Philip Wheatley and 'Direct Action'." *The Journal of Imperial and Commonwealth History* 17 (1989): 349–73.
East African Standard.
Good, Kenneth. "Settler Colonialism: Economic Development and Class Formation." *The Journal of Modern African Studies* 14, no. 4 (1976): 597–620.

Gregory, Robert G. "Churchill's Administration of East Africa: A Period of Indian Dissilusionment." *Journal of Indian History* 44 (1966): 397–416.

Hyam, Ronald. "The Colonial Office Mind, 1900–1914." *The Journal of Imperial and Commonwealth History* 8 (October 1979): 30–55.

Kenya Observer.

Kirk-Greene, A. H. M. "Canada in Africa: Sir Percy Girouard, Neglected Colonial Governor." *African Affairs* 83 (1984): 207–39.

The Leader of British East Africa.

Lonsdale, John, and Bruce Berman. "Coping With the Contradictions: The Development of the Colonial State in Kenya, 1895–1914." *Journal of African History* 20 (1979): 487–505.

———. "Crises of Accumulation, Coercion and the Colonial State: The Development of the Labor Control System in Kenya, 1919–1929." *Canadian Journal of African Studies* 14, no. 1 (1980): 37–54.

Maxon, Robert M. "African Production and the Support of European Settlement in Kenya: The Uasin Gishu-Mumias Railway Scheme, 1911–14." *The Journal of Imperial and Commonwealth History* 14 (1985): 52–64.

———. "Judgement on a Colonial Governor: Sir Percy Girouard in Kenya." *Transafrican Journal of History* 18 (1989): 90–100.

———. "The Kenya Currency Crisis, 1919–21 and the Imperial Dilemma," *The Journal of Imperial and Commonwealth History* 18 (1989): 322–41.

McIntosh, B. G. "Kenya 1923: the Political Crisis and the Missionary Dilemma." *Transafrican Journal of History* 1 (1971): 103–29.

Meredith, David. "The British Government and Colonial Economic Policy, 1919–39." *Economic History Review* 28 (1975): 484–99.

Nicolson, I. F., and Colin A. Hughes, "A Provenance of Proconsuls: British Colonial Governors 1900–1960." *The Journal of Imperial and Commonwealth History* 4 (1975): 77–106.

Overton, John. "The Colonial State and Spatial Differentiation: Kenya, 1895–1920." *Journal of Historical Geography* 13, no. 3 (1987): 267–82.

———. "War and Economic Development: Settlers in Kenya, 1914–1918." *Journal of African History* 27 (1986): 79–103.

Robinson, Ronald. "The Moral Disarmament of African Empire, 1919–1947." *The Journal of Imperial and Commonwealth History* 8 (1979): 86–104.

Savage, Donald, and J. Forbes Munro. "Carrier Corps Recruitment in the British East Africa Protectorate, 1914–1918." *Journal of African History* 7 (1966): 314–42.

Spencer, Ian R. G. "The First World War and the Origins of the Dual Policy of Development in Kenya 1914–1922." *World Development* 9 (1981): 739–47.

Spencer, Leon. "Church and State in Colonial Africa: Influences Governing the Political Activity of Christian Missions in Kenya." *Journal of Church and State* 31 (1989): 115–32.

The Times.

Wylie, Diana. "Confrontation Over Kenya: The Colonial Office and Its Critics, 1918–1940." *Journal of African History* 18 (1977): 427–47.

———. "Norman Leys and McGregor Ross: A Case Study in the Conscience of African Empire, 1900–1939." *The Journal of Imperial and Commonwealth History* 5 (1977): 294–309.

Yearwood, Peter J. "Great Britain and the Repartition of Africa, 1914–19." *The Journal of Imperial and Commonwealth History* 18 (1990): 316–41.

Youe, Christopher P. "The Threat of Settler Rebellion and the Imperial Predicament: The Denial of Indian Rights in Kenya, 1923." *Canadian Journal of History* 12 (1978): 347–60.

Index